An Introduction to Hearing

An Introduction to Hearing

DAVID M. GREEN

HARVARD UNIVERSITY

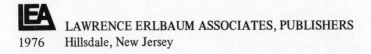

LAWRENCE ERLBAUM ASSOCIATES, PUBLISHERS
1976   Hillsdale, New Jersey

DISTRIBUTED BY THE HALSTED PRESS DIVISION OF

JOHN WILEY & SONS

New York   Toronto   London   Sydney

Lawrence Erlbaum Associates, Inc., Publishers
62 Maria Drive
Hillsdale, New Jersey 07642

Distributed solely by Halsted Press Division
John Wiley & Sons, Inc., New York

Library of Congress Cataloging in Publication Data

Green, David Marvin, 1932-
An introduction to hearing.

Includes bibliographical references and indexes.
1. Hearing.   I. Title.
QP460.G67   612'.85   76-20561
ISBN 0-470-15188-9

Printed in the United States of America

Contents

Preface

In recent years there have been many advanced treatments of various aspects of hearing: Möller, Plomp and Smoorenberg, Sachs, Terhardt and Zwicker, and the Tobias volumes. All contain admirable material presented by experts in their areas. Sadly, experience has taught me that students, even graduate students, can rarely start with this material or with articles in the current journals. They need some more general and basic introduction. The older general books are no longer suitable as introductory texts because of the enormous recent technical and conceptual advances in certain areas. Cochlear mechanics, single unit recordings, anatomy, and psychophysical methods have all undergone great change. The student cannot appreciate many of the issues and arguments raised in the current literature without at least a superficial understanding of these new developments. This is doubly unfortunate. First, since our current theories are no more complex than our previous ones, there is no reason to teach the older theories as our present understanding of the subject matter. Second, it robs him of some of the excitement and challenge we all feel in working in a discipline where new and quite revolutionary discoveries can appear in the next journal issue.

And so I have written what I call an introduction to hearing. Ideally, it should provide sufficient introduction to each of several subareas of hearing so that the serious student can read the more advanced treatments with greater appreciation and understanding. It is intended for upper undergraduate and graduate students. It assumes some mathematical sophistication—calculus, for example—but I have not hesitated to review some more basic concepts, for example logarithms, at least briefly. In my experience, certain mathematical tools are often rusty and a brief review is all that is needed. Undoubtedly some will still insist the level of presentation is uneven. I find this criticism difficult to defend. Ideally all material to be learned should be only a little difficult—but that ideal assumes a homogeneity in the background of the student that I have never found. My undergraduates are typically half from biological or social science and half from physical sciences. It is also hard to place an absolute scale on the difficulty of material. Modern algebra that used to be taught to upper-level undergraduates in mathematics is now taught in grade schools. Once a concept is widely understood, even a difficult one, it certainly appears less difficult in some sense, if not simple.

The student of the senses needs to know something from a variety of traditional fields—physics, physiology, psychology, anatomy, and, of course, mathematics. The field of hearing is no exception. Beginning students often become discouraged and decide that problems within the more traditional disciplines are safer and less anxiety-producing. One can sympathize with their feelings. Foreign concepts are initially threatening since one has little chance of knowing a priori whether a new concept is simple or complex. I have attempted to provide a brief treatment of the necessary material from the different disciplines—hardly enough to master it but enough at least to remove the strangeness of some of the concepts and terms and to show its relation to our study of hearing.

Finally I must thank the various people and institutions who helped me write this book. First let me thank the many people who commented on earlier drafts: F. W. Campbell, L. L. Elliot, N. Graham, I. Hafter, R. B. Henning, W. Jesteadt, J. Nachmias, John Robson, C. A. Smith, J. Tonndorf, W. D. Ward, and C. Wier, all commented extensively on various drafts of different chapters. Bert Rozin read the entire manuscript and has greatly contributed both to conceptual and grammatical clarification. Allan and Phillip Green are thanked for the drafting and photographs. Vivian Merritt, Ruth Roemer, and Ann Bello did most of the typing and retyping.

I must also credit several institutions for providing the time and means to work on this project. The bulk of the book was written while on sabbatical from Harvard University during a year as Visiting Fellow, St. John's College, Cambridge, England. During that year I also held a Guggenheim Fellowship. Some of the material was also accumulated while working on research grants from the National Institutes of Health and the National Science Foundation.

Finally, let me thank my students, whose questions and confusions provided the sustained motivation for the book's completion.

DAVID M. GREEN

An Introduction to Hearing

1
The Physical Nature of Sound

INTRODUCTION

The human senses are all remarkably acute. Under optimal conditions, the eye can detect a few photons. The skin can detect a vibratory stimulus that moves only a few microns. The ear can detect, at about 3,000 Hz (cycles per second), movements of the eardrum about a hundred times smaller than the diameter of a hydrogen molecule.

How is such sensitivity possible? How can the ear detect such minute vibrations? Why does the random vibration of the molecules in the air not obscure such faint sounds? These are some questions that arise in studying auditory perception. To understand in detail the answers to such questions, we must have a firm grasp of the physical nature of sound. Indeed, one of our goals is to understand the relation between what we hear and its physical properties.

We begin, then, by first considering what a sound wave is, how it is propagated, and what the rules are that govern its behavior. Answering these questions involves defining the units used to describe the intensity or energy of the sound wave. We review here several formulas specifying the intensity of the sound wave. We also discuss sinusoidal wave motion, in part because the absolute sensitivity of the ear depends strongly on the frequency of the signal. Finally, reflection of sound waves and resonance is discussed. This background material will permit us to answer some of our initial questions about absolute sensitivity. We begin by considering the nature of sound.

WHAT IS SOUND?

In ordinary usage the word "sound" refers to that which is heard. However, we want to understand the relation between what we hear and the physical aspects of sound. We therefore begin with a consideration of sound as a physical entity.

From a physical viewpoint, sound is a mechanical disturbance that is propagated through an elastic medium. This physical disturbance alters certain properties of the medium, and the rapid variation of one of them, for example, the variation of pressure as a function of time, might be called the *sound wave*. We are primarily interested in this mechanical disturbance as it moves in air, but sound can also move in liquid or solid structures as well. Air is composed of a mixture of molecules, the majority being oxygen, nitrogen, and hydrogen. The molecules of a gas move about freely in space, colliding with other molecules or any surface containing the gas. The mass of the molecules and the velocity of their motion determine the temperature of the gas. These factors, along with the number of molecules per unit volume, also determine how far, on the average, molecules travel before colliding with other molecules. The gas molecules wander about at random in an undisturbed state. As a result of their collisions with other objects, they create a net *static pressure* on an object placed in the gas. Pressure is defined as a force per unit area, and static pressure is essentially the pressure measured by a barometer. The "barometric" pressure represents the force produced by the impact of the moving gas molecules, averaged over both time and space.

The magnitude of the static pressure is determined by the speed of the molecules, their mass, and the density of the gas, that is, the number of molecules per unit volume. Air at sea level contains about 2.7×10^{19} molecules per cubic centimeter and is a mixture of different molecules the velocities of which depend on their mass. Hydrogen molecules are light, and their velocity is nearly 200,000 cm/sec (about 6,000 ft/sec).[1] Oxygen molecules are heavier, and their velocity is only about 48,000 cm/sec (about 1,600 ft/sec). The mean free path, that is, the average distance between collisions, is about 2×10^{-5} cm. The mass of a single molecule is very slight, of course, so the force generated by a single collision is very small. A large number of collisions is needed to generate a total force per unit area, which is the static pressure.

Now if we introduce a change in the position of some large object in the air by vibrating the cone of a loudspeaker, for example, then a mechanical disturbance is created in the gas near the cone. On one side of the cone there is a temporary increase in pressure, an increase above the average or static pressure. Accompanying this increase in pressure is a temporary increase in density. The local increase in pressure and density causes a temporary increase in the number of collisions among the molecules in the gas near the cone. The temporary increase in collisions spreads via a number of other collisions to other, adjacent areas, and so the local disturbance eventually spreads throughout the neighboring space. Thus, the initially local increase in pressure and density is propagated through-

---

[1] The metric system of units is used throughout this book. In this chapter, we occasionally convert the quantities to the British units but in later chapters only cgs units are specified. Appendix 1 contains a table defining and relating various quantities.

out the entire medium. This moving mechanical disturbance is called the "sound wave." Note that the mechanical disturbance can only be inferred by looking at the population characteristics of the gas. If we were to watch the movement of a single molecule, we would simply see it dancing about, striking the other molecules in the gas. An individual molecule would move unpredictably in different directions at different times. The direction of these motions only partially reflects external disturbance, such as the motion of the cone of the loudspeaker. "Sound," therefore, refers to population characteristics or averages computed over a large set of molecules. *Sound* is a change in average values; it is an increase (or decrease) in the average pressure or in the average density or a change in the average displacement of the individual molecules.

If we could measure the average quantities at several points in this space, we would see that a particular disturbance moved systematically. Suppose, for example, that a speaker cone moved quickly forward and then returned to a resting position. If we could measure the average pressure or displacement at some distance from the speaker, we would see the same quick increase and subsequent return to the previous average values.

We must appreciate the molecular aspect of sound to understand many important acoustic phenomena, particularly the incredible sensitivity of the ear to small average displacements, and we return to this problem later in Chapter 2. For the most part, however, sound is described solely in terms of population or statistical averages that often ignore the molecular basis of sound. To understand this description of sound, we must know how the average values change as they travel through the gas. We must know the velocity at which the sound wave travels and how it is influenced when it strikes objects of dissimilar composition, such as walls, and other similar facts. Let us therefore raise our level of analysis and consider these statistical or molar characteristics in more detail.

A MOLAR–STATISTICAL VIEWPOINT

The disturbance of the gas we call sound can be viewed from many different perspectives. For example, we can calculate the disturbance by measuring the change in the average position of the molecules of the air. A single molecule may move in any direction, but if a sound is present, then the molecules must, by definition, alter their average position. Similarly, we can look at the disturbance as an average change in pressure or density. The gas laws describe the relation between the average pressure, density, and temperature. Once we know the character of the gas, we can calculate the relation between these quantities. Therefore, pressure, density, temperature, or displacement can be used as our principal descriptor of sound, and the other quantities can be calculated. The most popular and convenient descriptor of sound, however, is *instantaneous pressure*.

We should be careful to distinguish between instantaneous pressure and static pressure. Both pressures are the result of collisions between the surface of some object and the molecules in a surrounding gas. Both pressures depend on some spatial averaging. They differ in the amount of averaging over time that is used in their computation. The diagrams in Figure 1.1 demonstrate this distinction.

Figure 1.1a shows a thin diaphragm located in the opening of a small box. This diaphragm is free to move either left or right. It is attached to the box by the spring. Inside the box is a vacuum, and hence no molecules collide inside to create a static pressure. Collisions between the molecules in air on the left side of the diaphragm push it to the right against the force exerted by the spring. Equilibrium between the static pressure and the spring force determines the average position of the diaphragm. The pressure is denoted as P_0 in the diagram in Figure 1.1b. If a sound occurs, then there may be either a brief increase or a brief decrease in pressure outside the box. The diaphragm of the box, if certain conditions are met, moves in proportion to the momentary pressure. Such rapid changes in pressure are called changes in "instantaneous" pressure. A change in instantaneous pressure produced by a sound is illustrated in Figure 1.1b. Instantaneous pressure, like static pressure, also results from an increase or decrease in the average number of collisions on the face of the diaphragm but the average is computed over a brief period of time—so brief we call it "instantaneous."

In practice, we can easily ignore the long-term or static pressure. This is illustrated in Figure 1.1c and d. We have simply added a small hole to the box. Air will fill the box, and, on the average, molecules within the box will bombard the diaphragm from the right side as much as from the left. Hence, the diaphragm rests at some neutral position. The net pressure on the diaphragm is zero, as illustrated in Figure 1.1d. Now, a brief increase and decrease in pressure produced by the sound wave will cause a change in pressure on the diaphragm. By assumption, the change is so brief that the pressure inside the box stays at static pressure and hence the change in pressure varies about zero, as the diagram to the right shows.

The only difference between instantaneous and static pressure, then, is the time scale we have in mind. If the increase or decrease in pressure is very slow, we ordinarily speak of it not as sound but as a change in barometric pressure.

Consider once more Figures 1.1c and d. If no sound is present, there are still random variations in the molecules of the air and in the total collisions occurring on each side of the diaphragm. Because of these random collisions, small movements are induced. However, if the diaphragm is reasonably large, there is an enormous number of collisions and their average effect, even when computed over a brief interval of time, is very nearly zero. There is practically no net displacement of the diaphragm, as Figure 1.1c or d illustrates. When sound occurs, however, there is an average increase in the motion of all the molecules in the same direction, say to the right, and the diaphragm, which may be part of a microphone, moves to the right. If this increase is averaged over a sufficient

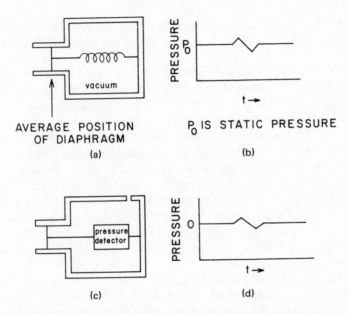

AVERAGE POSITION
OF DIAPHRAGM
(a)

P_0 IS STATIC PRESSURE
(b)

(c)

(d)

FIG. 1.1 Cross section of a box with a small diaphragm located at the only opening. A vacuum is created within the box and a string opposes the static or atmospheric pressure of the air outside the box. The average position of the diaphragm thus is a measure of P_0, and a sound wave causes changes about P_0 (b). A small hole has been added to the box (c), thus neutralizing the static pressure, and sound now is measured as fluctuation about a zero pressure level (d).

area, an easily detectable increase in pressure occurs at the diaphragm of the microphone. Therefore, the force exerted on the diaphragm of the microphone is an index of the instantaneous pressure in the gas. For the present, we describe the *sound wave* as the relatively rapid variation of pressure as a function of time. We shall denote this rapid change $p(t)$.

We now have some understanding of the physical nature of sound—it is an average of certain forces or pressures in a medium, such as air. To understand how the ear responds to such disturbances, especially how it is sensitive to very small average disturbances, we must consider how the sound wave moves and how these changes in pressure are measured. First, we analyze propagation.

PROPAGATION OF SOUND—THE WAVE EQUATION

A sound wave is a relatively rapid change in pressure. It should be clear from the molecular considerations that this rapid change in pressure can travel over some distance. The sound wave will spread from one point to another. We want to know the rules that wave obeys as it travels from one point to another. We want also to investigate what happens to the sound wave when it strikes a surface, such as a wall.

Perhaps understanding the next section will be easier if we first think about how the sound wave should behave. What properties should it have to make it useful for communication? We know, for example, that certain aspects of sound remain the same when we listen to the same source at different points in our environment. For example, we listen to music in a variety of different positions in a room and can still identify what is being played. Similarly, when we talk to people, we can move about and locate ourselves at various distances from the speaker and still understand the message. If we actually record these messages at different points in the room, the variations in pressure are seen to be different. These changes in the pressure wave occur because the sound wave encounters such objects as walls, floors, or ceilings and the reflections modify the pressure wave. However, if we listen to the recordings, they all convey the same message, for example, "Johnny, come here."

These intuitive examples show that some aspect of the sound wave must remain essentially invariant as we change distance. We know that the pressure variation is not always the same at different points in the acoustic environments, yet our perception of it is. We will consider this very interesting problem in perception in more detail later in the book (Chapter 12). For the present, let us return to the acoustics of the situation. Consider a very simple acoustic environment, an open space without any objects or reflecting barriers.

In a *free field* the pressure disturbance or sound wave radiates outward without encountering any obstacles or barriers. Therefore, no reflection or interaction among sound waves occurs. We simply have a source located somewhere in space and the sound waves are moving outward from it. We can think of the sound wave either as being completely absorbed at the edges of this free field or, because the field is imaginary, as having an unlimited extent. The surface of a quiet pond may provide a useful, tangible analog. Assume a source that creates a disturbance in the center of this pond. The wave initiated by the source radiates outward in an ever increasing circle. By "free field" we mean that the shoreline is so far away that we need not worry about reflections of the waves off the shoreline. A source may create a disturbance in the sound field by producing some change in pressure, $f(t)$. In our analogy of the pond, $f(t)$ would be a change in the water level. This disturbance radiates out from the source. Now, how should this disturbance change as it moves away from the source? For communication purposes we should like the disturbance to remain of the same form. In that case, if we send a signal by causing the source to execute a certain motion, we can then record essentially that same disturbance at any point in the space. Note that this is a peculiar requirement, because we want f to be of the same form at any distance and yet to be arbitrary. The function f must be able to say "Johnny, come here" or "Billy, come here" or "Mary, come here", etc. The peculiar property of an ideal communication wave therefore must involve the argument of f rather than f itself.

IDEAL COMMUNICATION WAVE

The ideal communication wave must move over distance so that the form of f is preserved. Mathematically, if we imagine the wave moving from left to right along a single dimension, then the wave obeys the following function:

$$f(t - x/c)$$

where t is time, x is distance, and c is a constant. Clearly, our ideal wave simply executes the same motion at any point in space if we wait long enough for the wave to travel from the source to that point. As Figure 1.2 shows, the disturbance created at $t = 0$ eventually reaches some point $x = k$ and then repeats itself

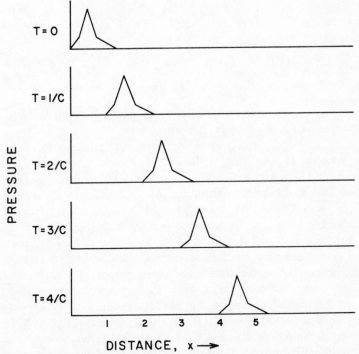

FIG. 1.2 An ideal form of a sound wave recorded at different times and distances. The constant c is the velocity of the wave. Since the form of the wave is independent of distance, the pressure disturbance is the same at source and receiver.

there at time k/c. The constant c is the velocity at which the sound wave travels. To see this, consider f at some point, t_1 and x_1, that same disturbance reaches another point x_2 at time t_2 when the two arguments are equal. Therefore

$$t_1 - \frac{x_1}{c} = t_2 - \frac{x_2}{c},$$

$$c = \frac{x_2 - x_1}{t_2 - t_1}.$$

The constant c is equal to the change in distance divided by the change in time or, by definition, the velocity of the wave motion.

We have been considering a wave that is traveling in the righthand direction, that is, for a constant value for the argument of the function, time and distance both increase. How can we represent a wave that travels in the opposite direction? Again, we assume an ideal communication wave, one that does not change in form as it travels over distance. The equation for a wave traveling in the lefthand direction is obtained by simply reversing the sign in the argument;

$$f(t + x/c).$$

Here, for

$$t + x/c = k,$$

$$t = k - x/c$$

or as t increases, x must decrease to keep the argument the same. Note once again, however, that the velocity of the wave is still c.

This concludes our discussion of an ideal communication wave, the form of which is invariant as a function of distance. There is an important difference between an ideal wave and any real wave. A real wave may retain essentially the same form but the size of the disturbance must diminish with distance. In the case of the water wave, this condition is obviously necessary from simple considerations of energy. As the wave moves away from the source, its circumference becomes larger and larger. For the form of the wave to stay the same, more and more water must be displaced as the circle of disturbance increases in radius. For a sound wave, the disturbance follows a spherical pattern about the source. The energy considerations are even more germane. In both cases the size of the disturbance must diminish as the wave moves out in space. Otherwise the energy required to propagate the disturbance would continually grow. In fact, as we shall see, the amplitude of a spherical sound wave decreases by the reciprocal of the distance it has traveled. Nevertheless, the form of the wave remains the same, and the same information can be recovered at all positions in space. This invariance of form with distance makes all wave phenomena important as carriers of information.

The analogy of the wave in the pond is apt except for one point. The difference between a sound wave and a surface water wave concerns how the mechanical disturbances are propagated. The particles of water move at right angles to the direction of the wave front. The surface wave moves along the horizontal component but the bulk of the particles actually move vertically. As the disturbance passes any point, the water moves down (the trough of the wave) and then up into the air (the crest). Waves of this kind are called *transverse waves*. In a sound wave the particles of the air move in the direction of the wave front. As the wave moves in a horizontal direction, for example, the gas molecules move back and forth, on the average, in that direction as well. Waves of this kind are called *longitudinal waves*.

WAVE EQUATION

The movement of a real sound wave depends on the interaction of the molecules of the gas when a disturbance occurs. Suppose a small source located in a homogeneous gas sends energy continually outward. Now assume there are no objects to reflect or disturb the outward flow of that energy. We can imagine the source as a balloon located at the top of a thin pole in the middle of a large field. The pole is so long that by the time sound waves travel downward and strike the ground, the wave amplitude is so small as to be negligible. Inflating and deflating the balloon very rapidly causes a disturbance in the pressure in the region of the source. How do these waves travel? Because of its elasticity, air can be likened to a mechanical system made up of a spring and mass. As the balloon expands, there is compression of the gas; this is analogous to the compression of the spring. An equal and opposite force is generated by the inertia of the air molecules caused by their mass. The interplay of these two forces causes a disturbance in the medium, the sound wave. The sound wave could be specified as a change in average pressure as a function of time at some fixed point in space, or, alternatively, time could be fixed and the average pressure measured at several different distances. If we do either or both of these things, we find that the sound wave obeys the following equation, called the *wave equation*:

$$\frac{d^2\,(x{\cdot}p)}{dt^2} = \frac{d^2\,(x{\cdot}p)}{dx^2}\,c^2, \tag{1.1}$$

where d is the derivative operator, p is some function representing variation in pressure, x is distance, t is time, and c is a constant.

The wave equation is a differential equation relating the second derivatives of the product of pressure and distance with respect to time and the second derivatives of the same product with respect to distance. It can be deduced from elementary physical considerations. In effect, it imposes conditions on the way in which the pressure waveform must vary as a function of time and space in order to move through the medium. The differential equation arises from consideration of the forces present when the gas is disturbed and dictates what waveforms can exist in this medium. Fortunately, the constraints are not at all severe; in fact, they are remarkably general and the following function satisfies the wave equation:

$$p(t, x) = x^{-1}g(ct \pm x). \tag{1.2}$$

The plus or minus sign simply indicates the direction in which the wave is moving. Clearly, g can be quite arbitrary in shape, as long as it is smooth enough to have second derivatives that exist with respect to time and space. The reader should verify that Eq. (1.2) actually provides a solution to the wave equation, Eq. (1.1). Readers who have trouble with this may consult Appendix 2, but the best understanding is gained by working the problem oneself. The reader should also verify that $(ct)^2 \pm x$ is not a solution to Eq. (1.1).

The important point of Eq. (1.2) is that the physical composition of a gas, in this case air, permits a pressure disturbance to move in the medium. It behaves exactly like our ideal communication wave, except that the amplitude of the disturbance diminishes with distance. The velocity of the wave is c. The wave travels either to the left or to the right, depending on the sign of x. The form of g remains the same at all distances.

The velocity of the wave, c, should be distinguished from the velocity of the gas molecules. We have discussed the velocity of molecules of air—the velocity of the individual elements that make up the wave. The *wave velocity, c,* is the velocity of the instantaneous displacement or instantaneous pressure. The wave velocity is about 330 m/sec or approximately 1,100 ft/sec. The wave velocity depends strongly on the medium, in particular on the compressibility of the medium. In a less compressible medium, the elements move only a short distance before they bump into their neighbors; in such a medium, therefore, sound travels much faster. Water, which is much less compressible than air, has a velocity of propagation about four times faster. The wave velocity also varies with temperature, being somewhat faster when the temperature is higher. In air this dependence is very slight; velocity changes only about 3% for a change of 30°F in the vicinity of 70°F.

The single most important property of the wave equation is its linearity. Because of this property, certain interference phenomena occur that are very important in the study of sound and hearing. The next section discusses this property.

THE LINEARITY OF THE WAVE EQUATION

Suppose we have two functions, g and h, and suppose each is a solution to the wave equation. When we substitute either g or h in Eq. (1.1), therefore, we obtain an identity. The linearity of the wave equation refers to the following fact: if both g and h are solutions to the wave equation, then their sum $(g + h)$ is also a solution. This follows because the differential of a sum is the sum of the differentials. The simplicity of this relation should not obscure its importance. Linearity allows us to express complicated waves as sums of simpler waves and hence allows us to analyze these complicated waves. For the present, however, we shall describe some other aspects of linearity.

Suppose we have two sound waves, g and h, moving in opposite directions. How do they interact? Figure 1.3 shows the results in graphical form. The various lines of the figure represent the waves at different instances in time. On the top two lines of the figure, the waves are sufficiently separated so that there is no interaction. Their sum is shown in the middle of the picture. Later in time, the waves have passed through one another and have interchanged positions along the line, completely unaffected by their encounter with each other. When the resulting sum produces a pressure at some point that is larger than either wave alone the waves are said to *reinforce* each other.

Another sort of interaction between two waves is shown in Figure 1.3 (left), where we have selected two waves of similar form but moving in opposite

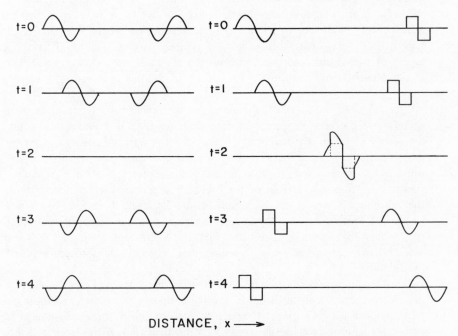

FIG. 1.3 An illustration of the interaction of two sound waves. On the left, two sinusoids of the same frequency but opposite polarity are traveling toward each other. As they meet, the instantaneous pressures of each wave simply add, thus completely cancelling both for one instant, $t = 2$. On the right, the interaction of two waves of quite different forms.

direction, that is, $g(ct - x)$ and $g(ct + x)$. These waves, as they move through each other, exactly *cancel* each other for a brief instant, shown in the middle part of the figure. They emerge again unchanged by the encounter.

How does the cancellation occur and how can pressures that are zero still propagate disturbances? To understand *cancellation* we must first recall that we are monitoring only one aspect of the mechanical disturbance, the instantaneous pressure. At the instant of interaction one wave has an excess pressure, whereas the other has a deficit; the net pressure at that point in space is therefore equal to the static pressure. If only pressure is measured, therefore, the two waves have cancelled each other. However, suppose we investigate other aspects of the mechanical disturbance that constitutes a sound wave. The displacements of the gas molecules at cancellation are in equal and opposite directions, because the net increase or decrease in pressure produced by the waves forces molecules either into (increased pressure) or away from (decreased pressure) a given region of space. The average velocity of the particles in the region of cancellation behaves differently. Given a static pressure, there is some average velocity caused by the collisions among the molecules. When two waves with equal but opposite instantaneous pressures enter a region, a number of collisions and the instantaneous velocity increases. One wave is applying a net force to increase the number of molecules in that area and another force, of equal size, is being applied to decrease the number of molecules in that same region. Therefore, the area of cancellation, zero pressure, is an area of greatest particle velocity. This is the aspect of the disturbance that conserves the energy in the two waves and that allows them to emerge from the encounter unmodified in direction or magnitude.

Interactions of sound waves frequently occur in most real environments. As a sound wave proceeds in space, consider what happens as it encounters a flat, hard surface. Unless the surface can yield in some way and absorb the energy inherent in the wave, reflections must occur in the same way that light or any other wave is reflected. Each reflection can be treated as another source transmitting from the surface of the object. The reflected waves interact with the originating waves in the linear fashion just discussed. Therefore, depending on the nature of the waves, there may be regions in space where the pressure is greater than that originally transmitted (areas of reinforcement) and other places where it may be considerably less than that originally transmitted (areas of cancellation).

The interaction between sound waves is called *interference*. This phenomenon makes sound extremely difficult to specify with any precision in an ordinary environment, such as a room. Although the description of the source—the wave emanating from the loudspeaker—may be straightforward, the reflection of this wave from the walls, ceiling, floor, and objects in the room makes it practically impossible to predict what the pressure wave will be at some arbitrary point in the room. In general, a complicated pattern of reinforcement and cancellation occurs. If the pressure waveforms in a room at two different points in space are measured, they are found to be quite different, despite the fact that both waveforms have arisen from the same source.

Although great differences are observed in the actual pressure waveforms at different points in reflective environments, some features of the waves must remain largely unchanged despite the transformations imposed by cancellation and reinforcement. Otherwise, communication would be impossible. How these invariances are detected is one of the central problems in speech perception. Another puzzle is how the direction of a source can be determined accurately. Reinforcement and cancellation may cause such alterations in the waveform that the largest sound pressure actually occurs at the ear opposite to where the source is located. These questions occupy us in Chapter 12. We must first discuss the intensive aspects of the sound wave; how the forces within the wave are measured and how these forces change as the wave moves in space. In some special, laboratory environments, the wave simply travels out from the source and is never reflected by any external object. In this case, it is somewhat easier to specify the pressure or energy in the wave because the inverse square law is true.

THE INVERSE SQUARE LAW

Let us review a few basic physical quantities, beginning with *energy* or work. In a mechanical system, such as a sound wave, *work* or *energy* is defined as the force exerted over a certain distance. For example, if we exert a certain force on a body and move it a certain distance, then we have done some work. In the centimeter–gram–second (cgs) system, the unit of force is the dyne and the unit of length is the centimeter. If a force of 1 dyne is applied to a body and moves it 1 cm, then 1 erg has been done. The erg is the basic unit of work in the cgs system. Perhaps a more familiar example of work or energy is the kilowatt hour (kW hr). Electricity is billed in those units. An erg is 10^{-7} watt seconds (W sec); so about 10^{14} ergs are equal to 3 kW hr, enough energy to keep a 100-W bulb burning 30 hr.

It is easy to confuse energy and power, but the distinction is important and must be kept clearly in mind. *Power* is the rate at which work is done. If the power expended is constant over time, then energy is simply power multiplied by time. Power is usually measured in watts. A familiar example from the home is the 100-W bulb. The same amount of energy is consumed if one 300-W bulb is burned for 1 hr, or six 100-W bulbs are burned for .5 hr. We should remark at this point that throughout this book we use the term *intensity* as synonymous with power. Some authors use "intensity" as a generic term to refer either to power or to energy. Although there is nothing wrong with such usage there is also no great advantage to be gained from it. Such usage occasionally causes confusion among those unfamiliar with the terminology. We shortly present some specific formulas specifying intensive aspects of the sound wave, but first let us take up the inverse square law and see why it is important for relative comparisons of the energy or power in different waveform.

The inverse square law follows almost immediately from elementary assumptions about an ideal acoustic environment. We first assume a homogeneous environment, so there are no irregularities in the space to disturb the propagation of energy created by the source. The wave generated by the source simply moves out uniformly in all directions at a speed determined by the nature of the gas. The wave is never reflected. Now, assume that the source is generating a constant power, say, 1 W each second. This power is radiated and moves out uniformly in all directions from the source. Imagine a sphere, of radius r, in this space with the source at its center. The amount of power passing through the surface of this sphere exactly equals that generated by the source because, by assumption, the environment is homogeneous and no more energy is concentrated in one region of space than in any other[2] the power passing through each unit area at the surface of the sphere is equal to the intensity of the source divided by the surface of the area of the sphere which is $4\pi r^2$. The amount of power intercepted by the diaphragm of a microphone placed at various distances from the source must vary inversely with the square of the distance. The ideal acoustic environment provides an easy way to compare two sources of unequal power. We need only find two distances where the power per unit area is the same. The power of each source then differs by the ratio of the square of the distances. Such comparisons lead naturally to statements of relative intensity with respect to some standard source. We can relate intensities via distances to a standard source of some kind and avoid the problem of absolute specification entirely. In light, the standard candle is a standard source and its illuminance is measured in foot candles. However, no standard "pin drop" has been developed in acoustics, in part, because the ideal environment is less easily achieved in acoustics than in optics. In most acoustic environments the wall, ceiling, and floor make the inverse square law a poor approximation, even if they are located at extreme distances from the source.

ABSOLUTE QUANTITIES

The inverse square law provides a convenient means of determining relative intensity. Such comparisons are useful but it is essential, especially when comparing results from one laboratory with those from another, to obtain

[2] Actually this is only true at reasonable distances from the source. The exact condition is that the frequency of the wave times the distance must be large, $f \cdot r \gg 1$. This condition defines the "far" field, as opposed to the "near" field. In the near field, the energy density is somewhat higher because of changes in the character of the medium (specifically the impedance); even in the near field, however, the energy density is the same for all points on a sphere of radius r.

absolute measures of the physical quantities involved. Absolute measures of sound intensity have been available for approximately the last 100 years. Prior to that time, only relative measurements were made. The absolute value of sound pressure in an acoustic wave was unknown, although various techniques to control relative intensity were employed. Lord Rayleigh, about a century ago, developed a thin disk, which he suspended by two thin wires in the sound field. A sound wave exerts a force on the disk and imparts a small torque on the wires. Thus, the torque, or force on the wires provides an absolute measure of sound pressure. Nowadays, precision microphones provide the most convenient and practical means of measuring sound pressure.

Sound pressure is simply a measure of force per unit area and the most common unit of pressure is dynes per square centimeter. A dyne is the force required to move 1 g with an acceleration of 1 cm/sec^2. One particular value of pressure is very important because it is often used as a reference sound pressure level in acoustic measurements. This value is *.0002 dyne/cm^2*. It is a convenient number when stated in terms of acoustic power. It is also near the level of the faintest audible sound.

To calculate how much work a sound wave performs, one must know the impedance of the medium. *Impedance* is a property of the medium of transmission, namely, the air itself.

A frequent formula for the power in an sound wave is the following:

$$I = \frac{p^2}{\rho_0 c},$$
(1.3)

where I is the power per square centimeter (W/cm^2) in the sound wave, p is the pressure in the wave measured in dynes per square centimeter, and the denominator, $\rho_0 c$, is the characteristic impedance of air.[3] The characteristic acoustic impedance of air, $\rho_0 c$, is simply the product of the density of the air ρ_0 and the velocity of the waveform c[4]. For those who know electrical measurements, this formula is exactly analogous to the $P = V^2/R$, where V is the voltage, R is the impedance or resistance, and P is power. For standard temperature and atmospheric conditions, $\rho_0 c = 40$ dyne·sec/cm^3.

It is always good practice to check a formula to see whether it is dimensionally

---

[3] $\rho_0 c$ has dimensions of

velocity $\dfrac{\text{cm}}{\text{sec}}$ times density $\dfrac{\text{g}}{\text{cm}^3}$, or $\dfrac{\text{cm} \cdot \text{g}}{\text{sec}^2} \times \dfrac{\text{sec}}{\text{cm}^3} = \dfrac{\text{dyne} \cdot \text{sec}}{\text{cm}^3}$.

[4] The sound is assumed to travel in a plane progressive wave in this environment. A more general definition of acoustic impedance is the ratio of averaged sound pressure to averaged volume velocity. In this form the ratio is usually a complex number and because the volume velocity is the product of the particle velocity and the area in question, acoustic impedance has the dimension dyne·sec/cm^5. In general then, acoustic impedance has the same structure as the complex ratio of voltage to current in electrical circuit theory.

correct. Equation (1.3) above is supposed to have dimensions of W/cm^2:

$$I \ (W/cm^2) \quad = \frac{\rho^2}{\rho_0 c} = (dynes/cm^2)^2 /(dyne \cdot sec/cm^3) = dyne/cm \cdot sec$$

$$= erg/cm^2 \cdot sec = W/cm^2 \times 10^7.$$

Now we can explain why the pressure value of .0002 $dyne/cm^2$ is used as a reference number. For normal atmospheric conditions $\rho_0 c$ is such that a pressure of .0002 $dyne/cm^2$ yields an intensity that turns out to be the relatively simple number of 10^{-16} W/cm^2 ($10^{-9}/erg/cm^2 \cdot sec$). Therefore, a spherical wave in an ideal environment with a pressure of .0002 $dyne/cm^2$ has an intensity of 10^{-16} W/cm^2.

These latter quantities are to have special importance when we consider some of the physical limitations that influence the absolute sensitivity of the ear. We should point out that Appendix 1, at the end of this chapter, reiterates the relation among the fundamental physical quantities and also provides some basic formulas for converting from one set of units to another. Although one can calculate the sound pressure or power in an acoustic wave, one rarely sees sound levels specified in absolute terms. Mainly, sound is specified as the ratio of one sound to some reference power. Often the logarithm of the ratio is taken and this quantity is proportional to decibels.

DECIBELS

By definition, one sound power I_1 is x decibels (dB) more intense than another sound power I_2 when

$$x = 10 \log_{10} \frac{I_1}{I_2}. \tag{1.4}$$

Briefly, I_1 is said to be x dB above (or below) I_2. Sometimes this relationship is expressed as I_1 is x dB re (with respect to) I_2. The reason for the widespread use of this logarithmic formula is primarily that practical sound intensities range over many orders of magnitude. Changes in sound power of less than 25%, or about 1 dB, are usually unimportant and, in fact, are barely discernible as different. The logarithm of the ratio of intensities is called a bel after Alexander Graham Bell. Ten times that quantity defines the decibel. The decibel is a convenient unit for practical application. Because $\log_{10} 10 = 1$, a difference of 10 dB implies an order of magnitude change in acoustic power. One should also remember that:

$$\log_{10} a \cdot b = \log_{10} a + \log_{10} b,$$

and therefore

$$\log_{10} a^b = b \log_{10} a.$$

Therefore, $\log_{10}$ 10^3 = 3 and hence sounds that differ by three orders of magnitude in power are 30 dB apart. Finally, one should memorize that $\log_{10}$ 2 = .3 (actually $\log_{10}$ 2 = .30103) and hence a factor of two in *power* is approximately equivalent to a 3-dB change. With these facts in hand it is easy to calculate that two acoustic powers having a ratio of 80 are:

$$80 = 2 \quad \cdot \quad 2 \cdot 2 \quad \cdot \quad 10$$

$$\|\qquad\quad\|\quad\|\qquad\quad\|$$

$$10 \log 80 = 3 \text{ dB} + 3 \text{ dB} + 3 \text{ dB} + 10 \text{ dB} = 19 \text{ dB apart.}$$

Often decibels are defined in terms of pressure ratios rather than power ratios. If our two pressures are p_1 and p_2, then using Eq. (1.3),

$$x \ (\text{dB}) = 10 \log \left[(p_1{}^2/\rho_0 c) / (p_2{}^2/\rho_0 c) \right]$$

$$= 10 \log (p_1{}^2/p_2{}^2)$$

$$= 20 \log (p_1/p_2) \qquad\qquad (1.5)$$

Note that either one can first square the pressure ratio and treat the result as a power ratio or, because squaring the argument of a logarithm is equal to doubling the logarithm, one can take the logarithm of the pressure ratio and multiply the answer by 20 to get decibels.

It is important to realize that decibels are dimensionless. They are neither powers nor pressures—just numbers. They are, in fact, proportional to the logarithm of the ratio of the two dimensional quantities. The differences in Eqs. (1.4) and (1.5) make it clear that one must know the dimensions of the quantities used in the ratio. If the ratios are acoustic powers, then the logarithm of the ratio is multiplied by 10 (Eq. 1.4), whereas if the ratios are pressures then the logarithm of the ratio is multiplied by 20 (Eq. 1.5).

The decibels remain the same; the ratios of pressure and power change. Consider the following example; suppose two sounds differ by 20 dB. Then, by Eq. (1.4), we know their acoustic powers must be in the ratio of 100 to 1. By Eq. (1.5), we conclude that their acoustic pressure must be in the ratio of 10:1. These results are consistent for, by Eq. (1.3), acoustic power is proportional to the square of pressure and $10^2 = 100$.

Decibels can also be negative. A value of −40 dB implies the ratio of acoustic powers (I_1/I_2) is 1/10,000 (Eq. 1.4), or the ratio of acoustic pressure (p_1/p_2) is 1/100 (Eq. 1.5).

Normally one pressure is used as the standard pressure. For example, if our reference pressure, p_2 in Eq. (1.5), is .0002 dyne/cm^2 then p_1 is said to be x dB *re* .0002 dyne/cm^2 or simply, x dB sound pressure level (SPL). If a peak acoustic pressure wave in air is .02 dyne/cm^2 then we say that the sound has a peak pressure 40 dB SPL. The use of SPL is simply a convenient way of specifying the reference pressure one is using. Knowing the SPL value of a sound wave in air one can calculate pressure in dynes per square centimeters, via Eq. (1.5), or its power in watts per square centimeters, via Eq. (1.4). To appreciate the magnitude of some sounds on the SPL scale Table 1.1 may be helpful. We assume in all cases that the acoustic power has been averaged over a period of 1 or 2 sec.

Sometimes in the study of hearing another reference level is used as the standard. If the reference is the pressure or power at which the sound first becomes audible, the scale is called *sensation level,* or SL. For example, if a sound is 40 dB SL, it is 10^4 times the power at which it is just audible or 10^2 times the pressure at which it is just audible. Obviously, such a specification is equivocal because it is not directly related to any physical standard, such as watts or dynes, but only to someone's judgment of what is just audible. It is therefore not very satisfactory as a means of specifying an acoustic level. Nevertheless, investigators have used it in the past. Decibels are sometimes a source of confusion, often because of unfamiliarity with the use of logarithms. It may be helpful for the reader to refresh his or her memory by working the problems at the end of the chapter.

Let us next take up a particular class of sound waves that is extremely important in acoustic analysis—sinusoidal waves. We must discuss the properties of these functions because they are often used as the elementary signals in acoustic analysis. Also, they must be discussed because, as we shall see, the ear is very sensitive to some sinusoidal frequencies but not to others.

SINUSOIDAL WAVES

At the outset, let us stress once more that an acoustic wave is not necessarily a sinusoid. An acoustic wave is a largely arbitrary function, g, constrained only by some minor technical restrictions on the derivative of g (see Eqs. 1.1 and 1.2, and the attendant discussion). The linearity of the wave equation lets us represent any wave as the sum of other waveforms. This technique is often

TABLE 1.1
Some Typical Sound Pressure Levels

SPL (dB)	Condition of measurement
0	Absolute threshold of a 3,000-Hz sinusoid measured in a free field
40	A very quiet living room
60	Average conversational voice measured in a typical room 5 ft from talker
80	Speaker shouting 5 ft away in a typical room
90–100	Platform of a subway station as the train arrives
130–150	100 ft behind an airplane jet engine

useful, because a complicated waveform can then be represented by a sum of simpler waveforms. Because sound obeys the wave equation and hence is a linear process, one can utilize this strategy in acoustic analysis.

One very useful, simple wave is the sinusoidal wave, a wave of the form

$$p(t) = A \sin(2\pi ft + \theta). \tag{1.6}$$

The constants are A, the amplitude; f, the frequency; 2π, a numerical constant; and θ, the phase angle. This is the function produced by taking a vector of the length A and mapping the projection of this vector as it rotates with uniform speed about the origin on the y axis. Figure 1.4 illustrates this motion for several values of θ. The number of occasions the vector rotates per unit time is the frequency f. Because $\sin(\alpha + 2\pi) = \sin \alpha$, the value of $p(t)$ is exactly the same each $t = 1/f$ seconds. At $t = 0$, the value of $p(0) = A \sin \theta$, so the initial value need not be zero at the origin. Two sinusoids of the same frequency and amplitude may have different phase angles and hence different instantaneous pressures. Also, because

$$\sin(2\pi ft_1 + \theta_1) = \sin(2\pi ft_2 + \theta_2)$$

if

$$t_2 = t_1 + (\theta_1 - \theta_2)/2\pi f,$$

we can also interpret phase as a shift in the time scale.

A sinusoidal acoustic wave is of the form

$$p(t_1 x) = A \sin[2\pi f(t \pm x/c) + \theta], \tag{1.7}$$

where x is the distance and c the velocity of the wave. From this equation we see that the pressure waveform is sinusoidal in both time and space.

The *frequency* of the wave is simply the number of times the wave repeats itself per unit time. Thus, a 1,000-cycle-per-second wave repeats itself 1,000 times in 1 sec. It has become standard terminology to use the European designation of cycles per second, Hz, after the German physicist, Henrich Hertz, who worked with another very important wave type, electromagnetic waves. The *period* of the wave is simply the time it takes to execute one cycle. For example, the period of a 1,000-Hz wave is 1 msec, 1/1,000 of a second. The period and frequency are reciprocally related, that is, the product of the wave's period and the wave's frequency is always equal to 1.

The *wavelength* of a sound wave is the quantity analogous to the period except that the wave is measured as a function of distance or space rather than time. In space the wave repeats itself whenever $x = c/f$ (see Eq. 1.7). Wavelengths can be measured in two ways. The velocity of sound in air is approximately 330 m/sec or 1,100 ft/sec. Hence we can determine the wavelength from the frequency by

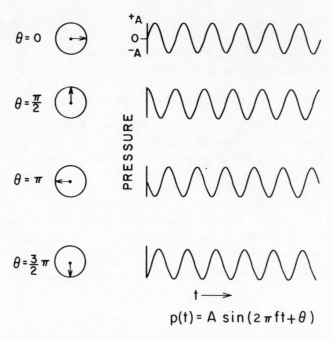

$$p(t) = A \sin(2\pi f t + \theta)$$

FIG. 1.4 Sinusoidal motion can be considered the vertical projection of the tip of the clock hand at each instant in time. The clock hand moves counter clockwise in this illustration. The time between epochs of the sine wave is exactly $1/f$. The four panels represent four starting phases for the sinewave, four values of θ.

simply dividing the velocity of sound by the frequency. A 1,000-Hz wave therefore has a wavelength of approximately 33 cm or 1.1 ft, for 1,000 cycles traverse 330 m or 1,100 feet in 1 sec. The second method of calculating the wavelength is to multiply the period of the sound by the wave's velocity. For example, if the wave travels 330 m in 1 sec, in one period, or 1/1,000 sec, it travels .33 m.

The size of the wavelength of a sound varies with frequency. For example, some of the lowest frequencies that the ear can hear are below 100 Hz. At 100 Hz the wavelength is approximately 3.3 m. Near the upper range of hearing, 10,000 Hz, the wavelength is about 3 cm.

We next consider the interaction of sound waves with other objects and themselves. These effects may seem surprising and even mysterious but are actually completely consistent with simple acoustic principles. The single most important principle is the linearity of the wave equation; if two sources generate two different waves, the resulting pressure wave is obtained simply by adding the two separate pressure waves. This is true of sound waves in general and hence is true of sinusoidal waves in particular.

One should also recall that complicated waves can be generated by adding sinusoidal waves. More important, as Fourier has proved, complicated waves can practically always be represented by a sum of sinusoidal waves. Therefore, in the material that follows we consider the response of various systems to sinusoidal waves. Because these systems are linear, the results obtained with sinusoids predict the response of these systems to complicated waves. This is the principle of superposition, and we have more to say about it at the end of the chapter. Its usefulness becomes apparent in the topics that follow.

A simple mechanical system will begin the discussion of the next topic, resonance. The properties of this mechanical system are more tangible and obvious than the motion of molecules in a gas. We will generalize the resulting principles to strings and, finally, to columns of air. The phenomena of standing waves will be introduced and the problem of nodes and antinodes in realistic acoustic environments will be discussed. Finally, the chapter ends with a discussion of linear system analysis and the principle of superposition.

RESONANCE

Acoustic resonance can produce startling results, such as the breaking of wine glasses, the sympathetic vibration of strings, or the enhancement of a particular frequency when it is listened to through a long tube. Resonance, however, is a general property of many mechanical and electrical systems. The potential for resonance is inherent in systems that can store energy in two different forms. First, consider a simple resonant system, the pendulum. The two different forms of energy storage are clearest in this system.

SIMPLE PENDULUM

Figure 1.5 shows a mass hanging straight down at the end of a long string of length L. Suppose we displace the mass a few degrees from the vertical. Because we have raised the mass slightly in height, we have imparted potential energy to the system. If we release the mass, it swings back and forth. At the bottom of its swing it has no potential energy. Because its velocity is fastest at that point, however, its kinetic energy is greatest. The pendulum therefore has two forms of energy, kinetic and potential. The mass moves sinusoidally as a function of time, if the displacement is not too great. (The maximum swing should be less than $15°$.) It can easily be verified that the period of the oscillation is proportional to the square root of the pendulum's length, L.

The period of the pendulum is independent of its mass. However, the amount of mass affects how long the pendulum swings once it is put in motion. This is

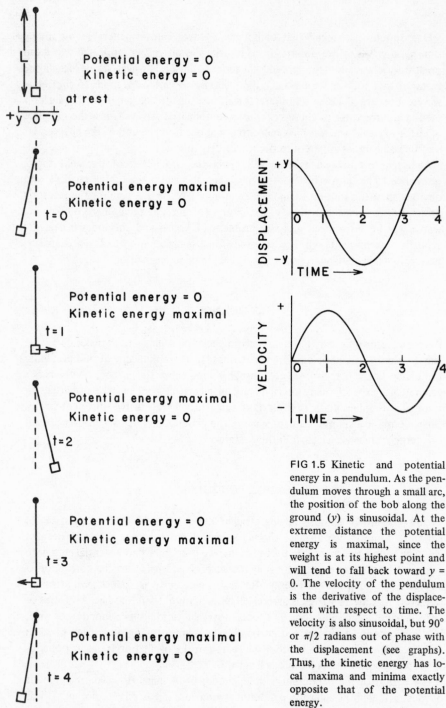

Potential energy = 0
Kinetic energy = 0

at rest

+y 0 ‾y

Potential energy maximal
Kinetic energy = 0

t = 0

Potential energy = 0
Kinetic energy maximal

t = 1

Potential energy maximal
Kinetic energy = 0

t = 2

Potential energy = 0
Kinetic energy maximal

t = 3

Potential energy maximal
Kinetic energy = 0

t = 4

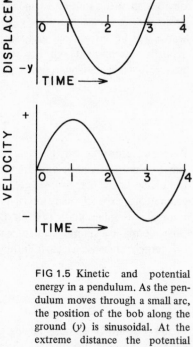

FIG 1.5 Kinetic and potential energy in a pendulum. As the pendulum moves through a small arc, the position of the bob along the ground (y) is sinusoidal. At the extreme distance the potential energy is maximal, since the weight is at its highest point and will tend to fall back toward $y = 0$. The velocity of the pendulum is the derivative of the displacement with respect to time. The velocity is also sinusoidal, but 90° or $\pi/2$ radians out of phase with the displacement (see graphs). Thus, the kinetic energy has local maxima and minima exactly opposite that of the potential energy.

because frictional forces reduce the energy in the system as it swings. These frictions take longer to dissipate the energy if the bob is massive. Figure 1.5 shows various phases of the pendulum's arc as well as the inherently sinusoidal motion it produces. Notice that the displacement of the pendulum and its velocity are 90° ($\pi/2$) out of phase with one another.

Now turn to the system illustrated in Figure 1.6. We have a pendulum made from a thin rod coupled to a wheel via a soft spring. As the wheel is rotated at a uniform velocity the spring is stretched in a sinusoidal fashion and a nearly sinusoidal excitation is applied to the pendulum. How does the pendulum respond to this force? The answer depends on the frequency of rotation of the wheel, that is, the frequency of the force exciting the pendulum. If the rotation of the wheel has a frequency much higher or lower than the natural frequency of the pendulum, then the pendulum responds very little. Only at the natural frequency of the pendulum will the wheel produce vigorous movement of the pendulum. Three cases are illustrated in Figure 1.7 and in Figure 1.8 the response amplitude is illustrated as a function of different frequencies.

What is the phase relation between the input force and the displacement of the pendulum? Assume that the driving force has been exerted a long time so that steady-state conditions exist. If the wheel turns very slowly compared with the

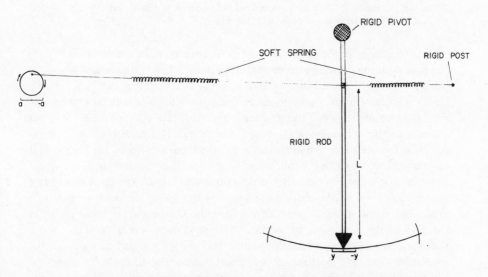

FIG. 1.6 Driving a pendulum with sinusoidal motion. The pendulum is being driven by a revolving wheel, shown to the left in the drawing. Since the wheel is at a great distance, the force it imparts is proportional to the distance of pin in the wheel measured along the horizontal distance (a to $-a$). The displacement of the pendulum (y to $-y$) is also measured along the horizontal component. By turning the wheel at a constant rate, a sinusoidal force is imparted to the pendulum.

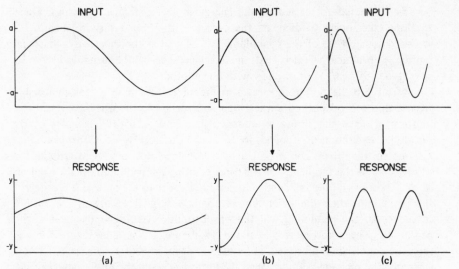

FIG. 1.7 Phase relation between the input force (a to $-a$) and the pendulum response (y to $-y$) for three different driving frequencies. The response is maximum at the resonance frequency (b), and the phase shift is $90°$ ($\pi/2$ radians). At frequencies below the resonance frequency, the amplitude of response is diminished but in the same phase (a). At frequencies above the resonance frequency, the amplitude of response is diminished and the response phase is $180°$ (π radians) out of phase with the input (c).

natural frequency of the pendulum, the displacement of the pendulum is exactly in phase with the displacement produced by the rotation of the wheel. When the pin on the wheel reaches the point labeled $-a$, the pendulum moves to $-y$, the maximal excursion to the right; as the pin moves to the point labeled $+a$, the pendulum moves to $+y$, the maximal excursion to the left, and so forth throughout the cycle. The response of the pendulum is small because the natural forces of the pendulum are in fact opposing the force applied by the spring. This can be understood from the following observation. Suppose the pin of the wheel were fixed at some position. The pendulum would stretch the right spring as it traveled from $-y$ to $+y$ and would compress the spring during the other half cycle. The energy needed would derive from the kinetic and potential energy in the mass of the pendulum. In contrast, if the pendulum were fixed at any point, the wheel would exert a stretching force only during one-half of its cycle, the revolution from the bottom of the wheel to the top through the point $+a$. Therefore, the input force and the pendulum would be in phase half of the time. Half of the time their forces would be in opposition. The argument used here should be familiar to anyone who has pushed someone in a swing. To produce the maximum motion one must time the pushes to be in phase with the ongoing motion.

In resonance, when the frequency of rotation of the wheel is equal to the natural frequency of the pendulum, the forces are in phase throughout the cycle.

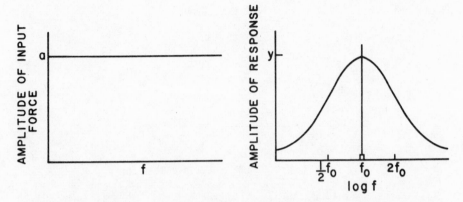

FIG. 1.8 The amplitude of response as a function of frequency. The amplitude of the input is the same at all frequencies. The maximum response occurs at f_0 and lesser response occurs at higher and lower frequencies. The shape of the curve for a simple resonance system is nearly symmetric when plotted against logarithm of frequency. The relative size of the response an octave above $(2f_0)$, or below $(\frac{1}{2}f_0)$ resonance is often used to indicate the degree of tuning.

The wheel moves from bottom to top, zero through $+a$ to zero, just as the pendulum moves from $-y$ through zero to $+y$. In terms of the input and response diagram the motions are 90° out of phase (see Figure 1.7). The response leads the applied force. Because the natural forces of the pendulum and the driving force of the wheel are exactly in phase throughout the cycle, the response is vigorous, as the middle diagram of Figure 1.7 illustrates.

At frequencies much above the natural resonance of the pendulum the response is again smaller, this time for reasons opposite to those true at lower frequencies. At very high frequencies the input displacement is 180° ahead of the response. Again, because the driving force and the response are largely out of phase, the response is small.

The size of the pendulum's response to a variety of input frequencies is summarized in Figure 1.8. The response is maximum at the natural frequency, f_0, of the pendulum, for the reasons we have outlined above; it is much less at frequencies above or below that value. The vigorous response of the system at the single frequency is called *resonance*. The curve shows how the system is tuned to selectively respond best at that single frequency. This is the simplest resonance system that can be constructed. Of course, more complicated systems, having a multitude of resonance peaks, can be constructed but the pendulum system is a good exemple of the simplest resonance system. The phase change of 180° between input force or displacement and the response to it as the input frequency moves through the resonance point is typical of all simple systems.

The frequency at which resonance occurs for the pendulum system depends only on the length of the pendulum. However, the exact shape of the resonance curve (Figure 1.9) depends heavily on the mass of the pendulum in relation to

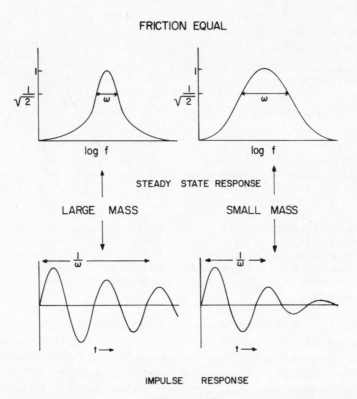

FIG. 1.9 Frequency response to equal amplitude sinusoids and temporal response to an impulse for two resonance systems. The figure illustrates that the highly tuned resonance system (left) will have a longer temporal response to brief excitation, such as an impulse, than will a less highly tuned system (right).

the frictional or damping forces inherent in the system. Suppose that the friction is held constant and the mass of the pendulum is varied. With a very light bob the motion of the wheel imparts a force that produces appreciable displacement at all frequencies, so that the resonance curve is fairly broad. With a large mass, however, only those frequencies very close to the resonance frequency induce a motion in the pendulum and those motions occur only after a long time.[5] In the case of the large mass, the resonance curve is sharply peaked. Figure 1.9 (top) illustrates the two conditions.

There is another consequence of the difference in the sharpness of the resonance curve. Suppose a brief force is applied, such as a tug on the spring. How do the two systems respond to such an impulse? First, the amplitude of the response of the system with the large mass is less because the massive

---

[5] We are assuming that, since the force is applied for a long time, steady-state conditions have occurred.

pendulum requires more energy to achieve the same displacement. However, the important fact is that the response continues for a longer period of time with the more sharply tuned system. In fact, for such simple resonance systems the time to reach half the initial response is nearly equal to the reciprocal of the bandwidth of the system. The *bandwidth* of the resonance system is the range of frequencies over which the system shows a vigorous response. It is convention-ally defined as the difference in frequency between the half power points. Since half power corresponds to a difference in pressure or force, or displacement, of $1/\sqrt{2}$, it is simply the range of frequencies within .707 times the peak response of the resonance system. Figure 1.9 illustrates the resonance curve of a sharply tuned and broadly tuned system and how the reciprocal of the bandwidth, $1/\omega$, is related to the impulse response of such systems.

WAVES IN A STRETCHED STRING

The preceding discussion should make it somewhat easier to understand the phenomenon of resonance in a stretched string. The stretched string tied to a rigid post provides a convenient example of wave propagation and reflection. Imagine a string of length L extending along the x axis as in Figure 1.10. Now suppose we introduce a wave at the left end of the string by moving it slightly along the y axis. This mechanical disturbance generates a wave that travels down the length of the string with some velocity V. The exact value of the velocity depends both on the character of the string and on its tension. At the end of the string a reflected wave starts traveling in the opposite direction with the same velocity V. Although the reflected wave is generally somewhat smaller than the incident wave, we shall assume perfect reflection.

Now we can deduce the conditions necessary for resonance by analogy with a swing or pendulum. Resonance can be achieved if we introduce energy that is in phase with the natural forces of the system. For example, if we momentarily move one end of the string, a wave runs down the length of the string and returns in exactly $2L/V$ seconds. If we excite the string by imposing a sinusoidal displacement of $V/2L$ cycles per second, then just as one wave returns from the opposite end, another wave starts exactly in phase with it. Actually, as the first wave returns to the source it is reflected to start yet another journey down the string. The mutual reinforcement of the returning wave and the new excitation should produce vigorous vibrations of the string at this frequency. The actual displacement of the string for this case is shown at the top of Figure 1.10.

By a similar line of argument it is also clear that a frequency twice as great as $f = V/2L$ can also provide energy exactly in phase with the wave traveling back and forth in the string. This is because at the higher frequency two waves are started before the first has returned but still one can stay exactly in step with the natural flow of energy in the system. Similarly, at frequencies equal to

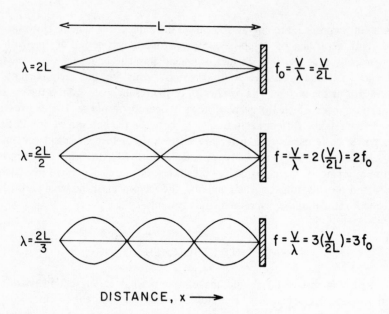

FIG. 1.10 Resonance modes in a stretched string. The displacement patterns for three frequencies are shown f_0, $2f_0$, and $3f_0$.

$n(V/2L)$, where n is any positive integer, the string can be excited easily. These other modes of vibration are illustrated in Figure 1.10.

Note that we have been discussing a wave that is traveling along the x axis but the response that we finally observe is perpendicular to that direction, namely a transverse wave. The transverse motion of the string is exactly sinusoidal. The wavelength of this sinusoid for the fundamental of first harmonic response is exactly $2L$. Note that the wavelength, λ, is also equal to the velocity of the wave divided by the frequency $\lambda = V/f$. The top line of the figure shows the fundamental or first harmonic. The other cases are called the second and third harmonics; that is, if f_0 is the fundamental then $2f_0$ and $3f_0$ are the second and third harmonics. When the second harmonic exists as the mode of vibration, there is a point half-way down the string that is literally not moving in the y direction. One can verify this by pinching the string there between one's fingers and noting that nothing changes. This is because of the interaction of the two waves. One wave travels down the string to the right and is exactly out of phase with the wave traveling to the left; hence complete cancellation occurs where they meet at the midpoint. This is the principle of cancellation, discussed earlier, and it is an important property of all waves. To the left and right of this midpoint, the waves are in phase and vigorous motion is evident.

We can better understand cancellation and reinforcement if we actually write down the equations that govern the motion in the string. The outgoing wave from the source travels to the right and has a form

$$y_1 = af[t - (x/v)], \qquad (1.8)$$

where t is time, a is amplitude, x is distance, and v is velocity. The reflected wave is traveling in the opposite direction and hence has the general form

$$y_2 = -af[t + (x/v)]. \qquad (1.9)$$

The fact that the displacement is zero where the string is tied to the wall means that the reflected wave must be opposite in sign from the incoming wave [i.e., at any time, for $x = L$, $y_1(t, L) + y_2(t, L) = 0$]. For the case of sinusoidal waves, then

$$y_1 = a \sin 2\pi f[t - (x/v)]$$

and

$$y_2 = -a \sin 2\pi f[t + (x/v)]$$

and the combined wave

$$y = y_1 + y_2 = -2a \cos 2\pi ft \sin 2\pi f (x/v) \qquad (1.10)$$

and so for the various resonant frequencies, where

$$f_n = n \; \frac{v}{2L} \quad , \qquad n = \text{integer},$$

$$\sin 2 \pi n \left(\frac{v}{2L} \right) \frac{x}{v} = \sin n\pi \frac{x}{L}$$

and so $y = 0$ at $x = L$ and $x = 0$ for any integer n. The displacement at other distances (x) is sinusoidal in time with frequency f_n (see Eq. 1.10), except where

$$\sin n\pi \frac{x}{L} = 0$$

for $n = 3$, this occurs at $x = \frac{1}{3}L$ and $\frac{2}{3}L$, as well as $x = 0$ and $x = L$, and produces the vibration pattern shown in the bottom of Figure 1.10.

RESONANCE IN CLOSED TUBES

Air columns in closed tubes behave in a similar fashion to our stretched strings. The wave, however, is longitudinal; that is, the motion of the particle of the gas is in the same direction as the wave motion. An important restriction concerns the width of the tube. The width of the tube must be much less than a wavelength. If this is true then the sound wave can be treated as a plane progressive wave; that is, the sound wave is exactly the same at all points in a plane perpendicular to the length of the tube. The wave is not spreading out, as it has been in our spherical wave, and hence its amplitude is constant and independent of distance. Actually, there is some loss, both at the sides of the tube and at the end where the wave is reflected, but these losses are slight in an enclosure with hard smooth walls.

The analysis of sound in a closed tube closely follows the arguments used in the case of a stretched string. If we have a closed tube, such as that illustrated in Figure 1.11, and we displace the gas molecules suddenly at one end, a longitudinal pressure disturbance moves down the tube. It is easiest to think of displacement or velocity of the gas particles rather than pressure. If we think of displacement of the sound wave then in the region of the end of the tube the reflected wave is equal to the incident wave and opposite in sign. Just as in a string, therefore, a sinusoidal vibration pattern may exist in the tube if the frequency of disturbance is equal to

$$f_n = n\left(\frac{c}{2L}\right), \quad n = 1, 2, \ldots, \text{integer},$$

where c is the velocity of sound in the gas and L is the length of the tube. For $n > 1$ there are regions inside the tube where the net displacement of the gas particles is zero. These points are called displacement nodes and are exactly analogous to the lack of vertical displacement at the nodes of a string. The reason there is no net displacement of the particles is that forces in that region of the tube are equal and opposite; these displacement nodes are therefore regions of maximum force or pressure. At other points along the tube the displacement is maximum and the pressure is exactly zero. At these pressure nodes one can, in principle, locate a microphone and find no sound present.

The principles governing the behavior of sound in larger containers are more complex but the basic phenomenon is similar to these described for the narrow closed tube. A sinusoidal source in a room or auditorium produces regions of maximum and zero pressure. These can easily be explored by exciting a sinusoidal source, such as a tuning fork, plugging one ear, and moving about while the source is sounding. A typical sound environment, such as the classroom or living room, is roughly analogous to a wall of mirrors in terms of reflections of the sound wave, but with ceiling and floor also acting as reflectors. Typical rooms also contain material, such as drapes or rugs, that absorb some of the acoustic energy. It is therefore virtually impossible to specify the exact distribution of sound pressure in such a real space except where the geometry of the room is extremely simple and there are no objects to absorb sound or break up the sound paths. For acoustic measurements a less complicated environment is needed.

ANECHOIC ROOM

To measure light in the laboratory, one typically uses dark rooms with the walls painted black to absorb stray light. This achieves an ideal optical environment, where the inverse square law should be valid. Similarly, in scientific studies of

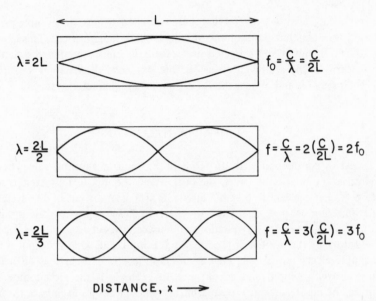

FIG. 1.11 Resonance in a closed tube. The patterns illustrated in the tube are values for average displacement of the molecules of gas. Three frequencies are illustrated, f_0, $2f_0$, and $3f_0$. Compare with Figure 1.10.

acoustics, one attempts to achieve the ideal acoustic environment by building a room with surfaces (walls, ceiling, and floor) that absorb as much sound as possible.

A source centered in the middle of such a room radiates sound in all directions. A minimum of sound is reflected at the boundary of the room. The room should produce no echos or reflections at the surfaces and is called *anechoic.* In an ideal acoustic room the inverse square law is valid. Anechoic rooms are constructed by covering the six surfaces of the room with sound absorbing wedges mounted perpendicular to the surface. If the wedges are of sufficient size, they break up the sound wave and absorb almost all of the incident energy. The amount of absorption depends on the frequency of the sound wave but is generally very large if the wave is short compared with the size of the wedge. A typical room may have wedges that measure a meter from base to apex. It becomes essentially echoless for frequencies above 100 Hz.

Anechoic chambers are very expensive and usually large. They are rarely employed in experiments on hearing. Instead, earphones that can deliver calibrated amounts of energy are employed. Because the ear channel, when covered by an earphone, is a closed tube, there are problems at high frequencies with standing waves and resonance. Most work with earphones is carried out below 4 kHz. For acoustic measurement or calibration, however, an anechoic chamber is often essential.

The preceding analyses of closed tubes, stretched strings, and simple pendulums used the fact that the systems were linear and time invariant. This allowed us to add the incident and reflected wave, for example, to predict the standing wave pattern in the stretched string. Before we close this chapter we briefly define such systems and discuss their most important characteristics.

LINEAR SYSTEMS

It is easiest to consider linearity in terms of an input and output rule. The rule that governs the relation between the output and the input of a system is some function F. Let us denote possible inputs as $x(t)$. The output of the system is another function of time, $y(t)$. Thus, the system takes as input $x(t)$ and produces as output $y(t)$. The exact way relationship between these two functions depends on the nature of the system or process. What is input and what is output is clear for a simple electronic circuit, such as an amplifier. Sometimes it is difficult to identify clearly an input and an output. An example is the closed tube. The definitions of input and output are arbitrary—they need not even have the same dimensions. In the pendulum the input can be regarded as force and the output as the displacement of the pendulum bob. One needs as a minimum two single-value functions $x(t)$ and $y(t)$, and a rule or law, F, relating $y(t)$ to $x(t)$. This function F defines the system

$$y(t) = F\left[x(t)\right]. \tag{1.11}$$

Consider several simultaneously presented inputs $x_1(t)$, $x_2(t)$, $x_3(t)$. These inputs are added together, each weighted by some constant. Our goal is to predict the output of the system given this input. If the system is linear, then we may express this relation between the input and the output very simply as

$$y(t) = F[ax_1(t) + bx_2(t) + cx_3 t]$$
$$= aF[x_1(t)] + bF[x_2(t)] + cF[x_3(t)], \tag{1.12}$$

where a, b, and c are constants.

This equation says that the output produced by an arbitrary weighted combination of these inputs is simply the same weighted sum of outputs to each alone. One can therefore always predict how the process responds to some new input, if that new input can be constructed from old, known inputs. This is the principle of superposition.

Often it happens that a system is both linear and time invariant. *Time invariance* simply means that the exact value of time plays no role in determining the output. The same output occurs whether the input is presented at 10 o'clock or at 11 o'clock. The output in the latter case, of course, occurs 1 hr later. Technically, time invariance means that if we shift the time scale at the input, then the output can be predicted by using the same shift at the output:

$$y(t + T) = F[x(t + T)]. \qquad (1.13)$$

If the system is both time invariant and linear, then its response to sinusoids provides a complete description of the system. By "complete" description we mean that we know how the system behaves for all possible inputs. This happens because any feasible inputs can be represented by a weighted sum of sinusoids (Fourier representation). One can predict the output of each sinusoid separately and then use Eq. (1.12) to predict the entire output.

Furthermore, the output of a linear, time-invariant system to a single sinusoid input is a sinusoid unchanged in frequency but possibly differing from the input in amplitude and phase. If we put any sinusoid into this system, we obtain only that same sinusoid frequency at the output. No other frequency will be present. Usually, one summarizes this by saying that the system produces no distortion. It generates no components other than those present at the input. By the same token, if the input is a set of different sinusoids, then one obtains only those sinusoids at the output. No other components appear at the output—no sum or difference frequencies.

The definition of linearity shows that the important defining property is *superposition*. This property is the basis of all linear analysis, and it is used repeatedly throughout this book. Before we close this chapter, let us emphasize again what this property allows us to do. Basically, it lets us use old answers to solve new problems. If we call the input causes and output effects, then we can summarize the situation as follows. Suppose that x_1 causes y_1, and x_2 causes y_2. Then $x_1 + x_2$ causes $y_1 + y_2$. To predict how the system responds to some novel input, one tries to represent the new input as some combination of old inputs. In most general cases, this may not be possible, although it often can be done. However, if the system is linear and time invariant, then one need only catalog the system response to a number of sinusoids. One can usually approximate any novel input by a linear combination of these sinusoids. Predicting the output involves only a linear combination of the separate effects.

If the system is linear and time invariant and one knows its response to sine waves, then one has the most general understanding one can have of the system. For any input one can predict the system's behavior. The generality of this understanding becomes clearer when we consider nonlinear systems. These systems are sometimes almost inscrutable. No matter how much one knows about their behavior to certain classes of input, the output to some novel inputs may be completely different and unexpected. By their very nature it is often impossible to provide a general description.

It is no accident that understanding and linearity are closely related. Often, one can understand complex systems by choosing the terms of analysis x and y judiciously, so that they are linearly related. One can make a case that scientific insight, such as defining force in terms of mass and acceleration, amounts to a shrewd choice of the terms of analysis. The use of linear analysis, and especially the concept of superposition, is an extremely important one in acoustics and its use in the analysis of sensory systems is stressed in this book. For some further remarks on this matter, especially the question of scientific strategy, Chapter 9 should be consulted.

SUMMARY

The physical basis of sound has been reviewed from both a molecular and a molar point of view. Sound is a mechanical disturbance obeying the wave equation. Two sounds combine by simply adding the pressure of each waveform. The intensity aspects of sound waves were discussed and several basic formulas were introduced. The decibel was defined and the standard reference level described. Sinusoidal vibrations were discussed and the terms "frequency," "wavelength," and "period" defined. Finally, the phenomena of resonance were discussed and the behavior of the simplest resonant system was explored.

APPENDIX 1: SOME COMMON FORMULAS AND DEFINITIONS

Energy (work) is force exerted over distance:

$$erg = dyne \cdot cm.$$

Dyne is a unit of force, the force needed to accelerate 1 g 1 cm/sec^2:

$$dyne = \frac{g \cdot cm}{sec^2}.$$

Pressure is the force per unit area:

$$\frac{dyne}{cm^2} = \frac{g}{sec \cdot cm}.$$

Characteristic acoustic impedance is simply the density of air ρ_0 multiplied by the velocity of sound, c:

$$\rho_0 c = 40 \frac{dyne \cdot sec}{cm^3} = \frac{g}{cm^3} \cdot \frac{cm}{sec}.$$

Power is the rate at which work is expanded. For a constant power over time, $E = PT$, where E is energy, P is power, and T is time.

$$10^7 \ ergs = 1 \ W \cdot sec.$$

Intensity is used to refer to power in this book. For a free field at some distance from the source

$$I = \frac{p^2}{\rho_0 c}$$

where p is pressure and $\rho_0 c$ is the characteristic impedance of the medium.

SPL (sound pressure level) of a sound with pressure p is

$$20 \log \frac{p}{p_{ref}}$$

where p_{ref} = .0002 dyne/cm². One dyne/cm² is 74 dB SPL, also called a *microbar.* In a free field p_{ref} corresponds to an intensity of 10^{-16} W/cm².

In a sonic boom the peak overpressure of the boom is commonly reported in foot-pounds, lb/ft². One foot-pound = 127.6 dB SPL.

APPENDIX 2

Given the spherical wave equation

$$\frac{d^2 \, (p \cdot x)}{dt^2} = c^2 \frac{d^2 \, (p \cdot x)}{dx^2}, \tag{A2.1}$$

where $p = p(ct \pm x)$ we wish to verify that

$$y = \frac{1}{x} p$$

solves this equation. Rewriting Eq. (A2.1) we have

$$\frac{d_2 y}{dt^2} = c^2 \frac{d^2 y}{dx^2}$$

where

$$y = \frac{1}{x} p(ct \pm x). \tag{A2.2}$$

Now the derivative of a function $y = f(u)$ with respect to z, where u is also a function of z, is simply

$$\frac{df(u)}{dz} = \frac{dy}{du} \cdot \frac{du}{dz},$$

the so-called chain rule. Therefore,

$$\frac{d^2 y}{dt^2} = \frac{d}{dt} \left(\frac{dy}{du} \cdot \frac{du}{dt} \right) = c^2 \frac{d^2 y}{du^2}$$

and

$$\frac{d^2 y}{dx^2} = \frac{d}{dt} \left(\frac{dy}{du} \cdot \frac{du}{dx} \right) = \frac{d^2 y}{du^2}.$$

Therefore, Eq. (A2.2) becomes

$$c^2 \frac{d^2 y}{du^2} = c^2 \frac{d^2 y}{du^2}$$

and

$$y = (1/x)\, p(ct \pm x)$$

is indeed a solution.

APPENDIX 3: EXERCISES ON DECIBELS

1a. If a portable radio has a peak output of 1 W and a high fidelity set has a peak output of 10 W, how many decibels is the peak output of the hi-fi above the portable?

1b. At the peak output levels, what is the difference in the peak pressure? (Assume the output is a sinusoid in both cases).

2. If the peak pressure of one sinusoid is 10 times the peak pressure of another, how many decibels is the larger above the smaller? How many decibels is the smaller below the larger? What is the intensity (power) ratio corresponding to this ratio of 10 in pressure?

3. If A is 20 dB above B and B is 20 dB above C, then how many decibels is A above C? What is the pressure ratio between A and B, B and C, A and C?

4. Recall that $\log_{10} 2 \approx .3$. If one sound pressure is four times another, by how many decibels do they differ? (Don't use a table.)

5. If one pressure is 50 times another, what is their difference in decibels? (Hint: 50 = 100/2).

6. Sound pressure level (SPL) implies a reference level of 0.0002 dynes/cm^2. How many db (SPL) is 1 dyne/cm^2?

7. Atmospheric pressure is about 10^6 dynes/cm^2 at sea level at 0°C. What is the sound pressure level of atmospheric pressure?

8. If 1 dyne/cm^2 is used as a reference pressure, then 2 dynes/cm^2 is said to be 6 dB *re* 1 dyne/cm^2. What is 10^{-2} dyne/cm^2 *re* 1 dyne?

9. Normal conversation is about 60 dB SPL. How many decibels is normal conversation *re* atmospheric pressure?

(*Answers given on page 338.*)

2
Absolute Sensitivity

INTRODUCTION

Normal hearing is most sensitive in the frequency region from about 2,000 to 5,000 Hz. At these frequencies the degree of sensitivity is especially impressive when stated in terms of linear displacements, such as the displacement of the eardrum. The absolute threshold for a 3,000-Hz wave, as discussed in Chapter 1, corresponds to displacements of the eardrum of less than 10^{-11} m or about one-hundredth the diameter of the hydrogen molecule.

Although the sensitivity of the ear is remarkably good, it is still a few orders of magnitude poorer than any fundamental limitation to such sensitivity that is determined by the random vibration of the molecules in the air (Brownian motion). To understand this limitation we must review thermal fluctuation and the concept of noise. A great deal is known about the detection of sinusoidal signals in noise, and that knowledge is applicable to the problem of absolute sensitivity. Finally, at the end of this chapter, we consider the definition of "normal" hearing in more detail and review the factors that influence the sensitivity of the average hearing adult.

ACOUSTIC POWER, DISPLACEMENT, AND FREQUENCY

Figure 2.1 shows human auditory sensitivity as a function of frequency for a signal of unlimited duration. The abscissa is the frequency of the sinusoidal signal. The ordinate is the sound pressure level of the sinusoid, measured in decibels and with respect to .0002 dyne/cm². Two sets of measurements are presented. One set, minimum audible pressure (MAP), is the threshold measured with earphones. The other set of measurements, minimum audible field (MAF),

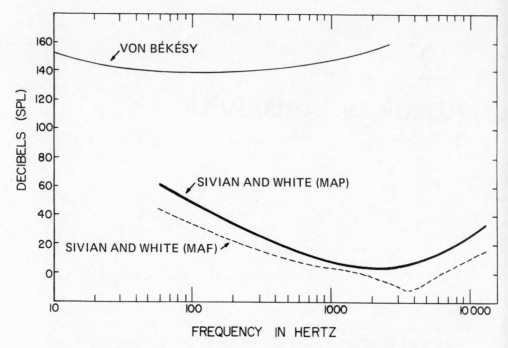

FIG. 2.1 The region of auditory experience. The lower graphs show the values of frequency and sound pressure level that can just be heard (absolute threshold). Sivian and White (1933) made the measurement in an anechoic chamber and measured the minimum audible field (MAF) or with earphones and calculated a minimum audible pressure (MAP). The upper curve is from von Békésy (1960) and represents the point at which the sound is so intense as to cause pain or discomfort.

is the free-field threshold. The difference in these two measures will be discussed later. The line at the top of Figure 2.1 is von Békésy's (1960) measurement of the pain threshold. The dynamic range of the ear, from just audible to pain, is about 15 orders of magnitude in power or about 7.5 orders of magnitude in pressure. We can hear best in the region between 2 kHz and 5 kHz and are less sensitive, by several orders of magnitude, at very low frequencies. Sensitivity can be stated in many ways. One can use the minimal acoustic power of a sine wave that is just audible, or the particle displacement at this threshold value. In addition, one can utilize the minimum pressure value, as we have in Figure 2.1. The power, frequency, and particle displacement of a free-field wave, such as the wave generated in our ideal acoustic environment, are related by

$$I = \rho_0 c (2\pi f)^2 d^2, \tag{2.1}$$

where I is acoustic power per unit area, the term $(\rho_0 c)$ is the density of the medium times the velocity of propagation, f is the frequency of the wave in hertz, and d is the rms[1] amplitude of the average displacement of the molecules, sometimes called the particle displacement. With $\rho_0 c = 40$ dyne sec/cm^3, f measured in hertz and d in centimeters, I has the dimensions erg/sec·cm^2 or 10^{-7} W/cm^2 (see Chapter 1). According to Eq. (2.1) at 0 dB sound pressure level (SPL), namely 10^{-16} W/cm^2, and $f = 3000$ Hz, then d, the rms particle displacement, is 2.64×10^{-10} cm.

Recall that particle displacement, d, refers to the average displacement of the molecules from their resting position. The main implication of Eq. (2.1) is that to keep a fixed intensity requires more displacement of the air molecules as the frequency of the source decreases. For example, if we decrease the frequency from 1,000 to 100 Hz, a factor of 10, we need to increase the displacement by tenfold to maintain the same intensity. This general relation is easy to verify if you notice the cone of a high-fidelity speaker. When reproducing predominantly high-frequency sound, the cone scarcely moves. At low frequencies the excursions of the cone are obvious. In fact, for very high sounds, a very small electromechanical transducer, called a tweeter, is usually employed. It is almost impossible to see the diaphragm of a tweeter move despite the fact that the acoustic power it radiates may be enormous.

The dependence between frequency, displacement, and power arises from basic physical principles. The force or pressure exerted by a certain mass is proportional to its acceleration ($F = ma$). The acceleration is the second derivative of the displacement with respect to time. For a wave whose displacement, x, is a sinusoidal function of time, the acceleration is proportional to the frequency squared times the original displacement. Let $x(t)$ be the displacement as a function of time, then

$$x(t) = A \sin[2\pi ft + \theta],$$
$$\frac{dx(t)}{dt} = -A \times 2\pi f[\cos(2\pi ft + \theta)],$$
$$\frac{d^2 x(t)}{dt^2} = -A(2\pi f)^2 \sin[2\pi ft + \theta].$$

Thus, the work or energy is proportional to $A^2 (2\pi f)^2$, the force times the distance the molecule of air has been displaced [$A(2\pi f)^2$ (acceleration) $\times A$

---

[1] For fluctuating quantities that change with time, the root mean squared (rms) value is often used to specify the degree of fluctuation. If $d(t)$ is the fluctuating quantity when its rms value is, as the expression implies,

$$d_{\text{rms}} = \left[\frac{1}{T} \int_0^T d^2(t) \, dt\right]^{1/2}$$

where T, the average time, is sufficient to achieve a good estimate of the mean. Those familiar with statistics will recognize the similarity of this quantity to the standard deviation of a statistical process with zero mean value. For a sinusoidal fluctuation the rms value of the sinusoid is $1/\sqrt{2}$ times the peak value of the sinusoid.

(distance)]. If, therefore, one lowers the frequency by a factor of ten the amplitude must be increased by the same factor to hold constant the work done by the sound wave.

Even small displacements such as 10^{-11} m should not be envisioned as the work expended in pushing the eardrum back and forth across this small distance over some long period of time, such as 1 sec. In fact, the drum is being pushed back and forth 3,000 times per second at 3,000 Hz. Hence, the work expended, which is proportional to f^2, is nearly 9,000,000 times larger than if the displacement took 1 sec. Nevertheless, the minute size of the displacement raises some questions about how such quantities have been measured or calculated.

CALCULATION OF EARDRUM DISPLACEMENT—LINEARITY

The limits of optical resolution are of the order of a half-wave length of light. Therefore, distances of about 10^{-7} m are the limits of what can be resolved even with the highest power optical systems. Displacements of 10^{-11} cannot be directly measured but must be inferred from other measurements. Within the ear, the system comprising the tympanic membrane and the small bones of the middle ear is remarkably linear. The movement of these structures is essentially proportional to the applied force, at least at reasonable pressure levels. The calculation of how much the drum moves at threshold is in fact based on measurements of drum displacement caused by signals of much higher pressure levels. These quantities are linearly extrapolated to the lower levels. Probably the best estimate of drum displacement is displacement of the stapes. The stapes is the last of three small bones connected to the eardrum (see Chapter 3) and its motion is essentially that of a piston. Hence, the stapes' linear displacement is easier to specify than the eardrum, a conical structure whose mode of movement is somewhat complicated. On the basis of anatomy it is safe to assume that some portion of the eardrum will move about as much as the stapes. The most careful measurements of stapes displacement are those of Guinan and Peake (1967) who studied the cat. At levels above 100 dB SPL, the displacements of the stapes are large enough to be observed with an optical microscope. Fischler, Frei, Spira, and Rubinstein (1964), using different techniques, also measured this displacement. Their figures are close to those of Guinan and Peake. Guinan and Peake found that the displacement of the stapes was about .2 μ (2 $\times$ 10^{-7}m) at 120 dB SPL and 3,000 Hz. Over the range 100–130 dB SPL their measurement showed that the displacement was nearly linear with the applied sound pressure level. A change of 20 dB in sound pressure level caused the amplitude of the displacement to change by a factor of ten. Guinan and Peake found district nonlinearity only above about 130 dB SPL. Most mechanical systems become more linear as the amplitude of the motion decreases. We shall therefore assume that the system is linear, since the amplitude of the displacements is much smaller. If we start with a displacement of 10^{-7} m for 120 dB SPL, we calculate a displacement of 10^{-13} m for 0 dB SPL.[2]

As previously stated, we assume that some portion of the drum membrane moves about as much as the stapes. Tonndorf and Khanna (1968) used a laser technique to directly measure the pattern of drum motion. The first detectable motion of a continuous surface, such as a membrane, is the so-called first mode of vibration. Here one part of the membrane moves out of phase with another. Tonndorf and Khanna detected the first mode of vibration at 100 dB SPL, 3,000 Hz. The amplitude of this motion was 3×10^{-8} m. Extrapolating linearly we arrive at 3×10^{-13} m at 0 dB, a value near Guinan and Peake's. Using the Mössbauer[3] technique, Gilad, Shtrikman, Hillman, Rubinstein, and Eviatar (1967) measured the movement of the joint connecting the incus to the stapes in the guinea pig. Their values at 5 kHz are very similar to Tonndorf and Khanna's and the results show a linearity between displacement amplitude and sound pressure level from 90 dB to 60 dB. Extrapolation of their measurements to 0 dB would yield a displacement amplitude of 2×10^{-13} m.

Clearly the tympanic membrane does not move very far at this very sensitive frequency. But the absolute size of the motion is only indirectly related to any fundamental limit of auditory sensitivity. As we shall see, the basic problem in hearing such small motion is determining whether the small motion is caused by the sinusoid or by the random bombardment of the molecules of the air. One can reliably hear such small motion because of the enormous amount of averaging that is taking place, over both time and space.

AVERAGE DISPLACEMENT

In one sense, the issue of the size of the displacement is irrelevant. Why should this quantity be any limitation to the sensitivity of hearing? The membrane moves back and forth a small amount, and to detect such motion, one need only compute with precision a quantity such as the average position of the membrane. The sheer size of the displacement is not a real limitation if the variability of the measurement is small, since one could then reliably detect small changes in the measurement. The amount of variability, in turn, depends on the amount of averaging. We can illustrate this point with the following analogy.

Suppose that the average increase in height of a young group of people was 10 cm/yr during a certain period of adolescence, which corresponds to an increase of about 2.7×10^{-4} m/day. Obviously, no one would actually try to measure the increase of .027 cm/day. Besides, the measurement of an individual's height is

[2] Fischler et al. (1967) measured at 250 Hz and found linearity from 60 to about 110 dB SPL.

[3] The Mössbauer technique is discussed in Chapter 6 in the section "Recent Mechanical Measurements."

probably no more accurate than ±.5 cm. But if a large number of people were measured on two different days, then such a trend might be reliably detected. In this example, probably 1,000 individuals would suffice to detect the trend. The change in the average would be small, but the precision of the average would be considerably greater than the precision of the individual measurements, especially if the average was computed using a sufficiently large number of individuals.

Detecting a change in the position of the eardrum is an analogous problem. The measurement of its position and the precision associated with that measurement is determined by the amount of averaging over both time and space. What then sets a limit on that precision? The answer is the irregular motion of the membrane itself, caused by the random bombardments of the molecules of the air. Recall our earlier discussion (Chapter 1) of static pressure and of the position of the microphone diaphragm located between gases of equal pressure. The diaphragm moves little because random collisions on one face tend to cancel the collisions on the opposite face. If the area of the diaphragm is decreased down to molecular dimensions, then these collisions occur more as individual events and the diaphragm tends to move quickly back and forth, especially if its inertia is small. In the limit it responds even to individual molecular collisions. If the area is large, however, only rarely does a difference occur in the proportion of collisions taking place on the two sides. The random motion of the diaphragm becomes too small to be observed.

Constant molecular bombardment occurs in the situation just described because the gas has a temperature greater than $0°K$. This bombardment is often called thermal noise. The greater the temperature of the gas, the faster the molecules move and, hence, the greater the average pressure they produce on the walls of a container. The effect of this molecular motion in air is to generate a low-level sound, or noise, that is best described in terms of its average power, or wattage. To understand the fundamental limitation this noise places on our ability to hear weak sounds, we need to relate the magnitude of this noise to the power of a sinusoidal signal that can just be detected in its presence. The thermal noise present in the pheriphery of the auditory system actually limits the potential sensitivity of the ear. The limit is not caused by the numerical magnitude of the displacement of some membrane or organ within the hearing system. What then is the character of the background noise?

NOISE

In everyday usage the word "noise" is used to describe unwanted sound. The hum of a motor, the roar of traffic, the sound of the wind, or even the cries of children at play, may be called noise. However, we will use the word "noise" in a very precise way. Noise is the sound produced if we amplify the random excursions of the diaphragm of a sensitive microphone placed in air. It is the sound one hears from tuning a radio off-station and turning the volume up—a steady, hissing sound. Such a sound is essentially random and unpredictable from moment to moment. Its general characteristics can be understood if we reconsider the diaphragm of the microphone, surrounded on both sides by air. Each side of the diaphragm is struck by molecules moving against the sides. The net position of the diaphragm is determined by whether the collisions from the left outnumber those from the right or the reverse. Over a very long period of time, the number of collisions on the two sides will be nearly equal since the differences in the number of collisions occurring from one side or the other will certainly be very small relative to the total. Thus, the diaphragm will be located on the average near its resting position. Suppose we consider smaller and smaller intervals of time, until we reach an interval where the number of collisions per unit interval is small, say of the order of ten or one hundred. Then there is a significant chance of an imbalance between the collisions against the two sides. Thus, the diaphragm will move in the direction of the predominant forces by an amount related to the relative mass of the diaphragm and the molecules. The next instant of time may produce the same or opposite motion. Thus, the position of the diaphragm or the instantaneous pressure on it, which is linearly related to that position, will be a random variable. Figure 2.2 shows how the pressure or displacement might change over some period of time.

Although the instantaneous position or pressure is irregular and unpredictable, noise shows statistical regularity. Of course the mean or average value of the displacement pressure is zero. If we take many instantaneous samples of the pressure or position of the diaphragm, then we would have the collection of points labeled x_i (see Figure 2.2). The distribution of such samples is Gaussian or normal, that is

$$f(x_i) = \frac{1}{\sigma\sqrt{2\pi}} e^{-1/2 \left(\frac{x_i}{\sigma}\right)^2},$$

where σ is the standard deviation of the distribution.

For a discrete set of independent samples (with zero mean) the standard deviation is computed as

$$\sigma = \left(\frac{1}{N}\sum_{i=1}^{N} x_i^2\right)^{\!1/2}, \tag{2.2}$$

where N is the number of samples. The average power of the noise can be computed from the instantaneous pressure by squaring the pressure and dividing by the characteristic impedance $(\rho_0 c)$ of the medium, namely

$$I = \frac{1}{\rho_0 c}\frac{1}{T}\int_0^T x^2(t)\,dt, \tag{2.3}$$

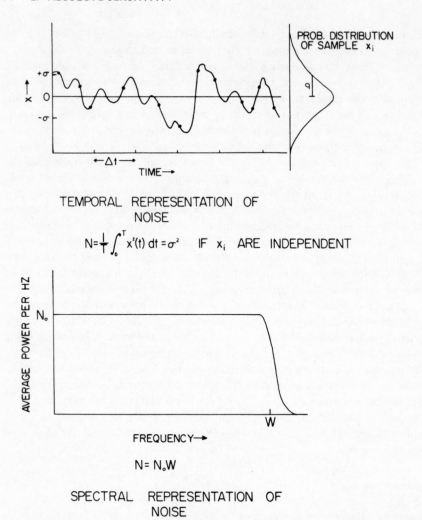

FIG. 2.2 Temporal and spectral representation of white Gaussian noise. The upper graph shows instantaneous pressure values for a sample noise waveform. The instantaneous pressure value follows a Gaussian distribution as illustrated on the right side of the temporal representation. The variance of that distribution σ^2 is equal to N, the average power of the noise. The bottom panel illustrates the spectral representation of the noise, where N_0 is the average noise power per cycle. Because there is equal power at all frequencies, the noise is called "white", after white light.

where T is the average time, x is the instantaneous pressure of the waveform, and I is the waveform's average power.

A very powerful noise (many watts per square centimeter) will have a large average power, that is, the instantaneous pressure excursions $x(t)$ are great, although their average value is still zero. The value of σ in Figure 2.2 will be large.

There is obviously a close relation between Eqs. (2.2) and (2.3). The summation in Eq. (2.2) is equivalent to the integral in Eq. (2.3). Thus, the average power and the standard deviation of the noise are related. In fact, they are proportional to each other, the constant of proportionality being the impedance of air. Equation (2.3) is straightforward and can be calculated for any waveform. Equation (2.2) is also straightforward, except for the important restriction of independence on the individual samples, x_i. In principle, there is nothing difficult about obtaining independent samples of a waveform $x(t)$. One need simply wait long enough between samples. But how long is long enough? As the interval between samples goes to zero we can see that successive samples will be highly correlated. For instance, if a given sample is positive, then the next is likely to be positive as well. This correlation between samples occurs because the microphone always has some finite inertia; the measuring device cannot have zero mass or infinitesimal area. In Figure 2.2, it is clear that if the time interval Δt is 1 msec, then it is certain that there are no noise components with a frequency greater than 100 $(1/\Delta t)$, or 100 kHz. At least in the sample in Figure 2.2, the fastest change in waveform occurs near the middle of the figure and represents a frequency no higher than about 20–30 kHz. This upper frequency limitation might occur because of the inertial properties of the microphone, since for any noise process an upper frequency limit exists. As long as the time between successive samples exceeds the reciprocal of that upper frequency limit, the samples are nearly independent, at least for noise with energy over a wide frequency band. The exact condition for independence depends on the details of the noise process.

In white or flat noise all frequencies below the upper cutoff are equally represented in the sense that the average power in any single band of frequencies, say, W Hz wide, would be the same wherever the noise band is located. The average noise power in a 1-Hz band (the noise-power density) is a very important quantity and is denoted N_0. It represents the density of noise in the same way that a density represents any quantity per unit of measure, for example, the density of matter is the mass per unit of volume. At the bottom of Figure 2.2 is a spectral representation of a flat noise process—the noise spectrum. All frequencies below the cutoff frequency have equal noise-power density, N_0. The noise-power density times the bandwidth, W, of the noise must therefore equal the total power, N, just as the total mass of a uniform material equals its volume times its mass per unit volume. In hearing, white noise refers to noise that has the same N_0 value over the audio spectrum, that is, noise whose spectrum is flat in the band from 100 Hz to 20 kHz. The value of N_0 is often called the spectral level of the noise.

We are now able to obtain independent samples from the waveform, $x(t)$. Let the highest frequency present in the noise be W_{max}. Clearly, we must sample at intervals no closer than $1/2W_{max}$ since that would represent times that are slow compared with the highest frequency present in the noise process. For example, if the highest frequency in the noise was 100 Hz, then $1/2W_{max}$ would be 5 msec and we cannot sample any faster than that interval. If we took samples with less time between, say, 1 msec, the fastest noise component could only change a little over that interval. Thus, considerable dependence would result among the successive samples. In certain cases sampling can be somewhat faster and still preserve independence, but the exact value depends on details of the noise, which, in turn, is related to its spectrum. For our purposes, the rule of sampling no faster than $1/2W_{max}$ is reasonable. If one sampled even slower at $3/W_{max}$ or $10/W_{max}$, one would obtain samples that are even more independent.

Before leaving our discussion of noise, one further observation is necessary concerning the dimensions of N_0. The spectral level, N_0, has the dimensions of energy per unit area, since it is defined as the ratio of a power per unit area divided by a bandwidth. A bandwidth has dimension cycles per second, and hence, its reciprocal has the dimensions of time, that is, $N_0 = N(\text{power/cm}^2) \times (1/W)$ (second cycle) or power·time/cm², hence, energy/cm². This should be kept in mind because noise is often described as a power occurring in some frequency band. Once that power is divided by the width of the noise band, an energy quantity is obtained.

BROWNIAN MOTION

The molecules of a gas are in constant motion. The velocity of their motion and hence the number of times they collide with other objects or themselves depends on the temperature of the gas. This motion is sometimes called "thermal motion." Of course the individual molecules are very small and the time between their striking a surface can be very short. Therefore the noise generated by this motion has a potentially very high frequency. In fact, the spectrum resembles that shown in Figure 2.2 and is essentially flat over the audio region. The highest frequency certainly extends beyond 20 kHz.

For standard temperature and atmospheric conditions the spectral level of this noise, in the region of 3,000 Hz, is about

$$N_0 = 10^{-21} \text{ W sec/cm}^2.[4]$$

[4] This value is nearly the same as that calculated by Sivian and White (1933). It is derived by considering the intensity generated on the side of a small piston exposed in a free field and at a temperature of 300° absolute. The wattage is 4 kT, where k is Boltzmann's constant and kT is 4 × 10⁻¹⁴ erg/sec at T = 300°. The power generated depends on the size of the piston, and its radius. The radius is assumed to be small compared with the wavelength of sound. This is probably reasonable at least up to 3,000 Hz where the wavelength would be somewhat larger than 10 cm. The value of the rms pressure is about 1.8 × 10⁻⁵ dyne/cm². This corresponds to an N_0 value of about 10⁻²¹ W sec/cm². Harris (1968) uses a value without the microphone present. We will base all our calculations on the assumption that the same microphone is used to measure the signal and noise. In any case, the factor of two is only 3 dB and the discrepancy has no practical significance.

Again we note N_0 has the dimensions of energy. Now we must compare this noise level to our nominal value for the absolute sensitivity of the ear at 3,000 Hz, which is about 10^{-16} W/cm^2. This threshold signal has the dimensions of power (e.g., watts) because its duration is indefinite. We cannot directly compare the noise and signal quantities because they have different dimensions.

A Dilemma

There are two ways out of this dilemma. One is to convert the noise-power density to a power, by assuming some effective bandwidth for the noise and multiplying it by N_0 to obtain the total effective noise power. We could then compare that quantity with the signal power or 10^{-16} W/cm^2. The difficulty in this approach is in making a conservative but realistic estimate of "effective" bandwidth. Sivian and White (1933) assumed an effective bandwidth of 5,000 Hz by examining human auditory sensitivity (Figure 2.1), and arguing that once the sensitivity rose by 10 dB the noise components would contribute so little that they could be ignored. The effective noise would then be 3×10^{-18} W/cm^2. The threshold value for the signal would only be 15 dB above the background noise. But Sivian and White's young group of subjects actually heard the signal some 10 dB below the nominal 0 dB level at 3,000 Hz. According to this calculation, therefore, the threshold signal is only about 5 dB above the background noise. Actually, there is considerable variation from subject to subject in this threshold value, as we will discuss in this chapter.

A second way to avoid the dilemma is to consider the detection of sinusoids in much higher levels of noise and proceed as follows: other experiments show that only a small fraction of the total duration of time effects the noise's detectability. For most frequencies, any duration longer than 200 msec will require about the same power to achieve threshold. Below this duration (excluding very short durations) the threshold depends on the energy of the signal, that is, the product of signal power times duration. Thus, the ear has an effective integration time of about 200 msec. We then take the signal power at threshold, multiply it by the effective duration, and obtain a signal *energy* at threshold. Finally, we directly compare this signal energy to noise-power density, since both have the same dimensions.

The basis of this approach is, of course, the assumption that the ratio of signal energy to noise-power density (E/N_0 is essentially independent of noise level, N_0. We know that this is true when the noise is clearly audible. For noise levels over a range of 90 dB, the signal-to-noise level is remarkably constant (see Figure 10.9, Chapter 10). At low levels the noise becomes inaudible while the signal energy is constant. We assume this constancy results because Brownian motion establishes a lower noise level that limits the detectability of the signal. The form of the graph of E/N_0 versus N_0 is consistent with the assumption of a low-level constant noise that simply adds to N_0, the noise introduced by the experimenter. We also have good evidence that the effective integration of time of the ear is independent of the level of the background noise and, second, that the threshold for a sinusoidal signal at a high level of noise is remarkably constant over all subjects. In fact, in the author's experience, the signal-to-noise ratio at threshold, stated in energy terms (E/N_0), rarely differs by more than 1 dB from one person to another. Let us therefore consider the detection of a sinusoidal signal in noise and how the effective duration of the signal affects the calculated signal-to-noise ratio.

Detection of Sinusoids in Noise

A large body of work exists on the detection of sinusoidal signals in a clearly audible background noise. Although the majority of this work has used a 1,000-Hz signal and a relatively short 1/10-sec signal, there are ample data at other frequencies and durations.

First, consider the question of duration. As one increases the duration of a signal from some very brief value, the power needed to just detect the signal drops and then reaches either a limit or region where the change in power for further increase in signal duration is very small. In the region from approximately 10 msec to 100 msec there is a reciprocal relation between signal duration and the detectable signal power, that is, the product of time and power (energy) is constant. At duration beyond about 100 msec, detection of the signal largely depends on the power of the signal. Certainly beyond 1-sec duration, detection is independent of signal duration.

The ratio of signal energy-to-noise power density (E/N_0) for a 3,000-Hz sinusoid at 100-msec duration in white noise (of sufficient intensity to be audible) is about 40; therefore, in terms of dB, about 16 dB. The advantage of this number is that it is nearly the same for most observers, although the absolute sensitivity of different people is different.

Nearly the same power will be required at longer durations than at 1/10 sec. Thus the total energy will actually be increased. To make sure our estimate is conservative we will assume that the ratio of signal energy to noise-power density (E/N_0) for detecting the sinusoid is 100, that is, 20 dB. This will also be a convenient value in making the comparison at absolute threshold.

E/N_0 at Threshold

Let us review the assumptions. We know from measurement of the detection of a sinusoid in noise at high levels of the noise that:

1. The effective integration time of the ear is not greater than about 1 sec—this is clearly conservative.
2. At frequency of 3,000 Hz the signal energy needed to just detect the signal in a flat noise corresponds to a ratio no greater than $E/N_0 = 100$ (10 log $E/N_0 = 20$ dB).

3. We assume that for a normal listener this ratio holds even in quiet. We know that it is constant over a wide range of noises. (Fletcher, 1953; Hawkins & Steven, 1950; and other articles cited in Green & Swets, 1974).

At a nominal threshold of hearing (0 dB SPL), the estimated energy of the signal, $E_s = 10^{-16}$ W sec/c^2. Our estimate of noise-power density is $N_0 = 10^{-21}$ W sec/cm^2. Thus, the ratio E/N_0 is 10^5. The previous discussion implies we need only a E/N_0 ratio of 10^2. We therefore conclude that the ear is not limited by thermal motion. In fact, it barely hears sound that exceeds that limit by about three orders of magnitude (30 dB).

The value of 30 dB is reasonable when considered in light of other evidence. First, the absolute threshold varies a great deal among even normal subjects. Young people are known to be 10 dB more sensitive than the nominal value of 10^{-16} W/cm^2. Second, cats and perhaps dogs have better sensitivity than men. The hearing of a domestic cat, for example, has been measured carefully and is about 10 to 20 dB more sensitive than man over most of the audible range (Watson, 1963). Thus, some animals' hearing may be nearly limited by the thermal agitation of the molecules of air.

In mammals other factors probably fix the absolute limit of sensitivity. Among those factors is the noise produced by the vascular system. A number of large arteries in the middle ear seem very injudiciously placed from the viewpoint of maximal sensitivity. Further, at the actual receptor site a blood vessel runs beneath the receptor elements. The turbulence that must accompany the flow of blood probably generates considerable noise. The situation is reminiscent of the vascular supply in the retina, where the vessels actually lie between the light source and the receptor elements, except in the fovea.

DYNAMIC RANGE OF HEARING

But even if the ear is not as sensitive as physical limitation would permit, it is still an impressive organ. The detection of very weak signals is only one challenge for hearing. Only in the most contrived settings can one be expected to hear a 10^{-16} W/cm^2 sinusoid. Most of the time wind noise or the noise due to machinery, light transformers, ventilation fans, and a variety of other artificial and natural noises make the detection of such a signal impossible. At the other extreme, man can endure in noise levels as high as 120 dB SPL, 10^{-4} W/cm^2, at least for short periods of time. He can even hear and understand speech presented in the 100 to 130 dB SPL range. Thus, the limit of absolute sensitivity deals only with one end of an enormous range of intensities that the hearing organ can span. The effective range of the ear is probably 100 dB or more. This is at least 10 and probably 20 to 30 dB better than the dynamic range associated with most hi-fi equipment. Most portable radios are built with a range no greater than 30 or 40 dB and even hearing aids often have less than a 40 dB dynamic range.

The dynamic range of hearing is almost instantaneously available. Unlike the eye, which requires twenty minutes or more to adapt to very dim illumination, the ear can adapt to and detect a near threshold signal within a few milliseconds after the termination of a moderately intense sound. Only if the previous sound is both intense and of long duration will it reliably increase the absolute threshold for a succeeding sound. One-tenth of a second after termination of a 10 sec 70 dB SPL signal, the ear's absolute threshold will be within 3 dB of the value obtained after a long period in quiet. This quick recovery, coupled with an enormous dynamic range, makes hearing a very impressive sense modality, even if it cannot hear the molecules dance.

NORMAL HEARING AND HEARING LEVEL

Throughout the preceding discussion phrases such as "normal hearing" have been used. But different individuals have different sensitivity to weak sounds and sizable variation occurs even within a so-called "normal" population. Younger people will often note that their grandparents or perhaps even their parents have somewhat less sensitive hearing. How is normal hearing defined and what are the ranges encountered in a normal population? Kryter (1970) describes normal hearing as follows: "Normal hearing is defined as the average auditory ability of persons who do not have pathological ears due to disease, injury from a blow, or exposure to intense sound [p. 109]." Thus, normal hearing is an average taken over a representative sample of subjects not obviously impaired. No absolute standard is implied; normal hearing is simply the average sensitivity of apparently normal subjects.

Actually, the most important "auditory ability" is probably the ability to understand speech since such an impairment has far-reaching social and economic consequences. But measurement of the ability to understand speech is a complicated problem. The stimulus itself is complex and responding properly to a speech message depends on a number of factors that are not strictly auditory. This problem cannot be avoided by adopting a standard speech message, since a talker's accent and the material of the message itself would make any comparison of individuals having different backgrounds and educations difficult. For this reason, nonspeech material is commonly used to measure general auditory ability. The usual stimuli are pure tones and their absolute threshold in a quiet environment is used as the index of auditory ability. But how is normal hearing defined?

Since about 1930 a number of hearing surveys have been made. The absolute sensitivity of large populations of subjects, all prescreened to remove any obviously abnormal participants, have been measured. A 1938 United States

Public Health Service study later became the American standard, and it seemed to be in reasonable agreement with a survey taken at the Wisconsin State Fair in 1955 and in good agreement with a survey taken at the World's Fair in New York (Steinberg, Montgomery, & Gardner, 1940). Since 1963, however, almost the entire world has adopted the International Organization for Standardizations (ISO) recommendations which specify levels about 10 dB lower than the initial United States standards. Table 2.1 gives the value for normal hearing levels in terms of SPL for several different countries. The numbers given for each country are the levels that should be used with that country's earphones and couplers to achieve 0 dB hearing level. They are somewhat different because of differences in each country's earphones or couplers. The values were obtained by pooling data from a large number of countries to establish the ISO standard.

A major reason for accepting the lower standards is the recognition that hearing sensitivity is different for different age groups. The Wisconsin survey clearly showed such age differences, and they have been confirmed by many studies since that time. To present data on this subject, however, we must define the term *hearing level* since the audiological literature invariably uses this measure rather than SPL.

Hearing level is simply defined as the number of decibels a sound exceeds the normal SPL at that frequency. Thus, if we accept the ISO levels of normal hearing, then +7.5 dB with respect to .0002 dyne/cm^2 (+7.5 dB SPL) is normal hearing at 3,000 Hz. If a subject required +17.5 dB to hear the 3,000 Hz waveform, then his hearing level would be 10 dB. Notice that one needs to know

TABLE 2.1
ISO Recommendation for 0 dB Hearing Level
Threshold [.0002 dyne/cm^2,
$(2 \times 10^{-5} \ N/m)]^a$

Frequency	United States	Great Britain	Soviet Union
125	45.5	47	55
250	24.5	28	33
500	11	11.5	14.5
1,000	6.5	5.5	8.5
1,500	6.5	6.5	8.5
2,000	8.5	9	9
3,000	7.5	8	10.5
4,000	9.5	9.5	11.5
6,000	8	8	18.5
8,000	9.5	10	9.5
Earphone	WE 705A	STC 4026-A	TD6
Coupler	NBS Type 9-A	BS 2042	IU-3

^{a}After Weissler (1968).

the standard or normal level at each frequency before one can interpret a hearing level in terms of sound pressure level. This issue is also discussed in Chapter 13.

Some typical data changes of hearing level with age are shown in Figure 2.3. The figure gives hearing level as a function of age for various frequencies. At lower frequencies these curves apply to both men and women. However, at higher frequencies there is clear difference among the sexes. Women invariably show less high-frequency loss as a function of age than men. The most plausible hypothesis for this difference is that women work in jobs having a lower average noise level than men, so that the greater loss for men is caused by the greater exposure.

Figure 2.4 shows the median hearing level of a 30- to 39-year-old group of men for three occupations that differ markedly in noise exposure. The medians are ordered as one might expect for this simple hypothesis.

Even an apparently normal group of subjects displays considerable variability. Typical standard deviations are about 6 dB at 3,000 Hz, even for normal subjects. Thus, roughly 5% of the population is better than normal by about 12 dB.

Obviously, in view of the effect of age and/or noise exposure the spread and form of the distribution changes as one measures the distribution of hearing level at older ages. Hinchcliffe (1959), for example, reports a median of 22 dB hearing level, an upper quartile of 12 dB, and a lower quartile of 45 dB for a group of 45- to 55-year-old men, measured at 4,000 Hz.

In relating these values for populations to our previous discussions of sensitivity, we should comment on the difference between thresholds measured with earphones (sometimes described as minimum audible pressures or MAP) and

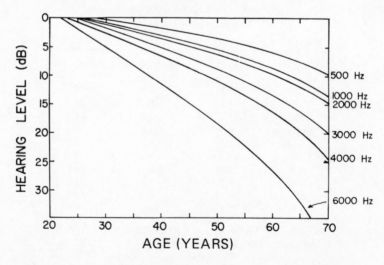

FIG. 2.3 Relation of average hearing level and age. (From Hinchcliffe, 1958.)

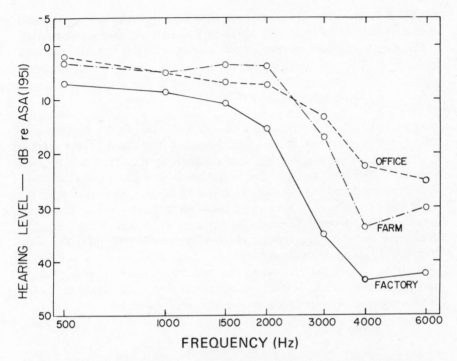

FIG. 2.4 Median hearing level of men 30–39 years of age working in various occupations as a function of frequency. The measured level for the left ear only appears in the figure. (From Glorig *et al.*, 1957.)

thresholds measured in a free field (minimum audible fields or MAF). The differences in these pressure readings are related to acoustic properties of the head, which acts as baffle in the field, and resonant properties of the external auditory meatus. These systematic differences have long been recognized and studied (Shaw, 1966; Wiener & Ross, 1946). The differences range from 6 to 20 dB with free-field results always being more sensitive than those obtained with earphones.[5] At 3,000 Hz the difference is about 6 dB, so the ISO standard based on measurement with earphones should be corrected to about 3.7 dB SPL at 3,000 Hz, a value very close to the 0 dB level, or 10^{-16} W/cm^2, that occupied

---

[5] Note once again that our calculation of a ratio of signal-to-noise energy at threshold nicely avoids these problems of changing MAP or MAF. Whatever the properties of the head and ear channel, they will modify signal and noise in the same way at any given frequency. Only if the impedance changes produced very sharply tuned resonance, which they do not, would our previous calculation need to consider the noise-power density integrated over some range of frequencies. For our purposes the noise spectrum is effectively flat, over a third of an octave or so, and this is the range of frequencies important in detecting a sinusoid in noise.

our previous discussion. One should also note that half the normal population is probably more sensitive at this frequency at least while they are young and before they are exposed to intense noises such as machinery or amplified music.

SUMMARY

We have considered the fundamental physical limitations on the absolute sensitivity of the ear. These physical limitations are established by the random motion of gas molecules, that is, by thermal agitation. A calculation of the limit imposed by this noise indicated that human hearing is well above this limitation. Even the most sensitive individuals are probably 20 dB above a lower limit. The most sensitive cat may be only 10 dB above the limit, but even in that animal thermal noise probably does not set the limit of absolute sensitivity. Also considered was the large dynamic range of the ear. The ear spans this range almost instantaneously, without the need for long adaptation times, as in vision. Toward the end of the chapter, we discussed the definition of normal hearing and presented evidence that hearing changes markedly with age. Exposure to intense sound causes even greater decline in sensitivity with age.

REFERENCES

Fischler, H., Frei, E.H., Spira, D., & Rubinstein, M. Dynamic response of middle ear structures. *Journal of the Acoustical Society of America*, 1967, *41*, 1220–12231.

Fletcher, H. *Speech and hearing in communication.* New York: Van Nostrand, 1953.

Gilad, P., Shtrikman, S., Hillman, P., Rubinstein, M., & Eviatar, A. Application of the Mössbauer method to ear vibration. *Journal of the Acoustical Society of America*, 1967, *41*, 1232–1236.

Glorig, A. Wheeler, D., Quiggle, R., Grings, W. and Summerfield, A., *1954 Wisconsin State Fair Hearing Survey: Statistical Treatment of Clinical and Audiometric Data,* American Academy Ophthalmology and Otolaryngology and Research Center Subcommittee on Noise in Industry, Los Angeles, California, 1957.

Green, D.M., & Swets, J.A. *Signal detection theory and psychophysics.* John Wiley & Sons 1966, reprinted R.E. Krieger Publishing Co., Inc. New York, 1974. New York: Robert E. Krieger, 1966.

Guinan, J., & Peake, W.T. "Middle Ear Characteristic of Anesthetized Cats," *Journal of the Acoustical Society of America*, 1967, *41*, 1237–1261.

Harris, G.G. Brownian motion in the cochlea partition. *Journal of the Acoustical Society of America*, 1968, *44*, 176–186.

Hawkins, J.E., & Stevens, S.S. The masking of pure tones and of speech by white noise. *Journal of the Acoustical Society of America*, 1950, *22*, 6–13.

Hinchcliffe, R., The pattern of the threshold of perception for hearing and other special senses as a function of age. *Gerontologica*, 1958, *2*, 311.

Hinchcliffe, R. The threshold of hearing as a function of age. *Acustica*, 1959, *9*, 303–308.

Kryter, K.D. *The effects of noise on man.* New York: Academic Press, 1970.

Shaw, E.A.G. (1966). Earcanal pressure generated by a free sound field. *Journal of the Acoustical Society of America*, 1966, *39*, 465–470.

Sivian, L.J., & White, S.D. On minimum audible sound fields. *Journal of the Acoustical Society of America*, 1933, *4*, 288–321.

Steinberg, J.C., Montgomery, H.C. & Gardner, M.B. Results of the world's fair hearing test. *Journal of the Acoustical Society of America*, 1940, *12*, 291–301.

Tonndorf, J., & Khanna, S.M. Submicroscopic displacement amplitudes of the tympanic membrane (cats) measured by a laser interferometer. *Journal of the Acoustical Society of America*, 1968, *44*, 1546–1554.

von Békésy, G. *Experiments in hearing* (E.G. Wever, Ed. and trans.). New York: McGraw-Hill, 1960.

Watson, C.S. Masking of tones by noise for the cat. *Journal of the Acoustical Society of America*, 1963, *35*, 167–173.

Weissler, P.G. International standard reference zero for audiometers. *Journal of the Acoustical Society of America*, 1968, *44*, 264–275.

Wiener, F., & Ross, D.A. The pressure distribution in the auditory canal in a progressive sound field. *Journal of the Acoustical Society of America*, 1946, *18*, 401–408.

3
Cochlear Excitation

INTRODUCTION

In the first two chapters, sound was treated largely from a physical viewpoint as a mechanical disturbance in air. Different physical aspects of sound, such as sound pressure, particle displacement, intensity, wave velocity, wavelength, and frequency were defined and discussed. For sound to affect man, however, it must excite some receptor system. In this process, the receptor system transforms the information contained in the acoustic wave. The information changes from a variation in pressure as a function of time to some spatiotemporal distribution of neural activity. In the transformation process some information may be lost. The next three chapters describe how sound stimulates the receptor elements, what anatomic and physiological structures are stimulated, and the electrical activity recorded in these structures. This chapter recounts the events that mediate the transduction of the sound wave from air to the fluids of the inner ear and treats the mechanical disturbance of the receptor elements themselves. Chapter 4 emphasizes the anatomic innervation of the receptor system and traces these anatomic connections back into the central nervous system. Chapter 5 emphasizes how the acoustic stimulus is coded, that is, the neural activity that occurs in response to the transformed sound wave. In essence, then, the next three chapters will study the first steps of auditory coding. How are the physical aspects of sound, such as frequency and intensity, encoded into neural events within the auditory system and what information is lost in this transformation? We shall also discuss the auditory pathways that carry this information through the central nervous system.

Our concern for these topics is easy to explain. The transformations imposed by the periphery may limit and restrict the information that the auditory system can appreciate. Any process of information transfer from one form to another runs the risk of information loss. For example, the physical description of the sound wave, as a variation of pressure as a function of time, clearly contains phase information. If the ear is largely a series of resonant systems tuned to different frequencies, then the phase of the various vibrations may be lost. In such a case only the amplitude of the vibration at each frequency would be available to the central nervous system. Ohm's acoustic law (1843) essentially suggested this, an observation which formed the basis of Helmholtz's (1863) resonance theory of hearing. In opposition to this theory, which was *the* dominant theory of hearing for nearly a century, various temporal theories have been proposed. These temporal theories maintained that the ear appreciates differences in the details of the pressure waveform, at least for low frequencies, and, consequently, that the ear was, to some extent, phase sensitive. The question of the ear's phase sensitivity stimulated auditory research for some time. Refinements of exactly how the question would be asked and evidence for and against phase sensitivity provide a good summary of much auditory research before about 1930. A major topic of interest was cochlear mechanics—how did the sound waves stimulate the receptor system and what was the best physical analogy to describe the pattern of mechanical vibration?

Those unfamiliar with sensory systems may find it peculiar that so much time and effort was devoted to understanding these peripheral processes and especially the limitations implied by them. Why not emphasize what the ear can hear rather than what it cannot? The answer to this question is very simple. There are usually several plausible mechanisms to explain why the ear can hear some aspect of the stimulus waveform. We are often uncertain as to exactly which explanation is correct. But suppose we can find some dimension or aspect of the stimulus to which the ear is insensitive. Then our understanding, especially in the early development of the science, is markedly increased. We can then, for example, develop new and unusual stimuli that are physically different, but perceptually identical. Analyses of these confusions can lead to very powerful descriptions of the stimulus itself and to an understanding of how the sensory mechanism processes the stimulus. The research tactic of trying to discover what we cannot sense has paid large dividends in other areas besides hearing.

The trichromatic specification of color is probably the best example of this general approach. Certain spectral distributions of light, while physically different, appear identical to the observer. The analysis of this confusion leads to a simple yet elegant specification of all color in terms of three numbers. We now know that it is possible to describe side-by-side matches of different luminance distribution with just three numbers because there are only three photochemical agents in the cone retina. Another example is the field of visual illusions. Here the attempt is to analyze and systematize those figures and forms that we incorrectly perceive. It is hoped that an understanding of these errors will provide insight into the transformation performed by our visual systems.

Similarly, the motivation for understanding the peripheral auditory system is to let us discard a number of plausible alternative theories and develop more precise tests among the remaining hypotheses about auditory perception. As this chapter proceeds we shall indicate how the peripheral limitations limit or restrict the information extracted from the pressure waveform. In particular, we shall discuss the older, classic theories of hearing as soon as some anatomic details have been presented.

OVERVIEW

The steps in the mechanical transformation of sound can be conveniently divided into three stages corresponding to the three gross anatomic structures that comprise the peripheral auditory system (see Figure 3.1). First is the *outer* ear, which includes the pinna located outside the head and the tube or meatus that penetrates the skull. This tube terminates at the eardrum or tympanic membrane which is the boundary between the outer ear and the middle ear. The *middle* ear is a cavity containing three bones (ossicles) that transport vibration from the tympanic membrane to the oval window. The oval window is the boundary between the middle ear and the inner ear. The *inner* ear contains both the auditory and vestibular receptors. The vestibular receptors are contained in the semicircular canals. The auditory receptors lie in a coiled tube having the form of a snail and called the cochlea. The cochlea is filled with fluid. It is divided along its length by two very thin membranes into two large chambers and a small third chamber. The latter is roughly triangular in cross section and is located midway between the other two. Sound causes these membranes to vibrate. The vibration of one of them, the basilar membrane, generates the mechanical forces that stimulate the receptor elements, which are called hair cells. The hair cells are located in a very intricate and regular geometric pattern along the basilar membrane. The hair cells are excited when the short stiff cilia or hairs protruding from their tops are deflected. The hair cells and their supporting structures are known as the organ of Corti. Mechanical deformations of the hair cells eventually initiate responses in the nerve fibers connected at the bottom of these cells. These neural signals represent the acoustic wave input in a coded form.

Briefly, the steps in this process are (1) the sound wave enters the external ear; (2) movement of the tympanic membrane is transferred by the ossicles of the middle ear to the oval window; (3) movement of the oval window generates a compression (sound) wave in the fluids of the cochlea, which, in turn, (4) moves the basilar membrane upon which the primary auditory receptors, the hair cells, are located.

In the following section, we will discuss the three major divisions of the auditory organ, the outer, middle, and inner ear. Most of our attention will be focused on the motion of the basilar membrane. This motion precedes the major transformation of the acoustic wave from a mechanical disturbance to a pattern of neural excitation. An understanding of the exact form of this motion is vital to any auditory theory.

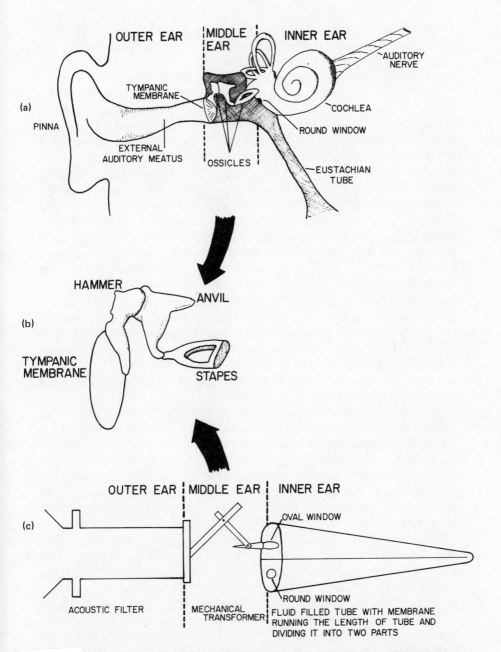

Major divisions of the peripheral auditory system: (a) the outer, middle and inner ear; (b) an enlarged version of the middle ear; (c) the mechanical analogs of the outer and middle ear.

THE OUTER EAR

The outer ear consists of the pinna, or external ear, and the tube leading into the head, called the external auditory meatus (see Figure 3.1). The most important functional property of the outer ear is the role it plays in sound localization. Obviously, by moving the head and pointing the pinna and meatus in different directions, one may selectively attenuate sound energy coming from different regions of space. Sounds are generally louder when we point one of our ears toward the source. The structure of the pinna makes it attenuate certain frequencies more than others. At frequencies below about 1,000 Hz, the auditory meatus has essentially no directional effect.

The ear canal itself ranges in length from about 2.3 to 2.9 cm. A reasonable average value seems to be about 2.4 cm. Any tube acts as an acoustic resonator, as we discussed earlier. The resonant frequency of a tube closed at one end occurs when the wavelength of the sound is four times the length of the tube (see Chapter 1). Under this circumstance reflections from the closed end are in phase with the incoming wave and reinforce it. For the ear then, a resonant wave would be 9–12 cm in length and therefore a frequency of about 2,700 to 3,600 Hz. The external auditory meatus is not a simple tube and its walls are not rigid. Wiener (1947) made direct measurement in the ear channel and showed a definite resonant peak of approximately 12 dB in the vicinity of 3,000 to 4,000 Hz. This peak is one factor that contributes to the ear's maximal sensitivity to frequencies in this region. Since the tube terminates at the tympanic membrane, which obviously is pliant, and since the walls of the tube absorb some energy, this resonance is not very sharp. Measurable enhancement of the acoustic signal extends from approximately 2,000 to 6,000 Hz.

Because of an accumulation of wax, for example, the ear channel often becomes blocked. Occasionally, a complete bony occlusion, called atresia, is found. The effects of such occlusions are thoroughly known. Complete atresia of the channel attenuates frequencies in the range of speech, 300 – 3,000 Hz, by about 60 dB. Other forms of occlusion with wax produce considerably less attenuation. Typically good fitting plugs yield 30 to 50 dB of attenuation. All produce better attenuation at high frequencies ($f > 2$ kHz) than at low frequencies ($f < 30$ Hz).

In the case of atresia, sound does not reach the cochlea by its normal path. One might ask how the sound is heard at any intensity. The answer is that sound waves vibrate the entire skull and are thereby transmitted to the fluids of the cochlea. Obviously, this route is very inefficient. However, the ability to hear anything with such bone conduction indicates that the normal pathway via the ear channel and middle ear is not essential; it is merely the most efficient pathway.

In summary, the external ear is important in directional hearing. The pinna in animals, such as horses or dogs, may be extremely useful and its control is marvelous to observe. Movement of the pinna is not well developed in man, but its convolutions may be important in certain situations. We will discuss these topics in Chapter 8. The acoustic properties of the ear canal, particularly its length, alter the incoming acoustic wave and enhance those frequencies in the range of 2,000 to 6,000 Hz.

THE MIDDLE EAR

Anatomically the middle ear contains the tympanic membrane and three small bones or ossicles that conduct sound to the oval window. The first is the *hammer* or *malleus* which is attached on one side to the tympanic membrane and on the other side to the *anvil* or *incus* which, in turn, is attached to the *stirrup* or *stapes*. The footplate of the stapes rests in the oval window. Motion of the tympanic membrane is transmitted through the ossicles and thereby exerts a force on the fluids of the cochlea. Figure 3.1b attempts to portray the anatomic arrangements from a side view. Figure 3.1c is a functional diagram of the entire system.

There are two important muscles in the middle ear. The *tensor tympani* muscle is attached to the malleus just above the point where the manubrium or handle of the malleus joins the tympanic membrane. The other muscle is the *stapedius* and runs from the posterior wall of the middle ear to the neck of the stapes. Activation of these muscles protects the ear from very loud sounds by changing the mode of vibration of the ossicular chain. The amount of this protection is equivalent to approximately 20 dB but may be greater for brief periods. This protective system is put in operation by an acoustic reflex whose latency depends on the intensity of the sound but is approximately 60–120 msec. The reflex, therefore, affords no protection to impulsive sounds such as gun shots or sonic booms.

The primary functional significance of the middle ear is easy to understand if we consider the physical properties of its two boundaries. Outside the tympanic membrane is air. Air, as a gas, has a characteristic *acoustic impedance* of approximately 40 dyne sec/cm^3. Recall that impedance is the denominator in the equation relating acoustic pressure and intensity or power (see Chapter 1). On the other side of the membrane the stapes rests on the oval window. Opposite the oval window are the fluids of the cochlea. Cochlear fluids resemble sea water in composition. Their characteristic acoustic impedance is therefore about 161,000 dyne sec/cm^3. The ratio of characteristic impedances of the air and the fluid is therefore about 4,000.

The formula for the energy transmitted from one medium to another is:

$$\beta = \frac{4r}{(r+1)^2},$$

(3.1)

where r is the ratio of the impedances. Note that r is a ratio of two dimensional quantities and is therefore, like β, a number having no dimensions. For the example in question, with r equal to about 4,000, β is equal to approximately .001. This means that a sound wave traveling in air and impinging on water transmits only about .1% of its energy into the water whereas 99.9% of the energy is reflected back into air. The same loss is true for a sound wave in water that we are trying to transmit into air. In other words, there is a loss of about 30 dB in going between these two media because of the differences in their composition. These numbers are only for characteristic impedances, that is, the impedance of the gas or fluid itself. Such impedance will only be measured in an acoustically ideal environment—a free field. The particular acoustic impedance of the outer or inner ear, that is, the ratio of pressure to volume velocity, can only be calculated by measuring these quantities at the tympanic membrane or in the cochlea. These impedances are complex numbers and their magnitude depends on frequency. The ratio of the magnitude of the measured values, at about 2,000 Hz, would be about 4,000 to 5,000, as we assumed by substituting in Eq. (3.1).

The primary function of the middle ear is to reduce this enormous impedance mismatch. It does this by mechanical tranformations using obvious physical principles to change the impedance.

The first is simple leverage, where a small force applied to a long lever exerts a larger force, acting through a smaller distance, at the other end of the lever. The ossicular chain acts as a small lever.

The second principle is to change the area over which the force is applied. This is illustrated by a hydraulic jack in which a small amount of force exerted over a small area imparts a larger amount of force on the larger area of the piston, except that the middle ear operates the other way around as the stapes has a smaller area than the tympanic membrane. At the tympanic membrane we have a pressure P_T or a total force $F_T = P_T A_T$, where P_T and A_T are the pressure and area at the tympanic membrane. The force at the stapes is the same or a pressure $P_S = F_T/A_S$, where P_S and A_S are the pressure and area at the stapes. The stapes has a smaller area than the tympanic membrane; thus, at the stapes $P_S = P_T$ (A_T/A_S) or a pressure amplification of A_T/A_S.

A third, more subtle principle is utilized in achieving a good impedance match. The tympanic membrane itself, by virtue of its curvature, acts as a mechanical tranformer, as Tonndorf and Khanna (1972) have established. All three principles are interdependent and it is not easy to isolate the effects of one from another. An example of this difficulty is illustrated when one attempts to calculate the "effective area" of the tympanic membrane that is conical in shape. To calculate the effective area one must first make assumptions about, or actually measure, how it moves. Tonndorf and Khanna (1972) have recently observed its vibration pattern using a time-averaged holographic method. Their observations are at variance with the more traditional views of tympanic membrane motion. Roughly speaking, the area ratio between tympanic membrane and stapes is about 20 to 1, the lever arm 1.3 or even 1 to 1, and the curvature of the tympanic membrane contributing even further. The net result of all these factors is to reduce the loss in energy transmission from about 30 dB to a value near zero.

We can verify the functional efficacy of these transformations by considering cases where the ossicle chain is broken. Such cases occasionally arise clinically. A sharp blow on the head may, for example, disarticulate the stapes, or occasionally an operation is performed that opens a hole so that sound passes directly to the inner ear, bypassing the bones of the middle ear. In such cases, the acoustic waves in air are directly transmitted to the cochlear windows without the mechanical advantage of the middle ear. Hence the wave in the fluid of the cochlea should suffer a corresponding loss in intensity. Measurements in such cases reveal that the loss ranges between 20 and 30 dB. This is approximately what one would expect from the character of the two media, air and something similar to sea water.

THE INNER EAR

To understand the action of the inner ear, we must first consider the anatomic arrangements of the structures within it. Then we can take up the pattern of vibration induced by the sound wave, and discuss the actual forces that stimulate the receptor elements themselves.

Anatomy

The cochlea, as the name suggests, resembles the interior of a snail shell. It is a small coiled tube of approximately 2.5 turns, with a length of only 3.5 cm. A special hard bone (the hardest in the body) makes up the walls of this tube. In cross section two membranes divide the tube near the middle. These membranes create three distinct chambers (see Figure 3.2a and b). The largest of these chambers is *scala vestibuli*; it has a total volume of approximately 54 mm^3. The next smaller chamber, *scala tympani*, has a volume of about 37 mm^3. Separating these two rather large chambers and running the length of the cochlea tube is the *cochlear duct*. It has a volume of only about 6.7 mm^3. Thus the cochlear duct is less than 10% of the total volume of the entire cochlea. Because the cochlear duct is so small one can think of the entire cochlea, as a first approximation, as simply a tube divided lengthwise by a single membrane.

The fluid in the two larger tubes, scala tympani and scala vestibuli, is the same. Two thin membranes form the boundary between the middle ear and the fluids of the cochlea. The oval window, to which the stapes is attached, is the membrane that seals one end of the scala vestibuli; the round window, another

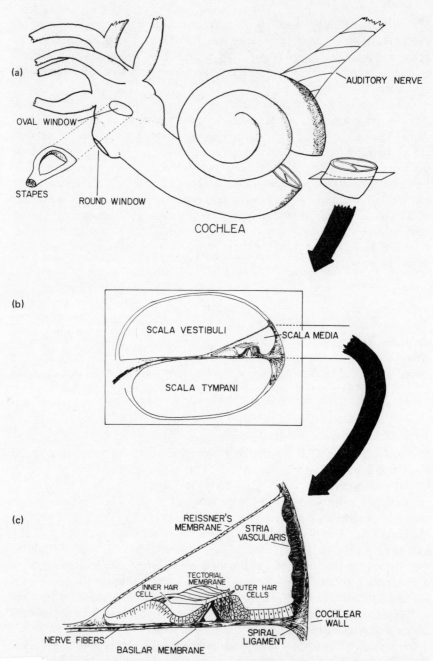

Structural and anatomical features of the cochlea: (a) the cochlea in relation to the middle ear, the vestibular channels (partially illustrated) and the auditory nerve; (b) cross section of the cochlea; (c) the structures within the scala media.

membrane-covered opening below the oval window, seals the scala tympani. These two ducts are connected at the upper end of the cochlea by a small opening near the apex called the helicotrema. The cochlear duct is separated by Reissner's membrane from scala vestibuli. The basilar membrane separates the other side of the cochlear duct from scala tympani. The fluid in the cochlear duct differs somewhat from the fluid in the other ducts.

The cochlear duct contains the receptor elements of hearing. Figure 3.2c is a highly magnified cross section of one of the cochlear turns. Remember that this duct occupies only 10% of the cochlea's total volume. It has been greatly enlarged in this figure so that the various structures lying on the basilar membrane are evident. Later, in analyzing the motion produced by sound waves, we will treat the cochlear duct, which includes all of the structures between Reissner's membrane and the basilar membrane, as a thin ribbon separating two tapered cylinders (see Figure 3.3).

Note that the entire blood supply to the cochlea comes from a single artery, the internal auditory artery. There is no collateral supply, so that the cochlear structures degenerate completely whenever this vessel becomes blocked. In the organ proper, two supply routes may be distinguished: one from vessels coursing below the basilar membrane and therefore outside the cochlear duct, and the other provided by a dense capillary network that lies along the lateral wall of this duct, the *stria vascularis*. Both of these are relatively far away from the hair cells. Opposite this wall on which the stria vascularis is located is a *bony promontory* that protrudes into the cochlea tube and to which the basilar membrane connects. Through this promontory course the nerve fibers that connect to the receptor elements, the hair cells. They enter the cochlea through small openings in the bone. The cell bodies of these nerve fibers are located in the spiral ganglion just inside the bony wall of the cochlea itself (see Figure 3.2a). The axons of these ganglion cells are twisted together to form part of the eighth cranial nerve. We will take up the physiology of the auditory nervous system in Chapter 4.

Within the cochlear duct and extending from above the plane of the basilar membrane is another membrane called the tectorial membrane. It lies just above the receptor elements. Moving along the basilar membrane from the bony promontory to the opposite wall, one first encounters the inner hair cell, the Arch of Corti, and on the other side of the arch, the outer hair cells, three in number in most mammals. The hair cells are oriented in a very regular and orderly fashion, one inner hair and three outer hair cells along each cross section. On top of each hair cell are fine cilia that give the structure its name. Each inner hair cell is topped by about 50 hairs and each outer hair cell by about 80 to 100 hairs. The hairs point upward toward the tectorial membrane and are also organized in a systematic, geometric pattern that we will discuss later. Continuing across the basilar membrane we find supporting cells both below and next to the outer hair cells and, finally, a carpet of low cells as the basilar membrane

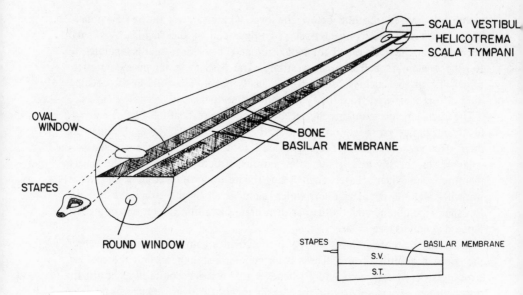

The major structural features of the uncoiled cochlea. Note that the basilar membrane is narrow near the round window and wider near the helicotrema, a taper opposite the cross-section area of the cochlea.

stretches to the opposite wall of the cochlear duct. On that wall is the vascular system we mentioned earlier, the stria vascularis.

Vibration of the Basilar Membrane

Structure of cochlea and the sound wave in the fluids. To understand how the basilar membrane vibrates, we shall make certain simplifying assumptions concerning the general structure of the cochlea. We will treat it as uncoiled and the equivalent of a tapered cylinder divided along the longest dimension by a thin membrane, which we will treat as the basilar membrane (see Figure 3.3). The upper half-cylinder represents the scala vestibuli and the other half-cylinder, the scala tympani. At the smaller end of the cylinder, the membrane terminates before the end of the cylinders is reached, permitting fluid to communicate between the two half-cylinders. The opening corresponds to the helicotrema. Closing off the large end of the half-cylinders are two membranes representing the oval and round windows. One of the half-cylinders is attached to a plunger which represents the stapes. In describing the motion of the basilar membrane we view the membrane from the side and describe the up and down displacements as a function of distance along the tube. Figure 3.3 portrays these relations schematically.

In explaining how sound waves cause the membrane to move, we must make a sharp distinction between the compressional sound wave that moves molecules in the water and the motion of the basilar membrane itself. To see this distinction, let us first calculate the wavelength of the pressure wave in the fluid. What we want to determine is whether the sound acts largely as a single force simultaneously over the entire basilar membrane or whether at any given instant there is appreciable variation in the force over the length of the cochlea. The fluids of the inner ear are similar in composition to sea water. The velocity of sound in sea water is approximately 160,000 cm/sec. Therefore, for a high-frequency sound, for example, 10,000 Hz, a wavelength is approximately 16 cm. The cochlear duct is 3.5-cm long and therefore, even for a very high frequency, only one-fifth of the wavelength of the sound. If we plot instantaneous pressure as a function of distance along the basilar membrane even at 10,000 Hz, there is at most a pressure difference of one-fifth of a cycle between any two points. At any instant then, essentially the same pressure extends from one end of the duct to the other, even for a high-frequency sound. At 1,000 Hz the duct is only one-fiftieth of the sound's wavelength. Thus, the duct is never pushed at one end and pulled at another, but rather nearly the same physical force is applied throughout the length of the duct as the stapes vibrates and creates a sound field in the fluids of the scala vestibuli. This observation suggests that the way in which the sound wave enters the cochlea is of little importance. The vibration induced in the membrane should be essentially the same, no matter how the sound wave starts in the cochlear fluids. The compressional force in the fluid has a wavelength that is long compared with the length of the basilar membrane.

Thus, sound may be treated as a pressure difference between scala vestibuli and scala tympani which, at any instant in time, is uniform over the entire extent of the membrane. Because of the variation of pressure as a function of time, energy is supplied to the basilar membrane which begins to be displaced in response to the pressure differences. The way in which it is displaced is now fairly well understood. The investigation of the vibration of the basilar membrane has had a long history culminating, at about 1928, with a remarkable series of experiments by von Békésy. With his work, for which he won the Nobel Prize, the mode of vibration was understood and the general pattern of basilar membrane motion became clear.

Classic views of membrane vibration. The discussion of basilar membrane motion will be more meaningful if the reader is aware of some of the historical antecedents of the recent investigations. The classic view of cochlear action was the resonance or place theory of hearing advanced by Helmholtz. Basically, this theory argued that the basilar membrane acted as a set of resonant devices, different parts of the membrane vibrating sympathetically to different sound frequencies. Thus, if one knew which place on the membrane was vibrating, one would know the frequency of the stimulus causing that vibration. The amplitude or some function of the amplitude of the vibration would then code the intensity of the sound. A complex wave, composed of several different sinusoids, would vibrate several different places along the membrane. In the simplest version of the theory the basilar membrane was compared with a harp. The different basilar membrane fibers, like the strings of the harp, were to respond to the different frequencies to which they were tuned. Hearing was a matter of detecting which strings were moving and thus it was essentially a complicated system of touch in which the locus of stimulation coded the frequency of the sound wave.

The opposing view was the temporal theory. There were a number of different versions of this basic position; Wever (1949) presents a good review of many of them. The basic idea of temporal theories was that frequency of a sinusoidal vibration was coded, not by place, but by the frequency of neural impulses. The intensity of the sound was coded by the number of fibers responding. Thus, temporal theorists believed that nearly the entire basilar membrane vibrated to nearly all frequencies. Complex sounds produced complex vibration patterns.

A number of problems were evident for both theories. The major difficulty with the temporal theory was the absolute refractory period of the neuron. After a nerve impulse has been initiated there is a period of time, approximately 1 msec in duration, during which it is impossible to excite the fiber, no matter how intense the stimulus. This absolute refractory period would limit the highest frequency that could be resolved. As it became apparent that this limit was about 1,000 to 2,000 impulses/sec, Wever (1949) proposed the volley theory. This theory held that the neurons broke into "squads," each firing on every second or third or even fourth period of the wave, thereby allowing the collection of fibers to initiate a spike on every epoch of the sinusoid. A number of fibers in such a collection could increase the upper limit of frequency resolution. For example, if ten fibers composed a squad, then 10,000 Hz could be coded if each fiber fired at 1,000 Hz in strict sequence. For such sequencing to code frequency successfully, firing must be maintained on a specific phase of the sinusoid. The question of phase-locking was therefore central for temporal theories. We will return to it in Chapter 5 when we discuss the electrical activity recorded from the fibers.

The place theory faced a series of more subtle problems concerning the degree and extent of mechanical resonance. First came the problem of determining whether the basilar membrane was sufficiently different in physical composition as a function of place to span the range of audible frequencies. Helmholtz argued that the length of the transverse fibers, the tension on them, and perhaps their mass changed sufficiently from one end of the cochlea to the other so that it could span two orders of magnitude change in frequency, which the ear appreciates. Second, there was the persistent problem of the degree of tuning. Resonance theory has always faced a dilemma. On one hand, it was desirable to assume the elements were sharply tuned since good frequency resolution and selection of individual components out of a complex periodic wave would be easily explained. On the other hand, such a high degree of tuning would imply a great deal of inertia and therefore the temporal response of the system would be very sluggish. In Chapter 1 we noted that for the simplest resonance system the response to an impulse lasts roughly the reciprocal of the bandwidth. Thus, if the bandwidth of the resonators is a few cycles, then the response to an impulse lasts several tenths of a second. Such a system could hardly track the brief, rapid, successive sounds such as occur in speech or music. The relation between degree of resonance and impulse response is a troublesome problem for resonance theory. These issues will guide the description of how the basilar membrane vibrates. We must particularly consider how it responds to sinusoidal vibrations, since this provides a measure of frequency tuning, and how it responds to impulsive stimuli, since this provides a measure of temporal resolution.

The traveling wave.   Let us describe how the membrane moves when excited by any sound; then we will consider why this particular form of motion occurs. The sound wave is a compressional wave in the fluids of cochlea. As we discussed earlier the pressure wave in the fluid has a high velocity (160,000 cm/sec) and may be treated as acting instantaneously over the entire membrane. In response to these forces the basilar membrane begins to move. This motion is a wave that moves from the stapes down the membrane toward the helicotrema. No matter what the nature of the sound wave, the membrane is first displaced near the base of the cochlea and the displacement moves toward the apex. This pattern of motion has been described as a traveling wave, which is simply a description of the form of the displacement. Traveling waves occur in various physical systems. An easy example to visualize is a rope tied to a door handle. We shake one end of the rope and thereby induce a disturbance that appears to travel down the rope toward the door handle. If the rope is long, the energy in the wave dissipates before reaching the end and no obvious reflections occur. Similarly, the waves induced in the basilar membrane disappear in the vicinity of the helicotrema. There is no obvious reflection back toward the stapes. The rope analogy is misleading because different physical processes are at work in the rope and the basilar membrane. Nevertheless, the form of the vibration pattern itself is similar in the two structures. The important point is that the displacement waves always travel from stapes where the area of cochlear duct is largest toward the helicotrema, where the area is smallest, never in the opposite direction. The velocity of this traveling wave is nonuniform. It travels very rapidly near the stapes, slows to about 15,000 cm/sec, 20 mm from the stapes, and then slows to about 1,000 cm/sec near the apex (von Békésy, 1960). Note that this velocity even at its fastest is very different from that of the compressional wave in sea water (160,000 cm/sec).

Sinusoidal input.   Next, how does the basilar membrane respond to a continuous sinusoidal vibration? The displacement of the basilar membrane as a function of time under these conditions also is a traveling wave. The amplitude of motion is small when the sinusoid first begins but the amplitude increases until a steady form of vibration occurs. Throughout this entire sequence the wave travels from the stapes toward the helicotrema. Even in its steady-state condition the vibration pattern appears as a wave traveling down the membrane. The position of the membrane at two different instants of time is shown in Figure 3.4. It is important to understand that this traveling wave is periodic, just as the source of excitation is periodic. The two instants displayed in Figure 3.4 represent the response of the basilar membrane at two times one-quarter of a wavelength apart. Were we to wait a full period the wave would be back to its initial position, indicated by the solid line in Figure 3.4. Thus, at any point on the membrane, the displacement as a function of time is periodic (in fact, sinusoidal). The phase relation between displacements at adjacent parts of the membrane is such that the wave appears to travel from stapes to helicotrema (left to right in Figure 3.4).

The preceding description is true for any sinusoidal excitation, but the location and form of the vibration pattern depends on the frequency of the sinusoid. If the frequency of the sound is high, say 8,000 Hz or above, the peak of the traveling wave occurs very near the stapes. For lower frequency sounds, the maximum of the traveling wave moves systematically toward the helicotrema and comparatively little vibration occurs near the stapes. All of the waves are similar in that they seem to move from stapes to helicotrema. The place of maximum vibration can be determined by measuring the peak excursion for each point along the membrane during a full cycle of vibration. This is indicated by the lightly dotted curve in Figure 3.4, which is called the envelope of the traveling wave. The shape of this envelope depends on the frequency of the exciting sinusoid. The correspondence between positions of the envelope's peak and the frequency of the stimulus is caused by changes in the physical structure of the membrane as we move from stapes to helicotrema. The membrane is wider at the helicotrema than at the stapes by approximately a factor of three or four. Note that this taper in the width of the *basilar membrane* is opposite the taper in the *cross-sectional area* of the duct. The wide end of the membrane is in the smallest part of the duct (see Figure 3.3). In addition to the change in width, the compliance of the membrane (the displacement in response to a constant force) varies by almost two orders of magnitude, being much stiffer near the stapes. These structural variables combine to make each region along the membrane move most easily to a narrow band of frequencies.

At any point along the membrane, the vibration pattern is sinusoidal and has a frequency exactly equal to the frequency of the imposed sound. Therefore, if one stood at any point along the basilar membrane, the frequency of vibration at that point would equal the frequency at which the stapes is being vibrated. Differences in phase of the membrane's motion produce the traveling wave.

Impulsive input. Next, consider the pattern of vibration of a very brief, impulsive sound. An impulse, by definition, contains all frequencies, and they

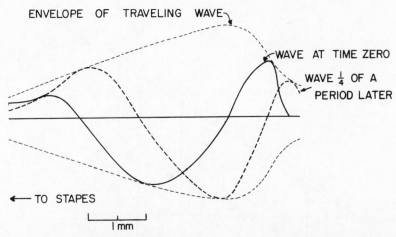

ENVELOPE OF TRAVELING WAVE

WAVE AT TIME ZERO

WAVE $\frac{1}{4}$ OF A
PERIOD LATER

← TO STAPES

1 mm

FIG. 3.4 The response of the basilar membrane to a sinusoidal signal shown in cross section (see Figure 3.3). The position of the membrane at two time instants is illustrated. The envelope of the travel wave is the point of maximum displacement reached during a full period of the sinusoidal excitation. (From von Békésy, 1960, p. 462. Copyright © 1960 by McGraw-Hill Book Company.)

are approximately equal in amplitude. One might expect from the frequency composition of an impulse that disturbance would be observed along the entire length of the cochlea partition. Such is indeed the case. Again, the displacement response travels from the stapes to helicotrema. The activity is less peaked than for steady sinusoidal vibration, however, and seems to involve almost the entire extent of the cochlea, although not at the same instant. At any local region, the response generated by the impulse as a function of time is first large and then decays gradually. The frequency of vibration of this decaying phenomenon depends upon the position along the basilar membrane. Near the stapes, a high-frequency vibration decays fairly quickly with time. Toward the helicotrema, the frequency of the vibration is much lower and the decay rate slower. Thus, the same association of a certain place with a certain frequency characterizes the response to impulsive sounds as well as to sustained sinusoidal vibration.

An Analogy for Basilar Membrane Vibration

It is important to understand the physical properties of the basilar membrane and how it vibrates. Von Békésy (1960) proposed an analogous system that provides a better intuitive feel for how the membrane responds to acoustic stimulation. Consider the series of pendula represented in Figure 3.5, each of different length. The top of each pendulum is connected to a rod and at its bottom is a weight that serves as its bob. Strings connect adjacent pendula with a mass attached to the connecting strings. These strings serve as couplers between adjacent parts of the system. Because the lengths of the pendula differ, the

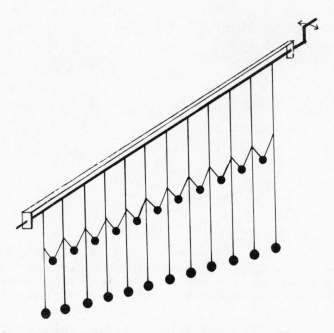

FIG. 3.5 A model of the cochlea after von Békésy. Pendula of various lengths hang from a rigid rod. Small masses hang by string connecting adjacent pendula. If the crank on the rod is moved back and forth in a regular rocking manner, a traveling wave will appear to move from the short pendula toward the longer ones.

natural frequency of each is different. The shortest pendula have higher natural frequencies than the longer ones. Thus, without the coupling strings, an impulse imparted to this system would make each pendulum vibrate at its own frequency. The vibration would slowly diminish over a period of time depending upon the damping of each pendulum. The cross-coupling adjacent pendulum, however, causes mutual interactions along the extent of this system.

Consider how the coupled system will respond when driven by a sustained sinusoid vibration. Note first that since the rod is rigid, the force it imparts acts on all of the pendula at the same time. This corresponds to the fact that the length of the compression wave in the cochlear fluids is long compared to the length of the membrane itself. As the rod is rotated back and forth regularly, the pendula begin moving in response to the sinusoidal driving force. The form of the vibration is a traveling wave. The wave travels from the short strings of the pendula toward the longer strings. This corresponds to the wave generated from the stapes to helicotrema along the basilar membrane. The vibration moves from structures with higher frequencies to structures with lower natural frequencies.

As one might expect, if the frequency of vibration equals the natural frequency of some pendulum, then that pendulum will vibrate maximally. Indeed, as one scans the series of pendula, one notices a locus of maximum movement. In this region the length of the pendulum is such that its natural frequency is near the frequency of the driving source. Thus, the frequency of the driving vibration changes the place of maximum vibration in this system.

Now consider what happens if we apply a brief impulsive stimulus. Since energy is imparted uniformly and instantaneously to the entire system, each pendulum begins to vibrate at its own natural frequency. Because of the cross coupling, however, these natural vibrations are constrained. Again, a traveling wave moves from the short pendula to the longer pendula. At each point along the system, of course, each pendulum vibrates in a sinusoidal fashion at a frequency nearly equal to its own natural frequency. These vibrations gradually decay since the energy provided by the impulsive stimulus is no longer present, but the damping in this system is not large.

In summary then, if the cochlea is excited by an impulsive stimulus, the basilar membrane vibrates at each point along its length with its own natural frequency. These vibrations are initially large in amplitude and decay with time. If a sinusoidal stimulus is the source of excitation, each point along the basilar membrane will vibrate at a frequency equal to that of input. The amplitude of membrane displacement depends upon the relationship of the driving frequency to the natural frequency of the membrane at that point. If the natural frequency and the driving frequency are nearly equal, then there will be a large amplitude of vibration. If the driving frequency and the membrane frequency differ widely from each other, then the vibrations will be much smaller. When viewed in time, differences in phase at particular points along the membrane produce a wave that travels from stapes to helicotrema in a regular progressive fashion. For sustained sinusoidal input, the location of maximum amplitude of this traveling wave depends upon the frequency of the driving source, since the point of maximum vibration occurs where the natural frequency of the membrane is equal to the frequency of the driving source.

Thus far, we have discussed the anatomic arrangements of structures within the ear and the pattern of vibration induced by the sound wave. Next, we must consider how the hair cells are stimulated. What excites the receptor elements?

Stimulation of the Hair Cells

We must first look more closely at the anatomy of the receptor elements themselves. The cross section of the basilar membrane is shown in Figure 3.2c, indicating the locations of both the inner and outer hair cells and of the tectorial membrane that lies immediately above the receptor elements. As the basilar membrane moves up and down in response to the sound wave, the organ of Corti is displaced to the plane of the basilar membrane in such a way that the position of hair cells relative to the tectorial membrane is altered. The small cilia on top of the hair cells are thus subjected to a mechanical force.

One hypothesis about how these forces operate is illustrated in Figure 3.6. This figure illustrates a cross section of the cochlea since we are now concerned with the displacement of the membrane along its width rather than length. In

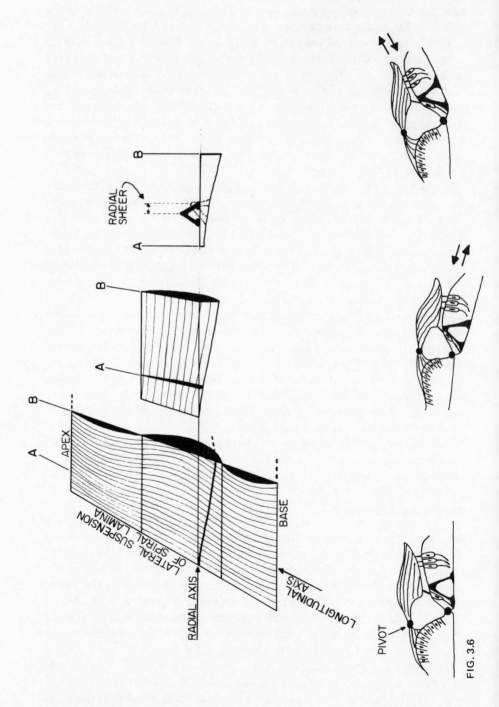

RADIAL SHEER

B

A

APEX

B

A

LATERAL SUSPENSION OF SPIRAL LAMINA

RADIAL AXIS

LONGITUDINAL AXIS

BASE

PIVOT

FIG. 3.6

this figure the basilar membrane and the tectorial membrane are represented schematically as two rigid surfaces hinged at slightly different points (marked with dark dots in the figure) along the horizontal axis. The Arch of Corti is represented by an inverted "V," and the hair cells are shaded in the drawing. As the membrane is displaced, either upward or downward, the two surfaces slide relative to one another. The directions of motion are indicated by arrows at the side of the drawings. This relative motion produces a shear force on the hair cells and bends them, as indicated in the drawing.

There may well be differences in direction and size of the forces that act on the inner and outer hair cells. As the drawing shows, the loci of the hinge points and the location of the cilia of the inner hair cell are especially critical. Several other hypotheses exist about the exact forces operating on the outer hair cell; each view is supported by some evidence but refuted by other evidence. There is better concensus about the forces operating on the outer hair cells and that is what Figure 3.6 illustrates. There also is general agreement that shear forces cause the hair cell to respond, not only in the cochlea, but also in other sense organs in which hair cells act as detectors. The shear force illustrated in the drawing is radially directed: if one thinks of the cochlea as a coil, the line of the shear force runs from the center outward toward the side of the coil.

In fact, the direction of the shear force may be either radial or longitudinal. Direction is somewhat confusing in the coiled structure, but a longitudinal direction is along the length of the membrane. A radial direction is one across the ribbon, from side to side (see Figure 3.7). The direction of the force depends on position along the membrane with respect to the maximum of the traveling wave. Von Békésy was the first to note that the direction of shear motions changes as one moves along the cochlea. The direction is mainly radial on the proximal or stapedial side of the maximum vibration and mainly longitudinal on the distal side toward the helicotrema. Tonndorf (1960) suggested a simple reason for the difference which Figure 3.7 illustrates. In Figure 3.7a a simple ribbon is shown unconstrained in the horizontal plane. The shear forces are entirely longitudinal, that is, along the length of the membrane. This is an inaccurate representation of the basilar membrane, since it is constrained along both sides, as illustrated in Figure 3.7b. Thus, the same traveling wave produces both longitudinal shear forces and radial shear forces. The figure suggests that the greatest longitudinal forces are on the low-frequency side of the membrane, toward the right in Figure 3.7b. The greatest radial forces occur on the side of the large deflection in Figure 3.7b, and thus on the high-frequency side of the traveling wave.

FIG. 3.6 Detailed view of the basilar membrane. The upper view defines the various terms, such as radial and longitudinal axes. The lower panels show how the tectorial membrane and basilar membrane may actually slide with respect to one another along the radial axis and establish a shear force on the tip of the hair cells.

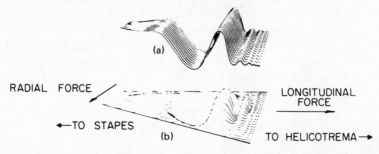

LONGITUDINAL   AND   RADIAL   FORCES
IN   COCHLEA

(a)

RADIAL   FORCE   LONGITUDINAL
                                                        FORCE

←—TO   STAPES   TO HELICOTREMA →
              (b)

FIG. 3.7   The usual cross-section view of the membrane (a) and a view illustrating the
correct boundary conditions at both sides of the membrane (b). Thus, displacement waves
produced by sound induce gradients in several directions and of different amounts on the
basal and apical sides of the maximum excursion. (From Tonndorf, 1960, p. 241.)

Electron microscopy has demonstrated that the cilia of the hair cells are
oriented in a very regular manner. The outer hair cells are grouped in three rows,
as we observed earlier. The cilia on top of the hair cells follow a "W" pattern,
with the bottom of the W pointing away from the center of the spiral, in the
radial direction. In this type of hair cell a so-called centriole lies at the bottom of
the W. In other preparations Lowenstein and Wersall (1959) have demonstrated
that motion of the hairs toward this centriole causes electrical depolarization of
the cell. These detailed findings suggest that the hair cells are particularly
sensitive to forces applied in certain directions.

SUMMARY

In this chapter, we have tried to trace the sound wave as it enters the external
ear up to and including the mechanical forces that initiate electrical activity in
the receptor elements of hearing.

The transmission of sound involves three gross structural stages, the external,
the middle, and the inner ear. The external ear is essentially a tube closed at one
end having a resonant frequency of about 3,000–4,000 Hz. The tube and the
pinna are important for directional hearing. The middle ear operates largely as a
transformer to match the acoustic impedance of air to that of the fluids of the
inner ear. In addition, the acoustic reflex provides some protection from loud,
sustained sounds via two small muscles attached to the bones of the middle ear.

In addition, the vibration patterns of the inner ear were discussed. These
patterns are traveling waves that result from the specific natural frequencies of
the various elements within the cochlea and the close cross-coupling between the

different elements. For sinusoidal stimuli, the maximum of the traveling wave lies at the place along the cochlea whose natural frequency equals the frequency of the sinusoid. For impulsive stimuli, the response at any point along the cochlea is nearly sinusoidal and the wave decays with time. The frequency of that motion is the natural frequency of that particular place.

Finally, we discussed the mechanical stimulation of the receptor elements themselves. The cilia on top of the outer hair cells are apparently maximally sensitive to a radial shear motion. This force is the ultimate mechanical stimulus for the auditory sense.

REFERENCES

Lowenstein, O., & Wersäll, J. A fundamental interpretation of the electron-microscopic structure of the sensory hairs in the cristae of the elasmobranch raja clavata in terms of directional sensitivity. *Nature,* 1959, *184,* 1807–1808.

Ohm, G.S. Über die Definition des Tones, nebst daran geknüpfter Theorie der Sirene und ähnlicher tonbildender Vorrichtungen. *Annalen der Physik und Chemie,* 1843, *59,* 513–565.

Tonndorf, J. Shearing motion in scala media of cochlear models. *Journal of the Acoustical Society of America,* 1960, *32,* 238–244.

Tonndorf, J., & Khanna, S.M. Tympanic-membrane vibrations in human cadaver ears studied by time-averaged holography. *Journal of the Acoustical Society of America,* 1972, *52,* 1221–1233.

von Békésy, G. *Experiments in hearing.* (E.G. Wever, Ed. and trans.). New York: McGraw-Hill, 1960.

von Helmholtz, H.L.F. *On the sensations of tone as a physiological basis for the theory of music.* (A.J. Ellis, trans.). New York: Dover, 1954. (Originally published, 1863).

Wiener, F. On the diffraction of a progressive wave by the human head. *Journal of the Acoustical Society of America,* 1947, *19,* 143–146.

Wever, E.G. *Theory of hearing.* New York: Wiley, 1949.

4
Anatomy
of the Auditory System

This chapter reviews the anatomy of the auditory system. Compared to the abundance of excellent anatomic information on this topic, it will be quite brief. This is simply because our main emphasis is on function. Despite some tremendous advances in our understanding of auditory anatomy in the last several decades, we still know comparatively little about relations between structure and function. A brief outline, however, is essential to understand the electrical activity recorded from the cochlea, a topic discussed in the next chapter.

We will first describe the innervation of the cochlea. We will then review the synaptic connections that the auditory system makes as it carries information into the brain. Finally, the last section of this chapter describes some of the changes in discriminative behavior that occur when certain of these pathways or structures are destroyed through ablation. Results of ablation and their relation to function are particularly difficult to interpret, and only a few of the findings will be presented.

INNERVATION OF THE COCHLEA

The system of connections and elements within the cochlea rests on a very orderly arrangement of receptor elements. The receptors do not appear at irregular points like the touch and temperature receptors of the skin; instead the receptor elements are arranged in an orderly fashion, one row of inner hair cells plus three rows of outer hair cells that continue along the extent of the basilar membrane from base to apex. Figure 4.1 indicates the general arrangement. The cross-sectional view (top) shows the width of the basilar membrane larger in the

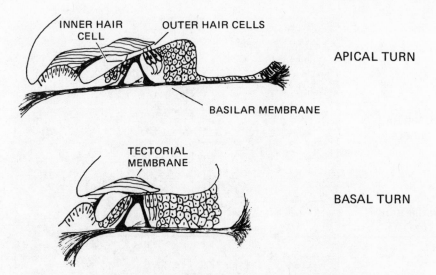

INNER HAIR CELL

OUTER HAIR CELLS

APICAL TURN

BASILAR MEMBRANE

TECTORIAL MEMBRANE

BASAL TURN

FIG. 4.1   A cross-sectional view of the basilar membrane and receptor cells in the apical and basal turns. Note that the basilar membrane is wide near the apex where the cochlear duct is narrower.

apex than in the base. Despite this change in size there is always an inner hair cell separated by the tunnel rod cells from three outer cells. Micrograph of this is shown in Figure 4.2.

Before describing how these cells are innervated we should recall that all nerve cells are generally composed of three parts: (a) a cell body, (b) dendrites, and (c) an axon. The electrical impulse, which signals the activity of the cell, is initiated at the dendrite and communicated down the axon. In the cochlea the hair cell itself is the primary receptor element. Dendrites surround the hair cell and initiate activity that is carried from the cochlea along those processes through the slitlike opening in the bony spiral lamina (which forms the support for one side of the basilar membrane). The dendrites are the peripheral processes of the cell bodies of neurons located in the spinal ganglion. The axons of these cell bodies are the twisted group of fibers that form part of the eighth (VIII) cranial nerve. This nerve also contains the axons from the vestibular system. All of the acoustic division of the VIII nerve terminates on cell bodies located in the cochlear nucleus, a collection of cells located in the lower brain stem.

It is important to understand that there are two separate and distinct systems of connections for the hair cells. One is the afferent (incoming fibers) branch, briefly described in the preceding paragraph. There is also an efferent (outgoing) set of fibers, whose cell bodies are located in the superior olive on both homolateral (same) and contralateral (opposite) sides. Their axons extend into the cochlea itself and terminate on or near the hair cells. The number of such fibers is relatively small but their extensive ramifications in the cochlear duct,

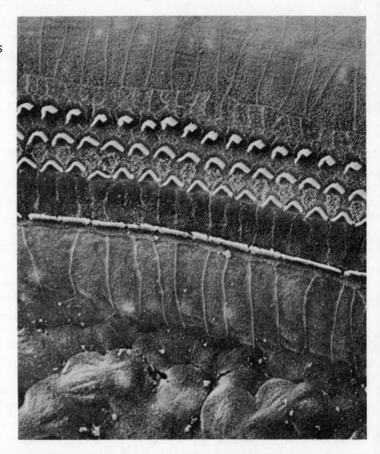

HENSEN'S CELLS

OUTER HAIR
CELLS

INNER HAIR
CELLS

INNER SPIRAL
SULCUS

FIG. 4.2   A top view of the organ of Corti as seen by a scanning electron microscope. The animal is a guinea pig. The regular arrangement of inner and outer hair cells is apparent (×825). (Photograph courtesy of Catherine A. Smith.)

particularly among the outer hair cells, have made it difficult for investigators to understand many details about the afferent connections. The efferent supply has particularly confused numerical estimates such as the number of afferent fibers that innervate inner and outer hair cells.

A quiet revolution has occurred in our understanding of cochlear innervation in the last twenty years. Although the general features of the organization of nerves have been known from the careful and patient studies of Retzius (1881, 1884), Lorente de Nó (1937), and Fernandez (1951), these investigators could not distinguish between efferent and afferent fibers. Rasmussen (1946, 1953) presented clear evidence of efferent fibers extending into the cochlear duct and extensively ramifying within the cochlea. Simultaneously, the use of electron microscopy (Engstrom & Wersäll (1958); Spoendlin (1966); Smith & Dempsey,

1957) has clarified what was obscure to optical techniques. In addition, one can remove the efferent fibers by transecting them and causing their degeneration within the cochlea. This procedure has materially improved our understanding of afferent innervation. But despite these improvements in technique and in clarifying the essential cause of past confusions, there are still numerous discrepancies among the descriptions. Many of these differences are undoubtedly attributable to differences among species. The animals most frequently studied are the cat, guinea pig, and chinchilla. The following account is based largely on Spoendlin's (1970) study of the cat. Although one might expect man to be similar, the variation among other mammals makes simple extrapolation hazardous. Certainly the number of fibers in the VIIIth nerve is quite different, being about 31,000 in man and monkey, about 24,000 in the guinea pig and chinchilla, and about twice those numbers, 50,000 in the cat (Gacek & Rasmussen, 1961). These warnings should be kept in mind in reading the next section.

One advantage of the following account is that it is numerically definite. If the goal of understanding anatomy is to build more specific hypotheses concerning the relation between structure and function, then such numerical estimates are needed on the anatomic side. While it is interesting to know that one structure connects to some other, it is ultimately essential to know roughly the number of such connections and how this number compares with estimates of connections along some other alternate pathway. Our present anatomic understanding is often not far advanced, although great progress is being made. More numerical estimates, particularly from different species, should be available in the next several decades. The present accounts are the best estimates that the author was able to find. In some cases where similar estimates are available from other animals, they will be quoted. With these caveats in mind let us begin the description.

AFFERENT INNERVATION

In the cat about 50,000 fibers enter the cochlea through the small openings in the basilar membrane called the habenula perforata. Since only about 2,500 of these are efferent fibers, the vast majority are afferent. The cell bodies of these afferents are located in the spiral ganglion, as stated earlier. About 20 separate fibers enter through each habenular opening. Outward from each habenular opening in the radial direction is one inner hair cell and, still further out, are three outer hair cells. There are about 2,500 such rows (one inner hair cell and three outers) along the membrane. There is no dispute about the preceding description. What is still not firmly settled is the ratio of afferent fibers that innervate the outer and inner hair cells.

According to Spoendlin, about 95%, or 47,500 of these 50,000 afferents terminate on inner hair cells! The fibers that innervate the inner hair cells are usually those that enter by the adjacent habenular opening. Each inner hair cell is therefore innervated by about 19 or 20 afferent fibers. They synapse on the hair cell by a small swelling that is attached to the base of the receptor element. In the cat, according to Spoendlin, only one or two of the 20 fibers might innervate a distant inner hair cell rather than the one nearest the habenular opening through which it entered the cochlear duct (see Figure 4.3).

The remainder of the afferent fibers, about 2,500 in number, cross the tunnel of Corti below the arch; they also turn after they cross the arch and run toward the base. As they run toward the base the fibers rise slightly and eventually send out branches to innervate the outer hair cells. These fibers are called external spiral fibers. One can estimate by measuring the angle of ascent of a spiral that it travels about 700 μ before reaching the first outer hair cell to be innervated. This means it runs along the side of at least 100 outer hair cells before sending off a small terminal collateral. The same fiber probably continues to travel toward the base, sending off one or two more collaterals to the first row of outer hair cells. The fiber then jogs radially and runs between the first and second row, again innervating three or four cells. Finally, it again jogs radially and again innervates three or four outer hair cells. Thus, the spiral fiber distributes its innervation to a few cells over about 100–200 μ distance. If each of these 2,500 fibers innervates about 10 outer hair cells on average, then, since there are roughly 7,500 outer hair cells, three or four different afferents must connect to each outer hair cell.

Figure 4.4 illustrates the afferent connections in the cat, according to Spoendlin. It is not difficult to draw the innervation of the inner hair cells since the

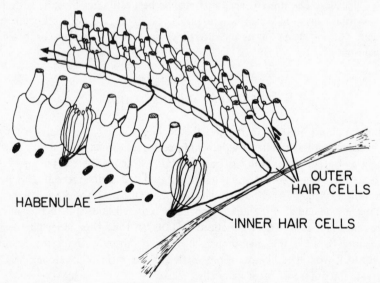

FIG. 4.3 Typical innervation pattern for the afferent fibers. (From Spoendlin, 1970, p. 33.)

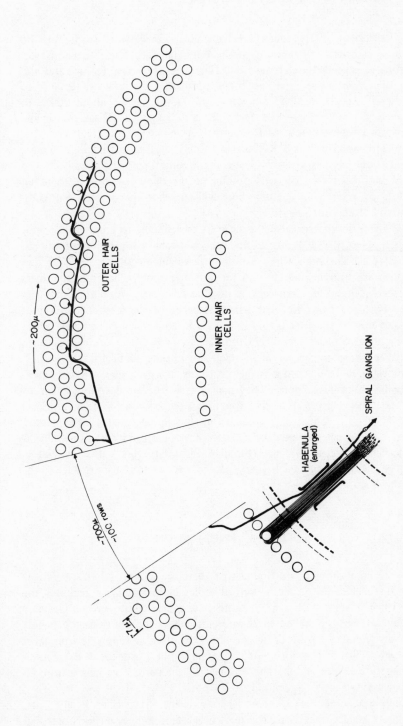

FIG. 4.4 Schematic view of cochlear innervation for afferent fibers in cat. (From Spoendlin, 1970, p. 33.)

majority of fibers, after leaving the habenula, immediately synapse on the neighboring cell. The connections of the outer hair cells are illustrated by a single fiber—a so-called external spiral fiber. As the drawing indicates the afferent fiber runs toward the base along the basilar membrane, a distance of nearly 700 μ, before making connection over a distance of about 200 μ to approximately 10 outer hair cells. Spoendlin and Gacek (1963) say that in the cat the only afferent supply to the outer hair cell is via this tract along the basilar membrane. Smith and Rasmussen (1963) say that in chinchilla afferents cross both along the basilar membrane and the central part of the tunnel. Since there are about as many afferents running to the outer hair cells as there are radial rows of outer hair cells, one fiber will innervate several outer hair cells. The figure illustrates one such fiber.

In chinchilla, Smith estimates the ratio of fibers going to inner versus outer hair cells is about 8 to 1. We could find no comparable estimate for guinea pigs. Smith has collected some statistics on the afferent innervation of the outer hair cells in the basal turn in guinea pigs. After emerging from the habenula the fibers run between 100 and 600 μ, at least in the first turn. They would therefore pass about 14 to 80 rows of outer hair cells. They then branch and innervate outer hair cells over a distance of 70 to 150 μ, or 9 to 20 hair cells. They yield about 20 nerve endings. Smith's data differ from Spoendlin's in that, for the basal turn, a single fiber tends to innervate only a single row of outer hair cells.

Finally, we should comment that these patterns, and particularly these numerical estimates are average figures. They may not be true for the entire extent of the cochlea. The innervation of the efferent system is known to be nonuniform and the afferent system is also nonuniform, but probably to a lesser degree. However, a numerical estimate of the degree of nonuniformity is not possible at this time. There is clear evidence (Smith & Sjöstrand, 1961) that, at least in guinea pigs, afferent innervation changes as one moves from base to apex in the outer hair cells.

EFFERENT INNERVATION

We know from Rasmussen's estimate that there are about 500 efferent fibers entering the cochlea in the cat. Their cell bodies are located in the region of the superior olive. The efferents ramify in the spiral ganglion but there are probably only a few efferent (compared to 20 afferents) emerging through each habenula because that number hardly decreases when the efferent supply is eliminated (Spoendlin, 1970). The majority of the efferent fibers arise from the contralateral superior olivary region. The estimate of the percentage ranges from 75 (Rasmussen, 1960) to 90 (Spoendlin, 1970).

Although the number of efferent fibers entering the cochlea is small, the ramifications are enormous, and the total number of endings on the outer hair cells is estimated to be about 40,000. The distribution is not uniform, however, and ranges from about 6 to 8 endings per cell near the base and decreases as one moves toward the apex. Also, the distribution is not uniform over the three rows of outer hair cells. The inner row receives efferent innervation throughout the length of the cochlea. In the second and third row the number of nerve endings gradually decreases as one moves apically. By the third turn there are often no efferent connections in the outer two rows.

The manner in which efferent fibers connect to the inner and outer hair cells is also different. The fibers of the efferent system terminate directly on the outer hair cells as do the afferents. In the case of the inner hair cells, the efferent synapses on the dendrite of the afferent fiber and only rarely contacts the hair cell itself. There are no estimates of the relative division of the 500 efferents between the inner and outer hair cells, nor of the number of efferent connections per inner hair cell.

Details about the pattern of innervation of the efferent system are still somewhat in doubt. Because of the large number of ramifications of such a small number of fibers, the innervation pattern is clearly diffuse and relatively undifferentiated. Both the ratio of hair cells to efferent fibers and the lack of a systematic pattern of innervation suggest that the role of the efferent system must be diffuse and general. Some evidence relating to the function of the efferent system will be discussed later.

We must now leave the cochlea and trace the fibers of both systems into the central nervous system. The mouth of a river is often better known than its source, so our understanding of where the auditory fibers begin and how they are controlled or monitored becomes progressively more vague as we ascend the central nervous system.

THE AUDITORY PATHWAYS

The traveling wave within the cochlea and the orderly arrangement of the receptor elements make it clear that a strong relation must hold between the frequency of the stimulating acoustic sinusoid and the place of the neural element. This principle is called tonotopic organization and it characterizes nuclei and tracts of the auditory system. Thus, the projection of the end organ to the cortex is orderly but this basic orderliness is complicated both by an increasing diversity of connections and alternate pathways and by an increasing number of elements. To penetrate this diversity and to understand the significance of the anatomy is often extremely difficult. Enormous gains have been realized in the last several years and continued advances can be expected. The following gives but a brief overview of a very complicated and complex story. We will begin our account with the afferent system and conclude with a description of the efferent pathways. Figure 4.5 shows the major pathways and can be used in the following description.

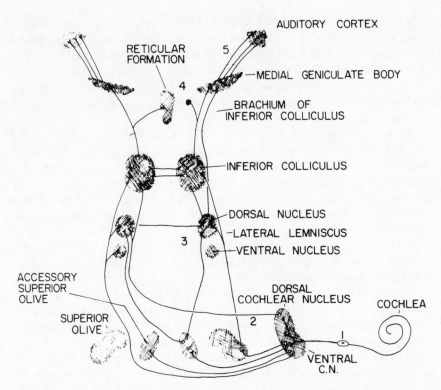

FIG. 4.5 Major structures of the auditory pathways and some of the connections. (From Gacek, 1972, p. 242.)

Afferent System

Cochlear nucleus. The axons of all the ganglion cells of the VIIIth nerve terminate in the cochlear nucleus. Thus, the cochlear nucleus represents the first synaptic stage in the passage of auditory information toward the cortex. The cochlear nucleus is the universal terminus of all the VIIIth nerve fibers. From this point upward there are a number of alternate routes until the medial geniculate body is reached. At the geniculate the universal rule is that all fibers synapse. Fibers from there carry auditory information to the cortex. Some of the diverse connections undoubtedly serve a reflex function; some interact at a low level with the efferent system, and some serve as points of binaural interaction with homological fibers from the contralateral ear.

The cell bodies of the cochlear nucleus comprise three major groups: (1) the dorsal cochlear nucleus, (2) the posteroventral nucleus, and (3) the anteroventral nucleus, the largest complex. Probably the best picture of how the cochlear nucleus is innervated comes from the work of Rose, Galambos, and Hughes (1960). They believe on the basis of electrical recordings from single fibers in this nucleus that an VIIIth nerve fiber enters the anteroventral part, divides into at least three collaterals, and innervates the three major groups. Based on the relation between best frequency of the fiber and location within the nucleus, it seems probable that an orderly map of location within the cochlea and location within the major divisions of the cochlear nucleus is preserved. Such an inference is also supported by degeneration studies (Sando, 1965).

The cells of the dorsal cochlear nucleus send their axons across the lower brain stem to a contralateral tract of the lateral lemniscus and then upward to the inferior colliculus or the dorsal nucleus of the lateral lemniscus. Some fibers from this nucleus also send collaterals that terminate in the contralateral superior olivary nucleus. In addition to this flow from the dorsal nucleus, the ventral part of the cochlear nucleus innervates both homolaterally and contralaterally the superior olivary complex and the accessory olivary nucleus.

Thus, after the first cell body of the spiral ganglion, a second cell carries the information from the cochlear nucleus as high as the inferior colliculus, although some fibers reach the inferior colliculus only after another synapse in the dorsal nucleus of the lateral lemniscus. Figure 4.5 shows a schematic diagram of these connections.

Inferior colliculus. The inferior colliculus receives input from as low as the accessory nucleus of the superior olive of the contralateral side and from the superior olive and accessory olive of the homolateral side. It is also innervated by the path from the contralateral cochlear nucleus previously mentioned. At higher levels it receives input from the lateral lemniscus of the same side and the inferior colliculus of the opposite side. There are also interconnections between the two lateral lemnisci, but the main interaction at higher levels is at the colliculus. The main output of the colliculus is to the medial geniculate, although other fibers branch into the reticular formation. A few fibers from the dorsal nucleus and the lateral lemniscus bypass the inferior colliculus and reach the medial geniculate directly.

Medial geniculate. The medial geniculate receives all afferent fibers that innervate the acoustic parts of the cortex. There are no neurons that cross to the other medial geniculate, so all subcortical interaction between the two systems must occur at lower levels.

Auditory cortex. The auditory cortex is not well known or as orderly as the visual cortex. Much of our information about it comes from electrophysiological studies. This information is at best indirect, since such activity only indicates that there is some pathway from one place to the other. There have been some anatomic degeneration studies but these have inferred a connection from the cortex to the geniculate from the degeneration of geniculate cells after cortical lesions (retrograde studies). Surer evidence is obtained by destroying the cell body and tracing the axonal degeneration thus created. This technique is laborious and probably impossible using light microscopy alone. At present we usually describe the main auditory cortex as two areas, AI and AII, lying in adjacent regions of the temporal lobe. Various other areas adjacent to these major ones are also sometimes described as auditory areas. There is also a third auditory area, denoted AIII, located in the head division of the second somatic sensory area.

There is considerable uncertainty about these various areas and their relation. The area AI appears to be a primary area of projection in almost all views. Whether the other areas are areas of secondary projection or "association" areas is not clear at this time.

Summary

Four and five synapses are needed to carry information from the cochlea to the auditory cortex. At each step in this ascending chain the interconnections increase in number and complexity. At each higher stage the number of cells increases sharply. Thus, in monkey the cochlear nucleus contains about 190,000 cells, the colliculus or geniculate about 400,000, and the cortex about 10,000,000 (Chow, 1951). This increase in number must reflect a more highly organized and more flexible processing system.

Superior Olivary Complex

In addition to the upward afferent flow of information that we have just discussed there is considerable afferent innervation of the superior olive. Some of these connections serve a reflex purpose. For example, this body controls the middle ear muscles and also the eye muscles, thus causing the eyeblink in reaction to sudden loud sounds. This latter reflex is among the fastest that can be reliably observed and has a latency of only 25 msec, (Landis & Hunt, 1939). In addition to these reflex functions, the medial part of the superior olivary nucleus contains cells that receive afferent connections from the cochlear nucleus and, in turn, send fibers to the ipsilateral lateral lemniscus. Because this nucleus is at the lowest level where binaural interaction occurs, it has been extensively studied using such stimuli.

In addition to these afferent aspects, the superior olivary complex contains the cell bodies of the efferent system whose axons extend into the cochlea itself. Let us now briefly review that system.

Efferent System

For our present understanding and appreciation of the efferent system, we owe a large debt of gratitude to the work of Rasmussen (1946, 1953). He described two separate systems of efferent control, both originating in or near the auditory cortex and traveling downward in the same tracts as the afferent bundle. One tract ends in the olivary complex that projects into the organs of Corti itself. The second system terminates in the dorsal cochlear nucleus.

The one system starts in auditory areas of AI or AII and descends through the medial geniculate to the inferior colliculus. New cell bodies start at the inferior colliculus, travel down to the level of the superior olive, and terminate on the multipolar cells that constitute the olivocochlear nucleus. This is the bundle of cells that start in the superior olivary complex and send axons that terminate in the cochlea itself.

The second system originates from both the primary auditory areas AI and AII as well as the associated areas. Most of these also end in the inferior colliculus, although side branches run into the reticular formation and the geniculate. From the colliculus, fibers run down the same tract as the ascending fibers but they bunch in a compact bundle running in the side of the tract. These fibers terminate in the preolivary nucleus on either side, but mainly on the ipsilateral side. In addition, other efferents start at various parts of the preceding tracts and end in the dorsal cochlear nucleus.

As with the ascending system in which both cochleas find representation in both hemispheres of the auditory cortex, so the efferent system is similarly a mixed one. Each hemisphere can affect either end organ.

EFFECTS OF DESTRUCTION OF PARTS
OF THE AUDITORY SYSTEM
ON DISCRIMINATIVE BEHAVIOR

Effects of the destruction of the two ends of the auditory system have received the most study. Damage to the cochlea and ablation of the cortical projection areas have been extensively explored in several species. While some of the effects are well known and agree nicely with our intuitions, many facets of this area still remain mysterious. This state of affairs is not wholly unexpected, for ablation does not provide precise analytic information concerning function. Loss of some behavior following ablation can be caused for a variety of reasons and it is certainly not evident that the ablated area is a center of such behavior. Similarly, the failure to find any behavioral change following the ablation of some neural tissue does not mean that this tissue is not intimately involved in the behavior pattern under question. Despite the lack of analytic precision inherent in these studies, they remain of value because of their clinical significance.

Cochlear Lesions

An extensive and conclusive series of experiments on the results of selective destruction of restricted areas of the cochlea have been carried out by Schuknecht. The experimental animal was the cat and the lesions were made by inserting a needle into the cochlear duct. After recovery from surgery, the animal's hearing was tested by using a pure tone to signal the onset of shock. The animal could avoid the shock by running to the opposite end of the cage prior to the presentation of the tone. Cats with cochlear lesions inevitably show abrupt pure tone hearing loss; changes in sensitivity of over 30 dB over a frequency range of one octave are not uncommon. Histological examination of the animal's cochlea confirms that the location of the lesions generally corresponds to the appropriate part of the cochlear duct. In fact, the correlation is so good that one can construct a map relating the distance along the membrane and the frequency at which the pure tone hearing loss begins. Schuknecht (1953) constructed such a map and it shows a logarithmic relation between the frequency of the pure tone and the distance along the cochlea, down to frequencies of about 500 Hz. Beyond this point, which represents the last 20% of the cochlea, the data are not sufficiently detailed to allow one to determine the relation. Over the higher frequencies, however, the correspondence is very good, a loss of half the basal part of the membrane will result in a sharp hearing loss above about 3,500 Hz.

Despite this very good correlation with pure tone threshold tests, there is little correlation between the size or extent of the lesions and other tests of auditory acuity. Frequency discrimination limens and even discrimination of a change of intensity seem remarkably unaffected. Schuknecht believes that frequency discrimination depends more upon a shift in activity among the frequency-dependent neural populations and is less influenced by the density of innervation.

Eighth Nerve Lesions

Restricted lesioning of the VIIIth nerve has long been a topic of study for a variety of reasons. First, the nerve is sometimes partially cut for relief from Meniere's disease in man. Dandy (1934) used such a procedure and found that patients often had only a slight change in the high-frequency hearing after such an operation. Several studies of similar results were reported on experiments with animals. Neff (1947) studied a number of animals. His results showed either little or no loss in a number of animals and, when hearing loss was found, it was inevitably in the high-frequency region. It appears now that the fibers cut were invariably afferents from the basal end of the cochlea, which tends to be twisted on the outside and bottom of the VIIIth nerve. These fibers are most vulnerable to the surgical approach used to make the lesions. This conclusion was supported by the histological examination carried out by Wever and Neff (1947). They remark on the failure of any of the lesions to destroy the fibers associated with the apical part of the membrane.

Thus, once more the lesion data support the tonotopic organization of frequency with place and the more general principle that widespread destruction is needed to produce noticeable behavioral effects. One should recall that a threshold discrimination task requires only one item of auditory information. In a system with many similar parallel channels, such as the ear, the preservation of a single channel may be sufficient to signal the presence of that one crucial item of information. Therefore, failure to produce a behavioral deficit is less informative than the reverse.

Other Receptor Damage

In addition to the two forms of insult just discussed, a variety of other causes produces abnormality of the peripheral receptor system. Systematic changes in the cochlea with age have been observed. In addition, the occurrence of sustained intense stimulation can cause dramatic changes in the cochlea. We shall take up the effects of intense stimulation in later chapters. Suffice it to say that intense sound causes destruction of the inner and outer hair cells and the frequency content of the sound determines the general locus of the destruction. For example, intense, high-frequency noise generally causes destruction in the basal end of the cochlea.

Cortical Damage

The results of cortical ablation on behavioral discrimination involve studies that stretch over a number of years. Neff has provided several brief reviews of this work and we will not elaborate beyond his summaries. Following bilateral ablation of the main auditory projection areas, which include most of the temporal lobe, the animal can generally learn to discriminate (1) onset of sound, (2) changes in intensity of a tone, and (3) changes in frequency of a tone. These results are in sharp contrast to similar studies in vision, where ablation of the cortical projection area severely impairs the animal. The usual reason given for the lack of similar dramatic changes in audition is that lower cortical centers provide sufficient alternative pathways to mediate these simple discrimination tasks.

The deficits that emerge reliably from cortical ablation appear to be failure to discriminate a change in the temporal pattern of a sequence of tones, that is, tasks in which the difference between a sequence, high, low, high, must be discriminated from its compliment, low, high, low (Diamond & Neff, 1957). Also, tasks in which the number of tone bursts in a pattern was the crucial stimulus element were extremely difficult to relearn. Similarly, a discrimination based on the duration of a tonal signal appears to be impossible to relearn after cortical ablation (Scharlock, Neff, & Strominger, 1965). Finally, it appears that localization is severely impaired. Any discrimination whose cues involve sounds in different locations invariably suffers.

Neff and his collaborators have conducted a number of studies based on the following simplified model. Any discrimination task in which the stimulus excites a new neural population, such as a task involving a change in intensity or frequency, is likely to be unaffected by cortical ablation. The vulnerable discriminations are based on different patterns of the same acoustic elements. In general, Neff and his co-workers' later work has supported this view although there are certain complications. One difficulty with this theory is, of course, the definition of acoustic elements—when can one say the patterning of sounds involves new elements?

The exact function of the auditory cortex is still largely a mystery. It is not needed for simple discrimination as Bromiley (1948) demonstrated. He found that a completely decorticated dog could learn to respond to a sound onset. Since this discrimination can be mediated by lower neural centers, it is believed that auditory cortex must be involved with more complicated operations. But how to characterize those more complicated operations is still largely unresolved.

ELECTRICAL STIMULATION OF HUMAN CORTEX

Finally, we should mention the data available on direct stimulation of auditory cortex in man. Penfield and Rasmussen (1950) have provided the only organized body of knowledge on this topic. Their information comes from a number of cases in which the cortex has been exposed, usually in operations for epilepsy or brain tumors. The patient is often alert and under only local anesthesia. As the surgeon stimulates certain portions of the cortex, sensory impressions are reported or motor responses occur. If the stimulating electrode is at the very top of the temporal lobe, close to the fissure of Sylvius, then stimulation causes a variety of reports such as buzzing, ringing, wind in the trees, or the sound of a motor. Occasionally some patients report sounds similar to single tones. Some patients also report that they feel deafened by the application of the stimulus. Auditory experiences such as these are not reported when stimulating other areas of the surface cortex. Insufficient data were obtained to correlate locus of stimulation with the apparent frequency of the sounds. The organization is not as neat as that found along the postcentral gyrus, where one can construct a map of the skin surface as one proceeds from top to bottom along the edge of the gyrus. Perhaps the main auditory projection area lies folded into the temporal lobe in an unaccessible region.

Surrounding the temporal region where these simple sounds can be evoked, electrical stimulation produces a variety of complicated auditory experiences or even evokes organized recollections of events. Some of these recollections may contain auditory sounds or images, but often they do not. Thus, there is fairly direct evidence that the temporal lobe does contain the main auditory projection area, although its organization, as we can measure it from surface stimulation, is not very well understood.

REFERENCES

Bromiley, R.B. Conditioned response in a dog after removal of neocortex. *Journal of Comparative Physiological Psychology*, 1948, *41*, 102–110.

Chow, K.L. Numerical estimates of the auditory central nervous system of the rhesus monkey. *Journal of Comparative Neurology*, 1951, *95*, 159–175.

Dandy, W.E. Effects of hearing after subtotal section of the cochlear branch of the auditory nerve. *Bulletin Johns Hopkins Hospital*, 1934, *55*, 240–243.

Diamond, I.T., & Neff, W.D. Ablation of temporal cortex and discrimination of auditory patterns. *Journal of Neurophysiology*, 1957, *20*, 300–315.

Engstrom, H., & Wersäll, J. Structure and innervation of the inner ear sensory epithelia. *International Review of Cytology*, 1958, *7*, 535–585.

Fernandez, C. The innervation of the cochlea (guinea pig). *Larynogoscope*, 1951, *61*, 1152–1172.

Gacek, R.R. Neuroanatomy of the auditory system. In J.V. Tobias (Ed.), *Foundations of modern auditory theory*. Vol. II. New York and London: Academic Press, 1972.

Gacek, R.R., & Rasmussen, G.L. Fiber analysis of the statoacoustic nerve of guinea pig, cat, and monkey. *Anatomical Record*, 1961, *139*, 455–463.

Landis, C., & Hunt, W.A., *The startle reflex*. New York: Farrar and Rinehart, 1939.

Lorente de Nó, R. The sensory endings in the cochlea. *Laryngoscope*, 1937, *47*, 373–377.

Neff, W.D. The effects of partial section of the auditory nerve. *Journal of Comparative Physiological Psychology*, 1947, *40*, 203–215.

Penfield, W., & Rasmussen, T. *The cerebral cortex of man; a clinical study of localization of function*. New York: Macmillian, 1950.

Rasmussen, G.L. The olivary peduncle and other fiber projections of the superior olivary complex. *Journal of Comparative Neurology*, 1946, *84*, 141–219.

Rasmussen, G.L. Further observations of the efferent cochlear bundle. *Journal of Comparative Neurology*, 1953, *99*, 61–74.

Rasmussen, G.L. Efferent fibers of the cochlear nerve and cochlear nucleus. In G.L. Rasmussen & W.F. Windle (Eds.), *Neural mechanisms of the auditory and vestibular systems*. Springfield, Ill.: Charles C Thomas, 1960, pp. 105–115.

Retzius, G. *Das Gehörorgan der Wirbeltiere, Vol. I. Gehörorgan der Fische and Amphibien: Vol. II. Das Gehörorgan der Reptilien, der Vögel und der Säugetiere*. Stockholm: Samson and Wallin, 1881, 1884.

Rose, J.E., Galambos, R., & Hughes, J. Organization of frequency sensitive neurons in the cochlear nucleus complex of the cat. In G.L. Rasmussen & W.F. Windle (Eds.), *Neural mechanisms of the auditory and vestibular system*. Springfield, Ill.: Charles C Thomas, 1960.

Sando, I. The anatomical interrelationships of the cochlear nerve fibers. *Acta oto-laryngologica*, 1965, *59*, 417–436.

Scharlock, D.P., Neff, W.D., & Strominger, N.L. Discrimination of tone duration after bilateral ablation of cortical auditory areas. *Journal of Neurophysiology*, 1965, *28*, 673–681.

Schuknecht, H.F. Lesions of the organ of corti. *Transactions of the American Academy of Ophthalmology and otolaryngology*, 1953, *57*, 366–383.

Smith, C.A., & Dempsey, E. Electron microscopy of the organ of corti. *American Journal of Anatomy*, 1957, *100*, 337–367.

Smith, C.A., & Rasmussen, G.L. Recent observations on the olivo-cochlear bundle. *Annals of otology, rhinology, and laryngology*, 1963, *72*, 489–506.

Smith, C.A., & Sjöstrand, F.S. Structure of the nerve endings on the external hair cells of the guinea pig cochlea as studied by serial sections. *Journal Ultrastructure Res*, 1961, *5*, 523–556.

Spoendlin, H., & Gacek, R.R. Electron microscopic studies on the efferent and afferent innervation of the organ of corti in the cat. *Annals of otology, rhinology, and laryngology*, 1963, *72*, 1–27.

Spoendlin, H. *The organization of the cochlear receptor, advances in oto-rhino laryngology*. Karger, Basel- New York, 1966.

Spoendlin, H. Structural basis of peripheral frequency analysis. In R. Plomp & G.F. Smoorenburg (Eds.), *Frequency analysis and periodicity detection in hearing*. Leiden: A.W. Sijthoff, 1970, pp. 2–37.

Wever, E.G., & Neff, W.D. A further study of the effects of partial section of the auditory nerve. *Journal of Comparative Physiological Psychology*, 1947, *40*, 217–226.

5

Electrical Activity of the Cochlea and Auditory Nerve

INTRODUCTION

Chapter 3 described mechanical action of the sound wave and forces that it generates on the various structures of the cochlea. The preceding chapter reviewed the anatomy of the auditory system, with particular emphasis on cochlear innervation. This chapter considers the electrical activity recorded from the cochlea. We remind the reader once more that we are not directly aware of the acoustic waveforms, rather we are aware of neural activity induced by the sound wave. Thus, the acoustic pressure wave is transformed or coded into neural activity. Our goal is to understand that neural code. In particular, we should like to know what aspects of the acoustic waveform are represented or ignored in the first transformation from acoustic to neural energy. We are fortunate that work in the last ten years has greatly advanced our understanding of these questions. Recent technical developments and computer technology have made it possible to obtain extensive recordings from single fibers in the auditory system. We can eavesdrop on the activity being transmitted from the receptor elements to the first synaptic station, the cochlear nucleus. Although the single-cell recordings represent only one class of electrical activity in the auditory system, these recordings will be particularly emphasized in this chapter. Many other kinds of electrical activity have been studied, and the data provide considerable insight into how the auditory system works. Fortunately, a recent book by Dallos (1973) summarizes this information in detail and our treatment will therefore be brief.

RECORDING TECHNIQUE

Electrical recordings fall into two classes: those employing gross electrodes and those employing microelectrodes. As their names suggest, the division between the two types of electrodes depends on the size of the electrode tip. There is, however, no sharp demarcation between the two types. Microelectrodes are supposed to be small enough to record electrical activity from single neural units, while the gross electrodes are designed to record activity over a large population of units.

Neural activity in the auditory system is like neural activity anywhere else in the body. An individual neural fiber or axon arises from a cell body, which may also give off dendrites. In the resting state there is a potential difference across the membrane of the cell, the inside is negative with respect to the outside. When stimulated the membrane switches potential rapidly and actually becomes somewhat more positive on the inside with respect to the outside. After a brief period of time, about .5 msec, the former potential is restored. This electrical impulse or "spike" potential is propagated down the axon of the cell. The size of the spike potential depends only upon the momentary conditions of the cell and its surrounding fluid, not on the intensity of the stimulus. The impulse or spike travels at a velocity that is determined by the diameter of the axon. Typical diameters of auditory fibers are about 7μ ($1 \mu = 10^{-6}$ m) or so and the conduction velocity is of the order of 50 m/sec. After a discharge has occurred there is a brief interval, the refractory period, during which no discharge can be initiated; then another spike potential may occur. The upper rate at which spike potentials can be generated depends upon momentary conditions of the cell, but rates as high as 1,000 impulses per second can be observed. For very short intervals, this upper limit may extend up to 4,000 impulses per second.

Microelectrodes have tip diameters of about .5 μ. If a microelectrode is inserted very close to an active neural unit, then one can detect electrical activity emanating from it. Usually the microelectrode is advanced by means of a micrometer, while noting the electrical activity recorded. If a microelectrode actually impales a nerve cell, then the recorded potential reverses in polarity. Once the microelectrode is resting within a cell body or axon the impulse is recorded as a brief positive wave.

Gross electrodes are as large as 100 μ or more and designed to record from a number of neural units. Such electrodes can be placed in the general vicinity of the VIIIth nerve to record the electrical activity present in the thousands of fibers of that bundle. They might also be embedded in the cochlea itself to record the changing potentials of the hair cells in response to sound stimulation. In all cases the gross electrode will record an average potential, weighted over space, of the potential of the individual elements in the vicinity of the electrode. At times the geometry of the structure, for example, the coil of the cochlea itself, makes interpretation of the gross-electrode response somewhat complicated. Thus, one often tries to locate two gross electrodes near each other in the same structure and record the differential voltage between the two electrode tips.

The choice of recording technique obviously influences the kind of information one can gain about the auditory system and the kinds of conclusions that can be drawn from the data. As in every other field of science one must choose whether to approach a subject from the molar or molecular point of view. Sometimes the detail on the molecular level is simply overwhelming and faster progress can be made by first describing the aggregate, average behavior of the process. Sometimes the opposite is true. Our current understanding of auditory electrophysiology is certainly incomplete, and the present account draws on both approaches. We will try to point out the difficulties of either approach. Besides the technical problems that are involved, clear limitations exist on the information that either type of recording can provide. The problem of interpreting results from a gross electrode, measuring as it does the response of an entire population of active elements, is not to be minimized. But it is equally true that until a large number of individual fibers has been studied under comparable stimulus conditions, the behavior of individual elements is about as informative as the anecdotes of case histories. Initially, the gross electrode may provide a useful, if crude, understanding of the process.

As stated earlier, we will devote more space to microelectrode work. This is in part because the research is more recent and thus not as widely quoted in secondary sources. But it is also because this area is presently very active. Some recent results are indeed impressive and the problems posed by these investigations are beginning to have a profound impact on our theories of auditory function. But let us begin historically so that the reader will have some appreciation of the development of information in this area.

COCHLEAR MICROPHONICS

In 1930 Wever and Bray at Princeton University were making gross-electrode recordings from a cat's ear. The electrode was placed near the auditory nerve of the anesthetized cat. The changes in the electrical potentials detected by this electrode were amplified and sent to a telephone receiver located in the adjoining, soundproof room. One can imagine their delight and amazement when they found that Wever, talking into the cat's ear, could be clearly understood by Bray listening on the receiver in the next room. There was initial confusion about the exact interpretation of this result. Wever and Bray thought that the potentials were responses of the nerve itself, but later work showed that the electrode was monitoring two different potentials. One of these potentials Adrian (1931) called the cochlear microphonic (CM). He pointed out that an electrode placed near the round window gave some of the best recordings. This potential faithfully follows the acoustic pressure wave in the same way that certain substances generate electrical potentials proportional to the force imposed on them. The second source of electrical potential recorded by Wever and Bray was the whole nerve action potential. This is an electrical potential generated by the combination of neural impulses within the auditory nerve.

It soon became clear that the first potential, the cochlear microphonic, was not summated neural "spikes." First, the amplitude of the potential varies proportionately with the amplitude of the sound input. If one increases the sound in amplitude a hundredfold, then the size of the cochlear microphonic increases by the same amount, at least up to some high sound pressure levels (80 to 90 dB SPL). At lower sound intensities the cochlear microphonic does not show a threshold as one would expect from a neural response, but gets continuously smaller as one decreases the amplitude of the sound input. One can further differentiate the cochlear microphonic from neural impulses by other criteria. It does not seem to be propagated in the same manner as the neural activity, it does not show fatigue, and it responds quite differently to a lack of oxygen, or to changes in temperature and/or anesthetic.

Nevertheless, the presence of this relatively large potential (.5 mV is possible) occurring in the general vicinity of the cochlea stimulated considerable interest and research. It was truly a landmark in auditory research.

Initially, some skeptics thought it might be some epiphenomenon of an almost artifactual nature. However, further studies showed that the presence of the CM was intimately linked to the presence of healthy and functioning hair cells. Von Békésy (1951) demonstrated that the electrical response of the CM follows the displacement of the basilar membrane. Thus, even if this potential was not neural in origin, it could provide information either about the vibration pattern of the membrane or the state of the primary receptor elements, the hair cells. Subsequent decades have seen it used in both ways. However, there is still not complete agreement as to the exact mechanisms responsible for this potential. Consensus is definitely with Davis' (1965) view that the CM represents a potential generated by changes in the receptor element itself and thus, as Dallos (1973) puts it, "these potentials are assumed to be the first electrical events in the sound stimulus–auditory perception chain [p. 218]."

We will review some of the main changes of this potential as a function of various parameters of the acoustic stimulus and will discuss some of the difficulties inherent in the correct interpretation of these potentials. Finally, we will present Davis' (1965) view on the origin of these potentials. This hypothesis has the most direct experimental support, although other hypotheses have been suggested (see Dallos, 1973).

Input–Output Relation

The first and probably most striking aspect of the CM is that for sinusoidal stimuli the amplitude of the CM changes linearly with the amplitude of the stimulus. Some typical results taken from Wever and Lawrence (1954) are shown in Figure 5.1. A sinusoidal stimulus is changed in amplitude over the range

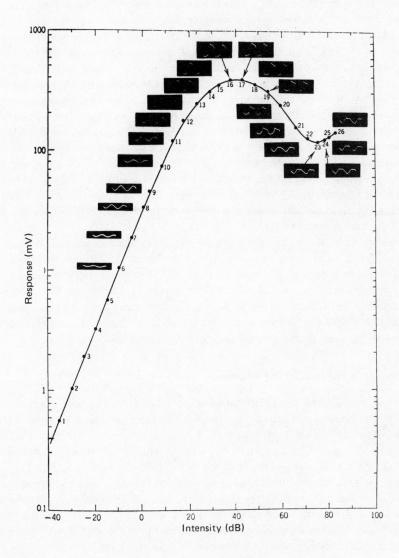

FIG. 5.1 Input–output of cochlear microphonic for sinusoidal stimulus. The inserts show the shape of the recorded signal at several points along the input–output curve. At low to moderate levels the response is linear and the waveform relatively pure. At about a 200-μV response, distortion becomes evident and amplitude no longer increases linearly with sound pressure level. At higher sound intensities the amplitude of the response actually diminishes. The amplification on the recorded insert is constant up to Point 9 and is reduced to one-half for all other points. (From Ernest Glen Wever and Merle Lawrence, *Physiological Acoustics* (copyright 1954 by Princeton University Press): Fig. 62, p. 167. Reprinted by permission of Princeton University Press.)

indicated in the figure. The cochlear microphonic recorded from the vicinity of the cat's ear is shown at various levels by small inserts in the graph. The reference pressure is 1 dyne/cm^2, so 0 dB on the graph represents a sound pressure level of 73 dB SPL. For this and all less intense sound the CM amplitude is almost exactly proportional to the amplitude of the input sinusoid (a 20-dB change in intensity produces a 20-dB change in CM amplitude). One can measure the extent of this linear response down to extremely low levels by averaging the responses to reduce noise present in the recording. Wever has measured response down to .005 μV and the relation is still linear. The linearity of the CM for sinusoidal stimuli has been demonstrated many times by many different investigators and is universally accepted. In fact, failure to obtain this linear relation strongly suggests recording artifacts (see Dallos, 1973, p. 240). At higher sound levels, about 70 to 90 dB SPL depending on frequency and where the recording is made, the waveform may show some distortion and second and third harmonics may be evident.

As intensity is increased the response increases proportionately. This gives the straight-line relation up to about 100 μV in Figure 5.1. Above that level the growth is no longer proportional but the total CM response, fundamental plus all harmonics, continues to increase. Finally a peak is reached and then both the amplitude at the fundamental as well as the total energy of the CM decrease, as the figure shows. This behavior is typical of all such recordings, although the reasons for these phenomena are still not fully understood.

Distribution of Locus and Frequency

Let us now consider the distribution of potential within the cochlea itself and how the frequency of stimulation and the locus of recording are related. This is an extremely critical topic because CM recordings, especially those made from the round window, are averages of all the potentials within the cochlea. Obviously, because of the proximity of the electrode to the basal end of the cochlea, basal potentials contribute disproportionately to the round window response.

The best quantitative measurements of the location and frequency distribution of the CM are those of Honrubia and Ward (1968). They inserted small electrodes into scala media via holes drilled in the region of the stria vascularis. Figure 5.2 shows their results for a number of different sound stimuli.

For each electrode position one can measure the magnitude of the response as a function of frequency for a fixed sound pressure level. As Figure 5.2 shows, a maximum is present at some point along the cochlear duct in such recordings. It is clearest at the lower sound pressure levels and can be interpreted as a region of maximum sensitivity. As the sound pressure level increases the CM maximum appears to shift its locus toward the round window. Figure 5.3 shows this locus of maximum sensitivity and of maximum voltage (the maximum of the maximum) for different frequencies. There is a systematic relation between fre-

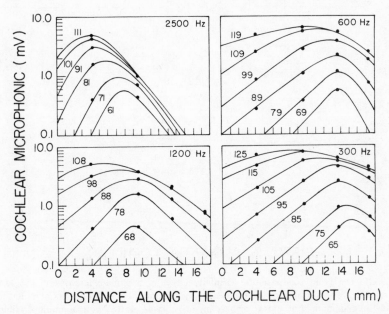

FIG. 5.2 Peak amplitude of cochlear microphonic at several distances along the cochlear duct. Each graph displays results for a different frequency. The parameter on the graph is the intensity of the signal. Note that the point of maximum CM appears to move toward the base as the level of the sound is increased. (From Honrubia & Ward, 1968, p. 953.)

quency and locus as one would expect from the envelope of the traveling wave. There are, however, discrepancies between the degree of mechanical tuning curves and these electrical measures. These discrepancies can probably be traced to the fact that the electrode integrates activity over a range of receptor elements. The differences between the locus of best sensitivity and maximum voltage probably reflect changes in position of the shear forces associated with mechanical vibrations of the membrane.

We can understand some of the complexities in interpreting CM data. Any single electrode averages the potentials generated in a population of elements having somewhat different characteristics. As the intensity of the stimulus is varied the contribution from various regions will change, as Figure 5.3 clearly demonstrates. Therefore, interpretation of CM response is a matter of some delicacy and deserves considerable caution. Whitfield, in several publications, has argued this point most effectively. He has used these arguments to caution against accepting even the apparent linearity of the response shown in Figure 5.1. An understanding of his views will clarify some of the disputes about the origin of the CM.

Whitfield's hypothesis. Consider the potential recorded by a single electrode located in the cochlear duct in response to a sinusoidal stimulus. The potential

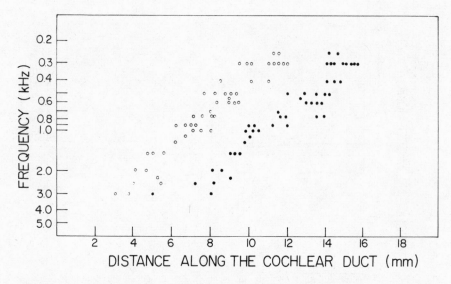

FIG. 5.3 The point of maximum sensitivity (locus of maximum response at low levels) plotted as a function of stimulus frequency (solid points). The point of maximum response (locus of maximum response at highest intensity level) plotted as a function of stimulus frequency (open points). (From Honrubia & Ward, 1968, p. 954.)

measured by the electrode is simply the space-weighted activity of the various elements in the vicinity. Hair cell potentials at a great distance contribute less to the potential than those near the electrode. At each hair cell, the forces and potentials generated are roughly sinusoidal, since that is the stimulus driving this array of elements. The finite velocity of the traveling wave, however, means that the potentials generated at the different distances are somewhat out of phase. This phase difference also affects the summed response. For example, if four loci at the same distance produced 1 mV each, then the total response will be 4 mV if all sources are in phase. If each source is 90° out of phase with the other, then no voltage will be observed since pairs of sources exactly cancel each other. At higher frequencies mechanical measurements indicate that the change of phase with distance is appreciable. Therefore, CM associated with the higher frequencies should be most heavily attenuated. Thus, the CM by its very nature acts as a low-pass filter. The recorded waveshape is then a false (conservative) indicator of the degree of nonlinearity. Higher distortion harmonics may be present in the vibration pattern, but because of the filtering these may not be apparent in the recording.

Pressing this point even further, Whitfield (1967) says "the cochlear microphonic, as normally recorded, is no guide either to the amplitude or waveform of the potentials produced by the individual hair-cell generators [pp. 43–44]."

Davis' theory of CM generation. Davis' theory of CM generation begins with the observation that the cochlea seems to contain two batteries or electrical sources causing a steady current flow across the organ of Corti (Davis, 1965). The first of these batteries is undoubtedly the stria vascularis, and a potential of about 100 mV can be recorded between scala media and either scala vestibuli or scala tympani. The substrates for the underlying metabolic process come through the vascular system of the stria (Davis, Deatherage, Rosenblut, Fernandez, Kimura, & Smith, 1958; Tasaki & Spiropoulos, 1959).

The second source of current is the intracellular potential of the hair cells themselves. When sound is introduced, mechanical force is exerted on the cilia of the hair cells and they are deformed and/or moved. The current flow through the receptor is thereby altered. Ciliary motion changes the resistance of the hair cell, which in turn modulates the constant current flow and generates a potential, the cochlear microphonic.

While the preceding argument is consistent with known facts, it is largely speculative since direct measures of the various critical quantities are not technically feasible. One very strong source of support for this theory comes from experiments by Honrubia and Ward (1969). They demonstrated two facts. First, if the DC potential is artificially altered by introducing experimental currents that augment or reduce the biological potential, then the magnitude of CM alters appropriately. By using anoxia to decrease the biological potential, they actually managed to reverse the DC potential present in scala media. The resistance hypothesis would predict the polarity of the CM reverses in accordance with the sign of the DC potential. These experiments provide convincing supportive evidence for Davis' hypothesis.

The Summating Potential

A further advantage of the resistance hypothesis is that it provides a natural explanation of another potential observed within the cochlea, namely, the summating potential (SP). The potential was observed by von Békésy (1951a) and by Davis, Fernandez, and McAuliffe (1950). The summating potential is a DC shift observable during a brief sinusoidal stimulus. The potential recorded through a wide-band DC amplifier shows both the CM, whose frequency equals that of the imposed sinusoid, and, in addition to the CM, a shift in the DC level. Although the original observations suggested the response was generally unidirectional, later work has shown that both stimulus (frequency and intensity) and recording conditions can influence the polarity of the response.

The easiest explanation of the summating potential is that the change in resistance of the hair cells produces a change in potential that is not exactly linear with the applied mechanical stimulation. This nonlinearity may be quite small, but since the DC potential has no phase, the cumulative effect over a wide area produces a noticeable potential change, especially at high sound levels. This hypothesis, while generally accepted, is still not very quantitative and cannot explain all of the various measurements made on this potential over the past two decades.

Evaluation of the Resistance Hypothesis

There is some skepticism about the resistance hypothesis stemming from the size of the displacement of the basilar membrane. At threshold we know these displacements are very small. Can these small displacements be responsible for noticeable resistance changes? The argument is clearest for threshold conditions, so let us review it here. Linear extrapolation of von Békésy's measurement implies that the basilar membrane moves only about 10^{-11} cm at absolute threshold. The hair cells themselves are roughly 10^{-5} cm in thickness while the diameter of a membrane pore is of the order of 3×10^{-8} cm. How is such a mechanism capable of detecting sound, especially at the lower sound levels?

Davis' reply is reminiscent of the line of argument taken in Chapter 2. After all, a number of hair cells are displaced, even if only by one-millionth of their thickness. If enough are so stimulated, the flow of ions may be altered to a sufficient extent that the sound can be reliably detected. We do not have enough information to calculate whether the ratio of mechanical energy to chemical change is within reasonable bounds. No quantitative calculations have been made that one would regard as compelling for either side.

A second viewpoint on this issue is Whitfield's (1967). He says "we now see that the whole extrapolation is based on false premises. The basilar membrane transducer system, does, indeed, act as a 'volume compressor,' responding relatively much more to small sound pressures than to large ones [Whitfield, 1967, p. 43]." He then suggests the nonlinearity is very sizable and estimates the change in displacement is only about 4 log units rather than the 7 one would expect from changes in pressure. Thus, at threshold he envisions the amplitude of motion at 10^{-8} cm, "still very sensitive, but now at least credible."

Coupled with this view he explains the apparently sinusoidal response of the CM to a sinusoidal input by the filtering arguments that we discussed earlier. Others, including Dallos, choose to emphasize the nonlinear aspects of the generation process.

Our knowledge is still far from certain in this area, but one fact strongly impresses this writer. The growth of the amplitude of the CM is almost exactly linear from subaudible pressures up to 80 or 90 dB SPL (see Figure 5.1). Given this huge range of linearity, which is a fact separate from theories about why the CM waveshape is sinusoidal, how is it possible that the hypothesized nonlinear processes do not seriously disturb that linear growth? Emphasizing such nonlinear processes in the face of 8 log units of apparent linearity rather ignores the obvious for the arcane.

This concludes our brief review of the topic of the cochlear microphonic. One can discern that experts still disagree among the exact origin of the potential. However, these disputes should not diminish the contributions that these recordings can make to solving certain auditory problems. The fact that the potential is intimately connected with healthy hair cells means that it is probably the first link in the conversion of mechanical vibration to electrical activity. It may play a vital role in the activation of activity in the fibers of the VIIIth nerve. Let us now turn to the second source of potentials recorded by Wever and Bray, namely, the whole nerve action potential.

WHOLE NERVE ACTION POTENTIAL

As we stated previously, two potentials were undoubtedly involved in the Wever–Bray experiment of 1930. One was the cochlear microphonic, a widespread potential, originating in the cochlea but recordable from many regions near the cochlea. The other potential originates from the simultaneous or near simultaneous discharge of the many fibers that make up part of the VIIIth cranial nerve. These fibers have their cell bodies in the spiral ganglion and terminate in the cochlear nucleus within the brain stem.

Imagine a single electrode in the vicinity of such a fiber, with an indifferent electrode being placed at some distance away, say at the mouth. Initially, the outside of a resting fiber is at a potential above the inside of the fiber. During a neural discharge, the outside becomes negative with respect to the inside. After about .5 msec it regains its initial condition. Suppose a large population of fibers undergoes this same change at nearly the same time. An electrode near this population will detect a momentary change in potential as a combined activity occurred. Such combined activity is shown in Figure 5.4. Note that the stimulus is the sharp onset of a sinusoid. The largest initial negative peak is called N_1;

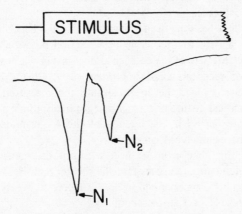

FIG. 5.4 Whole nerve action potential initiated by a tone onset (top trace). Recording is average response from scala vestibuli and scala tympani. The amplitude of N_1 will depend on many factors such as the condition and location of the electrode but $-200 \mu V$ is typical for moderate signal levels. The time between the peak of N_1 and N_2 depends on stimulus level but is between 1 and 2 msec (see Figure 5.5). (From Dallos, 1973, p. 28.)

later peaks, if they occur, are called N_2 and N_3. Typically, N_2 occurs about 1 msec after N_1.

Actually, the recording of whole nerve activity is more complicated than the preceding description would indicate. The single electrode described above would also record a large cochlear microphonic. There are various ways to remove this potential. Probably the most effective is to employ two electrodes, combining their outputs in various ways to estimate one or the other potential. Also, since the CM faithfully mirrors the acoustic waveform, one can alternate the phase of successive stimulus presentations and average the obtained output to effectively cancel the CM.

Independent of how the whole nerve activity is recorded, a stimulus with a sharp onset is needed to initiate a large response. This is because the electrode integrates activity over a population of fibers. The potential changes in every fiber must be nearly simultaneous to obtain a large response. Two factors militate against this occurring. First, the intensity of the stimulus may be insufficient to stimulate the entire population. Second, the fibers may not fire at the same time. Recall our previous discussion of cochlear motion. The very fact that the mechanical disturbance in the cochlea is called a traveling wave means that different parts of the membrane move at different times. The velocity with which the wave travels is also nonuniform. Its velocity is greater near the starting point, the stapes end, and slows as it travels toward the helicotrema. Because of this nonuniform velocity the distance between successive zeros in the displacement pattern grows shorter as one moves toward the helicotrema (see Figure 3.4, Chapter 3). The basilar membrane has larger areas in phase nearer the base than near the apex. This is true for impulse stimuli and for both high- and low-frequency sinusoidal waves.

For these reasons it has long been recognized that the basal end of the cochlea contributes most heavily to the whole nerve action potential. The mechanical wave travels across this part of the cochlea almost instantaneously and stimulates a large number of receptors nearly simultaneously. Obviously, the larger the amplitude of the stimulus, the more sizable the measured potential. Also, because the mechanical disturbance reaches a given amplitude sooner for a larger wave, some change occurs in the latency of the N_1 response with intensity. Some typical data are shown in Figure 5.5.

One model of the change in latency with intensity assumes some fixed threshold in the elements and argues that the shorter latencies result because the more intense stimulus crosses the threshold sooner. It is easy to calculate the expected size of this effect. Let the stimulus be

$$x(t) = A \sin \omega t.$$

We assume the threshold k is small and hence for $A > k$ we may approximate the sine by the usual power series expansion:

$$\sin \omega t = \omega t - \frac{(\omega t)^3}{3!} + \frac{(\omega t)_5}{5!} \ .$$

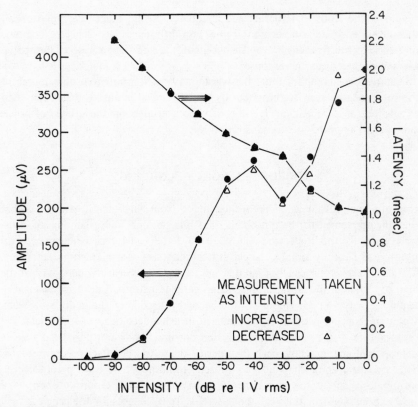

FIG. 5.5 Change of average latency and amplitude as a function of the intensity of a noise burst. Amplitude is measured between first negative and positive peak. The similarity of the measurements taken during stimulus increase and decrease indicate the stability of the measurements. (From Kiang *et al.*, 1962, p. 119.)

For small k the threshold is crossed when the amplitude of the displacement is equal to the threshold. Ignoring all the second-order terms we have

$$k = A\omega t.$$

Thus

$$\frac{k}{\omega A} = t.$$

Hence we expect the latency to vary inversely with signal amplitude A. An increase in amplitude by a factor of ten (20 dB) should produce a tenfold change in latency. Figure 5.5 certainly does not show such a change. A more complicated explanation is necessary. Note also the nonmonotonic relation between amplitude of response and the intensity of the stimulus. This is believed to reflect either a shift in the population of fibers generating the potential or a change in the mode of initiating neural activity. Again, exact interpretations of this dependence are complicated (1) because differences between phase or time of arrival of the traveling wave affect synchrony, and (2) because of the spatial averaging inherent in the response.

Despite these complications, the whole nerve action potential does represent the first neural activity initiated by the sound stimulus. It has been used extensively as a dependent variable in various studies on the effects of noise, anoxia, and a number of stimulus variables.

MICROELECTRODE RECORDINGS

One principal advantage of recordings made from single auditory cells is that they avoid some of the problems that plague our understanding of gross potentials. The microelectrode should record the activity of a single cell. This response is basically simple: the cell is either inactive or a spike potential occurs. The cell conveys a basically digital signal. If the cell is near the periphery of the auditory system, the signal represents an early transformation of mechanical to neural activity. Neural spikes are the language or code of the auditory system. We appreciate our acoustic environment through a decoding of such signals. The disadvantage of the microelectrode is that one must know not only what a single neuron is doing, but how each member of the entire population is responding. This objective is far beyond our present technology; we have practically no information about the simultaneous behavior of small groups of peripheral fibers. Some information can be inferred from changes in the single fiber's response when second stimuli are introduced. This line of attack is being pursued, but, by and large, we record from single cells, one at a time, and note characteristics that are common across the population of fibers. Sometimes rather bizarre and atypical responses are obtained. These may be a fluke of the particular preparation, for example, an injured or damaged cell. Only when a number of fibers show a particular pattern of behavior can we safely conclude that this response is typical.

The earliest work on this topic was the classic experiment of Galambos and Davis (1943). They made recordings from single fibers, probably second-order neurons of the auditory system. Many of the general features reported in their early paper have now been confirmed and the observations extended in some very systematic and thorough studies of the response of peripheral fibers. Two groups have been particularly active in recent times. One group is located at the Eaton Peabody Laboratory of Auditory Physiology in Boston, Massachusetts; the principal investigator is Nelson Y-S. Kiang. We will report their work carried out on the domestic cat, the primary experimental animal of this group. The other group, which we call the Wisconsin group, is located at the Laboratory of Neurophysiology at the University of Wisconsin and has included J. Rose, J.

Hind, J. Brugge, and D. Anderson. They use the squirrel monkey as the main experimental animal. We will review the work done by both groups in considerable detail, both because of the quality of the research and because these results indicate very clearly which aspects of the acoustic wave are coded in the neural signals. We begin by describing the results obtained by the Wisconsin group because they use primarily sinusoidal stimuli. Next, we will take up the work of the Boston group, who primarily use clicks as stimuli. Whatever the stimulus, whether a click or a sinusoidal burst, the neural response is an all-or-none potential change or "spike" discharge. Thus, the principal data are the times at which neural spikes occur. One carefully records these times over a large number of stimulus presentations. By comparing the times either with some epoch of stimulus, such as the onset, or by calculating intervals between successive neural firings, a picture emerges of how the fiber operates. Before discussing details of this analysis, however, let us consider how the data are acquired.

Although the animals used by the two groups of investigators are different, the general procedure is similar. The animal is first anesthetized and body temperature maintained at a normal level. An operation is then performed to expose the brain in the region of the cerebellum. The cerebellum itself is either removed or retracted so as to expose the VIIIth cranial nerve emerging from the hole in the skull called the internal auditory meatus. Once the auditory nerve is isolated, a microdrive is attached to the skull of the animal so that the microelectrode can be precisely manipulated and inserted into the VIIIth nerve. The placement of the electrodes is observed through an optical microscope also mounted on the preparation. The electrodes are either micropipettes filled with a salt solution or very fine wire electrodes embedded in glass. The tip diameters are less than one micron (10^{-6} m).

Various criteria are used to infer that the electrode is actually recording from an auditory fiber. The recorded response, the spike generated by the neural element, ranges between several hundred microvolts and 10 mV. The responses as measured are positive spikes of brief duration. They follow the all-or-none law. As these spikes occur, they are recorded either on magnetic tape or their time of occurrence is entered directly in a computer. Thus, the primary data of these experiments are a series of marks on a time line. Each mark indicates when a particular fiber fired. Transformations of these time marks are made into interval or period histograms, which we will discuss shortly.

The acoustic stimulus is presented to the animal through a probe tube inserted in the external ear canal. The signal is calibrated so that the precise physical characteristics of the stimulus are known.

Recordings Made with Sinusoidal Stimulation

Response area. As the earlier work of Galambos and Davis (1943) demonstrated, if the stimulus is a sinusoid, then each fiber responds to a limited range of frequency and amplitude. This limited range defines the *response area* of the fiber. There are two ways to present response areas and both have been used in the literature. One way is to plot the number of spikes per second generated as a function of frequency at each fixed sound pressure level. Figure 5.6 displays such plots for several different fibers. The *characteristic frequency* or *best frequency* is defined as that frequency to which the fiber responds with a maximum rate. As one can see from the figures, at low intensity levels, the rate functions are fairly peaked. It is easy to determine the best frequency. As intensity increases the rate at which the fiber responds reaches an asymptotic value. At a high intensity, a very broad response curve is obtained as a function of frequency and the maximum sometimes shifts to somewhat lower frequencies. All of the fibers show some level of spontaneous activity; rates of 10 to 50 spikes/sec are typical. Sustained rates greater than 300 spikes/sec are rare. A typical ratio for maximum-to-spontaneous rate is between 20 to 1 and 10 to 1.

The second way of depicting the response area of an auditory fiber uses a criterion of constant response, for example, a particular noticeable increase above spontaneous rate when the stimulus is applied. One can then determine the sound pressure level of different frequencies that will elicit this increase in activity. Figure 5.7 shows this type of response area. As far as we know, all fibers display such areas. They are routinely obtained in microelectrode work, mainly to identify the best frequency of the fiber under study.

Suppose we have isolated a fiber and have determined its best frequency. We stimulate that fiber with a sinusoidal stimulus of 1-sec duration at a constant sound pressure level, say 80 dB SPL. The frequency of the signal is systematically varied, and we record how the fiber responds at each different frequency of the signal. What is the temporal structure of the bursts elicited by the various stimuli?

Interval histograms. One of the most convenient ways to determine the temporal structure is to construct a histogram of the distribution of times between successive neural spikes. We then can determine how the distribution changes with the frequency of the stimulus. The bottom of Figure 5.8 displays such an interval histogram. The top two lines show how it is constructed. Along the top line is the stimulus, a sinusoid. The second line shows the output of the electrode with neural spikes indicated as small vertical lines. The measurements specify the times between successive neural spikes. Thus, t_1 denotes the time between the first and second spike, t_2 the time between the second and third spike, and so on. After a number of such times have been recorded, 1,000 in this example, one constructs the histogram shown in the bottom part of the figure.

FIG. 5.6 Firing rate versus frequency for constant sound pressure level. Four different fibers are shown having characteristic frequencies of 1700 Hz (a), 2100 Hz (b), 4100 Hz (c), and 17,000 Hz (d). The spontaneous rate of the fiber is indicated at the far right of each panel. (From Rose *et al.*, 1971, p. 687.)

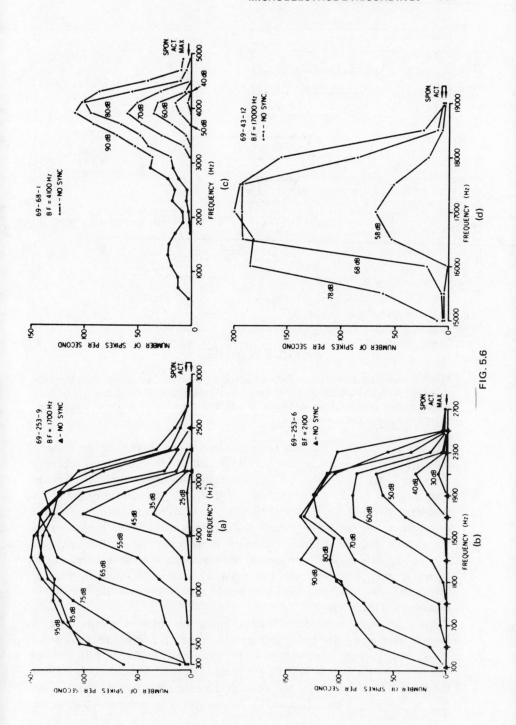

FIG. 5.6

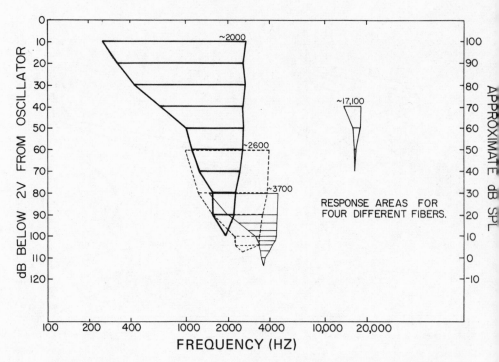

FIG. 5.7 Response area for four auditory fibers. A particular fiber is responsive to combination of intensity and frequency within the designated area. Each area is labeled by a frequency that represents the frequency to which the fiber is maximally sensitive. (From Galambos & Davis, 1943, p. 45.)

The abscissa indicates the time between successive spikes (t_i) and the ordinate indicates the frequency (number of times) with which that interval occurred. Thus, about 120 times out of 1,000, the interarrival time between two spikes was approximately t_2. As in the construction of all histograms, quantitizing of the time axis is critical for the appearance of the resulting histogram. If the time quantization was very gross, then t_1 and t_2 would occur within the same time bin and the shape of the histogram would be markedly altered. Note also that there is no definite limit imposed on the maximum time between successive pulses. A given histogram will only represent interarrival times up to some maximum value, and one usually notes in some other way the times that exceeded this maximum.

Figure 5.9 shows some actual interval histograms obtained in early work by the Wisconsin group. The histograms came from one fiber when stimulated by an 80 dB SPL sinusoid at several different frequencies. In Figure 5.9A the frequency of the stimulus is 412 Hz. The greatest number, approximately 120, of the interarrival times is near the value of 2.5 msec. [Note that x axis is given only on the bottom parts (E and J).] The number N in each part of the figure

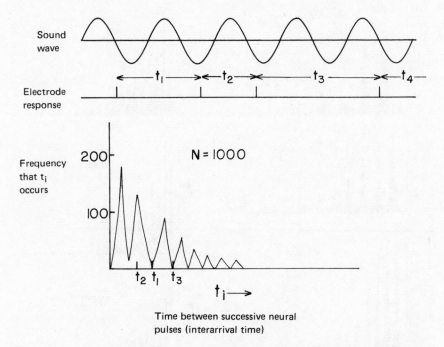

FIG. 5.8 An interval histogram. The top two lines show how the intervals between successive neural responses (t_i) are recorded without regard to epochs of the sinusoidal stimulation. The histogram at the bottom of the figure shows the frequency at which these intervals occur. (See Figure 5.9.)

refers to the total number of observations, broken down into the sum of two numbers. The first of these shows the observations that occurred within the time plotted in the histogram. The second number is the number of interarrival times exceeding the maximum value indicated on the abscissa. Thus, for example, at 412 Hz, 1,872 bursts occurred with interarrival times of 20 msec or less, and only three interarrival times exceeded this interval. The period is simply the reciprocal of the signal frequency. The small dots placed along the x axis of each part of the figure mark successive periods—note how the peaks of the histogram occur above these dots.

The form of the histograms shown in Figure 5.9 is extremely interesting. First of all, as Galambos and Davis initially found, the fiber tends to fire on only one phase of the stimulus waveform. The extent of this phase-locking revealed in the histograms is indeed impressive. The modes of the histograms occur at integer multiples of the period of the sinusoidal stimulus. For example, at 1,000 Hz, which is the best frequency for this fiber, the period is 1 msec. The first mode of the histogram appears at 1 msec, the next mode at 2, 3, 4, and 5, and so on out, until about the 14th value where the number of observations is very small.

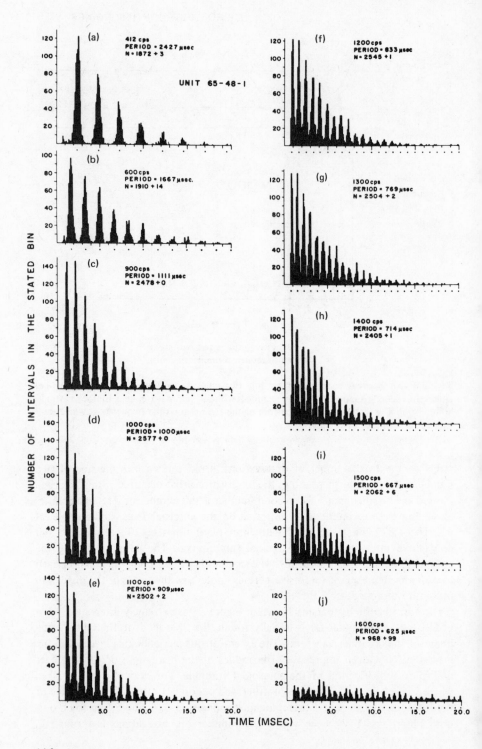

Notice also that the total number of nerve spikes, nearly 2,600, all occurred within a 20-msec interarrival time. As should be expected from the response area, the fiber can be stimulated by a variety of frequencies. An intriguing fact about these histograms is that their general form follows from a very simple probabilistic model.

Suppose we had a process that was independent from trial-to-trial with a fixed probability of success, p. Concretely, one might think of this as some sort of a biased coin, where the probability of a head was not .5, as in a fair coin, but some other value, p. Suppose we exercise this process and determine the probability that a certain number of trials will elapse between successive heads. Given that we have a success, the probability of a success in the next trial is simply p. The probability that we will have a failure and then a success is $(1 - p)p$. The probabilities are multiplied together because, by assumption, the trials are all independent. Similarly, the probability of having five failures and then a success is $(1 - p)^5 p$. The resulting distribution of intervals between successes is called a geometric distribution. The density of such a distribution for various values of p would look very much like the histograms shown in Figure 5.9. The neural data suggest very strongly that the underlying process is a simple renewal one, that is, the probability of a fiber firing is independent from trial to trial and has a constant probability of occurring that depends simply upon the intensity and frequency of the stimulating waveform. Notice that this description is valid even for the fibers responding to very high frequency sinusoids.

The preceding description is somewhat at variance with the classic concept of a threshold, which supposes a very slow recovery process such that a sufficiently vigorous stimulus would make the fiber fire earlier in the recovery phase rather than later. It appears that any relative refractory period for the neuron must be brief, and that once a neuron fires, it quickly regains a state of constant readiness to fire, which may be characterized by a fixed probability, p. Each cycle of the waveform then provides an opportunity, or trial, for this neuron. The distribution of the interarrival times resembles a geometric distribution.

The geometric form of the interarrival histogram is completely consistent with the fixed probability renewal process described above. It is not, however, the only way that this distribution could arise. The same type of histogram could result, for example, if the fiber fired initially very quickly and then slowed down appreciably. During the rapid phase, a number of interarrival times would pile up near the origin. During the slower phase, the fiber would skip several periods and

FIG. 5.9 Interval histograms taken at several different frequencies for the same auditory fiber. The time scale is the same for all panels. The frequency and period is indicated for each panel. The value N is the sum of two numbers. The first number is the total number of intervals used in plotting the histogram. The second number is the total number of intervals that exceed the longest interval plotted, in this case 20 msec. Note the peaks of the histogram occur at integer multiples of the period of the stimulating waveform. (From Rose et al., 1967, p. 772.)

many periods between successive spikes would fill out the tail of the distribution. To determine the accuracy of a simple renewal process in describing the data, we must compute the conditional probability that the unit will fire, given that it has not fired up to this point in time. According to our simple model, this probability should be independent of how long we have waited and simply be a fixed number, p. Studies of this conditional probability have provided fairly conclusive results (Rose, Brugge, Anderson, & Hind, 1967). The detailed analyses show that the probability of firing is remarkably constant and nearly independent of the number of cycles that have elapsed since the last firing. There is a slight tendency for the probability to be depressed immediately following a firing. These departures are relatively small, however. A good first approximation is to say that the probability of a fiber firing on any period of the stimulus is some fixed value, p, and that successive periods of the stimuli can be treated as independent events, at least for low-frequency ($f < 2,000$ Hz) stimuli.

Finally, we should note that there is some jitter in exactly when the neuron will fire. This variability in the firing time appears to be reciprocally related to the frequency of the stimulus. Thus, at very high frequencies, the distribution of interarrival times becomes relatively peaked and thin; at low frequencies the distributions appear to be somewhat more variable. This is somewhat counterintuitive because at low frequencies the fibers are firing less often, yet the variability is more than at high frequencies.

Another way to change the probability, p, of the interval histogram is to maintain the same frequency for the signal but to decrease its intensity. Figure 5.10 displays the results that occur when intensity varies. The fiber is stimulated by its best frequency over a range of 70 dB. At the high intensities the geometric form of the distribution of interarrival times is clear. As the intensity decreases, the grouping of the interarrival times at the period of the signal becomes more and more difficult to discern. However, we will present evidence later to show that even at these low levels the firing of a fiber tends to remain phase-locked to the stimulus. The fiber fires during a particular phase of the sinusoidal waveform.

The lower limit in intensity or the upper limit in frequency for which the fiber still remains synchronous with the waveform, is an important theoretical and practical question. It is difficult to answer because the data are recorded with finite precision in time. The size of the intervals used in constructing the histograms will always tend to obscure any high-frequency following that existed. The interval histogram only provides indirect evidence about this question since it is constructed from interarrival times between neural impulses. Another means of analysis is needed to probe the relation between time of occurrence of the impulse and some epoch of the waveform. The period histogram provides this means.

Period histogram. Figure 5.11 presents the details of how a period histogram is constructed. The top line shows the stimulus, a sinusoid, and the second time

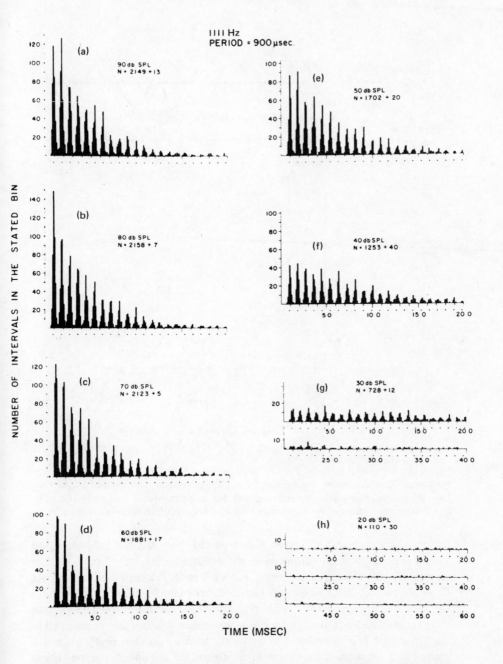

FIG. 5.10 Interval histograms taken from the same auditory fiber at several intensity levels. The signal frequency is 1111 Hz. The intensity level is indicated. At the lower signal levels the time scale has been expanded. For other details see Figure 5.9. (From Rose *et al.*, 1967, p. 784.)

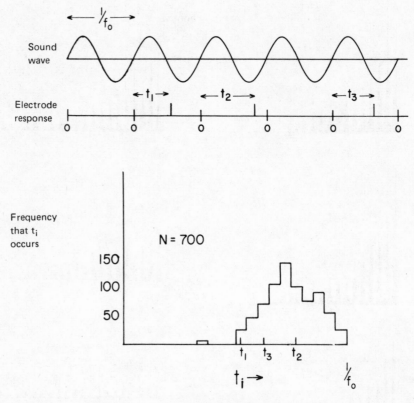

FIG. 5.11 A period histogram. The top two lines show how time is defined as zero at the positive-going zero crossing of the waveform. The intervals, t_i, are defined as the time between this positive-going zero crossing and the occurrence of a neural response. The histogram at the bottom of the figure shows the frequency at which these intervals occur.

line indicates when neural spikes were recorded from the fiber. As the figure shows, positive-going zero-crossings of the sinusoid define "zero" time. At each successive positive-going zero-crossing, a clock is reset. If a response occurs in the fiber, the time of its occurrence is recorded, for example, t_1, t_2, and so on. In the example indicated, 500 such responses have been obtained, and each response recorded as a time, t_i. A histogram is then constructed, as indicated in the lower part of the figure. The frequency with which each time occurred is plotted as a function of that time. In the figure, for example, there were about 100 responses that occurred t_2 msec after a positive-point zero-crossing of the waveform. Because time is reset after each positive-going zero-crossing no time can exceed the period of the waveform ($1/f_0$).

In the figure the spike is portrayed as occurring only on the negative portion of the sinusoidal signal. In fact, as a variety of evidence attests, the spike tends to be initiated on only one half-cycle of the basilar membrane movement. Exactly which part of the half-cycle causes activity is obscure because there is some delay between the waveform at the ear channel and the movement of the basilar membrane. Thus, the period histogram may tend to group in the middle or at either end of the stimulus period or be wrapped around the two ends. The particular phase delay will depend on the frequency of the stimulus and the best frequency of the fiber. The former determines the locus of the motion, and the latter the place along the membrane responsive to that motion. The exact relations will be discussed in more detail later in the chapter.

The period histogram provides valuable information about phase-locking. It also allows us to examine the highest frequency at which the fiber remains phase-locked to the stimulus, an important question in the dispute between place and temporal theories of hearing. Figure 5.12 provides some typical data on this question by showing some period histograms. The best frequency for this fiber was 4,000 Hz. The spontaneous rate of activity was approximately 64

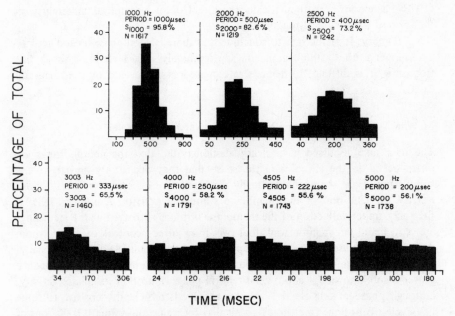

FIG. 5.12 Period histogram taken for several different frequencies from the same auditory fiber. Each panel indicates the signal frequency. N is the total number of neural responses recorded. S_f is a measure of syncrony (number of responses in the most responsive half period of the wave divided by N). At higher frequencies the degree of syncrony decreases. (From Rose *et al.*, 1967, p. 778.)

spikes/sec. This example shows that the decrease in phase-locking is gradual as the frequency of the stimulus is increased. For the fiber represented in Figure 5.9, the limit on phase-locked activity appears to be about 2,500 to 3,000 Hz.

We should point out a number of features that may limit detection of phase-locking at much higher frequencies. The first and obvious problem is possible injury to a fiber if it is pierced with a microelectrode, as in intracellular recording. Even extracellular recordings may not find the fiber in a completely normal state. One manifestation of this abnormal condition would be a drop in the high-frequency response of the fiber. Second, there is the general problem of precisely when the spike occurs. The spike itself occupies some time; its rise time is not infinitely fast but is about 100 μsec. Were everything in the preparation absolutely stable and no noise present at the recording site, then the fact that the rise time is finite would be of no consequence. Practically, of course, there is some variability in the base line and the signals are fairly small. Variations in the base line level coupled with the finite rise time will cause the detection circuit to misclassify the time of occurrence of spikes. At worst, the misclassification would err by the duration of the rise time, or 100 μsec. In this case any frequency having a period this small or smaller could not generate a phase-locked recording. The 100-μsec period corresponds to a frequency of 10 kHZ. Anderson (1973) has explored mathematically the effect of such temporal uncertainty on the form of the period histogram.

In summary, it seems safe to conclude that there is good phase-locked activity or following up to the regions of approximately 4,000 Hz/sec. Above this frequency it is difficult to demonstrate phase-locking, even though it may still exist.

To What Aspect of Membrane Motion is the Nerve Responsive?

The data just discussed have clearly demonstrated that the neural firings are phase-locked to the stimulus in the sense that they occur only on part of the stimulation cycle. As we have already discussed there is some ambiguity about exactly what motion of the membrane stimulates activity. A popular belief is that only upper deflection of the membrane initiates activity. But the recordings are not made in such a way that we have direct control of the motion. Acoustically we are AC, not DC, coupled to the membrane. Said less technically, we can wiggle the membrane, not push and pull it. Therefore, phase ambiguity prevents sure knowledge about what relative phase of motion stimulates activity, although phase-locking clearly indicates activity is principally sensitive to some half-cycle of motion. One should recall that for a sinusoid velocity is 90° out of phase with displacement and velocity is, in turn, 90° out of phase with acceleration. It is absolutely clear that *some* half-cycle of the motion is critical for initiating neural activity. We now take up the question of how best to describe the mechanism responsible for the phase-locking.

Two hypotheses immediately come to mind. The first, and simplest, is that the nerve acts as a simple threshold device. The nerve fires whenever the basilar membrane is deflected beyond a certain critical point. We call this mechanism an *amplitude threshold device* since the probability of firing is determined by the amplitude of membrane motion. A second alternative, somewhat more complicated to envisage in simple mechanistic terms, is a process that has an excitation value that varies with the phase of the stimulus. For example, given sinusoidal vibration the probability of excitation is near zero on the negative portion of the wave. It increases monotonically with the positive phase of the stimulus, reaches a peak at some point, and returns to zero as the negative phase begins. Such a mechanism might be thought of as amplitude sensitive, but with the variation in amplitude as a function of time normalized by the peak response of the vibration. Were such the case, then a small sinusoid and a larger one would produce nearly the same effective stimulus. The simplest designation of such a device is to call it phase-sensitive, since it is relatively unaffected by the amplitude of the stimulus and its response pattern largely follows the phase of the sinusoidal stimulation.

There is good experimental evidence that phase sensitivity best describes the fiber's behavior. Figure 5.13 shows a series of histograms computed for a 1,000-Hz burst over the period of that waveform. The best frequency of the fiber was 1,000 Hz and the intensity of the stimulus was systematically varied between about 10 and 90 dB SPL. Were the fiber purely amplitude-sensitive, then the distribution of spike activity within the period of the wave should clearly move toward the left as intensity is increased. This is because the fiber is initially quiet as it emerges from this phase of basilar membrane motion and, as it approaches the critical point, it is likely to fire. We can think of a threshold as fixed at some arbitrary amplitude, corresponding to a stimulus of 10 or 15 dB SPL. At low stimulus values this amplitude is seldom reached. Therefore, the resulting histogram is nearly flat because the firings are spontaneous and, consequently, largely independent of the phase stimulus. There also should be some variability in this threshold, and our classification of the time at which the nerve fires becomes a further source of variability. Nevertheless, as the stimulus is increased in amplitude, say by 20 or 30 dB, the fiber should fire almost immediately as the basilar membrane moves to this critical point. All of the spikes would then originate at a definite period during the stimulation cycle. Due to the enormous change in amplitude compared with the threshold value, the distribution of spike activity should move to the left and become extremely peaked. Figure 5.13 shows that this is not the case. At the higher levels, 30 dB SPL and above, there are intervals when practically no spikes ever occur. This indicates that the fiber has become largely phase-locked to the stimulus and the spontaneous activity has been nearly suppressed. Despite the clear control that the stimulus exercises on the firing times, the distribution of activity within the sinusoidal cycle is fairly broad and essentially independent of amplitude from 30

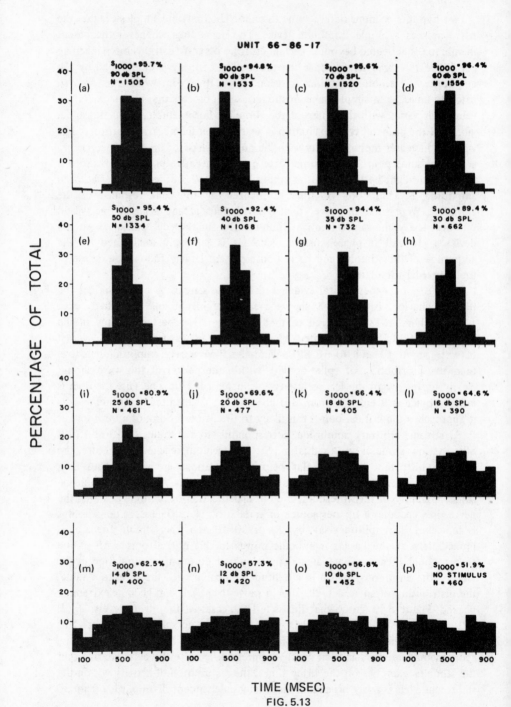

UNIT 66-86-17

FIG. 5.13

to 90 dB. More importantly, the mode of the distribution does not shift systematically with intensity from 14 to 90 dB SPL.

Another point to be noted in Figure 5.13 is how the total frequency of firing varies with the intensity of the stimulus. The total number of spikes recorded from the fiber (*N*) is listed in each panel. With no stimulus this number is 460 for the 10-sec sample, corresponding to a spontaneous rate of 46 spikes/sec. As the intensity of the signal is increased, the period histogram clearly shows an increase in the frequency of spikes in the middle of the panel—panels K and L in particular. Thus, at 18 and 16 dB SPL, the fiber is being influenced by the stimulus as shown in the modulation of the firing rate as a function of the period of the signal. Yet the total number of firings has actually decreased (*N* = 405 and 390) compared with the spontaneous rate. Turning *on* the stimulus has actually suppressed the total rate. This fact greatly complicates our interpretation of how stimulus intensity and rate of firing are related. For many fibers, especially those having a high spontaneous rate, the pattern of firing is more indicative of the signal's influence than the mere rate at which the fiber is firing.

Similar results also occur with complex stimuli. They generate displacement waves that are complex and multimodal. Such an experiment is shown in Figure 5.14. The stimulating waveform was the sum of a 1,000-Hz and 1,500-Hz sinusoid, each of the same sound pressure level. The period histograms obtained with this stimulus are shown for several different levels. The solid curves fitted to the histogram data are simply the amplitude of the sum of a 1,000-Hz and 1,500-Hz sinusoid waveform. The amplitude and phases of each of these sinusoids have been adjusted to fit the histogram data. Of particular interest is the ratio of amplitudes of these two "fitted" sinusoids. For the lower intensity conditions, 30 to 70 dB, the amplitude ratios of the fitted sinusoids are reasonably close to each other, approximately 1–1.5 on the average (see Figure 5.14D, E, F, G, and H). In order to fit the histogram for the higher intensities, this ratio is decreased and the low-frequency sine wave is assumed to have an amplitude approximately five times greater than the higher frequency amplitude. Thus, for this fiber at high intensities, the low-frequency wave largely controls the response of the fiber. As the insert at the lower right shows, at the highest intensities the lower frequency presented alone also produces a somewhat higher rate.

Despite rather enormous changes in the intensity (in the case of the last figure, a change of 10^7 in power), the distribution of spike activity resembles very closely the amplitude distribution imposed by the stimulus. Such distributions are completely inconsistent with the idea of a fixed amplitude threshold. One would expect on that basis that the resulting histograms would tend to gravitate

---

FIG. 5.13 Period histogram taken at same signal frequency at several different levels. The insert in the panel indicates the signal intensity. For other details, see Figure 5.12. Syncrony is noticeable even at intensities within 20 dB of threshold. (From Rose *et al.*, 1967, p. 788.)

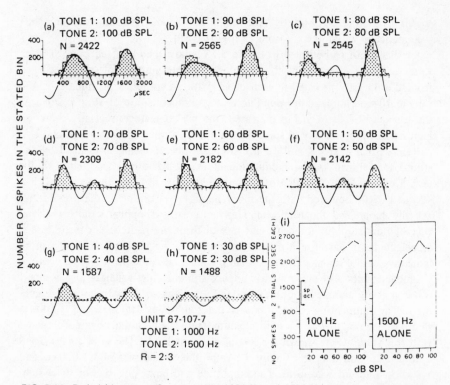

FIG. 5.14 Period histograms for two tones, 1000 Hz and 1500 Hz, at various combinations of relative and absolute intensity. The intensities of the two signals are indicated in the panels as well as the total number of responses, N. The solid line is a linear combination of the two sinusoids scaled in amplitudes and adjusted in phases to best fit the obtained histograms. The two panels at lower right indicate the rate functions versus intensity for each tone separately. (From Brugge *et al.*, 1969, p. 398.)

to a single point or to a few points of the complex vibration where this threshold value is first exceeded. The refractory state of the fiber and how it recovered would determine at which of these points the impulse would occur. A better description of the data is to say that the fiber is phase-locked. It follows the normalized amplitude of the stimulating waveform. The instantaneous firing rate of the fiber nearly mirrors the normalized variation in amplitude. The important point is that the distribution of firing times is nearly independent of stimulus amplitude in the case of a single sinusoidal stimulus, and largely so for complex stimuli, especially at moderate levels of stimulation.

All of the data on the response of single fibers to complex stimuli reveal that the distribution of firings within one period closely mirrors some phase in the displacement of the basilar membrane. The fiber seldom fires during one half-cycle of the motion. During the stimulating half-cycle the frequency of firing is nearly proportional to the instantaneous amplitude of the pressure. A given polarity of the pressure wave may be in phase with either an upward or downward motion of the membrane because of the phase delay associated with the traveling wave. We are, therefore, uncertain how this critical phase relates to actual membrane displacement.

We now leave the topic of the response of a fiber to sinusoidal stimulation and consider the results when the stimulus is an impulsive acoustic wave, that is, a click.

Response to Impulsive Waveforms

A stimulus often used by the Eaton Peabody Laboratory of Auditory Physiology in Boston is a brief acoustic click. Specifically, a rectangular pulse of electrical activity approximately 100 μsec in duration is applied to the acoustic driver coupled to the animal's ear. The click causes nerve impulses to occur which are analyzed using a poststimulus histogram. This type of histogram resembles the period histogram in being locked to the stimulus. Figure 5.15 illustrates how a poststimulus histogram is constructed. The occurrence of the click can be thought of as starting a clock. Some time after the click has been presented a neural firing occurs and one records this time of occurrence. If a second spike occurs, this time is also recorded. One can then construct a poststimulus histogram which displays the number of spikes having a particular latency following the application of the click. Kiang's group has recorded a large number of such histograms for a wide variety of stimulus conditions. The interested reader may find an excellent review of these results in a monograph by Kiang (1965). Figure 5.16 shows a typical set of poststimulus histograms from different fibers in a single animal. The different fibers have different characteristic frequencies, indicated to the left of each panel. At low characteristic frequencies, the data appear definitely multimodal, as did the sine wave data. A geometric characterization of the successive firing peaks appears to be fairly adequate. For fibers with higher characteristic frequencies, the modes become more difficult to discern, and finally, for a characteristic frequency of about 5,000 Hz, only a single mode is evident. In scanning this series of histograms, two quantities in particular should be noted. These quantities are defined in Figure 5.15. One is L, the latency from the onset of the click until the first neural activity occurs. The second quantity is Δp, the time between successive peaks in the poststimulus histogram. Let us return to Figure 5.16 with these two quantities in mind. The latency measure, L, is longest for the low-frequency fiber and shortest for the high-frequency fiber. The interpeak interval, Δp, appears to be closely related to the period of the characteristic frequency of that fiber. This impression is confirmed by calculating these quantities over a variety of such recordings, as Kiang has done.

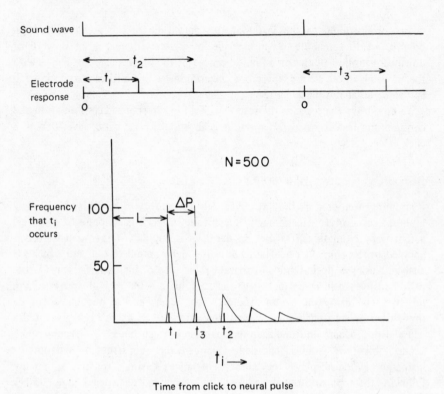

Time from click to neural pulse

FIG. 5.15 Poststimulus histogram. The top lines show how time is defined as zero at the time of the acoustic click. The interval between the onset of the last click and the neural event define the intervals (t_i). The histogram at the bottom of the figure shows the frequency at which these intervals occur. Two times are defined on the histogram, L, the time to the first peak, and Δp, the interval between successive peaks. (From Kiang et al., 1965, p. 25.)

Figure 5.17 is a plot of the characteristic frequency of the fiber in kilohertz versus the latency of the first peak in milliseconds. There is a strong inverse relation between these two quantities. This relation undoubtedly reflects the delay caused by the finite velocity of the traveling wave as it proceeds from stapes to helicotrema in response to the impulsive stimulus. This occurs because the characteristic frequency of a fiber is an indirect measure of its position in the cochlea. High-frequency fibers are located near the stapes, low-frequency fibers are located near the helicotrema. For the high-frequency fibers, the traveling wave affects the fiber very soon after the application of the stimulus. The latencies of firing are 1.5 msec or less. This latency is considerably longer than the period of the characteristic frequency of the fiber. Therefore, this first impulse partly represents the time of arrival of activity at that position in the

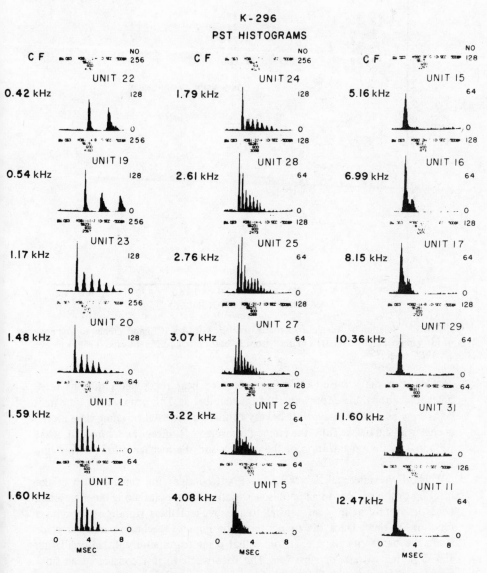

FIG. 5.16 Period histogram taken from several different units from a single cat. The frequency to the left of the panel is the characteristic frequency of that unit. Note that both the latency to first peak, *L*, and spacing between peaks (Δp) changes with best frequency. (From Kiang *et al.*, 1965, p. 28.)

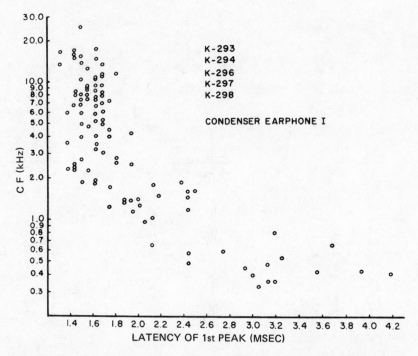

FIG. 5.17   Relation between characteristic frequency of fiber (CF) and latency to first peak of histogram, L. The data are obtained from several units in different cats. (From Kiang *et al.*, 1965, p. 26.)

cochlea. For the low-frequency fibers, located near the helicotrema, the wave must travel down the entire extent of the membrane. This propagation time may be as long as 2 or 3 msec. Von Békésy estimated the total traveling time up the cochlear as 2.6 msec. Thus, the latency measure, L, is nicely in accord with what we know of the organization of the cochlea and the mechanics of the traveling wave.

What of the interpeak interval, Δp? First, consider the general form of the reaction of the cochlea to an impulsive stimulus. Each point along the membrane tends to vibrate at its own natural frequency, and these vibrations decay as a function of time. Once the energy from the impulse reaches a particular place along the basilar membrane, it forces that place to respond with an oscillating and decaying pattern of vibration. The data we have just considered on sinusoidal excitation imply that some phase of the membrane deflection tends to elicit a neural response. Therefore the times between successive modes of the poststimulus histogram, Δp, should equal the reciprocal of the characteristic frequency. The rationale is simply that the characteristic frequency is excited by the impulsive stimulus. Figure 5.18 confirms these expectations. It shows that the interval between successive peaks, Δp, is a linear function of the reciprocal

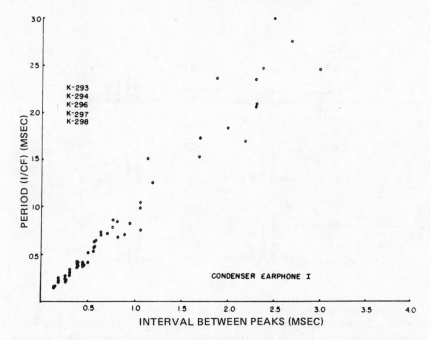

FIG. 5.18 Relation between the reciprocal of the characteristic frequency (or period = 1/CF) and the interval between successive peaks of the period histogram, Δp. (From Kiang *et al.*, 1965, p. 27.)

of the characteristic frequency of the fiber. The reciprocal of the characteristic frequency is, of course, the period of the sinusoidal vibration. Thus, the click data are completely consistent with what we know concerning the traveling wave in the cochlea.

Finally, how does the poststimulus histogram change as we alter the intensity of the stimulus? Figure 5.19 shows such a graph. At the lowest click level, the histogram modes are barely discernible. As the click level increases, the first mode of the histogram increases greatly. At still higher click levels, the first mode of the distribution occurs earlier in time. The latency of the fiber appears to be shorter, presumably because the first vibration of the cochlear partition becomes potent enough to excite the fiber as the intensity of the click increases.

The polarity of the click plays an important role in determining the form of the observed histogram. The click can be delivered as an outward excursion of the earphone, a condensation click, or as an inward motion of the earphone, a rarefraction click. The polarity of the click determines whether the first excursion of the basilar membrane is up or down. Since only one half-cycle of relative motion will excite the nerve fiber, the histogram obtained with a condensation click roughly equals that obtained with a rarefraction click, except the times are shifted by a half period, Δp/2. This fact has been used as an experimental

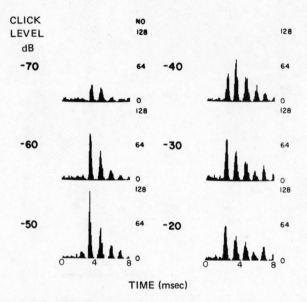

FIG. 5.19 Poststimulus histograms as a function of click intensity. The reference level is a constant high-level voltage, and so 70 dB is a level 50 dB below −20 dB. The characteristic frequency of the unit is .65 kHz. Note how the latency of the first peak is evident about one period (1/CF) earlier at the higher intensity levels. This undoubtedly explains some of the scatter in Figure 5.17. (From Kiang *et al.*, 1965, p. 33.)

technique by Goblick and Pfeiffer (1969). Figure 5.20 illustrates their technique. First, poststimulus histograms are obtained for each polarity of click stimulus. Next, a "compound" histogram is constructed by inverting the histogram obtained with the condensation click and adding it, in the proper time registration, to the rarefraction histogram. The compound histogram should resemble the pattern of vibration caused by the click stimulus. Thus, one attempts to fit the obtained histogram on the basis of the presumed pattern of vibration in the same way that the Wisconsin group attempted to predict the nerve's response to complex periodic stimulus (see Figure 5.14). The essential difference is that the compound histogram has removed the times during which the nerve is unresponsive and has constructed a bipolar histogram that is more convenient from the viewpoint of analysis.

SUMMARY

In this chapter we have reviewed the electrical activity associated with the application of acoustic stimulus to the ear. We have arbitrarily divided this electrical activity into two categories that we call gross and microelectrode

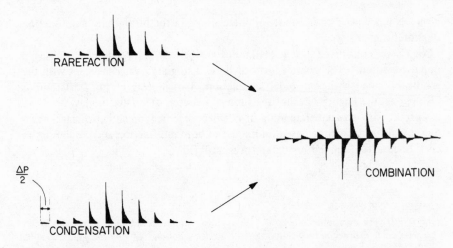

FIG. 5.20 Composite of rarefaction and condensation clicks. The receptors are maximally sensitive during a particular half-cycle of stimulation, and thus, opposite polarity clicks tend to generate poststimulus histograms that are similar but delayed from one another by one-half the period of the characteristic frequency. By inverting the histogram obtained with one polarity and adding to the other histogram, a combination histogram is obtained. This construction gives us a better picture of membrane response by, in effect, removing a major nonlinearity of the transduction process. (From Goblick & Pfeiffer, 1969, p. 925.)

recordings. The chapter has emphasized single-unit phenomena, since the recordings from single nerve fibers provide us with the sharpest insight into the mechanisms of stimulation as well as the mechanics of the cochlea. The more molar recordings are of value in a variety of circumstances, however, and we began the chapter with a brief discussion of their essential properties. These gross potentials include the cochlear microphonic, the DC potential of the scala media, the summating potential (a low-frequency shift in the DC potential in response to the acoustic stimulus), and, finally, the whole nerve action potential or average response of the group of nerve firings. The single-unit work occupied the bulk of the chapter, and we reviewed both the response of single nerve fibers to sinusoidal stimulation and to click stimuli.

Sinusoidal stimulation produces an excitation phase that is roughly proportional to the excursions of the basilar membrane. To a first approximation during each half-cycle of the membrane, motion establishes some probability, p, that the fiber will fire. The probability that the nerve will fire on the next excitation phase is independent of its behavior on the previous one. Thus a recording of interarrival times over a long number of presentations of a sinusoidal stimulus generates a nearly geometric distribution.

A more detailed consideration of the firing pattern within the positive period of vibration pattern established that the fiber's response is proportional to the normalized amplitude of the vibration pattern. A simple amplitude-threshold device is inadequate to account for the changes in the histograms as a function of stimulus intensity.

Next, we considered the poststimulus histograms recorded in response to impulsive stimuli. The general form of these histograms was consistent with the results obtained with sinusoidal stimulation. Two aspects of the poststimulus histograms, the latency, L, and the interval between successive modes, Δp, were consistent with our understanding of cochlear organization and cochlear mechanics. Finally, a technique based on the use of both rarefraction and condensation click to construct bipolar histograms was outlined.

REFERENCES

Adrian, E.D. The microphonic action of the cochlea: An interpretation of Wever and Bray's experiments. *Proceedings of Physiological Society, Journal of Physiology*, 1931, *71*, 28P–29P.

Anderson, D.J. Quantitative model for the effects of stimulus frequency upon synchronization of auditory nerve discharges. *Journal of the Acoustical Society of America*, 1973, *54*, 361–364.

Brugge, J.F., Anderson, D.J., Hind, J.E., & Rose, J.E. Time structure of discharges in single auditory nerve fibers of the squirrel monkey in response to complex periodic sounds. *Journal of Neurophysiology*, 1969, *32*, 386–401.

Dallos, P. *The auditory periphery*, New York & London: Academic Press, 1973.

Davis, H. A model for transducer action in the cochlea. *Cold Spring Harbor Symposium on Quantitative Biology*, 1965, *30*, 181–190.

Davis, H., Deatherage, B.H., Rosenblut, B., Fernandez, C., Kimura, R.S., & Smith, C.A. Modifications of cochlear potentials produced by streptomycin poisoning and by extensive venous obstruction. *Laryngoscope*, 1958, *68*, 596–627.

Davis, H., Fernandez, C., & McAuliffe, D.R., The excitatory process in the cochlea. *Proceedings National Academy Science, United States*, 1950, *36*, 580–587.

Galambos, R. & Davis, H. The response of single auditory nerve fibers to acoustic stimulation. *Journal of Neurophysiology*, 1943, *6*, 39–57.

Goblick, T.J., & Pfeiffer, R.R. Time-domain measurements of the cochlear nonlinearities using combinations click stimuli. *Journal of the Acoustical Society of America*, 1969, *46*, 924–938.

Honrubia, V., & Ward, P.H. Longitudinal distribution of the cochlear microphonics inside the cochlear duct (guinea pig). *Journal of the Acoustical Society of America*, 1968, *44*, 951–958.

Honrubia, V., & Ward, P.H. Dependence of the cochlear microphonic and the summating potential on the endocochlear potential. *Journal of the Acoustical Society of America*, 1969, *46*, 388–392.

Kiang, N.Y-S. Discharge of single fibers in the cat's auditory nerve. *Research Monograph*, 35. Cambridge, Mass.: MIT Press. 1965. 154 pp.

Kiang, N.Y-S., Goldstein, M.H., Jr., & Peake, W.T., Temporal coding of neural responses to acoustic stimuli. *Institute of Radio Engineers, Transactions on Information Theory*, 1962, *IT-8*, 113–119.

Rose, J.E., Brugge, J.F., Anderson, D.J., & Hind, J.E. Phase-locked response to low-frequency tones in single auditory nerve fibers of the squirrel monkey. *Journal of Neurophysiology*, 1967, *30*, 769–793.

Rose, J.E., Hind, J.E., Anderson, D.J., & Brugge, J.F. Some effects of stimulus intensity on response of auditory nerve fibers in the squirrel monkey. *Journal of Neurophysiology*, 1971, *34*, 685–699.

Tasaki, I., & Spiropoulos, C.S. Stria vascularis as source of endocochlear potential. *Journal of Neurophysiology*, 1959, *22*, 149–155.

von Békésy, G. DC potentials and energy balance of the cochlear partition. *Journal of the Acoustical Society of America*, 1951, *23*, 576–582.   (a)

von Békésy, G. Microphonics produced by touching the cochlear partition with a vibrating electrode. *Journal of the Acoustical Society of America*, 1951, *23*, 29–35.   (b)

Wever, E.G., & Bray, C. Action currents in the auditory nerve in response to acoustic stimulation. *Proceedings of the National Academy Science United States*, 1930, *16*, 344–350.

Wever, E.G., & Lawrence, M. *Physiological acoustics.* Princeton, N.J.: Princeton University Press, 1954.

Whitfield, I.C. *The auditory pathway,* London: Arnold, 1967.

6
Frequency Analysis

INTRODUCTION

The single most salient characteristic of the auditory sense is its analytic ability. With concentration, one can often listen to individual instruments in a concert orchestra or attend to but one speaker among many in a crowded room. One can also partially analyze a complex sound into its components and recognize differences among complex signals on the basis of slight differences in the amplitude of these components. This ability to perform at least a partial frequency analysis is the central tenet of Ohm's Acoustic Law.[1] This analytic ability was one of the first auditory abilities to be systematically measured once modern electronics allowed us to precisely control the stimulus.

In this chapter we review the topic of frequency analysis and begin with psychoacoustic experiments that measure the limit and extent of the observer's ability to analyze sound. Next, we take up the question of the mechanism responsible for this analysis. Resonance curves measured along the cochlear partition as well as tuning curves measured in peripheral fibers are discussed. Recent data on the resonant characteristic of the basilar membrane use a sophisticated technique arising from modern physics. We also report capacitor probe measurements.

---

[1] Ward has wittily characterized Ohm's Law as a quarter-truth (1970, p. 438). It is certainly true that the ear's ability to analyze the component frequencies is not perfect, but that some degree of analysis is possible is beyond serious doubts even by such illustrious skeptics as Dr. Ward. The issue is a quantitative one; those interested in this problem are referred to Plomp (1964) and Duifhuis, (1970, 1971) who made quantitative measurements in a situation very similar to those Ohm described in his formulation of the law. Pollack's (1964) results are also instructive; they cast doubt on the universality of the law.

For some years, the mechanical tuning of the basilar membrane has seemed to some insufficiently selective to explain either the data obtained from first-order nerve recordings or the degree of frequency analysis found in psychoacoustic results. Various suggestions have been advanced about how the mechanical pattern might be sharpened. We explore these hypotheses in some detail and also discuss some recent psychoacoustic work relevant to this point. Let us begin with the psychoacoustic experiments.

PURE TONE MASKING

Masking occurs when one sound makes another sound difficult or impossible to hear. One of the earliest and still most effective ways to study frequency analysis used this phenomenon of masking. When masking occurs, analysis has failed. Suppose, for example, we have two stimuli: the sound we are trying to hear, called the signal, and the interfering sound, called the masker. The signal and masker usually have somewhat different frequencies. We first establish the threshold value for the signal, that is, the intensity level for just hearing the signal with the masker absent. Next, we introduce the masker and measure the threshold for the signal with the masker present. The difference in these two intensities is, by definition, the amount of masking produced by the masker. If the threshold is unchanged, then the masker has no effect, and our ability to analyze the signal plus masker is good enough to ignore the latter. On the other hand, if the masker considerably elevates the threshold for the signal, then the masker has influenced detection of the signal and frequency analysis is incomplete or has partially failed.

As soon as the measurements were technically feasible, Wegel and Lane (1924) undertook systematic studies of the effects of pure tone masking. They used one of six sinusoids ranging in frequency from 200 Hz to 3,500 Hz as the masker. With the masker at some fixed intensity level, they measured the change in threshold of another sinusoidal signal at various frequencies. The most common summary of their results appears in Figure 6.1.

The solid line indicates for each frequency how many decibels the signal must be raised above its absolute threshold (sensation level) to be just detectable in the presence of a 1,200-Hz, 80-dB sensation-level masker. Below the solid line, only the masker can be heard. Above the solid line, both masker and signal are audible. Most masking occurs when the signal frequency is close to the masker frequency. As the signal and the masker frequency diverge, the amount of the masking diminishes. Sometimes there is an interaction between the signal and masker; for example, when the two signals are nearly equal in frequency, *beats* occur which are the main indication of the presence of the weaker signal. Note that beats apparently are audible in Wegel and Lane's data at the harmonics of the masker, namely, 2,400 and 3,600 Hz. The irregularities in the masking

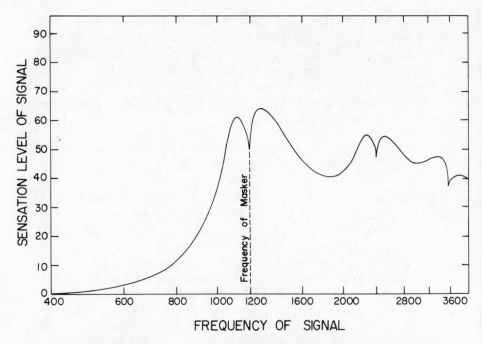

FIG. 6.1 Masking pattern produced by a pure tone at 1200 Hz at 80 SPL. The threshold in sensation level for a second tone is plotted as a function of frequency. Above the solid line two tones can be heard. Beneath the line only the 1200-Hz component can be heard. Because the ordinate is sensation level, masking represents an elevation in threshold caused by the masker. Note that the signal frequency is plotted on a logarithmic scale. (From Wegel & Lane, 1924.)

pattern have recurred in more recent investigations, but they often do not occur at harmonics of the masker. We will discuss this issue shortly. In any case, beats introduce irregularities of the masking pattern that complicate an interpretation of the results. To avoid these unwanted interactions between the signal and masker, several conditions of the Wegel and Lane experiment were repeated by Egan and Hake (1950) using a narrow band of noise rather than a pure tone as the masker. Because the masker was not a pure sinusoid, the signal would not beat with the masker. Hence, more precise determination of the form of the masking pattern could be made at all frequencies. Some data from Egan and Hake's experiment are reproduced in Figure 6.2.

The masking patterns produced with a noise masker are much more regular than those obtained with a sinusoid masker. With a noise masker, the irregularities around the center frequency of the noise band or its harmonics are not evident. The masking pattern of the narrow band noise is highly asymmetric even when plotted on the logarithmic scale of frequency of Figure 6.2. The 400-Hz masker produces about the same threshold elevation at 200 and 2,000 Hz.

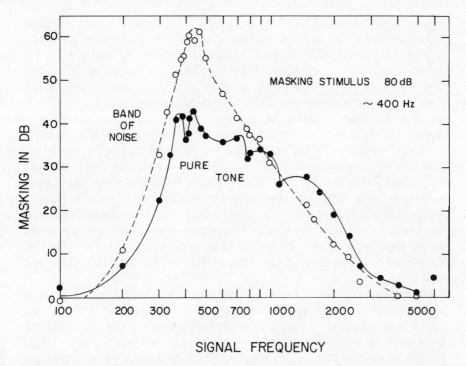

FIG. 6.2 The masking produced by a pure tone at 400 Hz and 80 dB and by a narrow band of noise. Many irregularities of the tonal masking pattern are removed when the noise masker is used. (From Egan & Hake, 1950, p. 628.)

Returning to the sinusoidal masker, the irregularities in the masking pattern observed at about twice the frequency of the masker bear further comment. In Wegel and Lane's original experiment, the masking patterns, especially at high intensity levels of the masker, showed definite irregularities at harmonics of the masker frequency. These irregularities were of the same form as those observed when the signal and the masker frequency were nearly the same. The simplest explanation is that harmonics of the masker frequency are generated in the ear at high intensity levels and these components interact with the signal. Later investigations of pure tone masking both by Ehmer (1959) and Small (1959) also show irregularities in the masking pattern when the masker and signal frequencies are in the ratio of about 3 to 2. Thus, a masker at 800 Hz produces an irregular masking effect near 1,200 Hz. This result is clearly not caused by harmonics of the masker. The results are inconsistent with this simple distortion hypothesis. We postpone a detailed discussion of the phenomenon at this time, however, Chapter 9 explains these irregularities in terms of a more general distortion hypothesis and, in particular, in terms of the cubic difference tone.

The general picture to emerge from a consideration of the pure tone masking data is that the ear behaves like a set of narrowly tuned filters or a series of resonant systems, each of which responds selectively to some frequencies while attenuating those frequencies outside its acceptance band. The asymmetry seen in Figure 6.2 implies that the attenuation rate of those frequencies above the center frequency of the filter is much steeper than that below. A typical measure of a filter's attenuation as a function of frequency is the decibel decrease, or increase, per double in frequency (dB/octave). These attenuation characteristics are typically called the skirts of the filter. The ear's filters apparently have asymmetric skirts with the high-frequency skirt much sharper than the low-frequency skirt. Thus, if the signal is located below the masker frequency, the filter located on or near the signal frequency has a steep high-frequency skirt which largely rejects the masker. If the signal frequency is above that of the masker, then the low-frequency skirt of the auditory filter rejects the masker, but since its attenuation rate is less, more masking occurs in this condition. Even this simple summary is complicated because the amount of asymmetry depends on the level of the masker. We will postpone discussion of this level effect for the present and take up a related series of experiments employing noise as a masker.

While the experiments of Wegel and Lane clearly establish that the ear may act as a tuned filter, it remained for Fletcher (1940) to indicate the generality and utility of this concept in understanding the process of masking. Fletcher used noise as his masker. The bandwidth of the noise masker was the independent variable of the experiment. The signal, a sinusoid, was located in the center of the band of noise for all conditions of the experiment. Fletcher started by measuring the threshold energy for the signal in the wideband noise of some constant noise power density, N_0.[2] Thus, the first data point in the experiment is the threshold value of the signal when the masker is a wideband noise. The next condition of Fletcher's experiment was to decrease the bandwidth of the noise holding the noise-power density constant and determine if the change in bandwidth had any influence on the threshold for the signal. If the threshold of the signal remains unchanged, we may infer that the noise masker energy attenuated by our filtering operation is ineffective in masking. If, on the other hand, the threshold of the signal is lowered and the signal becomes easier to hear, then we may infer that the attenuated energy is effective in masking. The width of the noise masker at which the signal first begins to become easier to hear measures the width of the auditory filter. Figure 6.3 shows data from a replication of the original Fletcher experiment conducted by Swets, Green, and Tanner (1962). The inserts on the graph show the power spectrum for the noise for several conditions of the experiment. As the width of the noise band is narrowed, the signal becomes easier to hear. We may arbitrarily select the point at which the signal becomes 3 dB easier to hear as the effective width of the filter. According to these data, the effective width of the filter is about 40 to 60

---

[2] Noise-power density is defined in Chapter 2.

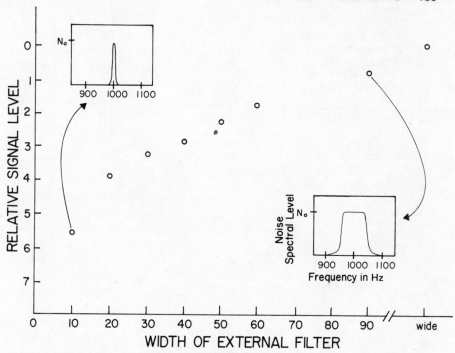

FIG. 6.3 Masking a pure tone by a narrow band of noise centered at the signal frequency. The spectral level of the noise is held constant and the bandwidth is varied as indicated. The signal threshold, expressed as relative attenuation in decibels, is the ordinate. The two inserts show the spectrum of the noise for two conditions of the experiment. (Data average over three subjects from Swets *et al.*, 1962.)

Hz around a signal frequency of 1,000 Hz. Fletcher called this bandwidth at which the signal becomes easier to hear the *critical band*.

We should note that through the experiment the noise-power density, N_0, that is, the noise level in a 1-Hz band near the signal frequency, is held constant. Thus, as the bandwidth of the noise is reduced, the total power of the noise is also reduced. In fact, the change in noise bandwidth from roughly 10,000 Hz to 90 Hz reduces the noise power by more than 20 dB. Such a reduction in power produces a dramatic decrease in the loudness of the noise, but the threshold level of the signal remains nearly unchanged. Were we to hold the bandwidth constant and change the noise-power density by 20 dB, the threshold for the signal would also change 20 dB.

In Fletcher's original experiment, a number of signal frequencies were used. Estimates of the width of the critical band varied with signal frequency. Figure 6.4 shows his estimates (triangles) of the width of the critical bands as a function of frequency. As one can see from the right-hand ordinate, the bands increase in width as a function of frequency. Fletcher estimated the critical band to be about 60-Hz wide at 1,000 Hz and about 200-Hz wide at 4,000 Hz. We postpone

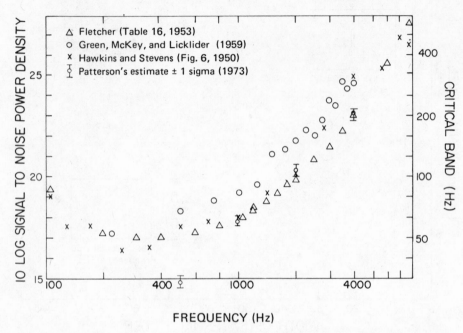

FIG. 6.4 Change in signal-to-noise ratio for a signal just detectable in a wide band masking noise. The threshold ratio has also been converted to an estimate of the critical band width (see ordinate on the right) according to the critical ratio hypothesis. The results of several studies are presented. (From Patterson, 1974, p. 803.)

for a moment a discussion of the other data included in Figure 6.4 and the left-hand ordinate of that figure.

Fletcher's original experiment stimulated a number of similar experiments, all investigating various aspects of the critical band phenomenon. One of the most notable is the experiment by Schafer, Gales, Shewmaker, and Thompson (1950). They constructed their noise masker by adding together a large number of sinusoidal components. Thus, the edges of their noise bands were extremely sharp. Despite this change in the details of the masker, the results are essentially similar to those obtained by Fletcher. Their estimate of the critical band at 800 Hz is approximately 65 Hz. Different assumptions concerning the exact shape of the auditory filter can change this number by about a factor of 2. Another important experiment is the obverse of the original critical band experiment. It was performed by Webster, Miller, Thompson, and Davenport (1952). They filtered the noise in such a way as to leave a gap in the noise near the signal frequency. They measured the detectability of the signal in the region of the gap and, by varying the width of the gap, made inferences concerning the width of the auditory filter. Again, their results are in rough agreement with those obtained by Fletcher.

Finally, an experiment conducted by Patterson (1974) attempted to infer the entire shape of the auditory filter. Patterson employed both high-pass and low-pass noise and varied the edge of the cutoff frequency of the noise in relation to the signal frequency. Assuming that the auditory filter is centered at the signal frequency, the noise stimulates one side or the other of the auditory filter. From detailed measurements of the change in the threshold, one can estimate the entire shape of the auditory filter. Patterson predicted a number of other results from this estimate. Figure 6.5a, b, and c shows his predictions based on three previous masking experiments. In the first panel, we have his fit to the data of Egan and Hake, discussed earlier in this chapter. The assumed bandwidth is about 50 Hz. In the second panel, Figure 6.5b, the data of Webster, Miller, Thompson, and Davenport are fitted by the same procedure. They estimated the masking produced by a noise gap. Finally, in Figure 6.5c we have Patterson's prediction data from Greenwood (1961). In Greenwood's experiment, the noise was a nearly rectangular band of noise at the frequency indicated on the graph. The threshold for a sinusoidal signal was measured at various frequencies near the noise. The bandwidth of the filter used to predict Greenwood's data is 150 Hz. This is about the value one would expect from Figure 6.4. Patterson's filter shape and the bandwidth estimates as a function of center frequency shown in Figure 6.4 provide a reasonably satisfactory account of a wide range of masking data.

Location of the Auditory Filter

Our review of noise masking demonstrates that a great deal of data can be predicted from the assumption of an internal filter. This leads us to reconsider the pure tone masking data. From a theoretical viewpoint, the pure tone data are difficult to interpret. The essential problem is our uncertainty about how the various different auditory filters will be utilized in this situation. Suppose the masker is 1,200 Hz and the signal is 1,000 Hz. What auditory filter should be used in order to maximize the possibility of detecting the signal? Should one interpret the results of this experiment as if the observer was using a filter centered at the signal frequency? To see why this might not be the case consider the following hypothetical example that illustrates the essentials of the problem. In Figure 6.6, we construct two hypotheses. In Figure 6.6a, we center the auditory filter on the signal frequency and compute the signal-to-noise ratio. Our assumptions concerning the skirts of the auditory filter are purely hypothetical but a variety of assumptions would lead to a similar conclusion. Figure 6.6a shows that the signal-to-masker ratio at the output of the hypothesized auditory filter is −10 dB. Figure 6.6b shows the auditory filter centered not at the signal frequency but at a slightly lower frequency. Because of the falloff of the high-frequency skirt the signal level is attenuated; but as the calculations show, the masker has been attenuated even more and hence the signal-to-masker ratio

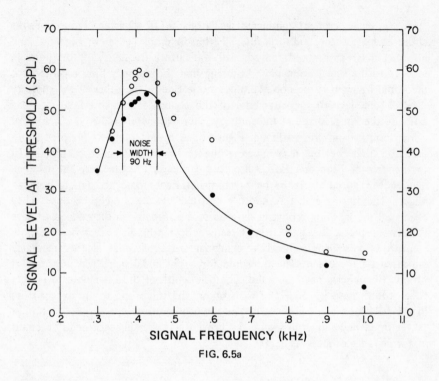

FIG. 6.5a

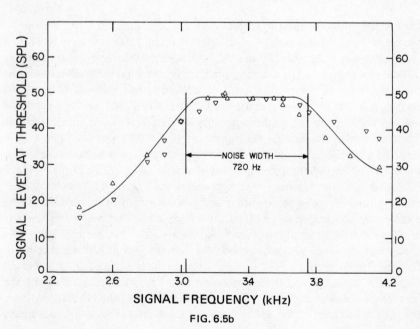

FIG. 6.5b

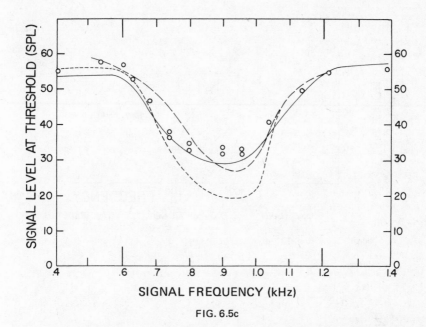

FIG. 6.5c

FIG. 6.5 (a) The data are masking produced by a narrow band noise (Egan & Hake, 1950). The open and closed symbols are data from two observers. The noise spectrum level is 40 dB. The theoretical function (solid curve) is from Patterson (1974, p. 808). (b) The data are from Greenwood (1961), the masking produced by a nearly rectangular noise band of 720-Hz width. The solid curve is from Patterson (1974, p. 808.) (c) The data are masking in the vicinity of a notch in a noise, from Webster *et al.* (1952). The solid curve is the prediction from Patterson filter. The dotted and dashed curves are predictions based on rectangular and simple-tuned filters. (From Patterson, 1974, p. 803.)

has improved. Obviously, there is a limit to how much we can improve the signal-to-masker ratio with this procedure. At some point we will drive the signal level to so small a value that it would be inaudible no matter how great the signal-to-masker ratio. However, in practically all cases, with pure tone maskers we can improve the signal-to-noise ratio by detuning, that is, by listening not at the signal frequency but in some off-frequency region. This hypothesis is not merely a formal mathematical construction. Since frequency and place of maximum excitation along the basilar membrane are related, this hypothesis amounts to assuming that the observer weights most heavily the information from that place along the basilar membrane where the signal-to-noise ratio is maximal. This place is not, in general, the place associated with maximal displacement when the signal is presented alone.

This "off-frequency" listening will generally be advantageous wherever the masker and signal frequency occupy different regions of the spectrum. It is especially effective for those cases where the masker spectrum is narrow relative

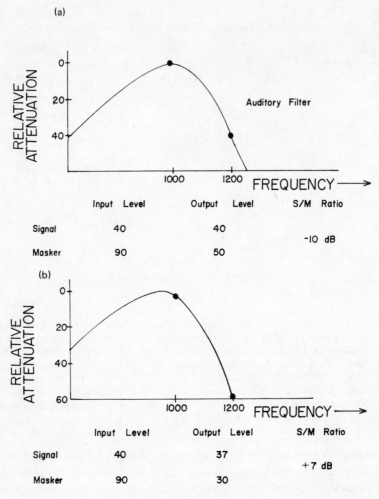

FIG. 6.6 Hypothetical auditory filter and the signal to masker ratios produced in a sinusoidal masking situation. The signal is the 1000-Hz component presented at 40 dB. The masker is the 1200-Hz component presented at 90 dB. In the top panel the filter is centered at the signal frequency. The signal-to-masker ratio is −10 dB. In the bottom panel the center frequency of the filter has been moved to a slightly lower frequency and the signal-to-masker ratio improves to +7 dB.

to the signal spectrum. The phenomenon of off-frequency listening is not only important for pure tone masking but for any relatively narrow band masker. Leshowitz and Wightman (1971) demonstrated this point in a variety of experimental settings.

Because we are uncertain about the degree of off-frequency listening in pure tone masking studies such as those of Wegel and Lane, it is difficult to use these results as a basis for inference about the auditory filter. The best theoretical successes are with data from those situations where the masker is relatively broad, as in experiments using wideband noise and very narrow signals. In these cases, some generality has been achieved by employing the idea of an auditory filter.

Other Studies of the Critical Band

Since about 1950, a number of investigators have studied other phenomena assumed to reflect the critical band mechanism. These experiments have not concentrated on masking phenomena. They have used such techniques as the loudness matching of complex signals as a function of spacing between components of the complex, and the perception of phase effects in a complex signal as a function of the separation of the components. In all of these experiments, one can determine a frequency interval such that within it, certain effects occur, whereas, outside the critical interval, other different phenomena are observed. The width of this interval is another estimate of the critical band or the Frequenzegruppe (Scharf, 1961; Zwicker, Flottorp, & Stevens, 1957). The width of the Frequenzegruppe found in these loudness and phase studies is roughly three times the width of the critical band estimated by Fletcher.

An excellent summary of this material is presented by Scharf (1970). Scharf is especially careful to distinguish between empirical phenomena—"the critical band is that bandwidth at which subjective responses rather abruptly change [p. 159]"—and a more theoretical interpretation of this frequency region as an auditory filter. The bandwidths of the auditory filter depend, as we have pointed out, on an assumption concerning its mode of operation. Many of the discrepancies between the calculated bandwidths can be traced to different theoretical assumptions. There are, however, some areas where discrepancies in the data exist (e.g., Green, 1965; Zwicker, 1954). Furthermore, a largely arbitrary definition of a masking bandwidth also affected early critical band estimates and needs to be treated briefly here.

Critical Ratio Hypothesis

In his original investigation, Fletcher (1940) noted the following empirical rule: for wideband noise conditions the product of the critical bandwidth and the noise-power density, (i.e., the total noise power at the output of the assumed auditory filter) is nearly equal to the signal power at threshold. In symbols,

$$S_t = W_c N_0 \quad \text{for } W > W_c, \tag{6.1}$$

where N_0 is the noise-power density, S_t is the threshold power for the signal, W_c

the critical band, and W the bandwidth of the noise. If the noise bandwidth is less than a critical band, the threshold signal level would simply vary as the product of the noise band and the noise-power density as follows:

$$S_t = WN_0, \quad W \leqslant W_c. \tag{6.2}$$

If this generalization is true, then one may calculate the critical band quite simply from any data gathered in a wideband masking condition. Since both N_0 and S can be measured at threshold we can calculate the critical bandwidth (W_c) from Eq. (6.1). Since the estimate is obtained from the ratio of S_t divided by N_0, it is called a critical ratio estimate. In fact, many of the "critical band" estimates obtained from Fletcher's (1953) book are undoubtedly based on such a method. Such estimates are certainly arbitrary, as Zwicker, Flottorp, and Stevens (1957) have observed. It is important to remember that the duration of the signal plays a role in the estimated signal threshold. Fletcher (1940) used a continuous signal, as did Hawkins and Stevens (1950) in their later study. Using a .1-sec signal, however, Green, McKay, and Licklider (1959) obtained results similar in shape to the older studies (see Figure 6.4). On the left-hand ordinate of Figure 6.4 we have plotted the ratio of signal power to noise-power density needed to just hear the signal in a wideband noise. Despite their use of an unlimited signal duration, Hawkins and Stevens obtained about the same threshold as Green and his colleagues (1959). This is probably because Hawkins and Stevens asked the subject to adjust the signal level until it had a definite pitch rather than until it was just audible. Note also Patterson's estimates.

If an even shorter duration was used for the signal, then more signal power would be required [since the ear is sensitive to energy (power × duration) in this temporal region] and the critical bandwidth would appear to widen. Whether such a result is to be taken seriously or not is a question of current debate (see Scharf, 1970, Section 5). We will not pursue the matter here. General consensus is that the critical ratio approach is largely arbitrary and should be given little weight as a critical band estimate. We saw earlier, however, that the use of Fletc er's estimate of the critical bandwidth and an assumed auditory filter shape can be used to fit a considerable amount of noise masking data. All of these critical band estimates are about a factor of three smaller than the corresponding Frequenzegruppe.

In summary, then, a wealth of psychophysical data indicates that the ear can achieve a partial analysis of the frequency spectrum and can ignore or at least partially suppress the effects of unwanted sounds. What are the mechanisms responsible for this ability? Where in the auditory system is the information processed in such a way that the effect of masking can be explained? These are the topics of the next section. The first filtering process considered is the mechanical tuning as seen in the displacement of the basilar membrane.

MEMBRANE DISPLACEMENT TUNING CURVES

Békésy's Curves

We have already seen that sinusoidal stimulation produces a displacement wave on the basilar membrane that travels from base to apex. Each point on the membrane vibrates sinusoidally at the frequency of the input sinusoid. From von Békésy's observation we know the place of maximum amplitude of vibration depends on the frequency of the imposed sound. As one moves away from this place of maximum vibration the magnitude of the vibrations diminishes, an effect equivalent to filtering action. Let us first investigate the degree of tuning present in this mechanical system. To do this we need to measure the amplitude of the basilar membrane displacement, in particular, the amplitude of the sinusoidal excursions at each point along the membrane. One can then plot these amplitudes as a function of distance along the basilar membrane. This amounts to plotting the envelope of the traveling wave, since the value of the envelope at some point on the basilar membrane is the maximum excursion observed there.

Békésy made the first systematic observations of this kind. Some of his data showing actual patterns of vibration observed in a cadaver specimen are reproduced in Figure 6.7. Note the restricted range of frequencies observed; only the apex, or third, turn of the cochlea was accessible. To view the first or second turns of the cochlea would have required destruction of the third. This might seriously alter the natural mode of response. While this graph displays some of the required information, it is not terribly informative. A large change in response across a few millimeters of the basilar membrane could represent either very narrow or very broad tuning. To determine the *frequency* selectivity present in the system, another series of measurements was taken. A given point on the membrane was selected and the amplitude of this point was observed while the input frequency was changed, holding the amplitude of motion at the stapes fixed. The point of maximum vibration was taken as unity, and the relative amplitude was taken to be the amplitude at that point relative to that produced by the maximally effective frequency. Figure 6.8 displays data on these scales, again, taken from von Békésy. The figure shows that the tuning is remarkably broad. Given a sinusoidal stimulus of 800 Hz, we see that the basilar membrane vibrates with nearly half the amplitude of the maximum vibration for all frequencies in the range between 500 and 1,200 Hz (see the third curve from right in Figure 6.8). The degree of mechanical tuning seems relatively broad and probably insufficient to account for the frequency analysis ability displayed in psychoacoustic data. (Recall Fletcher's critical band is only 60 Hz wide at 1,000 Hz).

A quantity convenient for these discussions is the degree of tuning or Q of the resonance system. The quantity Q is defined as the ratio of two numbers: the

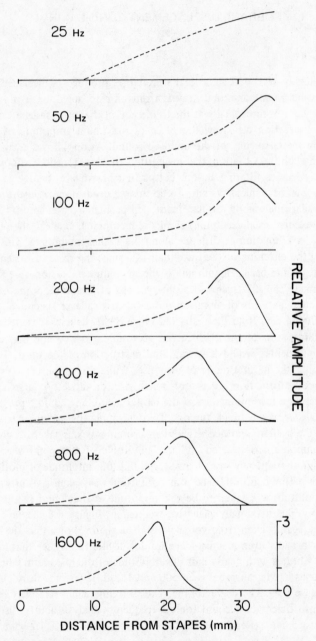

FIG. 6.7 Von Békésy's observations of basilar membrane displacement as a function of distance for several different frequencies. The observations in the second turn are only possible if the third is destroyed and this may alter the pattern of vibration, hence are plotted as dotted lines. (From von Békésy, 1960, p. 448. Copyright © 1960 by McGraw-Hill Book Company.)

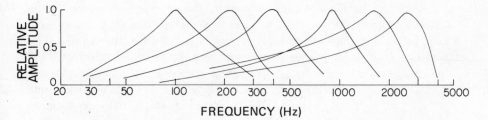

FIG. 6.8 The relative amplitude of basilar membrane response plotted as a function of frequency. (From von Békésy, 1960, p. 454. Copyright © 1960 by McGraw-Hill Book Company.)

frequency at which the resonance system is maximally responsive (the *center* frequency of the filter) divided by the bandwidth of the response of the system. The latter is the frequency region over which the response of the filter is at least some fraction of its peak response. Traditionally, one uses the half-power width, or 3-dB width, that is, the range of amplitude that corresponds to a response equal to $\sqrt{2}$ times the peak amplitude. Other measures are sometimes seen. In single fiber recordings, because the peak is difficult to measure precisely, a range of response within 10 dB of the peak is used. The mechanical tuning shown in Figure 6.8 is low, a Q of about 1. The psychoacoustic data at 1,000 Hz are a much higher Q, about 16.6 (1,000/60).

Recent Mechanical Measurements

Von Békésy's classic measurements of the basilar membrane motion used an optical microscope. He could measure distances of approximately 1 μ (10^4 Å) with such a technique. To obtain sufficient amplitude of motion of the basilar membrane, sound intensities around 120 dB SPL and above were needed. For nearly 20 years Békésy's measurements provided the sole available data, and only in the last decade have several new techniques been introduced to obtain more data. The first of these is the Mössbauer technique used by Johnstone and Boyle (1967).

The Mössbauer technique depends upon the fact that the frequency of wavelength of the radiation emitted from an excited atom is extremely stable. Essentially, one needs a source and an absorber. The source bombards the absorber with gamma rays of a certain frequency. If the source is exactly tuned to the absorber, then practically all the gamma rays will be absorbed and none will be available to activate a scintillation counter located behind the absorber. If, however, one detunes the source in some way, then less radiation is absorbed and gamma rays can be detected at the counter. If one plots the number of gamma rays absorbed as a function of frequency of the source, the resulting resonance curve has a Q of about 10^{10}. Because of this extremely high degree of tuning, one of the most highly tuned filters known in nature, slight changes in frequency can be induced simply by moving the source with respect to the absorber. The relative motion produces a change in frequency known as a Doppler shift. A similar acoustic effect can be heard when listening to a train approaching or receding while sounding its horn. To measure basilar membrane motion, a small source is placed upon the membrane and an absorber is located near it. A count is then made of the number of gamma rays with no sound being applied. When sound is applied the membrane moves, thereby producing a changing velocity difference between source and absorber, hence a changing frequency and thereby a modulation in the gamma radiation absorbed. The technique is so sensitive that a relative velocity of the order of 1 mm/sec can be detected. Once the velocity is inferred from the change in radiation and because the frequency of a sinusoidal sound source is known, one can calculate the amplitude of the basilar membrane vibration by simply dividing the measured velocity by the frequency.[3] Unfortunately, in order to obtain accurate measurements of the counts, which are Poisson events, a large amount of absorption must occur. Thus, in practice, a single data point may take several minutes to obtain. Further, because a measurable change in radiation occurs only over a restricted frequency range, the dynamic range of measurement is about 10 − 20 dB.

Johnstone and Boyle (1967) and Rhode (1971) have presented some measurements using this technique at sound levels of approximately 70 − 100 dB SPL. There are some discrepancies between their measurements. The chief difference is the matter of linearity. Johnstone and Boyle found the amplitude of the response to be roughly linear with sound pressure level at least up to about 95 SPL. Rhode found considerable nonlinearity and the degree of nonlinearity depended on the relation between frequency of the signal and the best frequency for that particular location on the membrane. If the signal frequency was near the peak response or slightly above it, then nonlinearity was apparent even at levels as low as 70 dB SPL. Both investigators, using the Mössbauer technique, conclude that the tuning is somewhat sharper than that observed by von Békésy. However, as all investigators have mentioned, the Mössbauer measurements were made at much higher frequencies than were the optical observations and this may be responsible for the somewhat sharper tuning. Békésy remarked that he believed the degree of tuning, or Q, increased with frequency. There were also differences in the species, the preparation, and, of course, in the locus of measurement. Figure 6.9 shows a rough comparison of these measurements.

The information in Figure 6.9 is not sufficiently precise to compare with other sorts of data, especially tuning curves from the auditory nerve. We must transform the basilar membrane motion to determine the amplitude of vibration for constant sound pressure levels.

Before making these transformations we will briefly describe one other tech-

---

[3] Since if $d(t) = A \sin wt$, then $d'(t) = Aw \sin wt$.

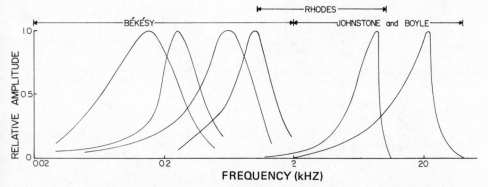

FIG. 6.9 Comparison of the response of the basilar membrane as a function of frequency for three different investigators. (From Johnstone & Sellick, 1972, p. 20. Copyright © 1972 Cambridge University Press.)

nique that has recently provided new measurements of basilar membrane displacements. This is the capacitive probe technique, employed by Wilson and Johnstone (1972, 1975). They built a miniaturized version of Békésy's first probe, with a tip diameter of only .15 mm. The procedure rests on the principle that capacitance varies inversely with the distance between the tip of the probe and a surface whose motion is to be measured, in this case the basilar membrane. If an electrical signal of very high frequency is applied between the end of the tip and the biological specimen, then the amplitude of the potential measured at the tip depends on the value of the capacitance. Hence, it is a direct measure of the distance between the tip and the basilar membrane. Refinements in this technique have allowed Wilson and Johnstone to make measurements in the 1 Å (10^{-4} μ) range, that is, at sound pressure levels as low as 40 dB SPL. The most serious discrepancies between Rhode's and Wilson and Johnstone's results again concern the matter of linearity. Rhode found considerable nonlinearity. Figure 6.10, taken from Wilson and Johnstone, shows the response of the basilar membrane measured at several different frequencies. This very impressive collection of data shows that the response is linear over a range of nearly 80 dB. Just why a discrepancy occurs on this point among different investigators is not clear. There are also serious discrepancies in the measurements of the phase response. It is easier to make comparisons among the different phase measurements because they are less influenced by differences in the calibration procedures. The phase discrepancies are therefore even more perplexing than the amplitude measurements.

One problem with capacitive probe measurements is that they require an air gap between the probe and the tissue. The fluids in the scala tympani must be removed before the measurements are made. This may change the mode of vibration, as Robertson (1974) claims in a recent publication. Robertson showed

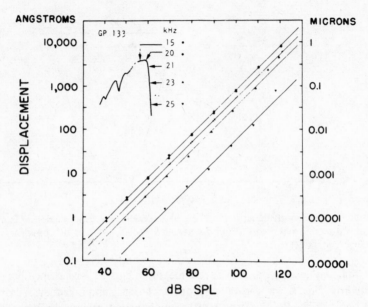

FIG. 6.10 Amplitude of basilar membrane displacement versus sound pressure level for several different frequencies near the place of peak response. The insert shows the relative response as a function of frequency. The 45° lines fitting the data represent a linear relation between displacement amplitude and sound pressure level. (From Wilson & Johnstone, 1975, p. 714.)

the tuning curve for a peripheral fiber changed as the fluid was removed. Wilson and Johnstone (1972) and Evans (1972) report no change in whole nerve action potential as a function of presence or absence of fluid.[4] Von Békésy often investigated cochlear models with fluid on only one side of the membrane, saying the presence of liquid on the other side only changes the fluid mass. In summary, issues remain unsettled in measuring the displacement of basilar membrane.

Let us now take a closer look at the results on the amplitude of basilar membrane displacement. Any student in the area should be cautious about comparing data and should make sure that the measurement procedures are indeed comparable; we will illustrate some of the problems shortly.

Figure 6.11 shows the displacement of the basilar membrane for a variety of different frequencies at a constant 80-dB SPL input level. Three sources of data have been used in constructing the figure: Rhode (1971), and Johnstone, Taylor, and Boyle (1970) used the Mössbauer technique but different species, namely, squirrel monkeys and guinea pigs, while Wilson and Johnstone (1972) used a

---

[4] Johnstone, Johnstone, and Yates (in preparation) have confirmed Roberston's findings but claim the degree of dryness needed to change the tuning curve was much greater than that used in the mechanical measurements.

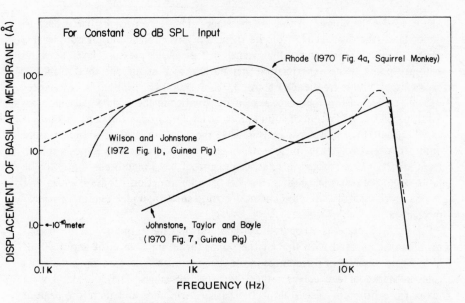

FIG. 6.11 Displacement of basilar membrane, in Angstroms, as a function of frequency for constant sound pressure level. The three different sources are indicated on the graph. The measurements are taken at different frequencies but the general form of the curves can be compared by mentally sliding the curves to the left or right.

capacitive proble and a guinea pig. The data then are taken with different techniques at different locations along the basal membrane and from different animals. Nevertheless, the available data of the displacement of the basilar membrane for constant sound pressure level input show a remarkably flat frequency response. Rhode's data come from the basal turn of the squirrel monkey, an area thought to be tuned at a frequency of around 6,000 Hz. Yet, as the figure shows, the maximum displacement occurs around 2,000 Hz. Similarly, the measurements of Wilson and Johnstone are taken from an area that shows maximum response to relatively high frequencies, at least something about 10 kHz. Nevertheless, there is a relatively broad maximum response and a secondary maximum in the region of 1 kHz. Taylor and Boyle's data are an idealization of a series of measurements and are more orthodox in showing a single peak and considerably less response at other frequencies. All curves show a very sharp decline in the high-frequency portion and relatively little low-frequency attenuation. From all displacement measurements taken at constant sound pressure input, we conclude that the basal membrane has a relatively sharp high-frequency cutoff and a very slight to nonexistent low-frequency cutoff.

The recent literature on this topic does not show the broad tuning curves displayed in Figure 6.11 but rather more conventional tuning curves with single maxima and appreciable falloff on both the low- and the high-frequency side. This is because the measure commonly reported is the ratio of the displacement of the basilar membrane to that of the stapes. The reason for its use is easy to understand—the displacement of the stapes for any given sound pressure level is easier to obtain than the actual value of the sound pressure level at some arbitrary point in the experimental preparation, such as the entrance to the ear canal. Especially at frequencies above 3,000 or 4,000 Hz, probe tube resonances become critical, as do the exact size of the cavities in the middle and inner ear. Thus, precise specification of sound pressure level over large frequency regions is very difficult to achieve. No matter what the absolute level of sound pressure input, it is relatively easy to note stapes motion. For this reason stapes displacement is often used to give a relative measure of basal membrane motion. The ratio of these two measures is also the transfer function of the cochlea and therefore a quantity of fundamental significance in understanding cochlear mechanics.

Figure 6.12 presents some typical data showing the response of the basilar membrane compared with that of the stapes for an input level of about 80 dB SPL. Again, because of differences in the species, one should compare simply the general shapes of the curves rather than specific values. The recordings were taken from different places along the basilar membrane and therefore peak at different frequencies. One can mentally move the curves left or right and observe considerable agreement among the measurements. These curves are more representative of basilar membrane mechanics than the absolute measurements in Figure 6.11 because we are more certain of both the input and the output quantities. Figure 6.12 indicates something of the transfer function imposed by the mechanics of the cochlear itself. We should, however, remember that the displacement of the stapes is not constant for all sound pressure level inputs and, in fact, changes by several orders of magnitude above about 2,000 Hz.

The basic problem in evaluating tuning curves is determining what the effective stimulus really is. It may be that displacement of the basilar membrane is not the relevant measure. With simple sinusoidal motion, amplitude, velocity, and acceleration of any physical object depend on the frequency of the input. Suppose that the force on the membrane is the real stimulus rather than displacement. Force is proportional to the square of the frequency of a sinusoidal vibration. For constant displacement then, the force would increase with the square of frequency. Thus, if constant force is plotted as the ordinate in Figure 6.11, we would find the force increasing 6 dB for each doubling of frequency (6 dB = 10 log 4) or about 20 dB per decade of frequency. Similarly, the velocity of motion would increase proportional to the frequency of the signal or at a rate of 3 dB per octave or 10 dB per decade. Thus, if either velocity or acceleration of the basal membrane were more relevant input variables than displacement in determining the response of the hair cells, then one should mentally tilt Figure 6.11 by either 10 or 20 dB per decade to see the effective tuning as viewed by the hair cells. Since the high-frequency slope of the tuning curves is so great, tilting

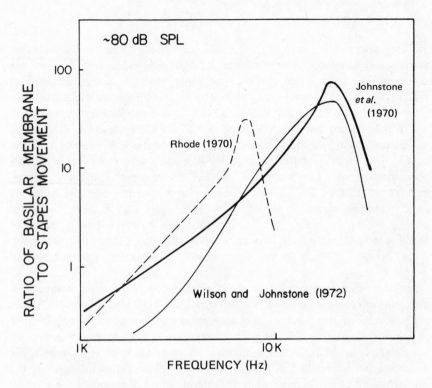

FIG. 6.12 Ratio of amplitude of basilar membrane motion to amplitude of motion at stapes for a constant 80 dB. Same measurements reported in Figure 6.11. Note how much more similar the curves are in these coordinates than those used in Figure 6.11.

the spectrum by 10, 20, or even 50 dB per decade will only slightly influence the high-frequency slope. The low-frequency side, on the other hand, will be greatly altered. Since the exact mechanical factors responsible for the stimulation of the hair cells are at present unclear, it is difficult to know what transformation of the data to employ in describing the mechanical tuning of the basal membrane.

Given these uncertainties it is apparent why workers in the field will continue to employ basilar membrane displacement compared with stapes displacement. The advantage is that both displacements can be directly measured, often at the same time. The measurements, which are fundamentally concerned with the mechanics of the inner ear, will be independent of any hypothesis about the "effective" stimulus for the hair cell. But to convert these relative measurements to some hypothesis about "effective" hair cell stimulus, one must first calculate how the stapes response changes as a function of frequency for constant SPL and then calculate how the "effective" hair cell stimulus varies.

Neural Tuning Curves

We have reviewed the evidence for mechanical tuning along the basilar membrane. The exact shape of the tuning curves depends on what dependent variable one employs. Neural tuning curves are more uniform in their method of presentation in the literature. The definition of the tuning curve was discussed in a previous chapter but it is perhaps well to review it briefly here. First, a single cell in the auditory pathway is located with a microelectrode. Then short bursts of sinusoids with different frequencies and intensities are presented to the animal. The response of the cell is noted. Practically all cells have some level of spontaneous activity, even with no input, but certain combinations of frequency and intensity cause a noticeable alteration in that spontaneous discharge. At each frequency presented the lowest signal intensity that causes a noticeable change in the response defines a point on the tuning curve. Finally, a plot of sound pressure level versus frequency reveals the tuning curve for that fiber. Figure 6.13, from Kiang (1965), shows a set of such curves taken from a single cat.

Different investigators have obtained their tuning curves using a variety of different schedules of intensities and frequencies. These procedural differences are not critical; the tuning curves are approximately the same (± 5 dB). The definition of a noticeable change in spontaneous activity is also treated somewhat differently in different laboratories. As we pointed out in Chapter 5, the first noticeable effect of a very faint tone is to alter the period histogram of the unit. The unit responds more frequently during one half-period of the sinusoid and less during the other. The net effect of this synchronization may be to decrease the firing rate. If one uses a criterion of an increase of 15–20% above spontaneous activity, then this level will yield a tuning curve 10 to 25 dB higher than that obtained by noting the beginnings of synchronous discharge in the period histogram. The general shape of the tuning curve will, however, be very similar—the more sensitive tuning curve simply occurs at 10 to 20 dB lower sound levels at all frequencies (Littlefield, 1973).

One often sees some measure of tuning derived from neural tuning curves. The measure is usually defined as the ratio of the frequency at the most sensitive place on the tuning curve—the characteristic frequency—divided by the frequency range or bandwidth within 10 dB of this point. Such Qs range from about 2 near 500 Hz to about 10–20 at the higher frequency regions. There is general agreement that the high-frequency slope is very steep with typical values of 100-dB octave or greater. The low-frequency slope is less steep. As we will discuss shortly there are really two segments to the low-frequency skirt of the tuning curve. For frequencies near the characteristic frequency the curves shown in Figure 6.13 are typical. A recent study by Kiang and Moxon (1974) shows that at more extreme low frequencies there is little or no tuning (see Figure 6.17).

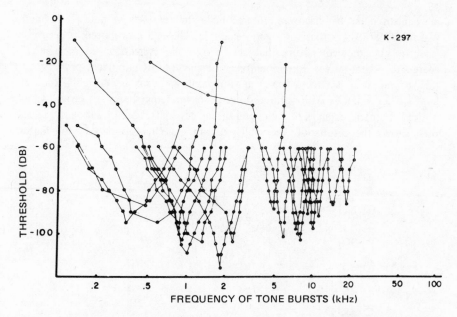

FIG. 6.13 Tuning curves taken from the auditory nerve. Threshold response as a function of frequency is shown for several different units. (From Kiang, 1965, p. 87.)

A number of investigators have attempted to compare the degree of mechanical and neural tuning. They believe the latter is much sharper than the former. The basis of their comparisons is usually the Q obtained at comparable frequencies or the slopes of the sides of the tuning curves. Such comparisons become the basis of the search for "sharpening" mechanisms of various kinds to reconcile the apparent discrepancies between mechanical and neural tuning. While we concede that there are many important and unsolved problems in this area, we must approach numerical comparisons between the apparent tuning obtained from such different sets of data with great caution. As discussed above, it is not clear what mechanical quantity is relevant to plot. Displacement of basilar membrane at a fixed sound pressure level certainly yields tuning curves so broad as to scarcely deserve the name. If one considers velocity, acceleration, and so forth, rather than displacement, then each successive derivative of displacement simply tilts the spectrum 6 dB per octave. Different mechanical theories about the effective stimulus for the hair cell can alter numerical arguments considerably. A variety of mechanical theories has been proposed; one notable example is by Huggins and Licklider (1951). Such theories may well reconcile the differences between the degree of tuning seen in mechanical and neural studies and, in fact, predict the neural response curves from the mechanical one.

But at present the majority of investigators believe that the discrepancy between neural and mechanical tuning is so great that some new and different mechanism must be discovered to reconcile the two sets of data. Evans and Wilson's (1973) hypothesis is a good example. They have proposed a "second" filter of physiological nature that acts before the conversion of mechanical energy to neural spikes. Experimentally the single most important property of this second filter is its physiological vulnerability. Evans and his collaborators have treated animals with various drugs or have changed oxygen levels. They noticed dramatic changes in the neural tuning curve after such treatment. Figure 6.14 shows the results of one such experiment. The top part of the figure

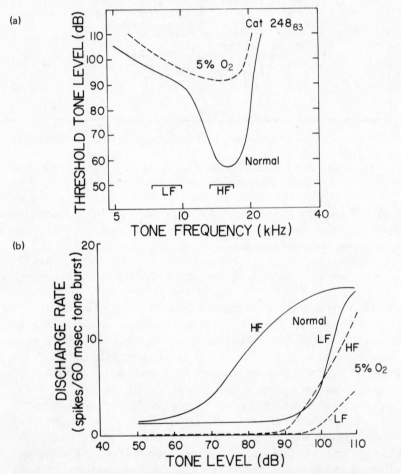

FIG. 6.14   (a) Tuning curve taken during normal conditions and under hypoxia. (b) Rate of discharge as a function of sound pressure level for a low frequency (LF) and high frequency (HF) under both conditions. Note the depression in the spontaneous rate under hypoxia. (From Evans, 1974. Copyright © 1974 Cambridge University Press.)

displays two tuning curves. The lower curve, marked control, is from a normal animal. The upper curve was obtained from the same fiber during hypoxia. Lack of oxygen is known to have a deleterious effect on hair cell function. Thus, the loss of tuning under hypoxia is interpreted as the failure of the physiologically vulnerable second filter. In the lower part of Figure 6.14 are some firing rate versus intensity curves. The frequency used to drive the fiber was either low (LF) or high (HF), as indicated. Note that the maximum rate at which the fiber fired was nearly the same in both the control and hypoxia condition at the extreme sound pressure level. Thus, the change induced by anoxia appears to be associated with frequency selectivity and does not simply reflect the general responsiveness of the neuron. Other treatments using certain drugs have shown similar effects.

Another suggestion to resolve the apparent discrepancy between neural and mechanical tuning curves is that of interaction occurring among the neural elements themselves. One kind of analogous interaction frequently studied in vision is lateral inhibition. As we pointed out in Chapter 5, no studies have recorded simultaneously from several auditory fibers. Therefore, information on any direct interaction among the peripheral fibers is slight. Furthermore, since no fibers interconnect between the afferents of the VIIIth nerve before the cochlear nucleus, any chance for interaction is limited to presynaptic potentials or ephaptic effects among neighboring fibers. Nevertheless lateral inhibition is very useful in understanding both the skin and visual senses. Its potential application to auditory phenomena should therefore be understood in some detail. We will devote the next section to a detailed consideration of this process. This analysis will demonstrate that lateral inhibition need not necessarily result in any direct sharpening of the neural pattern. It may, however, alter the pattern.

LATERAL INHIBITION

The original impetus to the investigation of the phenomenon of lateral inhibition was a series of very elegant experiments by H. K. Hartline (1949) on the horseshoe crab, or *Limulus*. The advantage of the Limulus is its faceted eye with a separate optical system for each facet. It is thereby possible to stimulate only one facet at a time and to determine the mutual interaction of adjacent receptor elements. Hartline's work indicated that the behavior of a single receptor can be accounted for by an excitation quantity characteristic of that receptor and an inhibitory quantity derived from the activity of adjacent receptors.

An increase in the frequency of firing is a measure of excitation while a decrease in that firing rate, below the spontaneous rate, serves as a measure of inhibition. Investigation showed that the following simple equations nicely describe the behavior of two adjacent fibers, designated a and b:

$$F_a = e_a - K(F_b - \theta_b),$$
$$F_b = e_b - K(F_a - \theta_a),$$

(6.3)

where F_i is the frequency at which the fiber fires, e_i is the excitation produced by the ith receptor (either a or b), K is the constant of inhibition, and θ is the threshold value. If, for example, θ is 20, K is .10, e_a and e_b = 200, then F_a and F_b = 192. The size of K reflects the amount of neural inhibition between the fibers. We assume for simplicity that K is the same for both fibers, that is, the inhibition is symmetric.

If F_i is treated as the output and e_i as the receptor input, then the fiber frequency F is a nonlinear function of the two receptor inputs, e_a and e_b. It is nonlinear rather than linear because of the thresholds, θ_i. If e_b is smaller than θ_b, then changes in it will not affect F_a, whereas if e_b is larger than θ_b, a linear influence will be evident. To understand a large array of such elements some simplifying assumptions are needed to make the analysis manageable. One attractive approach is to assume the firing rates are high enough so that the threshold effects can be ignored. In this case, Eq. (6.3) becomes

$$F_a = e_a - KF_b$$
$$F_b = e_b - KF_a,$$

(6.4)

and by combining the two equations we have

$$F_a = \frac{e_a - Ke_b}{1 - K^2},$$

$$F_b = \frac{e_b - Ke_a}{1 - K^2}.$$

(6.5)

This last form is particularly useful since it means that the frequency of the fiber (output) is a linear function of the excitatory receptor influences (input). This greatly simplifies the analysis of the behavior of this system. We can now calculate the effect of lateral inhibition on input pattern and determine exactly how the neural response is altered as a result of the interplay between mutual inhibitory processes.

Suppose we have a linear array of elements, that is, a set of adjacent elements spaced equally apart. Suppose each element of the array has the following properties: excitation of any element is given unity weight, and inhibition of the two adjacent receptors is given a weight of .4. The response of three adjacent units when excitation is applied to the center unit is shown in Figure 6.15a. Suppose further that the array is stimulated by the input pattern drawn in Figure 6.15b. In Figure 6.15c we have computed the output of each receptor $R(y)$. For example, to determine the response at position 4, we have 300 units

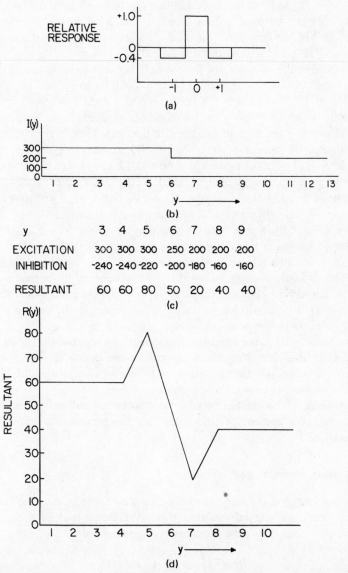

FIG. 6.15 The output (d) produced by a linear array of elements having the receptor response indicated (a) to an input which is a step change in intensity (b). The table (c) shows the excitatory and inhibitory contributions when the receptor element is centered at the positions indicated. For example, at $y = 9$, the receptor is stimulated by 200 units of excitation from the center and −160 units of inhibition [.4(200) = 80 from each side]. The resultant is therefore 40.

of excitation *(E)* and 240 units of inhibition *(I)*, 120 each from the two adjacent receptors. Thus, the total output is 60, as indicated in the column labeled "Resultant." In position 6, we listed the excitation as 250 since it is the average of 300 and 200. We have plotted the output of this array at discrete points in Figure 6.15d and have connected the points by straight lines. Note that the main change from original to transformed pattern has been to add an irregularity on each side of the discontinuity, at Positions 5 and 7. At Position 5, the fiber is responding somewhat more than its neighbors to the left. At Position 7, the fiber's response is less than its neighbors to the right. Thus, in the vicinity of the discontinuity, the change is about 4, from 80 to 20. The average rate for the entire array is about 50, the average of 60 and 40. The *change* at the discontinuity relative to the average is about 1.2 (60 to 50). At the input the change at the discontinuity is 100 but the average rate is 250; and, thus, the relative change is only about .4. The effects of inhibition can be appreciated if we vary the value of K (see Eq. 6.5). For $K = 0$ the resulting frequency would simply be the excitation. Comparing these values to the resultant obtained with $K = .4$ in our example we see two effects. First, the total range of firing frequency is diminished. This property is compressive: there is less change in the output than there is in the input. Note that this property depends on the ratio of inhibition and excitation. If the inhibition is increased, for example, to the value of .5 rather than .4 in our example, then there would be zero rate to any constant input pattern. Second, there is a relative enhancement of discontinuities in the pattern in the sense that the change in firing rate at the discontinuities is increased relative to the average. In our example the relative change is about 1.2 at the output as opposed to about .4 at the input.

The preceding analysis has derived the "excitation pattern" of an array of adjacent receptor elements. We may also view this process as a simple filter, as we next show.

The Receptor Element as a Filter

To demonstrate that the array of similar receptor elements can be considered a filter we write an integral equation that gives the output of the array as a function of the input $I(y)$ and the element response $h(y)$:

$$R(y) = \int_{-\infty}^{+\infty} h(z)I(y - z)\,dz. \qquad (6.6)$$

To test whether this equation is correct, we can compute an approximation to the integral at several discrete values. For example,

$$R(4) = h(-1)I(4+1) + h(-0)I(4+0) + h(+1)I(4-1),$$
$$R(4) = -.4(300) + 1(300) - .4(300) = 60.$$

We need not consider terms beyond $h(-1)$ or $h(+1)$ since they have $h(z)$ equal to zero and do not contribute to the sum. Similarly,

$$R(7) = h(-1)I(7+1) + h(0)I(7) + h(1)I(7-1),$$

$$R(7) = -.4(200) + 1(200) - .4(250) = 20.$$

Equation (6.6) is known as a convolution integral, since it convolutes or mixes all input values with a weighted response from the receptor element. If the input is a single narrow line of excitation, then the output $R(y)$ is essentially the same shape as $h(z)$. This is easily verified if we let $I(y) = 1$ when $(y - z) = 0$ and $I(y) = 0$ elsewhere. The integral will be nonzero when its argument is equal to unity and hence as z varies, the successive values of h will be obtained. Because of this property, the function, h, in vision is called a line-spread function. In audition, a brief transient stimulus is the input and the response is called the impulse response. Thus, $h(z)$ is known as the unit impulse response or the line-spread function. The principal advantage of this point of view is that we may analyze the receptor array from the standpoint of spatial frequency as well as of space. This suggests an entirely new set of experimental techniques that might be brought to bear on the issue of determining the shape of the response of the individual receptor elements. Campbell and Robson (1964) and others have used this approach in determining the functional response of visual receptor elements.

To understand this spatial frequency approach we need only take the Fourier transform of both sides of Eq. (6.6). The results are very simple. Denoting the transform of $R(y)$ as $R(w)$, and so on, we have

$$R(w) = H(w)I(w). \tag{6.7}$$

In other words, the Fourier transform of the output is the product of the Fourier transform of the input $I(w)$ and the Fourier transform of the receptor element response $H(w)$. If one can arrange sinusoidal inputs to the system, then $I(w)$ is nonzero only at a single frequency. The response $R(w)$ then is simply proportional to $H(w)$ and we can determine $H(w)$ precisely by measuring the system response at several frequencies. The Fourier transform of $H(w)$ is $h(z)$. Once we know $h(z)$, then we can use Eq. (6.6) to predict the output of this system to any input.[5]

Applications to Audition

Several problems arise in applying this approach to condition. One is the matter of phase. Actually, we must know both the phase and amplitude of the response to determine $H(w)$ precisely since $H(w)$ is in general a complex number. Second,

[5] A very readable introduction to this material is *Visual Perception,* by T. Cornsweet (1970).

assuming the system is linear, as can be seen from Eq. (6.6), superposition holds. This assumption assures us that when we drive the system with a certain frequency only that same frequency will be present at the output.

We will not pursue the details further; there are many difficulties, as one might expect. It is appropriate to review at least one application of these ideas to the area of hearing, that of Houtgast (1974). Houtgast treated the basilar membrane as a linear spatial array. We know that a single sinusoidal input stimulates a large area of the membrane (see Figure 6.7). What we would like to determine is the effective impulse response, that is, what is $h(z)$ where z is position along the basilar membrane. Since each place on the membrane is maximally responsive to one frequency we will transform position to frequency and try to determine the effective response as a function of frequency, similar to the displacement function shown in Figure 6.9.

Figure 6.16 is taken from Houtgast. The functions are the apparent weight, h, given to different frequencies in the neighborhood of 1000 Hz. The parameter D refers to different input amplitudes. The relative constancy of the weighing function, h, implies that the system is reasonably linear as a function of intensity.

These curves are derived from the measurement of the threshold value of a pure tone presented in a masking noise whose spectrum level changes sinusoidally with frequency (rippled noise). As the sinusoid is presented in various phases of the rippled noise, its threshold varies depending on how well the system resolves the ripple. If the noise ripples much slower than h, then we can resolve the peaks and valleys of the noise level and the threshold for the sinusoid should change a large amount. If the noise ripples much faster than changes in h, the peaks and valleys will be smeared together and the threshold for the sinusoid will change little as it is presented in different phases of the noise. $H(w)$ can thus be inferred from measurements of the detectability of the sinusoid in noise having different frequencies of ripple. The results on the left of Figure 6.16 show when the noise and signal are presented simultaneously, what Houtgast calls "direct masking." Note there is no evidence that h contains any negative inhibitory portion. The panels to the right of the figure describe the results obtained when the signal is presented a few milliseconds after the termination of the noise, or alternately between noise bursts. This nonsimultaneous masking technique, basically the results of forward masking, makes the negative portion of the curve evident, giving some direct psychophysical evidence for an inhibitory mechanism.

Lateral inhibition is a popular theoretical concept in both vision and the skin senses (Ratliff, 1965; von Békésy, 1967). Perhaps because of this popularity it is often discussed as a possible mechanism in explaining psychoacoustic phenomena. Regrettably the application of this theoretical concept in hearing has been relatively vague, the exception being Houtgast's work. Direct experimental evidence in psychoacoustics is slight, Houtgast (1972, 1974), Shannon (1974).

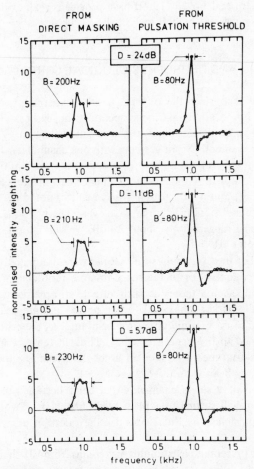

FROM DIRECT MASKING

FROM PULSATION THRESHOLD

D = 24dB

B = 200Hz

B = 80Hz

D = 11dB

B = 210Hz

B' = 80Hz

D = 5.7dB

B = 230Hz

B = 80Hz

normalised intensity weighting

frequency (kHz)

FIG. 6.16 The relative weighting as a function of frequency of the auditory receptor element derived from Houtgast's measurements. The amplitude of the ripple in the noise was set at three different values (top to bottom in figures). The similarity of the inferred receptor shape is evidence of the linearity of the technique. The panels on the left are results obtained when the noise and signal are simultaneously present. There is no negative region in the receptor response, indicating no lateral inhibition. The curves at the right are obtained from measurements when signal and masker are presented alternately. The negative region to the right of the peak in the receptor weighting function is evidence of an inhibitory process. (From Houtgast, 1974, p. 66.)

Carterette, Friedman, and Lovell (1969) have provided weak evidence and even this has been challenged by Rainbolt and Small (1971).

MASKING AND NEUROPHYSIOLOGICAL CORRELATES

Finally, we should reconsider the original masking experiments in light of our understanding of how peripheral fibers operate. The earliest concept of the physiological mechanism of masking was the so-called "line busy" analogy. This general notion stems directly from systems with one channel per terminus, such as a simple telephone or railway system. It proposes that certain fibers or neural channels become occupied by the masker and hence become unresponsive to the signal. Serious doubts about this notion arise when it is noted that the signal-to-noise ratio for masking is essentially the same over a nearly 90-dB range, yet the nerve fibers' dynamic range is only about 30 dB. We will consider this point in more detail in Chapter 10.

As explained earlier the psychophysical theories were dominated by the notion of a filter and by calculations of the signal-to-noise ratio at the output of the assumed filter. While such a theory is fairly effective in predicting performance with a broad band masker, the single filter notion has great difficulty with sinusoidal masking. For a sinusoid or narrow band masker, the critical filter need not be the one tuned to the signal frequency. Thus, at the very least, one must consider the signal-to-noise ratio over an array of filters. Do the neurophysiological data have any bearing on this?

No simple notion of a single channel, either being occupied or altered in its signal-to-noise ratio, will suffice to explain single fiber data. Two examples will illustrate some typical results. First, consider the question of noise masking a pure tone.

Kiang (1965) has presented poststimulus histograms from VIIIth nerve fibers for a number of signal-to-noise ratios. Without noise the spike frequency increases when the tone is first turned on, but then decreases over the 100 msec of its presentation. The mean rate is about 60 spikes/sec for one fiber and about 110 for another fiber. When the signal is added to a continuous noise, the activity over the poststimulus histogram becomes more uniform. Finally, at very high noise levels, the activity is essentially the same during the entire signal. The overall rate of firing decreases slightly for one of the fibers, from 60 to 55 spikes/sec; and in the other case the decrease is even greater from 110 to 80 spikes/sec. Whatever the effect, the simple line-busy theory is clearly wrong. More noise produces *less* overall activity, not more!

Recent data by Kiang and Moxon (1974) show the effect on the tuning curve of adding a noise background. Figure 6.17 gives their results. The noise essentially changes the tip of the tuning curve. The similarity of the effects of noise and hypoxia (see Figure 6.14) on the tuning curve is striking. As yet we have little data indicating what the response of a fiber is at a constant noise

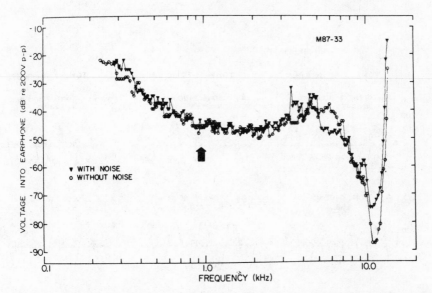

FIG. 6.17 A tuning curve for a high-frequency fiber with and without low frequency masking noise. First, note that the fiber is responsive over an enormous range of frequencies even though its characteristic frequency is above 10 kHz. Second, note that the major change induced by the masking noise is on the tip of the tuning curve. The noise is 500 Hz wide centered at 1 kHz (see arrow). (From Kiang & Moxon, 1974, p. 623.)

background at different signal levels. Obviously, we need to know something more than how the rate of firing is altered, since the changes are far from simple or straightforward.

The other neurophysiological data on masking concern the effect of one tone on another. A very clear way to study this effect uses the period histogram. The Wisconsin group has done this. First, a fiber is isolated that will respond to two different frequencies. Then the relative levels of the two signals are varied and the resulting period histograms measured. Figure 6.18 shows some results of these measurements. At the top of each column is the response to the higher frequency signal at three different absolute levels. The rows present data as the level of the second (lower) frequency signal is increased. At the bottom of each column the period histogram has become phase-locked to this lower frequency signal. In the middle of the diagram the histogram shows a mixed pattern of response partially influenced by both frequencies. The solid lines indicate the best fitting combinations of the two frequencies as the relative weights of the two signals change as one moves down each column. At the two extremes of each column the response of the fiber is determined by only one input. Thus, the masking effect is best described as a change in the pattern of response of the fiber as the relative signal levels are altered. Just exactly what aspect of this change is related to psychophysical masking is unclear. One should also recall that this change in pattern is being reflected in different relative amounts and at

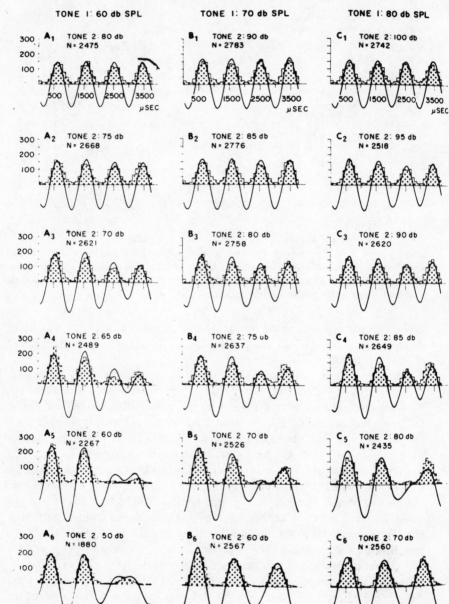

UNIT 67-135-7

TONE 1: 798 Hz
TONE 2: 1064 Hz
R = 3:4

TONE 1: 60 db SPL   TONE 1: 70 db SPL   TONE 1: 80 db SPL

NUMBER OF SPIKES IN THE STATED BIN

A₁ TONE 2: 80 db   B₁ TONE 2: 90 db   C₁ TONE 2: 100 db
    N = 2475   N = 2783   N = 2742

A₂ TONE 2: 75 db   B₂ TONE 2: 85 db   C₂ TONE 2: 95 db
    N = 2668   N = 2776   N = 2518

A₃ TONE 2: 70 db   B₃ TONE 2: 80 db   C₃ TONE 2: 90 db
    N = 2621   N = 2758   N = 2620

A₄ TONE 2: 65 db   B₄ TONE 2: 75 db   C₄ TONE 2: 85 db
    N = 2489   N = 2637   N = 2649

A₅ TONE 2: 60 db   B₅ TONE 2: 70 db   C₅ TONE 2: 80 db
    N = 2267   N = 2526   N = 2435

A₆ TONE 2: 50 db   B₆ TONE 2: 60 db   C₆ TONE 2: 70 db
    N = 1880   N = 2567   N = 2560

FIG. 6.18

168

different relative levels by all the neighbors of this fiber. Thus, the change produced by altering the relative intensity of two sinusoids is a complicated pattern difficult to summarize. How this pattern is related to psychophysical masking is unclear at present.

SUMMARY

The central topic of this chapter has been frequency analysis. The ear's ability to partially analyze complex sounds is the basis of Ohm's initial statements concerning the auditory sense. We first reviewed this ability as reflected in psychoacoustic studies of masking. The signal was a sinusoid, the masker either noise or another sinusoid. We discussed a possible filter model in an attempt to understand these data. Next we turned to an examination of possible physiological mechanisms that might provide the frequency selectivity seen in the psychoacoustic data. We first looked at mechanical tuning as the first filtering process in the auditory system. Békésy's original observations as well as the more recent measurements were discussed and summarized. Next, tuning as measured in VIIIth nerve fibers was discussed and summarized. The differences in degree of tuning of the mechanical and the first stage neural processes are interpreted by some as indicating the presence of some second stage of tuning. One possible candidate for this apparent sharpening of the filter characteristic is lateral inhibition. The basis of this process was discussed and some of its properties illustrated. We returned to the molar level of analysis to consider some of the evidence for lateral inhibition available from psychoacoustic data. Finally, the chapter concluded with a brief review of interactions between different sounds as observed in single fiber recordings. A large gap remains between the masking as observed on the psychophysical level and the neurological events corresponding to that process.

REFERENCES

Brugge, J.F., Anderson, D.J., Hind, J.E., & Rose, J.E. Time structure of discharges in single auditory nerve fibers of the squirrel monkey in response to complex periodic sounds. *Journal of Neurophysiology,* 1969, *32,* 386–401.

FIG. 6.18   Period histograms (see Figure 5.11) for different combinations of two sinusoids: Tone 1, 798 Hz, Tone 2, 1064 Hz, ratio = 3 to 4. The level of Tone 1 at 798 Hz sinusoid is varied across the columns. The level of Tone 2 at 1064 Hz sinusoid is varied along the rows. Tone 2 at the top is 20 dB above the level of Tone 1; at the bottom it is 10 dB below. The solid line is the combination (sum) of the two frequencies adjusted in relative amplitude and phase to best fit the histogram. At the top the higher frequency tone is more evident, at the bottom the lower frequency component is present in the greater amplitude. (From Brugge *et al.,* 1969, p. 394.)

Campbell, F.W., & Robson, J.G. Application of Fourier analysis to the modulation response of the eye. *Journal of the Optical Society of America*, 1964, *54*, 581.

Carterette, E.C., Friedman, M.P., & Lovell, J.D. Mach bands in hearing. *Journal of the Acoustical Society of America*, 1969, *45*, 986–998.

Cornsweet, T. *Visual perception.* New York and London: Academic Press, 1970.

Duifhuis, H. Audibility of high harmonics in a periodic pulse. *Journal of the Acoustical Society of America*, 1970, *48*, 888–893.

Duifhuis, H. Audibility of high harmonics in a periodic pulse. II, Time effect: *Journal of the Acoustical Society of America*, 1971, *49*, 1155–1162.

Egan, J.P., & Hake, H.W. On the masking pattern of a simple auditory stimulus. *Journal of the Acoustical Society of America*, 1950, *22*, 622–630.

Ehmer, R.H. Masking patterns of tones. *Journal of the Acoustical Society of America*, 1959, *31*, 1115–1120.

Evans, E.F. Does frequency sharpening occur in the cochlea. Paper presented at the Symposium on Hearing Theory, Institute for Perceptual Research, Eindhoven, Holland, 1972.

Evans, E.F. The effects of hypoxia on the tuning of single cochlear nerve fibers. *Journal of Physiology*, 1974, 238(No. 1), 65P–67P.

Evans, E.F., & Wilson, J.P. The frequency selectivity of the cochlea. In A.R. Möller (Ed.), *Basic mechanisms in hearing.* New York and London: Academic Press, 1973.

Fletcher, H. Auditory patterns. *Review of Modern Physics*, 1940, *12*, 47–65.

Fletcher, H. *Speech and hearing in communication.* New York: Van Nostrand, 1953.

Green, D.M. Masking with two tones. *Journal of the Acoustical Society of America*, 1965, *37*, 802–813.

Green, D.M., McKey, M.J., & Licklider, J.C.R. Detection of a pulsed sinusoid in noise as a function of frequency. *Journal of the Acoustical Society of America*, 1959, *31*, 1446–1452.

Greenwood, D.D. Auditory masking and the critical band. *Journal of the Acoustical Society of America*, 1961, *33*, 484–502.

Hartline, H.K. Inhibition of activity of visual receptors by illuminating nearby retinal elements in the *Limulus* eye. *Federation Proceedings*, 1949, *8*, 69.

Hawkins, J.E., Jr. & Stevens, S.S. The masking of pure tones and of speech by white noise. *Journal of the Acoustical Society of America*, 1950, *22*, 6–13.

Houtgast, T. Psychophysical evidence for lateral inhibition in hearing. *Journal of the Acoustical Society of America*, 1972, *51*, 1885–1894.

Houtgast, T. Lateral suppression in hearing. Unpublished doctoral dissertation, Institute for Perception, Soesterberg, The Netherlands, 1974.

Huggins, W.H., & Licklider, J.C.R. Place mechanisms of auditory frequency analysis. *Journal of the Acoustical Society of America*, 1951, *23*, 290–299.

Johnstone, B.M., & Boyle, A.J. Basilar membrane vibration examined with the Mössbauer technique. *Science*, 1967, *158*, 389–390.

Johnstone, B.M., & Sellick, P.M. The peripheral auditory apparatus. *Quarterly Reviews of Biophysics*, 1972, *5*(Pt. I), 1–57.

Johnstone, B.M., Taylor, K.J., & Boyle, A.J. Mechanics of the guinea pig cochlea. *Journal of the Acoustical Society of America*, 1970, *47*, 504–509.

Kiang, N.Y-S. Discharge of single fibers in the cat's auditory nerve. *Research Monograph.* Cambridge, Mass.: MIT Press, 1965, *35*, 154 pp.

Kiang, N.Y-S., & Moxon, E.C. Tails of tuning curves of auditory-nerve fibers. *Journal of the Acoustical Society of America*, 1974, *55*, 620–630.

Leshowitz, B., & Wightman, F.L. On frequency masking with continuous sinusoids. *Journal of the Acoustical Society of America*, 1971, *49*, 1180–1190.

Littlefield, W.M. Investigation of the linear range of the peripheral auditory system. Unpublished doctoral dissertation, Washington University, St. Louis, Missouri, 1973.

Patterson, R.D. Auditory filter shape. *Journal of the Acoustical Society of America*, 1974, *55*, 802–809.

Plomp, R. The ear as a frequency analyzer. *Journal of the Acoustical Society of America*, 1964, *36*, 1628–1636.

Pollack, I. Ohm's acoustical law and short-term auditory memory. *Journal of the Acoustical Society of America*, 1964, *36*, 2340–2345.

Rainbolt, H. & Small, A.M. Mach bands in auditory masking: An attempted replication. *Journal of the Acoustical Society of America*, 1972, *51*, 567–574.

Ratliff, F. *Mach bands: Quantitative studies on neural networks in the retina.* San Francisco: Holden Day, 1965.

Rhode, W.S. Observations of the vibration of the basilar membrane in squirrel monkeys using the Mössbauer technique. *Journal of the Acoustical Society of America*, 1971, *49*, 1218–1231.

Robertson, D. Cochlear neurons: Frequency selectivity altered by parilymph removal. *Science*, 1974, *186*, 153–155.

Schafer, T.H., Gales, R.S., Shewmaker, C.A., & Thompson, P.O. The frequency selectivity of the ear as determined by masking experiments. *Journal of the Acoustical Society of America*, 1950, *22*, 490–496.

Scharf, B. Complex sounds and the critical band. *Psychological Bulletin*, 1961, *58*, 205–217.

Scharf, B. Critical band. In J.V. Tobias (Ed.), *Foundations of modern auditory theory*, Vol. I. New York: Academic Press, 1970. Pp. 159–202.

Shannon, R. Suppression of forward masking. Unpublished doctoral dissertation, University of California, San Diego, 1974.

Small, A.M. Pure-tone masking. *Journal of the Acoustical Society of America*, 1959, *31*, 1619–1625.

Swets, J.A., Green, D.M., & Tanner, W.P. Jr. On the width of critical bands. *Journal of the Acoustical Society of America*, 1962, *34*, 108–113.

von Békésy, G. *Experiments in hearing.* (Edited and translated by E. G. Wever.) New York: McGraw-Hill, 1960.

von Békésy, G. *Sensory inhibition.* Princeton, New Jersey: Princeton University Press, 1967.

Ward, W.D. Musical perception. In J.V. Tobias (Ed.), *Foundation of modern auditory theory.* Vol. I. New York: Academic Press, 1970. Pp. 407–447.

Webster, J.C., Miller, P.H., Thompson, P.O., & Davenport, E.W. The masking and pitch shifts of pure tones near abrupt changes in thermal noise spectrum. *Journal of the Acoustical Society of America*, 1952, *24*, 147–152.

Wegel, R.L., & Lane, C.E. The auditory masking of one pure tone by another and its probable relation to the dynamics of the inner ear. *Physical Review*, 1924, *23*(2), 266–285.

Wilson, J.P., & Johnstone, J.R. Capacitive probe measures of basilar membrane vibration. Paper presented at the Symposium on Hearing Theory, Institute for Perception Research, Eindhoven, Holland, 1972.

Wilson, J.P., & Johnstone, J.R. Basilar membrane and middle-ear vibration in guinea pig, measured by capacitive probe. *Journal of the Acoustical Society of America*, 1975, *57*, 705–723.

Zwicker, E. Die Verdeckung von Schmallbandgeräuschen durch sinustöne. *Acustica*, 1954, *4*, 415–420.

Zwicker, E., Flottorp, G., & Stevens, S.S. Critical band width in loudness summation. *Journal of the Acoustical Society of America*, 1957, *29*, 548–557.

7
Pitch Perception

INTRODUCTION

When we listen to a complex tone, such as that played by a musical instrument, two attributes of the sound are immediately apparent. First, the loudness of the sound is an attribute closely related to the energy or acoustic power of the waveform. Second, we hear the pitch of the note that the instrument is playing. Variation in this latter attribute as a function of time creates the tune or melody of a musical pitch, and this is exactly the process that the instruments in an orchestra undergo when they tune up before a performance. Tuning two different instruments to the same pitch seems such a simple and uncomplicated procedure that it is a little difficult to appreciate the problem it creates for understanding pitch perception. Often, of course, it is fairly easy to predict the pitch of the waveform. Although the pressure waveform may be complex, it is often periodic, repeating itself in time. If the period of repetition is relatively short, say 10 msec or less, so the waveform repeats itself 100 times per second or faster, then its pitch usually corresponds to the rate of repetition. The shape of the pressure waveform is not particularly crucial for the apparent pitch. This is why a piccolo, a piano, and a trumpet can generate the same pitch despite differences in the acoustic waveforms they produce. One can, however, radically alter the pressure waveform in various ways without greatly disturbing the pitch. For example, reducing the period of a waveform from say 200 to 10 repetitions per second may produce relatively minor changes in its pitch. Thus, the fundamental problem of pitch perception is one of invariance. What aspects of properties of the waveform cause perception of a certain pitch and how can that pitch be predicted? Before looking at the problem in more detail, however, and briefly tracing some of its history, we had best begin by defining some key terms.

DEFINITION OF TERMS

A *periodic* waveform is one that always repeats itself after some interval of time. The time interval is called the *period*. The reciprocal of the period is called the *fundamental frequency*. If the period of a wave is 10 msec, its fundamental frequency is 100 Hz. Fourier was the first to prove that a frequency analysis of a periodic waveform always yields a unique sum of sinusoidal waves. The amplitude of the various sinusoidal components and, hence, the distribution of energy in the wave as a function of frequency is called the *amplitude spectrum*. Any complex, periodic waves will have energy both at the fundamental frequency equal to the reciprocal of the period, and at integer multiples of the fundamental called *overtones* or *harmonics* of the fundamental. Further, a periodic waveform cannot have energy at any frequencies other than the fundamental or integer multiples of it. Thus, a periodic waveform is often represented as a *line* spectrum because only components at a discrete set of frequencies are present—usually the fundamental and integer multiples of the fundamental. The amplitude spectrum of a periodic wave is therefore a series of lines whose heights represent the amplitudes of the sinusoid at different frequencies. The frequency of successive harmonics is equal to an integer multiple of the fundamental frequency. A periodic waveform need not have energy at its fundamental frequency. For example, a waveform consisting of the sinusoidal components at 1,000, 1,010, 1,020, and 1,030 Hz is periodic. Its fundamental is the greatest common denominator of the four frequencies, 10 Hz, although there is no energy at this frequency. Its period is therefore .1 sec.

Figure 7.1 shows the amplitude spectra for two waveforms. The top waveform is a simple sinusoid, the second is a sum of five sinusoids, with the fundamental at $1/T$ and the first four overtones or harmonics.

The *pitch* of a complex waveform is a subjective attribute. It cannot be directly observed. Rather, one must observe something about the pitch of a sound by comparing or matching it to other sounds. For some sounds the pitch is so obvious one can easily give it a value by matching it to a pure tone. The frequency of the pure tone is then said to match the pitch of the sound under consideration. The ease with which this match is accomplished varies greatly with the sound to be matched. Often the sound is complex and has many frequency components. In such cases the match is sometimes easier when made against another complex waveform. Often the standard waveform is a pulse train, a set of brief pulses of equal amplitude and spaced equally in time. The period of a pulse train is simply the time interval between the pulses. The amplitude spectrum of a pulse train is the fundamental, equal to the reciprocal of the period, and all harmonics of that fundamental. If the pulse itself is brief, the fundamental and all the harmonics have nearly equal amplitude. Figure 7.2 shows both the time waveform and the amplitude spectrum of our standard waveform. We may imagine that the subject listens to a complex waveform and

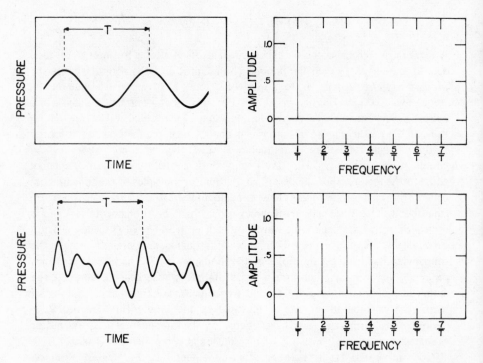

FIG. 7.1   The temporal (left) and spectral (right) representation of two waveforms having the same period (*T*). Top, a simple sinusoid; bottom, a complex wave produced by adding a fundamental, $1/T$, and the first four harmonics. As Fourier proved, a periodic wave only has energy at components which are integer multiples of the fundamental. (From Wightman & Green, 1974, p. 208.)

adjusts the frequency of the pulse train (the spacing between the pulses) so that it sounds equal in pitch to the complex waveform. The fundamental frequency of the pulse train is then taken as the numerical index of pitch for the complex waveform. Although this matching procedure is standard it is sometimes unsatisfactory. Often the complex sound does not have a very strong pitch, or sometimes it has several different pitches that can be matched. One must then present data about the distribution of matches taken at different times with the same subjects or taken from different subjects. From the character of such distributions one may infer something about the strength and clarity of the pitch matches. As yet there is no accepted definition of the strength of clarity of a pitch match, although variation on this dimension is obvious to anyone who has worked in this area. Although some matches are difficult to make, even a difficult match may yield a standard deviation less than 1 Hz. The precision of these judgments (often better than 1%) has been a spur to experimental investigation of this topic. In summary, the important concepts for pitch are period, fundamental, harmonics or overtones, amplitude spectrum, and our operational

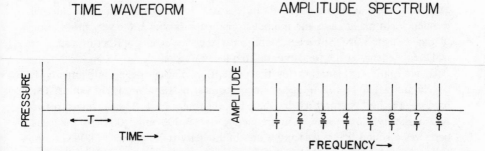

FIG. 7.2 The temporal and spectral representation of a simple periodic pulse train. Each harmonic contains approximately the same energy. The number of components present in the spectrum depends on the duration (width) of the pulse. If the pulse is ΔT long the components extend to about $1/\Delta T$, e.g., a .1 msec pulse has components up to about 10 kHz.

definition of the numerical index of the pitch of an arbitrary, complex waveform.

BRIEF OVERVIEW

These basic definitions lead us to the general problem of pitch perception and the two major theories that have been concerned with it over the past century. The history of the problem begins with the following demonstration. Consider our standard waveform, as shown in Figure 7.2. Suppose we filter the pulse train, removing the fundamental and the first four or five harmonics. Remarkably, the pitch of the waveform is hardly affected! We have all observed this phenomenon firsthand when we listen to a human voice speaking on the telephone. Certain sounds, such as the "a" in father, are periodic waves whose fundamental is 100–120 Hz for a male speaker. The telephone transmits only frequencies of about 300 Hz, yet the pitch of the vowel is the same whether heard live or over the telephone.

The fact that the pitch of a sound can correspond to a fundamental frequency that is not present is called *the problem of the missing fundamental.* Two schools of thought have tried to explain this apparent paradox. Place theorists argue that the fundamental is, in fact, not missing if one calculates the energy present at the relevant locus along the basilar membrane. They assume that the transduction of acoustic energy prior to the basilar membrane is nonlinear and that the nonlinear transformation generates sum and difference tones. Since all difference tones of adjacent harmonics of a periodic wave equal the fundamental of the waveform, distortion reintroduces considerable energy at the fundamental frequency. Thus, place theory claims the pitch of a complex periodic waveform, even with the fundamental filtered out, is still determined by the fundamental frequency. In many cases the nonlinear distortion occurs in the very production of the acoustic wave. Sufficient nonlinearities either in an amplifier or a speaker will create energy at the fundamental frequency.

An alternative explanation for the perception of the missing fundamental is largely unrelated to the frequency composition of the complex stimulus. The basic idea is best exemplified by the phenomenon of beats. If one listens to two sinusoids very close together in frequency, say 1,000 and 1,002 Hz, then one perceives a sound that waxes and wanes in intensity twice per second. We do not feel compelled to argue in this case that a difference tone of 2 Hz is responsible for the perception. Indeed, such an explanation seems highly artificial and unlikely. Rather, one observes that the auditory system simply seems responsive to gross fluctuations in amplitude that occur at a slow rate. We can imagine, for example, that many nerve fibers fire when the amplitude of the complex waveform is large and that few fire when the amplitude is small. One simply detects this waxing and waning of neural activity as beats. Similarly, if the difference in frequency between the two sine waves is increased, and especially if additional pairs of sinusoids are introduced having the same common difference frequency, then the periodicity in the waveshape becomes so evident as to be the basis of the apparent pitch. For example, in a complex waveform containing components at 1,000, 1,200, 1,400, 1,600, and 1,800 Hz, periodicity in the waveform occurs at a 200-Hz rate. The periodicity is visible, for example, upon observing this waveform on the oscilloscope. A temporal theorist asserts that the nerves fire in response to this periodicity. Thus, the ear is said to be responsive to this waveform periodicity in exactly the same way that it reacts to a 2-Hz beat.

Historically, Helmholtz (1863) advocated the place theory, whereas Seebeck (1841, 1843) and others favored the temporal theory. In more recent times, Schouten (1938) has been the champion of the temporal theory. Much of the modern work on this topic was either initiated by Schouten or by his collaborators in the Netherlands. No one name can be associated with the modern version of the place theory. Although there is no question of a correlation between place of stimulation and waveform frequency, as von Békésy and others have demonstrated, the issue is whether or not pitch is mediated by place. The physiological evidence makes it quite clear that at least at low frequencies the peripheral fibers do "follow" the epochs of stimulus in the sense of being phase-locked to the stimulus. We will shortly review evidence for low-frequency pitch perception occurring without stimulating the proper place along the basilar membrane. Such evidence has definitely put the classic place theorists on the defensive. But nonlinearities do exist—a variety of interesting ones have been demonstrated recently and will be reviewed in another chapter. However, no one has presented a systematic account of how these nonlinearities could be used to save the classic place theory. Temporal theory has also been placed on the defensive by recent experimental evidence. The two newest theories of pitch perception make no appeal to timing information to explain pitch perception.

We now turn to the central experimental phenomenon—the missing fundamental.

THE MISSING FUNDAMENTAL

As we mentioned in the Introduction, it is relatively simple to predict the pitch of periodic waveforms that contain significant energy at the fundamental frequency. The pitch is invariably equal to the fundamental frequency.[1] This class of waveforms is basically uninformative about how pitch is perceived. One can maintain either that the pitch is equal to the fundamental frequency or to the reciprocal of the period of the waveform. Since these two quantities are the same, each remains viable for determining the waveform's pitch. The first interesting case arises when we construct a waveform with little or no energy at the fundamental. In fact, Seebeck (1841, 1843) made the first experimental attack on this problem. He used a siren to generate his stimuli (see Figure 7.3). A siren is built by spinning a disk in front of an airstream such as that produced at the end of an airhose. By cutting holes in the disk in certain places, the air can pass through these holes and different acoustic waveforms can be generated. Seebeck constructed disks with a variety of different properties. The main thrust of his work, however, was to construct waveforms containing little or no energy at the fundamental frequency.

Suppose we cut only one hole at some point in the disk and spin it at a certain rate. Obviously, we will produce a pressure pulse each time the hole comes in front of the airhose. This will generate a periodic wave similar to that shown in Figure 7.4a. The period is equal to the reciprocal of the number of revolutions of the disk per second. Suppose we now construct another disk having two holes, the second placed $180°$ from the first exactly across the center of the disk. If we spin this disk at the same rate as the first, the pressure pulse will occur at exactly twice the rate of the first disk and produce a waveform similar to that shown in Figure 7.4b. The amplitude spectra of these two waveforms appear on the right side of the figure. Finally, let us construct a third disk again with two holes. This time, however, we place the second hole at some other position than $180°$ away from the first. To be specific, suppose we locate the second hole $162°$ away from the first, that is, $18°$ away from halfway across. Now the period of the waveform is simply the reciprocal of the rate of rotation

[1] We are assuming that the frequency of the fundamental is about 50 Hz or above. At lower frequencies the sensation is more a rumble or periodic thumping. According to our operational definition we might set a pulse train to the correct frequency, but these would not be the sensations traditionally treated as pitch.

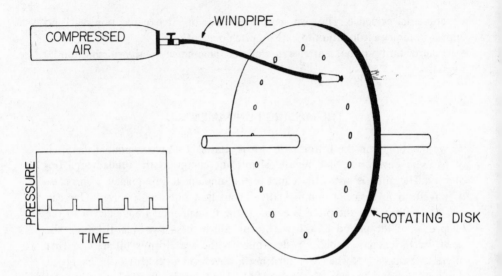

Fig. 7.3   A schematic of a simple siren that can be used to produce a pulse train, see Figure 7.2. (From Wightman & Green, 1974, p. 208.)

of the disk, just as it was with the first, single-hole disk. Although two holes are encountered on each revolution of the disk, the wave exactly repeats itself only when the disk has gone through a full cycle. The pressure waveform as well as the amplitude spectrum for this third disk is shown in Figure 7.4c. The interesting property of this third disk is that although its period and, hence, its fundamental is equal that of the first disk, very little energy occurs at this fundamental frequency. What is the pitch of the waveform produced by the third disk? Is it like that produced by the first disk because the periods are equal? Or is it like that produced by the second disk because the largest low-frequency component of the amplitude spectrum is the same, namely, the component at $2/T$.

The pitch of the third disk is a much better match to the pitch of the first than to the pitch of the second. We should clarify the exact nature of this result to prevent any misunderstanding. None of the three waveforms sound identical to each other. The sound produced by the third disk clearly differs from that produced either by the first or the second. But if we must choose, the pitch of the third waveform more closely resembles the pitch of the first waveform than that of the second. The third waveform contains some quality that resembles the pitch of the second because the pitch of the second disk is an octave above the pitch of the first. Ambiguity among octaves is a serious problem in the study of pitch perception and has never been successfully handled by any existing methodology. An observer may say that the predominate pitch, that is, the

SEEBECK'S EXPERIMENT

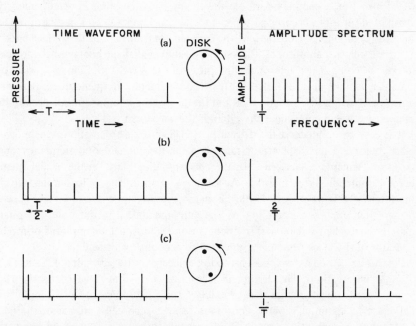

FIG. 7.4 The three waveforms and spectra used by Seebeck to challenge classical place theory. The disk of a siren used to produce the wave is shown in the center of the figure. Note that (a) and (c) have the same period, but (b) and (c) have the largest low-frequency component at the same frequency, namely $2/T$.

strongest percept, matches some particular frequency, but often may find other pitches weaker than the first simultaneously present.

There can be many quarrels with the details of Seebeck's experiment. The siren produces waveforms with fidelity far short of what we expect today. But a repetition of Seebeck's experiment with the best available equipment generating spectra very similar to those shown in Figure 7.4A–C will produce the same results. The predominate pitch of the third waveform appears to depend more on the period of the waveform than on its most intense low-frequency component. This, in a nutshell, is the problem of the missing fundamental. To maintain a convincing account of pitch perception, place theory must address itself to this experiment.

Place Theory Account of the Missing Fundamental

According to place theory, the acoustic stimulus undergoes a limited frequency analysis caused by the mechanical resonance properties of the cochlea. This analysis distributes the various frequency components of the complex waveform to different places along the basilar membrane. Excitation of a certain place along the membrane signals the presence of that frequency in the acoustic waveform. For a complex periodic waveform, the membrane is simultaneously stimulated at places corresponding to the fundamental and its harmonics. According to Ohm's acoustic law, the listener can hear each of these frequencies and their relative amplitudes. Place theory assumes that the energy at the lowest frequency component determines the pitch of the waveform. In many cases, for example, various musical instruments, the fundamental frequency of a periodic tone is noticeably less intense than the first or second component but despite its smaller size it still determines the pitch of the waveform.

It is easy to understand the difficulty that Seebeck's observations create for a place theory. There is little or no energy at the fundamental frequency and receptor elements associated with the corresponding place on the basilar membrane presumably do not vibrate. According to place theory in its simplest form, the pitch of this waveform should be at the first overtone or a pitch one octave higher than that corresponding to the fundamental. But the observed pitch match equals the fundamental frequency. Some additional assumptions or modifications of the place principle are needed to account for these data.

Helmholtz (1863) gave the orthodox place theory account of Seebeck's original observations. His argument is so ingenious that it lasted nearly 100 years, despite the fact that it is probably wrong. The longevity of Helmholtz's defense is a testimony to the enormous respect accorded him and to the fact that technical limitations made it impossible to provide convincing contrary evidence. Helmholtz's basic principle was to assume significant amounts of nonlinear distortion in the hearing mechanism. Since we will treat this topic in a separate chapter later, we will review only the essential features of the argument here. Once these are understood, its application to the problem of the missing fundamental is straightforward and we can proceed with our discussion of pitch perception.

Nonlinear distortion. Consider the functional relation between the input and output of some system. To be concrete, let us take the relationship between the displacement of the tympanic membrane and displacement of the basilar membrane. If we push the tympanic membrane in by a certain amount, the basilar membrane will be displaced. We can construct a graph as that shown in Figure 7.5a which indicates along the x axis the displacement of the tympanic membrane, and along the y axis the displacement of the basilar membrane. The zero

---

FIG. 7.5 (a) A hypothetical input–output curve for middle ear. The dotted line shows a nonlinear relation, the solid curve shows a linear relation. (b) A similar input–output curve using pressure as the input variable and emphasizing range of relations (see the top of the logarithm scale).

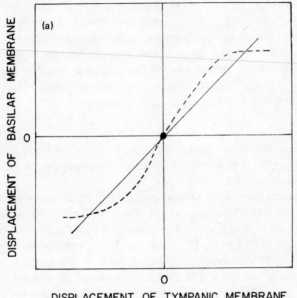

DISPLACEMENT OF BASILAR MEMBRANE

(a)

0

0

DISPLACEMENT OF TYMPANIC MEMBRANE

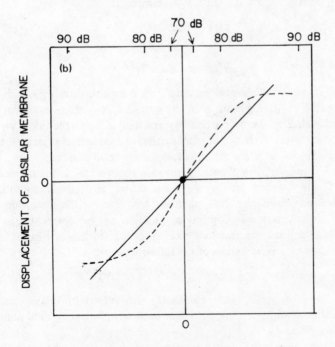

70 dB

90 dB   80 dB ↓ ↓ 80 dB   90 dB

DISPLACEMENT OF BASILAR MEMBRANE

(b)

0

0

SOUND PRESSURE LEVEL

FIG. 7.5

on each axis simply represents the resting position of each structure. Positive numbers represent motions in one direction from that resting state, whereas negative numbers represent displacements in the opposite direction.

Were the relation between tympanic membrane and basilar membrane displacements perfectly linear, then a straight line passing through the origin, like the solid line of Figure 7.5a, would represent the relationship. The equation for such a relationship is the simple linear one, namely,

$$y = a \cdot x, \tag{7.1}$$

where y equals the displacement of the basilar membrane and x, the displacement of the tympanic membrane. The constant, a, represents the gain $(a > 1)$ or attenuation $(a < 1)$ in the system.

If the tympanic membrane moves, we can describe that motion as a function of time, $x(t)$. Similarly for a movement of x there is a corresponding movement of y, and we let $y(t)$ describe that motion. A simple linear relation between x and y such as described in Eq. (7.1) makes it easy to describe the motion at both input and output. For sinusoidal stimulus, such as one might encounter in a complex acoustic wave, the transformation between the tympanic and basilar membranes would only change the amplitude of the vibration. The frequency would, of course, remain the same. For example, if

$$x(t) = A \sin 2\pi(ft + \theta),$$

then

$$y(t) = a \cdot A \sin 2\pi(ft + \theta). \tag{7.2}$$

Similarly, if we simultaneously stimulate the tympanic membrane with two sine waves at different frequencies, then the output also contains only two frequencies, both scaled by the proportionality constant a. Thus, the rule is very simple if the system is linear. Only that combination of frequencies present at the input appears at the output. Only the amplitude of vibration changes.

Consider, however, a nonlinear relationship between the input and output of a system. If the function relating input and output is relatively smooth, such as the dotted line in Figure 7.5a, then we can describe the distortion in quite general terms. Almost any continuous function can be represented as a power series. Thus, any smooth function such as the dotted line in Figure 7.5 can be approximated by a power series of the following type:

$$y = ax + bx^2 + cx^3 + dx^4 + ex^5 + fx^6 \cdots, \tag{7.3}$$

where $a, b, c, d, e, f, \ldots$ are constants. The output of this system can be calculated by determining the output of each term separately and summing the separate outputs.

The distortion here involves a simple, nonlinear relation between the amplitude at the input and the amplitude at the output. Other, more complicated forms of distortion might be considered, but this simple case suffices for our purposes. We can prove a very general property of such distortion, namely, a single frequency introduced at the input of a nonlinear system yields other frequencies at the output of that system. The proof is easiest if we consider each different power law distortion separately.

Consider first a simple square law distortion:

$$y = bx^2. \tag{7.4}$$

If we now use an input waveform

$$x(t) = A \sin 2\pi(ft + \theta), \tag{7.5}$$

then the output will be

$$y(t) = (bA^2/2) - (bA^2/2) \cos 2\pi(2ft + 2\theta). \tag{7.6}$$

Thus, with square law distortion a sine wave of one frequency, f, at the input yields a constant or dc (direct current) term at the output, $(bA^2/2)$, plus a sine wave of twice the frequency, $2f$, having amplitude $(bA^2/2)$.

Next, consider an input, $x(t)$, consisting of the following two sinusoids:

$$x(t) = A_1 \sin 2\pi f_1 t + A_2 \sin 2\pi f_2 t. \tag{7.7}$$

We have set the phase term $\theta = 0$ to simplify the derivation, but this restriction does not change the general conclusion. The output is

$$y(t) = (A_1 \sin 2\pi f_1 t)^2 + 2A_1 A_2 \sin 2\pi f_1 t \sin 2\pi f_2 t$$
$$+ (A_2 \sin 2\pi f_2 t)^2. \tag{7.8}$$

We have already seen that the squared terms produce a constant term and frequencies of $2f_1$ and $2f_2$, but what does the cross product term yield?

Recall that

$$\sin \alpha \sin \beta = \tfrac{1}{2} \cos(\alpha - \beta) - \tfrac{1}{2} \cos(\alpha + \beta). \tag{7.9}$$

Thus, the cross product term is proportional to

$$A_1 A_2 \cos 2\pi(f_1 - f_2)t - A_1 A_2 \cos 2\pi(f_1 + f_2)t. \tag{7.10}$$

Even if $f_2 - f_1$ is negative, a component still occurs at the difference frequency $f_2 - f_1$ because $\cos -x = \cos x$. Similarly, there is always a component at frequency $f_1 + f_2$.[2] For our present purposes the existence of the difference frequency is critical.

---

[2] The sine is an odd function, so the sine of minus x is equal to the minus sine of x, that is, a negative frequency term simply indicates that the phase of the sine wave has been flipped $180°$ and the frequency is the same. For a cosine term, since the $\cos(-x) = \cos(+x)$, there is no change in the phase for the negative argument.

Consider the case of a cubic distortion

$$y = cx^3. \qquad (7.11)$$

If the input is a single frequency, f_1, then the output will contain the original frequency, f_1, plus a component at three times that frequency, $3f_1$.[3] Similarly, if the input consists of two frequencies, f_1 and f_2, then the output will contain the following: f_1, $3f_1$, f_2, $3f_2$ (from the cubic terms) and $3f_2 + f_1$, $2f_2 - f_1$, $2f_1 + f_2$, $2f_1 - f_2$ (from the cross product terms). In a similar fashion, the results of the other power law distortions can be calculated. For example, x^4 is $x^2 \cdot x^2$. Thus, the input of a single sinusoid of frequency f_1 yields a DC plus $2f_1$ from the x^2 term and the product $x^2 \cdot x^2$ yields a constant term, $2f_1$ and $4f_1$. In a like manner x^5 can be decomposed into $x^3 \cdot x^2$, and the various frequencies determined.

In summary, then, many forms of nonlinear distortion can be represented by a power series of the form

$$y = ax + bx^2 + cx^3 + dx^4 + \cdots.$$

All terms beyond the linear one introduce energy at the output at frequencies other than those present at the input. The amount of energy is determined by the coefficients b, c, d, and so on. For a complex input the terms such as x^2, x^4, x^6, and so on, produce sum and difference frequencies, that is, frequencies at the output equal to the sum and difference in frequency of the components at the input.

The Missing Fundamental and Nonlinear Distortion

The mechanical details of the hearing organ and the wide dynamic range of the sense make some nonlinearity more than likely. This is because as the pressure in the acoustic wave increases the various mechanical parts will necessarily reach some limits of their displacement. For example, the tympanic membrane will only move so far before it begins to rip or tear apart. Before that extreme is reached the displacement begins to limit. A graph relating sound pressure level to membrane displacement will resemble the solid line of Figure 7.5b. Intuition also suggests that at lower sound levels the linear approximation will be much better, that is, the amount of distortion will be less at low sound levels. For example, if a level of 80 dB corresponds to the limiting points in a graph, such as Figure 7.5b, then sound pressure levels of one-third of that amount represent 70 dB and one-tenth of that amount 60 dB (see the upper scale in Figure 7.5b). A sound of 30 dB represents a reduction in amplitude of three orders of magnitude, so the entire displacement is only one one-thousandth the total distance shown on the graph. Over such a small range, a linear segment should provide a

---

[3] The basic trignometric relation is $\cos^3 \alpha = \tfrac{3}{4} \cos \alpha + \tfrac{1}{4} \cos 3\alpha$.

good approximation to the input—output function and hence the degree of distortion will be very small. Certainly, the above argument describes a variety of simple mechanical and electrical systems. One reason for quoting distortion figures at high levels of output is simply that many systems are linear at low power levels. Such arguments, although plausible, should be recognized as mere possibilities. The exact form of the auditory nonlinearity is not known in detail. The mechanical linkages are, in fact, remarkably linear, even up to very high sound intensities. More details will be found in the chapter dealing with nonlinear distortion.

As noted above, if some nonlinear distortion is present, we may be able to represent it by a power series containing terms such as x^2, x^4, x^6; each term will produce frequencies at the output that equal the differences in the frequencies of the components present at the input wave. If we now take a periodic waveform, the difference frequency between the higher harmonics is equal to the fundamental frequency. For a waveform consisting of 2,000, 2,200, 2,400, 2,600, 2,800, and 3,000 Hz, sufficient nonlinearity will produce a large difference frequency at 200 Hz in the output since that difference frequency originates from five different pairs of adjacent sinusoids. Other difference frequencies might be present as well, for example, 400, 600, and 800 Hz. The amplitude of these components should be smaller, however, because there are not as many pairs of input sinusoids that will produce them. According to the place theory, then, the missing fundamental is only missing at the ear's input. If one calculates the spectrum of the stimulus along the basilar membrane, then the missing fundamental would in fact be present. The energy at this difference frequency corresponds to the missing fundamental and would stimulate receptors located at the appropriate region on the basilar membrane.

At the time that Helmholtz advanced this argument, practically nothing was known about the amount of nonlinear distortion present in the hearing organ. Later measurements indicated a great deal of distortion, but certain technical flaws in those experiments have been uncovered. Recent experiments, especially by Wever and Lawrence (1954), have indicated that mechanical transformation through the bones of the middle ear is remarkably linear. Let us now turn to later psychoacoustic experiments that attempted to explore the topic of pitch perception.

Replies to the Nonlinear Distortion Hypothesis

From the mid-1800s until about 1940, there was comparatively little progress on the topic of pitch perception. The issue of the missing fundamental was unsettled. If there was sufficient nonlinear distortion, then place theory could handle the problem as easily as periodicity theory. About 1940 another set of experiments was initiated, largely by Schouten, in Holland. These new experiments began by casting doubt upon the extent or amount of nonlinear distortion; in addition, some completely new stimuli were generated. The former line of attack involved either lowering the stimulus to a level where it was unlikely that distortion would occur[4] or, by masking the low-frequency regions with noise so that even if distortions were producing a difference frequency, it could not be detected via the low-frequency region of the basilar membrane. The second line of attack consisted of constructing new and more complex stimuli that would yield pitch matches at values other than those predicted by the nonlinear distortion hypothesis.

Periodicity pitch at low intensity levels.   It is certainly true that at sufficiently high intensity levels, some part of the transduction process is nonlinear and significant distortion products are produced. These distortion products can be perceived by the ear. The question at issue is whether or not the distortion products are always the sole reason for perceiving the pitch associated with periodic waveforms. Thus, one line of attack is to demonstrate that periodicity pitch, associated with the period of the waveform, occurs even at intensity levels too low to produce significant distortion products. But just how low is low? At what intensity level can we be reasonably sure that the distortion products are minimal?

This problem can be tackled by using two-tone sinusoids at 2,000 and 2,200 Hz. The level of the combination is raised until a 200-Hz component is clearly audible. We can try to assess the magnitude of this component by the method of *best beats.*

In this method we introduce a third sinusoid, say 201 Hz, and note that a beat of 1 Hz is audible. The beats are most prominent when we set the amplitude of the 201-Hz component to a certain value. If the amplitude is too large or too small no beats are heard. Other experiments show that two sinusoids beat best when their amplitudes are roughly equal. Thus, we infer that the amplitude of the 201-Hz tone must approximately equal that of the nonlinear difference tone of 200 Hz when we hear best beats in the situation described above. Using this method, von Békésy (1960), Plomp (1965), and others have indicated that about 60 dB SPL is approximately the lowest level at which listeners can detect any difference tone, between tones in the region of 1,000 to 2,000 Hz, using the method of best beats. Thus, it would seem safe to generate a missing fundamental stimulus at a level below 60 dB SPL and determine if the pitch remains the frequency of the missing fundamental.

A number of studies have used extremely low sound pressure levels and yet have clearly produced a periodicity pitch. Thurlow and Small (1955) and Small and Campbell (1961) heard clear periodicity for a signal as low as 20 dB SPL in

---

[4] The general approach concerning the level of distortion and amplitude rests on approximating and continuous function by a straight line over a small enough range. At low sound pressure levels the entire motion of any part of the hearing mechanism is so small that it would be approximated by a linear function.

the region of 1,000 Hz. Practically all work in Schouten's laboratory was conducted at an intensity level of about 40 to 50 dB.

Schouten (1940) investigated this problem in a slightly different manner, but with a similar thrust to his argument. He generated a complex tone whose pitch matched the fundamental of the waveform. He then introduced a second stimulus, a sinusoid at the fundamental frequency. He adjusted the phase and amplitude of this second stimulus until it canceled the energy produced at the fundamental in the complex waveform. The pitch of the complex waveform, nevertheless, remained the same. To demonstrate that no energy was present at the fundamental frequency, he introduced another sine wave slightly off the fundamental frequency and varied it in amplitude in an attempt to make it beat with the fundamental. No beats were perceived and consequently he concluded there was no energy present in the stimulus at the fundamental frequency. The judged pitch remained equal to the reciprocal of the period of the complex waveform. Schouten called this pitch a *residue* pitch. One often finds "periodicity" pitch called "residue" pitch, especially in the literature from Holland.

A number of difficult experiments were aimed at demonstrating that the periodicity pitch remains even though the missing fundamental is not present either externally or through the introduction of distortion products. But advocates of a place theory remained unconvinced. Perhaps the estimate of the amount or extent of nonlinear distortion was inadequate or perhaps something was wrong with the method of best beats. No less an authority than von Békésy (1960) has questioned the technique of best beats. It was natural, then, to search for more evidence concerning periodicity pitch.

Masking studies. Probably one of the most compelling demonstrations of periodicity uses a low-frequency masker. The experimental demonstration uses a complex stimulus produced by a number of components in the region from say 2,000 to 3,000 Hz. Varying the spacing between the high-frequency components produces different low-frequency, periodicity pitches. For example, components at 2,000, 2,200, 2,400, and 2,600 produce a 200-Hz pitch, while components at 2,100, 2,400, 2,700, and 3,000 produce a 300-Hz pitch. Different combinations of the high-frequency stimuli can be programmed to play a simple melody. According to the place theory, this melody is perceived through difference frequencies located in some low-frequency region of the basilar membrane, say in the region corresponding to the octave between 200 and 400 Hz. If this hypothesis was true, these distortion products should be masked by introducing a low-frequency noise. However, masking noise in the low-frequency region, for example, in the band below 1,000 Hz, is almost completely ineffective. The melody produced by the high-frequency complex is still evident and remains clear until the masker is increased to such an intensity that it interferes with the high-frequency components themselves. The conclusion from this demonstration is that the low-pitch information depends on receptors associated with the high-frequency region of the basilar membrane; the receptors maximally sensitive to sound in the region of 2,000 to 3,000 Hz. The apparent low-frequency periodicity pitch is encoded by these high-frequency fibers—a situation clearly contrary to the postulates of place theory.

Variants of this now classic demonstration have been conducted by Licklider (1954), Small and Campbell (1961), and Patterson (1969). The essence of the demonstration is nicely presented in a record prepared at Eindhoven. The record uses both a high- and a low-frequency noise and generates the same melody both with complex, high-frequency stimuli and with low-frequency sinusoids. The low-frequency sinusoid is masked by the low-frequency noise, of course, and is completely unaffected by the high-frequency masker, while the reverse is true for the complex waveform. Either low or high-frequency receptors can code pitch sufficiently to convey a simple melody. The exclusive association of pitch with place of stimulation along the basilar membrane is incorrect. Although the masking demonstration is extremely compelling, further experiments by the Dutch investigators provided even more crushing evidence against the place theory.

Pitch Shift of the Residue

The easiest way to understand the basic phenomenon is to begin with the original stimulus actually employed by Schouten (1938). It consisted of a carrier frequency, f, multiplied by another signal consisting of a constant voltage, that is, a dc term, plus a sinusoid of frequency g. Multiplying the carrier by a constant simply modifies the amplitude of the carrier by the magnitude of the constant voltage. The modulation sinusoid g produces two components, called sidebands, at frequencies $f + g$ and $f - g$. The size of the modulating sinusoid g relative to the constant voltage also determines how much fluctuation occurs in the carrier.[5] Figure 7.6a illustrates about 100% modulation so the amplitude of the sinusoid is about equal to the constant dc voltage. The right of the figure shows the spectrum of the resulting waveform. It consists of a carrier frequency, f, and two sidebands located at $f + g$ and $f - g$.

The pitch of the resulting waveform depends upon the frequencies f and g. Consider first the simplest case. Suppose f is some integer multiple of g; for example, suppose the carrier frequency is 1,000 Hz and the modulating fre-

---

[5] Modulation in general refers to the multiplication of one waveform by another. In our case, the higher frequency sinusoid, f, is multiplied by a sum of two waveforms, a dc plus a sinusoid of frequency g. Thus let $x(t) = A \sin 2\pi ft$, where A is a constant.

The waveform $x(t)$ is called the carrier. The other waveform, called the modulation waveform, we denote as $y(t)$: $y(t) = D + m \sin 2\pi gt$, where D and m are constants.

The result, $z(t) = x(t) \cdot y(t)$, is

$$z(t) = A \cdot D \sin 2\pi ft + \tfrac{1}{2} mA \cos 2\pi(f-g)t - \tfrac{1}{2} mA \cos 2\pi(f+g)t.$$

The quantity, $(m/D) \cdot 100$, is referred to as the percent of modulation.

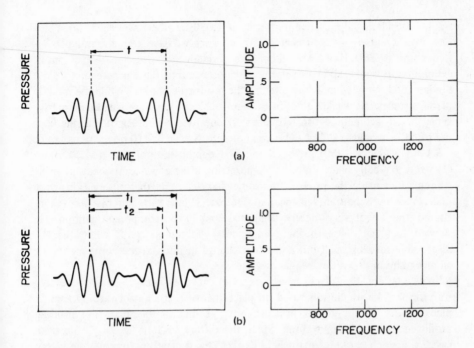

FIG. 7.6 Waveforms and their spectra used in pitch shift experiments. The top panels show a three component complex: the fourth, fifth, and sixth harmonics of 200 Hz. The period, *t* = 5 msec, is the reciprocal of 200 Hz. In the bottom panels all frequencies have been moved up 50 Hz. The fundamental is now 50 Hz or a period of 4*t* or 20 msec. (About half a period is represented, note the two segments are similar but not identical in the bottom left panel.) The t_1 and t_2 are slightly longer and shorter than 5 msec. (From Wightman & Green, 1974, p. 213.)

quency is 200 Hz. The resulting waveform had three components at 800, 1,000, and 1,200 Hz. The fundamental frequency, the greatest common denominator, is 200 Hz, but there is no energy at the fundamental. A peak amplitude of modulation waveform occurs every 5 Hz of the carrier frequency, as shown in Figure 7.6a. Because there is an integer relation between the modulation and carrier frequency, the fundamental is 200 Hz and hence the waveform is exactly periodic every 5 msec. The fine structure of the waveform repeats itself exactly 200 times per second, so it is not surprising that the pitch of this waveform is approximately 200 Hz.

What is surprising is how the pitch changes when we alter the carrier frequency. Suppose we move the carrier frequency from 100 Hz to 1,050 Hz. In Figure 7.6b, we have illustrated a few cycles of the waveform (not an entire period) as well as the spectrum. The spectrum is relatively simple. It consists of the components at the carrier frequency, *f*, and at the carrier frequency plus or minus the modulation frequency *g*, just as in the previous case. In the example we are considering the carrier frequency is 1,050 Hz, the lower sideband is 850 Hz, and the upper sideband is at 1,250 Hz, since we have kept the modulation frequency at 200 Hz. Notice that the fundamental, the greatest common denominator, is now 50 Hz. As in the previous example, there is no energy at the fundamental. Now what is the pitch of the resulting complex? While the pitch is perhaps somewhat weaker than in the previous example, observers unanimously agree that it has increased in frequency. If one took a number of judgments of the pitch, it would match a pulse train of approximately 210 pulses per second.

Schouten (1938–1940) provided the first demonstration. But it was deBoer (1956) who greatly elaborated the phenomenon using a five-component complex stimulus that made the pitch match somewhat easier. Further observations were undertaken by Schouten, Ritsma, and Cardoza (1962). Patterson (1973) demonstrated the effect very clearly using six- and twelve-component stimuli. He showed that the phase of the components was unimportant. What, then, is responsible for this small but consistent change in pitch as the components are all moved up or down the frequency scale?

First consider the place theory account of the perception of these two waveforms. The prediction based on place theory is straightforward. Orthodox place theory would argue that the pitch is due to the distortion product produced by the different tone. Since the difference tone is 200 Hz in both cases, the pitch should remain at 200 Hz. This is clearly wrong. If one listens alternately to the waveforms shown in Figure 7.6a and b, the pitch of the waveform with the 1,050-Hz carrier is definitely higher than that of the waveform with the 1,000-Hz carrier. About this fact there can be no doubt.

If place theory cannot explain this phenomenon, can we account for it in terms of periodicity? DeBoer (1956) attempted an explanation in his original paper. He emphasized the details of the waveshape. First, he considered how the fundamental frequency had been altered by shifting the components up in frequency. With components at, say, 850, 1,050 and 1,250, the fundamental of the waveform would be 50 Hz. Thus, the small sample of the wave in Figure 7.6b would represent about one-half of the total period of the waveform. The waveform would repeat itself only after 21 oscillations of the carrier frequency. If we were to ask for the time between successive maxima of the carrier frequency, there would be no unambiguous answer. As illustrated in the figure, the distance between some of the adjacent maxima is about 4 periods of the 1,000-Hz carrier, between others 5, and others 6. These correspond to frequencies of about 250, 200, and 166 Hz. The average frequency, then, is about 206 Hz, a value close to the pitch match of the subjects.

While the preceding discussion has been stated in terms of local maxima, other aspects of the waveform, for example, zero crossing, might also be the crucial variable. The important point is that some detail of the waveform determines pitch. In the pitch-shifted waveform, because the fundamental is so low, the distance between successive markers of the fine structure changes from period to period of the envelope modulation. Several pitch matches are possible, and the pitch should be ambiguous.

One aspect of this ambiguity is immediately apparent if we continue to raise the frequency of the carrier. Suppose we move the frequency of the carrier up a full 200 Hz. At this point the component frequencies would be 1,000, 1,200, and 1,400 Hz. The carrier is then an integral multiple of the modulation frequency and the pitch is 200 Hz once more. Thus, an upward shift in carrier frequency causes an increase in pitch; yet, when we increase it by a full 200 Hz, the pitch is back to where it began. Clearly, something has gone wrong and it is this: as we increase the carrier frequency there comes a point, usually at about half the modulation frequency, where the pitch becomes ambiguous. The pitch of the shifted version may be judged either higher or lower than the unshifted version.

To understand this phenomenon in more detail, we need to consider the entire set of results one might obtain with the shifted carrier. Figure 7.7 plots the possible results obtained starting at three different carrier frequencies in the range 1800–2200 Hz. The data fit the dotted lines are described by the following equation:

$$\Delta p = (g/f)\, \Delta f, \tag{7.12}$$

where Δf is the amount the carrier is shifted, Δp is the apparent change in pitch, and g and f are the modulation and initial carrier frequencies, respectively. For example, with $g = 200$ Hz and $f = 2,000$ Hz, $g/f = 1/10$. Thus, for a positive increase of 100 Hz in f, $\Delta f = 100$ Hz, the change in pitch is roughly 10 Hz or 210 Hz. This point is plotted as a large circle in Figure 7.7.

This point also lies in a region of considerable ambiguity. If one shifted the frequency up another 100 Hz, then the complex would be 2,000, 2,200, and 2,400, and the pitch would be 200 Hz. This ambiguous region becomes even more pronounced if one uses multiple component stimuli to produce the complex. For example, the combination 1,500, 1,700, 1,900, 2,100, 2,300, and 2,500 can be viewed as an upward shift of 100 Hz from a lowest component of 1,400 Hz or a downward shift from 1,600 Hz. In the former case the increment in pitch is $100/7 = 14.3$. In the latter case, the decrement in pitch is $100/8 = 12.5$. These shifts correspond to frequencies of 214.3 or 187.5 Hz. Highly trained subjects can generally hear both pitches and will adjust the standard stimulus to match either pitch on command.

If f is continuously increased for a fixed value of g, the low-frequency pitch of the complex tone cannot be heard at high values of f. The pitch matches become erratic or impossible. Ritsma (1962) studied this phenomenon explicitly and mapped out what he called the "existence region" of the residue. He used the three-component stimulus that we have described and varied both f and g as well as the modulation depth, m. For $m = 100\%$, the existence region of periodicity pitch is largest. The general rule is that as frequency, f, is increased, g is increased

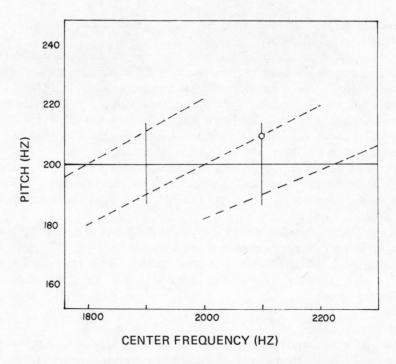

FIG. 7.7 Some possible results of a pitch shift experiment. At the point marked by the open circle (o) the frequencies can be interpreted as an upward shift from 2000 or a downward shift from 2200.

to maintain a residue. At very high frequencies of the carrier f, one can only hear relatively high-frequency residues; at 1,000 Hz, for example, one can hear residues from about 50 to 300 Hz, whereas at 4,000 Hz, matches can be made only from about 250 to 800 Hz. Above about 5,000 Hz it is extremely difficult to make any pitch matches. There is, however, considerable variability between subjects in the locus of the existence region, although the preceding generalizations apply to all subjects.

Probably the most convincing demonstration of the pitch shift occurs when we abandon the technique of amplitude modulation and generate multicomponents, all of equal amplitude. Patterson (1973) used such stimuli in his investigation of the pitch shift of the residue. The advantages of multicomponent stimuli are several. First, the pitch of the complex sound is much stronger than that produced by the three components of the amplitude modulation wave. Matches of a pulse train to the pitch of the complex wave have a standard deviation of less than a part of one cycle. Second, one can independently manipulate the phase of the various components and generate a variety of quite different waveshapes having the same spectral components. Figure 7.8 provides a good

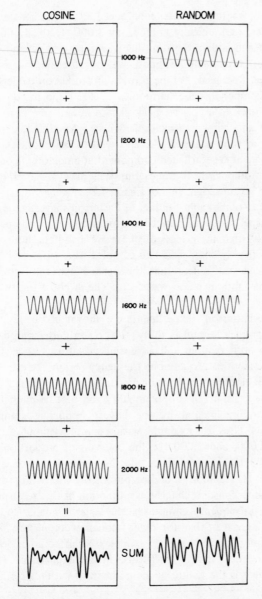

FIG. 7.8 Two complex waveforms caused by adding the same components in two different phase relations. (Left) all components are in cosine phase and a peak is evident in the complex sum. (Right) the components are in different random phase and the periodicity of the complex sum, although the same as the waveform to the left, is much less evident. (From Wightman & Green, 1974, p. 214.)

example of the advantage of this technique. Let us take six sinusoids of equal amplitude that are harmonically related, say 1,000, 1,200, 1,400, 1,600, 1,800, and 2,000 Hz. When added, the resulting waveform will depend upon the phase of the individual components. Suppose we use all cosine phases, starting each waveform at a positive peak at time zero, as illustrated on the left side of Figure 7.8. Since the components are harmonics of 200 Hz, 5 msec later (1/200 Hz) they will all be back to a positive peak. The resultant (see bottom, left side of Figure 7.8) will also show a peak each 5 msec. At other times the individual components are at various amplitudes and tend to cancel one another. Consider next what happens if we start each component at a random phase. The resultant will still be periodic each 5 msec, but will have a smoother envelope, as illustrated at the bottom, right side of Figure 7.8.

One of the most remarkable findings of Patterson's investigations was that the detailed waveshape hardly influenced the pitch match of the complex stimuli. This is not to say that the effects of phase are inaudible, but, rather, they are subtle. Only by quickly comparing two complex waveforms such as those shown in Figure 7.8 can one notice that the peaked waveform sounds somewhat rougher than the random phase waveform. The *pitch* of the two waveforms is identical.

The results of Patterson's experiments are shown in Figure 7.9. The fundamental of the complex stimuli is always 200 Hz in Patterson's experiment. The figure combines both random and all cosine waveforms since the pitch of the two appear to be identical. At any one frequency region, the pitch shift increases linearly with the increase in frequency, Δp is proportional to Δf. Patterson suggests that the constant of proportionality can best be predicted by dividing the approximate fundamental by the lowest frequency component of the complex stimulus. Thus, for example, with a complex stimulus of 1,200, 1,400, 1,600, 1,800, 2,000, and 2,200 Hz, the constant of proportionality is 200 Hz divided by 1,200 Hz, or 1/6. Thus, if this entire complex is shifted up in frequency by 12 Hz, the corresponding pitch shift will be approximately 2 Hz. The proportionality constant changes as a function of the frequency locus of the complex. For high-frequency complexes, the slope is smaller and less change in pitch occurs for a given Δf than for lower frequency complexes.

Ambiguity in pitch occurs when the complex is shifted up or down by half the fundamental frequency, that is, by 100 Hz in this experiment. This is indicated in two ways. There is the failure of the point to fit within a certain tolerance of

FIG. 7.9 Some results of a pitch shift experiment for three different observers. Six- and 12-component harmonic complexes of a 200 Hz fundamental were shifted by an amount that can be inferred from abscissa, for example, 1,700 Hz means 1,700, 1,900, 2,100,.... The apparent pitch can be read along the ordinate. Those points connected by solid lines are conditions where the pitch judgments were reasonably consistent (±1 Hz). Those uncorrected points show more variability. Note at some points the same stimulus has a pitch both somewhat greater or lower than 200 Hz. (From Patterson, 1973, p. 1569.)

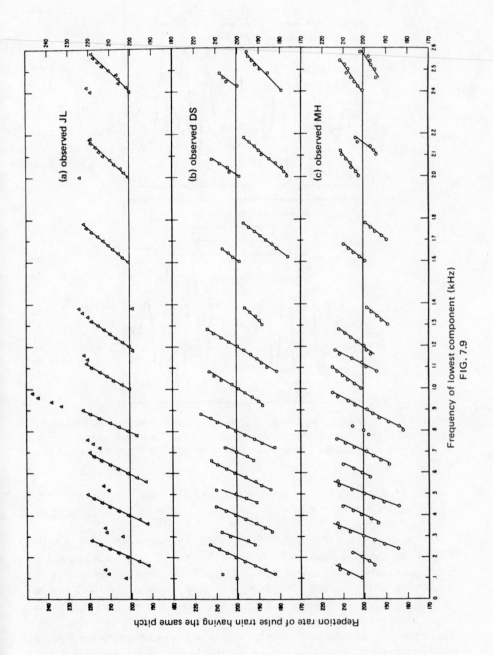

(a) observed JL

(b) observed DS

(c) observed MH

Repetion rate of pulse train having the same pitch

Frequency of lowest component (kHz)

FIG. 7.9

195

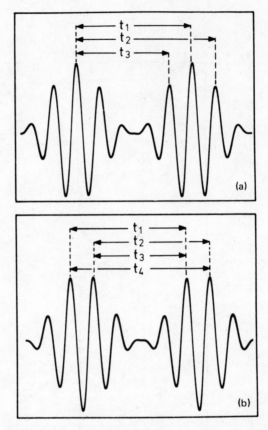

FIG. 7.10 Two waveforms, one an inverted version of the other, having identical pitch. The waveforms cannot be distinguished. Any theory maintaining that local maxima or minima are crucial would predict these waveforms should sound different. (From Wightman, 1973, p. 399.)

the line. In this case the line is not drawn through the point. Second, two points are occasionally plotted at a single frequency, indicating the distribution of judgments is bimodal.

Not all periodic waveforms that differ in phase are discriminable. Wightman has pointed out that the waveforms shown in Figure 7.10 are indiscriminable from one another, yet the waveform in Figure 7.10a is the inverted version of that shown in Figure 7.10b. Naturally, they have identical pitch. This fact in itself should surprise theories that claim the time between local maxima is important, for the distribution of such times is different in the two waveforms. No matter how the maxima are selected, one would expect t_1 in the top panel to be the most preferred pitch match. In the bottom panel t_1 is the same time, but one would expect more pitch matches at t_3 and t_4 of the bottom panel.

The issue of whether phase influences residue pitch has had a checkered history. Hoogland (1953) found no evidence of a residue pitch in experiments he conducted in 1953. The discrepancy between Hoogland and Schouten's observation led Licklider (1959) to suggest that the difference might be phase, since Schouten used all cosine phase for his complex wave and thus produced fairly peaked waveforms. Licklider (1955) also listened to some multicomponent stimuli and reported that he could hear differences among the waveforms dependent only on phase. Licklider never reported that the pitch depended on phase; in fact he advanced an autocorrelation model for pitch perception that is independent of phase. Hoogland's failure to hear the residue pitch was probably because of the high frequency of his carrier, about 5,000 Hz. This is outside the "existence" region of the residue, as Ritsma (1962, 1963) has shown. Thus no evidence suggests that the phase of the complex stimuli affects the apparent pitch.[6] Patterson's evidence is quite clear to the contrary.

HOW IS PITCH DETERMINED?

At this point it would be nice to present a comprehensive theory of pitch that would account for all the known data and suggest some interesting new observations. Unfortunately this is not possible. It is clear that a simple place theory, such as the original resonance theory with nonlinear distortion, cannot account for the data, especially those collected over the past 25 years. For a time there was hope that a simple temporal theory would evolve, such as that based on the fine structure of the waveform. But such theories are generally phase-sensitive, and it is increasingly clear that phase plays little role in determination of pitch. Two new theories have recently been suggested. Both return to the frequency or place principle by assuming that the complex periodic waveform is spectrally analyzed to determine at least roughly the frequencies of the various components of the complex.

Goldstein's (1973) theory claims that the auditory system tries to find a greatest common divisor for the set of components. When the wave is periodic,

---

[6] A recent experiment by Brunnen, Festen, Bilsen, and van der Brink (1974) has shown an effect of phase. Three component stimuli are used, f_1, f_2, and f_3. The lowest component is 10 dB less intense than the other two components, which are equal in amplitude. As the relating phase among the components changes, the pitch of the complex varies systematically. The probable cause of this effect is that the ear generates a distortion product via f_1 and f_2 that is located at f_1. The relative phase of the distortion product changes as the relative phase among the components changes, and the interaction of the distortion product and the less intense component f_1 cause the pitch change. Distortion measurements confirm this conjecture and the highly contrived stimulus conditions were, in fact, selected to demonstrate this effect. Note that even this demonstration gives little comfort to a temporal theorist. Its entire rationale is grounded in place principles.

this is always possible. Most of the time this greatest common divisor yields the matched pitch value, for example, 200 Hz is the greatest common divisor of 1,000, 1,200, and 1,400 Hz. Problems arise, however, in the pitch shift experiment when all the frequencies are raised a small amount. The components 1,050, 1,250, and 1,450 have a period of 1/50 Hz, but a pitch of 210 Hz. Goldstein claims that the pitch extractor rejects the 50 Hz as an impossible candidate, and fits 210 Hz or something near that number as the best of a bad job. Certain criteria are established in the theory to explicate how these compromise solutions are achieved, but these are details that will not concern us here.

Wightman's (1973b) is the second of the recent theories; he treats the problem of pitch matching as a pattern recognition problem. He suggests that the ear first performs a rough spectrum analysis, computes the Fourier transform of that spectrum, and looks for the lowest maximum in the resulting function, which is roughly an autocorrelation function. That lowest maximum, including the correlation of unity at zero, yields the pitch of the waveform. Again, the details of the theory are omitted here.

Note that both recent theories agree on a number of critical points. The first stage of each theory is essentially a power-spectrum analysis, making phase unimportant. Second, both admit that the pitch can vary in clarity in the sense that pitch matches will be easier or harder to make. In Wightman's model the correlation may be imperfect, in Goldstein's theory integer multiples of the greatest common divisor may miss some of the spectral components in frequency. Both agree that there might be more than a single solution, so that multiple pitches are possible. We may, therefore, expect that the next generation of experiments on pitch perception will try to measure the goodness of the match as well as the value assigned to pitch itself. Such new data may allow us to refine our theories of pitch perception and probably will contribute generally to our understanding of auditory processing as well. Pitch perception is a fascinating area because it appears so simple and yet is a process of considerable subtlety and complexity. It has certainly perplexed auditory theorists over the past century and seems likely to be an area of major importance for some time to come.

REFERENCES

deBoer, E. *On the residue in hearing.* Doctoral dissertation, University of Amsterdam, 1956.
Brunen, T.J.F., Festen, J.M., Bilsen, F.A., & van der Brink, G. Phase effects in a three-component signal. *Journal of the Acoustical Society of America,* 1974, *55,* 297–303.
Goldstein, J.L. An optimum processor theory for the central information of the pitch of complex tones. *Journal of the Acoustical Society of America,* 1973, *54,* 1496–1516.
Helmholtz, H.L.F. *Die Lehre von den Tenepfindungen als physiologische Grundlage fur die Theorie der Musik.* New York: Dover, 1954. (Originally published, 1863)
Hoogland, G.A., The missing fundamental. Doctoral dissertation, University of Utrecht, 1953.

Licklider, J.C.R. Periodicity pitch and place pitch. *Journal of the Acoustical Society of America*, 1954, *26,* 945(A).

Licklider, J.C.R. Influence of phase coherence upon the pitch of complex periodic sounds. *Journal of the Acoustical Society of America*, 1955, *27,* 996(A).

Licklider, J.C.R. Three auditory theories. In S. Koch (Ed.), *Psychology: A study of a science* (Vol. 1). New York: McGraw-Hill, 1959.

Patterson, R.D. Noise masking of a change in residue pitch. *Journal of the Acoustical Society of America*, 1969, *45,* 1520–1524.

Patterson, R.D. The effects of relative phase and the number of components on residue pitch. *Journal of the Acoustical Society of America*, 1973, *53,* 1565–1572.

Plomp, R. Detectability threshold for combination tones. *Journal of the Acoustical Society of America*, 1965, *37,* 1110–1123.

Ritsma, R.J. Existence region of the tonal residue, I. *Journal of the Acoustical Society of America*, 1962, *34,* 1224–1229.

Ritsma, R.J. Existence region of the tonal residue, *Journal of the Acoustical Society of America*, 1963, *35,* 1241–1245.

Schouten, J.F. Five articles on the perception of sound. Eindhoven, The Netherlands: Institute for Perception, 1938–1940.

Schouten, J.F., Ritsma, R.J., & Cardoza, B.L. Pitch of the residue. *Journal of the Acoustical Society of America*, 1962, *34,* 1418–1424.

Seebeck, A. Beohachtungen über einige Bedingungen der Entstehung von Tönen. *Annalen der Physik und Chemie*, 1841, *53,* 417–436.

Seebeck, A. Über die Sirene, *Annalen der Physik und Chemie*, 1843, *60,* 449–81.

Small, A.M., & Campbell, R.A. Masking of pulsed tones by bands of noise. *Journal of the Acoustical Society of America*, 1961, *33,* 1570–1576.

Thurlow, W.R., & Small, A.M. Pitch perception for certain periodic auditory stimuli. *Journal of the Acoustical Society of America*, 1955, *27,* 132–137.

von Békésy, G. *Experiments in hearing* (E.G. Wever, Ed. and trans.). New York: McGraw-Hill, 1960.

Wever, E.G., & Lawrence, M. *Physiological acoustics*. Princeton, N.J.: Princeton University Press, 1954.

Wightman, F.L. Pitch and stimulus fine structure. *Journal of the Acoustical Society of America*, 1973, *54,* 397–406. (a)

Wightman, F.L. The pattern-transformation model of pitch. *Journal of the Acoustical Society of America*, 1973, *54,* 407–416. (b)

Wightman, F.L., & Green, D.M., The perception of pitch, *American Scientist*, 1974, *62,* 208–215.

8
Binaural Phenomena

INTRODUCTION

The phenomena covered in this chapter depend upon the fact that we have two ears. Auditory localization is the first topic considered. Our two ears located at opposite sides of the head allow us to determine fairly accurately the locus of sound sources in space. Originally, this ability probably contributed considerably to our survival as a species. It is still helpful when as pedestrians we use it to avoid motor vehicles. A second, less obvious, facet of our two-eared existence is that we can use the somewhat different information provided by our ears to attend selectively to particular sources. Thus, we can pick out one voice from another in a crowded room. Some of this ability arises from monaural cues such as frequency, timing, or syntax of the source, but the binaural capacity improves the range of situations in which voice communication is possible.

Few studies of auditory localization and selective attention have used natural acoustic environments. Rather, the bulk of our data comes from refined laboratory tests employing artificial stimuli. These data are generally more reliable than can be obtained in naturalistic environments. They are more reliable because fine stimulus control can be achieved and because a variety of contaminating variables can be avoided. Many of the generalizations obtained in the artificial situations will help isolate the cues used by the binaural system in realistic settings. In reviewing these laboratory studies, however, we should try to remember the differences between the highly controlled but artificial testing environment and the actual problem facing an individual in a naturalistic environment who tries to infer the location of a sound source or to attend to one source amidst other conflicting sources.

Earphones are often employed to study the cues used by subjects to localize sources. Earphones generally produce an auditory image that people describe as within or near the head. This exact locus of the image depends on the stimulus conditions. We call this a lateralized image, rather than a localized one. Studies of lateralization have contributed important information about binaural processing. They also provide much of our data on binaural selectivity. One can actually measure the amount of selectivity in terms of the amount of binaural masking in decibels. This area is called masking level difference and it has been extensively studied in recent years because it provides a controlled and precise paradigm in which to study selective attention. Localization, lateralization, and masking level differences, then, are the main topics of this chapter.

AUDITORY LOCALIZATION

The problem of auditory localization is the understanding of cues used to localize a sound source in space. Most presentations of this topic first discuss sinusoidal source and how two obvious cues, namely, interaural intensity and interaural time, influence judgments of localization. The reason for this approach is partly historical. During the period from about 1930 to 1940, a number of studies, basically physical in nature, investigated how those cues changed when sinusoidal sources of various frequencies were directed at the head from a variety of different positions in an anechoic (echo-free) environment. The impetus for these studies arose from the basic generalization stated first by Lord Rayleigh (1907) in the Sidgwick lecture given at Cambridge, England. He stated that sources of low-frequency sinusoids are localized on the basis of interaural temporal differences, while sources of high-frequency sinusoids are localized on the basis of interaural intensity differences. This is the so-called "duplex theory" of sound localization. All of our present empirical evidence supports this theory.

Before reviewing this evidence and theory in detail, however, it is important to consider the problem of localization in a real space when listening to naturalistic stimuli. First of all, in naturalistic situations, stimuli are rarely if ever sine waves. Most sounds are complex and often transient signals such as clicks or thumps. Frequently one is trying to localize a human speaker. Because the sounds are complex, there are sharp onsets and offsets. Even in the sustained, quasi-periodic portion of speech or music, many frequencies are often simultaneously present. Thus, the localization of an actual source in space may be based on a combination or interaction of different cues.

Another acoustic characteristic of natural environments is that they are generally not anechoic. Unless one is trying to localize a sound in the middle of a vacant field, echoes and reverberations will be produced by reflections of the pressure wave from objects or walls in the environment. These echoes make the problem of localizing the sound source very difficult. Even an open field generates appreciable reflection from the ground. If the acoustic environment is the inside of a room or an auditorium, then the problem becomes immeasurably more complex. The reflections from the walls, ceilings, and floors produce a number of successive wavefronts or echoes at the listener's ear. Although the echoes may occur at comparatively long delays and with amplitudes nearly equal to those of the original wavefront, the hearing mechanism suppresses most of these echoes. In fact, one usually does not perceive the echo as a separate and distinct sound unless the delay is extremely long, of the order of 500 msec or longer. The multiple reflections do, however, act as "phantom sources" located within the room. They increase the problem of locating the actual sound source, just as a room whose walls are covered with mirrors would hinder the location of a light source.

Additionally, in localizing real sound sources, the listener usually can move his head. This allows one to resolve initial ambiguities concerning the possible location of the source.

The laboratory research on sound localization has understandably sought to simplify the conditions of localization in order to isolate the different factors that can contribute to the final localization judgment. But these factors are potential cues. No matter how sensitive we are to slight changes in certain aspects of the stimulus, this sensitivity is no guarantee that the cue is utilized in the naturalistic environments. Exquisite sensitivity to interaural phase of a steady sinusoid may play little role in natural localization. These studies do provide information about the binaural process and delineate what is and is not a cue. But the preceding caveat should be recalled when one moves to the realm of application.

Localization of Sinusoidal Signals

Interaural time differences. The most careful and systematic experimental analysis of cues for localizing sustained sinusoidal signals comes from studies conducted in anechoic environments. The signals used are generated without audible onsets or offsets so that the subject can utilize only information in the sustained sine wave to localize the source. Physically, these cues are differences in amplitude and/or phase that may arise because the two ears are located at different places on the head. To a first approximation the two ears of the human subject can be treated as point receivers located on opposite sides of a uniform, solid sphere. A distance source therefore generates sound waves that may arrive at the two ears at different times because of the difference in pathlength from the source to each ear. A simple way of computing this difference appears in Figure 8.1, a diagram first presented by Woodworth (1938). The difference in length of the sound path is given by

$$\Delta d = r(\theta + \sin \theta), \tag{8.1}$$

where r is the radius of the circle (head) and θ is in radians. Since θ is a pure number, Δd has the same units as r. Assuming that the radius of the head is equal to 8.75 cm and the speed of sound is 34,000 cm/sec, the difference in time

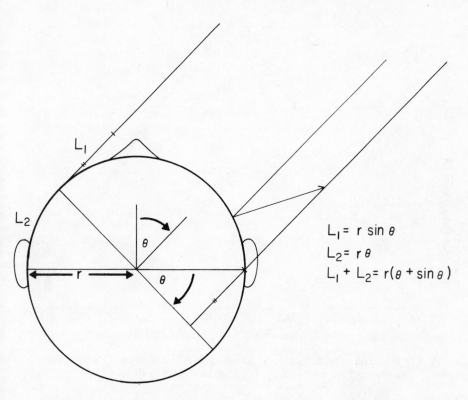

$$L_1 = r \sin \theta$$
$$L_2 = r \theta$$
$$L_1 + L_2 = r(\theta + \sin \theta)$$

FIG. 8.1 Path length difference ($L_1 + L_2$) between the two ears for a distance source at an azimuth θ. Reflections from the head will interact with the direct ray paths. One such interaction is illustrated on the right side of the drawing. (After Woodworth, 1938.)

to reach the two ears is given by

$$\Delta t = 257 \,(\theta + \sin \,\theta), \tag{8.2}$$

where Δt is in microseconds. Thus, if the source is straight ahead, $\theta = 0$, and there is no time difference between the two ears. If the source is at $90°$, $\theta = \pi/2$, and the difference in time is approximately 660 μsec. This formula is an approximation, since it neglects reflections from the head and neglects the interactions of these reflections with the wavefront proceeding directly to the two ears. (Note the interaction of the two sound paths illustrated near the right ear in Figure 8.1.) The reflected wave and the arriving wave will interact and cancellation or reinforcement may result. The resulting waveform may be phase shifted, which in turn would affect the time of arrival at the two ears. Thus, Eq. (8.2) is not equally valid at all frequencies. However, for transient signals, which contain all frequencies, it is a remarkably good approximation, as Figure 8.2 indicates.

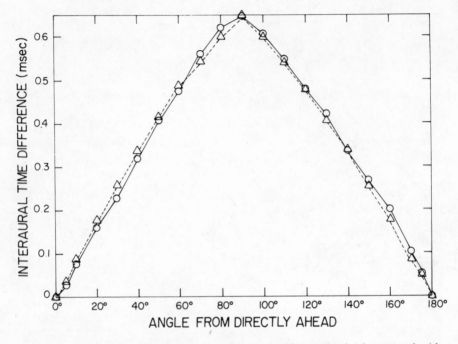

FIG. 8.2 Interaural time differences as measured on a human head (○) compared with Woodworth's formula (△), see Eq. (8.2). (From Feddersen *et al.*, 1957, p. 989.)

Interaural intensity differences. While the geometric argument presented above provides a simple and direct way of determining the interaural time differences for a distant source, there are also interaural differences in intensity. These intensity differences depend heavily on the frequency of the source. The amount of sound shadow produced by an object depends on the size of the object and the wavelength of the sinusoid. The head is roughly 16.5 cm in the widest dimension; 16.5 cm corresponds approximately with one wavelength at 2,000 Hz (∿34,000 cm/sec/16.5 cm). Above this frequency, the head is large compared with the wavelength of the sound and will therefore produce a noticeable sound shadow. At low frequencies, for example, 200 Hz, the head is small compared with the wavelength of sound and is therefore essentially transparent. No simple formula summarizes how the amount of sound shadow depends on frequency. Figure 8.3 presents some empirical data collected at different frequencies. Several aspects of these data should be noticed. First of all, as we might expect, the position of the source hardly affects interaural intensity differences at 200 Hz, where the head width, being only about one-tenth of a wavelength, plays little role. At 6,000 Hz, however, the extent of the sound shadow is sizable, about 20 dB difference at the two ears for a source

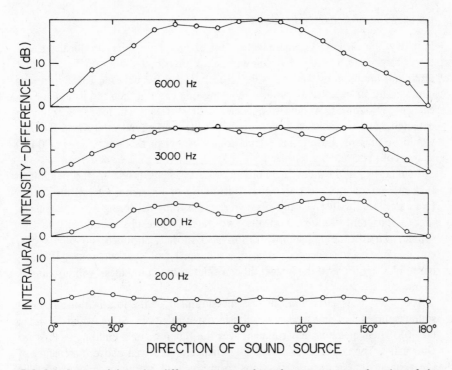

FIG. 8.3 Interaural intensity difference measured at the two ears as a function of the position of the sound source. At 200 Hz there is essentially no sound shadow, whereas at 6000 Hz it is nearly 20 dB when the source is located directly to the side. The lack of symmetry about 90° is caused by the pinna. (From Fedderson *et al.*, 1957, p. 989.)

located 90° to the side. Note that at high frequencies there is a marked asymmetry in the intensity difference at the two ears from a source that is located at 30° (slightly off line in front) as against 150° (slightly off line in back). These asymmetries depend upon the pinna, which also produces sound shadows that are frequency dependent.

A sustained sine wave in an echoless environment provides appreciable cues of interaural intensity and interaural differences that vary systematically with the position of the source. We should note one restriction on this generalization, namely, all the sounds have been generated by sources in the horizontal plane, which is roughly determined by the tip of the nose and the two ear canals. In a simplified model any sound source in the medial sagittal plane, which lies perpendicular to the line connecting the two ears and halfway between them, will produce no difference either in interaural time or intensity. This is because the head is essentially symmetric about the midline. Later we will consider the problem of localizing sounds in this medial sagittal plane.

Localization of Actual Sound Sources

Probably the earliest systematic statement of how pure tones are localized was Lord Rayleigh's (1907). His knowledge of physics led him to believe that interaural intensive differences were critical at high frequencies. This hypothesis could easily be checked by simply blocking one ear at a time and listening for a change in loudness. At low frequencies little difference in loudness could be detected, and his calculation indicated that little interaural intensity difference would be present. Despite his calculations it was clear that a very low ($\sim$90 Hz) source could be reliably localized.

Reluctantly, as he himself admits, Lord Rayleigh considered the possibility that the ear could detect the phase difference or interaural arrival time at the two ears.[1] He finally overcame his own skepticism by delivering two sinusoids of slightly different frequency to the two ears. As the phase between the two sources varied, the apparent location also moved, although, he points out, considerable care is needed to assure the purity of the two tones. If many harmonics are present, the image, though fluctuating in loudness, will not appear to move in space.

About 30 years later more precise measurement of the localization of actual sound sources was undertaken in classic experiments by Stevens and Newman (1936). Their anechoic environment was the flat roof of a building at Harvard University. The subject was seated in a chair elevated well above the surface of the roof so that acoustic reflections from the roof would be minimized. The measurements were made during the small hours of the morning to avoid the disturbance of external sources. The sound source the subject attempted to localize was positioned in a horizontal plane at 15° intervals about the subject. Sinusoidal signals of different frequency, as well as clicks and noise, served as stimuli. It soon became apparent that front-to-back reversals were common, especially for low-frequency sounds. If errors are calculated by discounting these front-to-back reversals, then the scores varied with frequency in a systematic way. The number of errors peaked around 3,000 Hz and declined at higher and lower frequencies. The usual explanation for these data is the duplex theory. Basically, the theory maintains that there are two separate processing systems. One process is effective at high frequencies, the other at low frequencies, and in

---

[1] Rayleigh was reluctant to admit that phase differences were perceptible because he agreed with Helmholtz's supposition that the ear was largely phase-deaf. As he points out, "... when we admit that phase differences at the two ears of tones in unison are easily recognized, we may be inclined to go further and find less difficulty in supposing that phase relations between a tone and its harmonics, presented to the same ear, are also recognized [*Scientific Papers of Lord Rayleigh*, Vol. V, p. 357, New York: Dover, 1964. P. 357]." This question, the phase perception of complex tones, is discussed more fully in Chapter 7.

the midfrequency range, at about 3,000 Hz where neither system is very effective, the errors are maximal.

The basic results of Stevens and Newman have been confirmed in more recent experiments, for example, those of Sandel, Teas, Federson, and Jeffress (1955). The later experiments used a second source, in this case a noise stimulus, which the subjects adjusted to the apparent location of the pure tone source. Error curves (inferred from the precision of the settings of the noise source) show maxima in the midfrequency range, about 1,500–3,000 Hz, and better localization at the extremely high or extremely low frequencies.

Mills (1958) measured the minimum *change* in the second source that the subject could reliably detect as a function of the initial position of the source. He called this measurement the minimum audible angle since it represents the minimum change in angle of the source that is reliably detectable. The subject listened in an anechoic chamber with his head restrained to prevent movements. Figure 8.4 shows the minimum audible angle as a function of frequency for different initial positions, that is, different initial azimuths of the source. As one

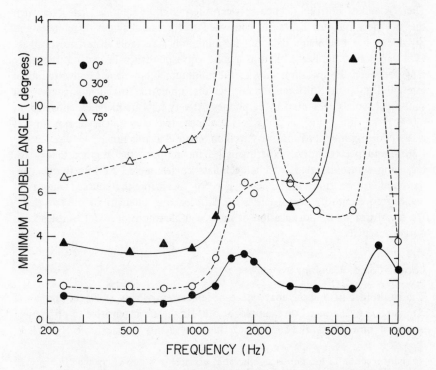

FIG. 8.4   The smallest change in the angle of a source that is just detectable as a function of frequency. The initial angle of the source is indicated in the key. (From Mills, 1972, p. 310.)

can see from the graph, the best discrimination of a change in the position of the source occurs when the source is straight ahead of the observer (0° azimuth). Although this is true at all frequencies, errors increase in the midfrequency range. At other initial azimuths, the discrimination of a change in the position of the source is harder and interacts strongly with signal frequency.

One argument for maintaining that temporal cues are responsible for the discrimination of low frequencies and intensity cues are responsible for the discrimination at high frequencies is the close correspondence between data obtained in an anechoic field and measurements of the discrimination of temporal and intensity cues made with earphones. Mills (1960) made a direct comparison between the minimum audible angle measurement and two psychophysical experiments employing earphones and sinusoidal stimuli. In the first earphone experiment, Zwislocki and Feldman (1956) measured the ability of subjects to discriminate a change in the phase of the stimulus at the two ears while holding the intensity of the two sine waves constant. In another earphone experiment, Mills (1960) measured the ability of subjects to discriminate a change in intensity at the two ears while holding the phase of the two sine waves constant. There is a close correspondence between the minimum audible angle data when the free-field measurements are converted to interaural phase differences and Zwislocki and Feldman's data on the minimum detectable difference in phase with earphones. Similarly, there is a good correspondence in the midfrequency range between the measurements of the minimum audible angle converted to an interaural intensity difference and the discrimination of such a change for sinusoidal signals presented by earphones. At very high frequencies, above about 6,000 Hz, a discrepancy appears between these two curves. The reason for this lack of correspondence is not very well understood at this time.

In summary, extensive experimental data support the duplex theory for localizing sinusoidal signals in an echoless environment. At low frequencies, temporal information is the major cue for localizing the source, whereas at higher frequencies the major cue is the difference in intensity at the two ears.[2] We next turn to the localization of more complex nonsinusoidal transient and noiselike signals.

Localization of Transient Signals

The sinusoidal data show that one can detect remarkably small differences in interaural arrival time. For example, at 500 Hz the ear is sensitive to differences in arrival time of about 15–20 μsec. This same acuity is evident for two clicks

---

[2] The perception of location is an interesting example of a case where the differences in discriminative processes are not apparent to introspection. The acoustic source is simply out there. No subjects report that the process or content of their percepts of location depend on the frequency of the source.

presented via earphones and separated in time by some short interval. Depending upon the frequency composition of the click, the threshold for interaural time disparity in this situation is of the order of 20–30 μsec, although well-trained subjects can go as low as 10 μsec. Again, performance depends on the frequency content of the signals. If the clicks are filtered to contain only energy at frequencies below about 1,000 Hz, interaural temporal disparities of approximately 20–30 μsec can be detected. If this low-frequency information is excluded by high-bandpass filtering the click, then greater interaural temporal disparity is needed to detect the difference in onset time. If the click is filtered to contain only frequencies above about 4,000 Hz, approximately 100–200 μsec are needed to reliably detect an interaural time difference (Yost, Wightman, & Green, 1971). This result is surprising, especially in view of the temporal waveforms generated by these clicks. High-frequency filtering of the clicks produces very brief spikes. Thus, the total duration of the signal is very short. Low-frequency filtering of the click produces a long transient response. The waveform resembles a damped sinusoidal vibration with a frequency equal to the cutoff frequency of the filter. Thus, if the low-pass filter is 500 Hz the signal lasts at least 2,000 μsec. Despite long total duration, an interaural difference of 20–30 μsec can be detected. With high-pass filtering, for example, above 5,000 Hz, the signal duration may last only 200 μsec. Yet the interaural temporal difference must be about as long as the total signal duration to be detectable.

Headphone Data

Headphones can be used in discrimination experiments without making any assumptions about the basis of the discrimination. Consider the experiment just discussed, namely, two clicks with some interarrival time, Δt. If the leading click is randomly assigned the left or right earphone and the subject can reliably report which was leading, then clearly the discrimination can be made at that value of Δt. One may report that the sound image appears to be located near the leading ear, but the report is independent, and may even be irrelevant to the discriminatory behavior. But headphones do produce a phenomenal impression of an image close to one or the other ear or centered in the head. As parameters of the signals are changed the source may move and be located slightly left of center or about halfway between center and the left ear, but such judgments are difficult and precise representations are obviously difficult. Von Békésy (1960) had the subject draw a mark on a schematic view of the top of the skull, a circle with two ears, the nose, and so on such as in Figure 8.1. Such judgments can be made, but the precision is not very great. In any case, the precision is not as good as pointing to an external source in a free field. We generally call judgments of position made with earphones *lateralization* rather than *localization* judgments.

OPPOSING CUES—TRANSIENT
VERSUS STEADY-STATE CUES

The advantage to be gained from the use of the lateralized image is that one can use it to achieve null adjustment. For example, we can pit a difference in interaural transient disparity with an ongoing disparity of the opposite direction. We can then ask the subject to adjust one of the disparities so as to bring the sound image back to zero (that is, the center of the head). Tobias and Schubert (1959) used noise as a stimulus and gated the noise in one earphone to start slightly ahead of that presented in the other earphone. The difference in onset time was one of the disparities. It was varied from 0 to 400 μsec. In addition, the noise waveform was passed through a delay line so that the fine structure of the noise also arrived at the two ears with a temporal disparity. The latter disparity was in the opposite direction to the onset disparity and could be varied systematically by the subject in an attempt to achieve a noise burst that appeared centered. Various noise burst durations ranging from 10 msec to 1,000 msec were used. As the noise bursts became shorter, more fine structure disparity was necessary to balance the onset disparity. As the noise duration increased, for example, to 1 sec, then the onset disparity had comparatively little effect on the centering judgment and essentially no trade-off occurred between the two conflicting cues.

We should again emphasize that this experiment was conducted using ear-phones and that the task of the subject was to center the subjective image by adjusting two conflicting cues. Such judgments are difficult to make and may reflect quite different processes from those used in a natural environment. In fact, when we consider the perception of actual sound sources in real space our general conclusion will be that onset information is far more important than the steady-state information. No one, however, has conducted an experiment ex-actly analogous to that of Tobias and Schubert in a natural environment using noise as the stimulus.

Time—Intensity Trade

The evidence that time and intensity differences are the principal interaural cues to location, and the use of earphones whereby each cue could be independently manipulated led inevitably to experiments in which these cues were placed in opposition. In this situation sound arrives earlier at one ear while in the opposite ear the same sound is more intense. Numerous experiments have used some combination of these conditions and several experimental techniques have been employed to assess the trade between time and intensity. In some experiments, the position of the lateralized image was indicated on a schematic drawing. In other experiments a second indicator, such as noise, was time-delayed in one ear by the observer until the indicator lay in the same position as the test image.

Many experiments used a "centering" technique in which one parameter of the interaural difference, such as interaural intensity, ΔI, was held fixed and the subject adjusted the other parameter, in this case interaural time, Δt, to bring the auditory image to the center of the head. Ambiguity concerning the exact location of "center" can be reduced by reversing the inputs to the two earphones. If the auditory image does not move when the inputs are interchanged, then center has been achieved. These experiments led to a value for the ratio, the interaural time, (Δt), needed to offset a given difference in intensity, ΔI. It is often called the time–intensity trading ratio.

In an early parametric study Harris (1960) used a click filtered to restrict the signal energy to a relatively narrow frequency region. He then measured the time–intensity trading ratio at several different center frequencies of his filter. His data clearly indicated that the time–intensity trading ratio $(\Delta t / \Delta I)$ depended on the frequency region of the transient signal. At low frequencies below about 1,500 Hz, a relatively small change in interaural arrival time offset a difference in intensity of a few decibels. At higher frequencies the ratio was much greater. The exact value of the trading ratio depended on a variety of circumstances, an important one being the overall level of the two signals. The value of the trading ratio was also quite variable from one subject to the next, but typical values from Harris' study were 25 μsec/dB in the low-frequency region to 90 μsec/dB at the higher frequencies.

Rather than review the many parameters studied with this experimental paradigm, let us consider the theoretical ideas behind these experiments. Why has the time–intensity trading ratio been so frequently studied? The basic motivation has been the possibility that only one cue system actually operates in binaural judgments of localization. The single mechanism might, for example, be a time-of-arrival comparator. If this were the case, how would intensity difference influence judgments of localization? Intensity could alter the latencies of neural response and hence within the binaural system interaural intensity differences would become interaural time differences. Figure 8.5 shows the simplest form of this idea. We assume a fixed threshold neural element triggered on an upward swing of the basilar membrane. The threshold value of the fiber is indicated along the ordinate. If the intensities are unequal in the two ears, then the fibers associated with the more intense side would fire earlier and create a net time of arrival difference in the binaural system. The difference in arrival time could be offset by starting one waveform slightly before the other, thus achieving a situation where the threshold is reached in each ear at the same instant (right side of figure). This simple scheme obviously generates strong predictions concerning other variables in the situation. For example, if the threshold level is fixed, then raising the intensity of both signals by several orders of magnitude should materially reduce the size of the time–intensity trading ratio. In fact, if the initial threshold is near the origin, as indicated in the figure, then raising the intensity in both ears by a factor of ten should decrease the trading ratio by nearly the same amount.

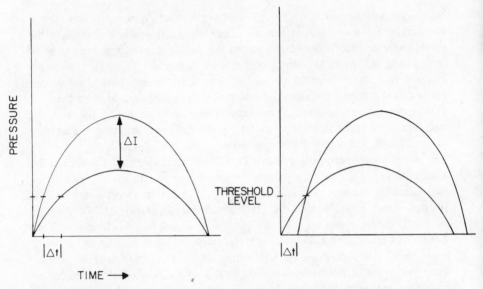

FIG. 8.5 A time–intensity trade arising from a fixed threshold device. To the left, a difference in amplitude causes a difference in the time at which the threshold is crossed. At the right the more intense signal has been delayed by Δt to compensate for the difference in intensity.

One does not need to think of intensity directly affecting latency. An alternate theory is that more intense signals simply produce shorter latencies at some central comparator. The mechanism would involve stronger signals increasing the rate of bombardment of some synaptic junction. The synapse is crossed if enough impulses arrive within a certain time. Thus, intense sounds would increase the probability that the neural message will be passed on to the next stage. If many messages are sent repetitively, then increasing the probability decreases the delay. This idea predicts a time–intensity trade, but the exact form of the relationship is not specified except that more intense signals generate shorter latencies.

These theories in their simplest forms would predict that several combinations of interaural time and interaural intensity exist that should be indistinguishable. If only one mechanism is operating then a null stimulus ($\Delta t = 0$, $\Delta I = 0$) should be indistinguishable from one caused by balancing some interaural time difference by some interaural intensity difference. Early studies by Whitworth and Jeffress (1961) and then by Hafter and Jeffress (1968) suggested that this was not the case. If interaural time or intensity differences were introduced, two images seemed to be present. The subject could listen to either or both images depending on the degree of training and skill he had acquired at this task.

One of the more convincing demonstrations of this ability to distinguish among lateral images is the experiment by Hafter and Carrier (1972). They used a 100-msec burst of a 500-Hz sine wave and systematically compared (Δt, ΔI)

pairs with a null stimulus. The subjects were asked to discriminate a stimulus having a particular $(\Delta t, \Delta I)$ value from the null stimulus. For a particular value of interaural time delay, Δt, the percentage of correct discriminations showed a minimum as ΔI varied. This indicated that a particular $(\Delta t \; \Delta I)$ pair was the most difficult to discriminate from the null stimulus. This minimum, however, did not necessarily reach the chance level. In fact, as Δt increased, the minima moved further and further from chance. The existence of a minimum clearly indicates that some values of $(\Delta t, \Delta I)$ resemble the null stimulus more than others. The fact that the most similar values are not indistinguishable means that other aspects of the stimulus are detectable from the null condition. Thus, the simple time–intensity trade models described previously appear to be oversimplifications of the actual process. This conclusion would be much stronger were it not for a recent study by Babkoff, Sutton, and Barris (1973). They essentially repeated Hafter and Carrier's study but used a wideband click stimulus in a three-alternative test: two null conditions and one pair with opposing time–intensity parameters $(\Delta t, \Delta I)$. They also found the discrimination function showed a minimum at one particular pairing of opposing cues. But for their conditions, if ΔI were less than 7 dB the minima actually equalled 33% or the chance level. Unlike Hafter and Carrier they found that their subjects could not distinguish between the null condition and the best Δt, ΔI paring. It seems particularly confusing that Babkoff and his colleagues could achieve perfect cancellation with a broadband stimulus. One might have expected a priori that a narrowband stimulus such as that used by Hafter and Carrier would make complete cancellation easier to achieve.

On a more general level the idea of a single cue system is difficult to defend. Consider the processes involved in localizing a sinusoid. Subjects *can* localize sinusoids at very high frequencies and they appear to do so on the basis of difference in intensity. Timing information is simply not present in the nervous system at very high frequencies. Even if it was, it would be unreliable as a localization cue at high frequencies because the periods, such as 200 μsec (5,000 Hz), are small compared with the headwidth delay (660 μsec). Thus, the waveform can be delayed several periods before the sound reaches the more distant ear and an ambiguous lead or lag occurs. A single cue system such as that described in the timing model must ignore the data on the localization of sinusoidal signals. While intensity can affect latency (as dozens of studies attest), it seems an extreme and dubious position to this author to maintain that a theory based on only one system can handle all of the known facts about binaural localization and lateralization.

Localization in the Medial Sagittal Plane

We have restricted our discussion of localization to sources located in the horizontal plane. Experiments have concentrated on this plane because localization is most precise there. An orthogonal plane can be investigated—the medial sagittal plane—which is midway between the two ears and perpendicular to the line connecting the two ear canals. It runs directly in front of the observer's nose, over the top of his head, and to the back of his head. Because of the head's bilateral symmetry, sound sources in this plane arrive at the two ears with very small interaural phase differences. In fact, insofar as the head is exactly symmetric, the waveforms at the two ears are identical. Nevertheless, localization judgments can be made in the medial plane, although not with the accuracy associated with the horizontal plane ($\pm5°$ as opposed to $\pm1°$). Since the waveforms at the two ears are virtually identical, judgments of localization in the medial plane must be based on monaural cues. These monaural cues are changes in the spectrum of wideband stimuli, that is, changes in intensity as a function of frequency.

The spectrum of a wideband sound changes with its location in the medial plane due to interaction of the sound with the pinna, that peculiar convolution of tissue outside the ear canal. Some animals, such as horses and cats, can move the pinna to point at the apparent location of the sound. Man largely lacks this ability, but the shape of the pinna provides some acoustic filtering of the sound. This provides cues for locating a source. One of the most interesting speculations concerning the role of the pinna is that of Batteau (1967). He suggests the pinna introduces various delay paths that transform the incoming signal. The amount of the delay determines the spectral change made in the sound.

Roffler and Butler (1968) have investigated this general hypothesis by studying how the spectrum of a noise influences the observer's ability to localize in the medial plane. They found that localization was best when the sound contained high-frequency information, for example, frequencies 8,000 Hz and higher. Gardner and Gardner (1973) performed a series of tests in which they progressively modified the pinna by occluding it with wax moldings. In one of their conditions they occluded everything except the opening to the external ear canal. Error scores were then very large—in fact, little better than chance. As they progressively occluded less and less of the pinna, the error scores diminished rapidly. With the unoccluded pinna, the subjects could correctly localize with about 90% accuracy one of nine speakers located in front of the observer and spaced 4.5° apart. Gardner and Gardner also confirmed Roffler and Butler's finding that the high-frequency portion of the noise signal was the crucial part of the spectrum. For example, if the source was an approximately one-tenth octave band of noise centered at 2,000 Hz, localization was seldom better than about 25% correct. Gardner and Gardner also demonstrated that sources directly behind the subject but still in the medial plane were harder to localize than those situated directly in front of the subject.

In summary, on the basis of changes in the spectrum brought about by acoustic filtering of the pinna, the ear apparently can compute the approximate location of a signal in the medial plane even when the waveforms are nearly identical at the two ears.

Localization in Nonanechoic Environments:
The Precedence Effect

One can exploit cues such as interaural arrival time or interaural amplitude differences in localizing sine waves or transient signals in anechoic chambers. The use of such cues in natural environments is far more complex. The essential problem is that of echoes. For example, if one listens to a source in a room with ordinary plaster walls, approximately 80–90% of the energy of the acoustic wave will be reflected by the walls and arrive at the ear as an echo. The reflections are not even single in number; a wave bouncing off the wall will strike other walls in the room, losing only about 10–20% of its energy with each reflection. Thus a multiplicity of such echoes and reverberations occurs. This is especially true if the dimensions of the room are small, for then little energy loss occurs because of the inverse square law. The problem is analogous to standing in a room with mirrors on all sides. A candle is illuminated and one is asked to indicate the location of the candle. Because of multiple reflections from the mirrors, the candle may appear to be in many different places.

The preceding description of acoustic echo is physically accurate but certainly does not agree with our experience. Our usual acoustic environments do not appear filled with echoes. Admittedly, the quality of the sound is somewhat different out of doors or in an anechoic chamber compared to a lecture room. One reason we are relatively insensitive to echoes is that they arrive at the ear appreciably later in time than does the first wavefront. Sound travels about a meter in 3 msec, so the echo from a wall 1 m behind a subject arrives about 6 msec later than the original wavefront. The original wavefront strikes the subject's ear, travels the meter to the wall, and returns as an echo about 6 msec later. The analogy with the mirrored room is faulty because the speed of sound is exceedingly slow compared with the speed of light. If the auditory system could suppress the later arriving echoes, one very difficult problem of localization would be largely solved. To some degree the auditory system seems to do this. The general name given to suppression of echoes is the precedence effect, which simply indicates that the preceding or first waveform is much more important in localizing the source than later or echo waveforms. Thus, in an environment with prominent echoes, which occurs anywhere that walls are not good sound absorbers, the first waveform contains the only veridical information concerning the locus of the source. The later wavefronts generally give a false impression of location because they originate from objects that have reflected the first wavefront.

This argument indicates that there are really two processes in localizing a source in a reverberant room. One is echo suppression, the other is maximally weighting the earliest arriving information. Since the acoustic environment will not even appear stable unless echoes are suppressed, we discuss it first.

Precedence Effect: Echo Suppression

The occurrence of echo suppression is easily observed. We seldom hear echoes in normal-sized rooms, although the time between the first waveform generated by a brief click and its succeeding reverberations may be 20 or 30 msec. Echoes are usually heard only at much, much longer durations—500 to 1,000 msec. At these long durations, the reflecting wall must be a distance of 500 feet or more. The echoes *are* noticeable and are a source of either great amusement or distress! Failure to notice echoes when the delay between the initial and reflected sounds is a few tens of milliseconds is not due to poor auditory acuity. Consider the following experiment, which can be carried out with earphones. Two pulses or clicks are presented in succession, separated by about 10 msec. Virtually all subjects report two distinct sounds. One must separate the clicks by less than 2 msec to make them sound qualitatively similar to a single click. Thus these data imply we should hear echoes if we are standing about a meter from a wall and we clap our hands to make a transient signal. (The echo will arrive about 6 msec later.) Yet no one would claim to hear an echo in such a situation. In the realistic case, the amplitude of the echo is somewhat attenuated (1 or 2 dB) from the initial waveform. But this is not the crucial difference: attenuating the second click in the earphone presentation by an appropriate amount leaves it still noticeable and distinct, even at delays of 5–10 msec. In fact, one can attenuate the second click by nearly 20 dB before it becomes unnoticed. This would correspond to a wall with nearly 99% energy absorption.

A more systematic series of observations the reader can make on the suppression of echoes requires an audio system employing two loudspeakers. The bane of two speaker systems is that stereo listening is enjoyable only in a relatively restricted region along the midline between the two speakers. This fact makes it easy to demonstrate the following (monaural listening can be used, since our binaural condition has essentially no relevance here). First, turn the program material to monaural, so that the same sound originates from both speakers. You will notice that in a relatively narrow region directly on the midline between the two speakers you are conscious of the sound emanating from both loudspeakers simultaneously. If you move a little to the left or right of the spot between the two speakers, only one of the speakers appears to be broadcasting. One simply cannot be sure that the far speaker is even active. If possible, have a friend disconnect the far speaker, and you will immediately notice a change in the quality of the sound. If asked to localize this sound source, however, even when both speakers are operative, you will observe that the near speaker generally sounds like the entire source of the program material. Moving off the midline by only a few feet can cause the source to jump to the near speaker. Since sound travels about a meter in 3 msec, the far speaker is delayed by only a few milliseconds as you move 1 m toward the nearer speaker. The difference in intensity of the sound reaching the two ears is the ratio of the square of the distances between the two speakers. If the two distances are 4 and 5 m, then the ratio of intensity is only 2 or 3 dB. Despite this relatively slight difference in intensity and relatively small temporal delay, the far speaker is largely suppressed as the apparent locus of the source material. Again, we must emphasize that suppression only affects localization. The second speaker is not inaudible, since its removal changes the quality of the sound. The second speaker gives the near speaker a fuller, more expansive quality. But for localization, these observations convince us that the auditory system tends to suppress later arriving echoes and attends mainly to the first wavefront.

Precedence Effect: Localization

General consideration of echoes in a natural environment shows that only the first wavefront indicates the true source location. The cues associated with the second and third reflections do not necessarily point to the sound source, because the arrival at the ear depends on a variety of other objects in the field. Thus it should be possible to demonstrate that the cues associated with the first wavefront get more weight in judgments of localization than the cues associated with the later echoes. A classic experiment performed by Wallach, Newman, and Rosenzweig (1949) showed this fact.

First recall that two clicks presented in brief succession within an interval of about 2 msec will be heard as one single transient sound. In the Wallach, Newman, and Rosenzweig experiment, the temporal onset disparity of a pair of clicks to one ear was fixed and the temporal onset disparity of a second similar pair presented to the other ear was varied in order to achieve a centered image. The temporal waveforms used in these experiments are shown in Figure 8.6. As the time-line drawings show, the first two clicks to arrive should appear to the left, since the onset of the initial click in the left ear slightly precedes the onset of the initial click in the right ear. The second pair of clicks is, however, arranged in the opposite order. The onset of the final click in the right ear precedes the onset of the final click in the left ear. Because the total duration of all clicks is 2 msec, the ear hears a single transient. By fixing the first disparity, Δt_1, and varying Δt_2 to achieve a centered image, one can estimate the relative importance of these two conflicting sources of information. The first pair of clicks obviously points left, the second pair of clicks points right. When the image is centered, the ratio of the two Δts tells the relative importance of the two temporal cues. In the Wallach *et al.* (1949) experiment, the value of this ratio was typically between 6 and 10, so an initial disparity of 30 μsec in the leading pair needed a balance of almost 200 μsec in the second pair in order to center the image. Note that a necessary condition of this experiment is that the two

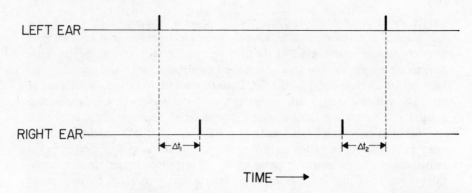

LEFT EAR

RIGHT EAR

$\leftarrow \Delta t_1 \rightarrow$ $\leftarrow \Delta t_2 \rightarrow$

TIME $\longrightarrow$

FIG. 8.6 Stimulus conditions in the precedence experiment. Two clicks are presented within a brief interval to both ears. The first click to the left ear arrives Δt_1 before the first click to the right ear. The second click to the right ear arrives Δt_2 before the second click to the left ear. The subject hears a single sound, and by adjusting Δt_2, can "center" the image, thus offsetting Δt_1.

pairs of clicks must fuse to form a single image. If we waited 10 or 20 msec between the pairs of clicks, then they would sound like two distinct pairs, the first pair located to the left and the second located to the right.

This concludes our discussion of localization. We turn now to binaural selectivity—the ability to attend to one source in the middle of other competing sources. The most precise paradigm for the study of this phenomenon is the masking level difference.

DETECTING OR RECOGNIZING SIGNALS
IN A BACKGROUND NOISE:
THE MASKING LEVEL DIFFERENCE

The importance of two ears in localizing the position of a sound source is obvious. The most important physical variables that influence this ability were discussed in the previous section. What is equally obvious, especially when one ear is not properly functioning, is that two ears permit selective attention to certain parts of auditory space and thus ameliorate the masking effects of distracting noises. The most common example of this selectivity is conversing with another person at a crowded party. Many different processes undoubtedly operate in selectively attending to one voice and ignoring others. Some of these factors are much more complex than the sensory ones. They include the redundancy of the conversation, the ability to recognize certain qualitative features of the speaker's voice, and long- and short-term memory. But some of these selective processes are entirely sensory and could not operate if we had but one ear instead of two. The systematic study of these processes started comparatively recently and became a very popular topic of research in the past several years. The original studies date from about 1945.

J.C.R. Licklider at the Psychoacoustic Laboratory at Harvard was attempting to improve voice communication over headphone systems used by pilots in aircraft. The problem was twofold. First, the quality of the voice communication was not the best. Second, the communication was occurring in a very noisy environment. Licklider (1948) found a simple way to improve the pilot's ability to receive and understand messages in the midst of this noise. He merely reversed the wires leading to one earphone. This reverses the phase of the signal in the two ears. Thus if one earphone diaphragm moves outward causing a rarefraction wave at one ear, then the diaphragm on the opposite earphone moves inward causing a condensation wave at the other ear. The efficacy of this procedure rests on the fact that the masking noise is largely external to the earphones and produces waveforms in the same relative phase at the two ears, independent of the polarity of the earphone connections. This improvement in the reception of signals when noise and signal are in different phase relations at the two ears has been called the *masking level difference* (MLD). The name is hardly apt because many procedures improve the detectability of signals. Specifying this particular binaural phenomenon by such a general name leads to confusion, both theoretical and empirical. For this reason, the term "binaural masking level difference" is frequently used, but the improvement is only slight. Elsewhere we (Green & Yost, 1976) have suggested the term "binaural analysis." Whether this term will gain acceptance is still uncertain, and so we will retain the more traditional terminology.

About the same time as Licklider's discovery, Hirsh (1948 a,b), started a systematic exploration of the phenomenon at the same laboratory. He used a sinusoid as the signal rather than speech. This allowed him to precisely control the frequency content of the signal. As we saw previously, the signal frequency is an extremely important variable in binaural effects. Let us turn to Hirsh's experiments.

Basic Paradigm

Since the effect is basically an improvement in the detectability or recognizability of some signal, we must first start with a monaural condition or one in which no binaural cues are available. Monaural listening is awkward experimentally because absolute quiet is necessary to avoid distracting the subject via the unmasked ear. Therefore, a binaural listening task, as illustrated in the top part of Figure 8.7, is often used. Both the noise, which is the masking waveform, and the signal—a low-frequency sinusoid—are identical in the two ears. The subject adjusts the signal level so that it is just barely detectable. The frown on the listener's face in the figure indicates this state of affairs. Next we turn the signal off in one ear as illustrated in the bottom part of the figure. Now we have a

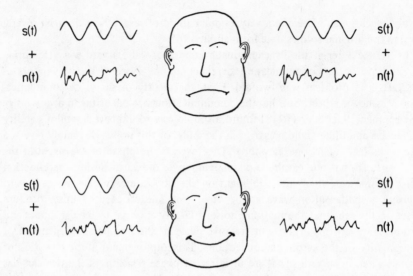

FIG. 8.7 The basic conditions of the masking level difference experiment. (a) Both noise and signal are presented in phase at the two ears. The frown on the subject's face indicates the signal is inaudible. (b) The signal to the left ear has been removed. Removing the signal from one ear has made it audible in the noise, as the smile indicates.

binaural situation where the waveforms are different in the two ears. The smile on the observer's face shows that the signal is now plainly evident. In fact, the improvement in detectability amounts to about 10 dB in this situation.

Given this improvement in detectability, questions immediately arise concerning other configurations of the noise and signal at the two ears. To answer some of these questions efficiently we need some notation to indicate various interaural configurations. We can then quickly summarize what is known about these various conditions. The conventional notation uses a subscript to denote the interaural condition. The subscript m means monaural, o denotes the same input to the two ears, and u means the noise or masker is uncorrelated at the two ears, that is, one ear listens to one noise source and the other listens to a different, uncorrelated noise source. The various conditions that we will consider and the binaural experience associated with these conditions are:

S_o: Signal presented to both ears with no interaural differences (lateralized image in center of head).

N_o: Noise presented to both ears with no interaural differences (lateralized image in center of head).

S_m: Signal presented to only one ear, no signal presented at the other ear (sound image at one ear).

N_m: Noise presented to only one ear, no noise presented at the other ear (sound image at one ear).

S_π: Signal presented to both ears but the waveform inverted at one of the ears (sound image at both ears or on a thin line from center toward both ears—distinctly different from S_o).

For a sinusoid this amounts to $180°$ phase delay between the two ears.

N_π: Noise presented to both ears but inverted at one of the ears, that is, if $n(t)$ presented to the right ear then $-n(t)$ presented at the other (sound image at both ears definitely different from N_o).

N_u: Noise uncorrelated at the two ears (sound image in center of head but very diffuse compared with N_o).

The above conditions are not exhaustive but summarize what can be achieved with minimal equipment. If one measures the threshold of a low-frequency sinusoidal signal, say 500 Hz, of brief duration, say 100 msec, in noise $N_o > 10$ dB SPL for all of the combinations listed above, then the following facts emerge:

First, the signal is never harder to hear than in the situation illustrated at the top of Figure 8.7, the N_oS_o condition. Let us denote that condition as our zero (0 dB) reference since all other conditions improve or do not alter the detectability of the signal. As long as the noise is about 20 dB over absolute threshold, then N_mS_m and N_uS_m both yield the same signal detectability as our base condition, namely, N_oS_o.

In all of these conditions, N_oS_o, N_mS_m, and N_uS_m, the only discrepancy between waveforms at the two ears is the N_u condition, where the noise is unrelated. This is a reasonable and comforting result, because it means that the crucial element is whether the information present at the two ears is similar or different.

There is one important exception to this summary. If the external noise level is very low, then listening with two ears is better than listening with one. Also, S_π is somewhat more detectable than S_o if no external noise is used. This result presumably arises because internal noise such as breathing, heartbeat, or spontaneous neural activity limits the detectability of the signal. This noise is partially uncorrelated at the two ears (Diercks & Jeffress, 1962; McFadden, 1968).

How do the various other combinations of interaural signal and noise conditions rank in detectability as compared with the reference S_oN_o? Table 8.1 gives our best summary of the many results.

The two missing conditions, S_oN_m and $S_\pi N_m$, are not usually included in a discussion of binaural masking level differences. Unless the noise in the one ear is extremely loud, the signal's detectability in the other ear with no noise hardly differs from its detectability in quiet. In effect one can simply turn off one ear and listen with the ear where the signal-to-noise ratio is best.

Several other remarks should be made about the pattern of results. The difference between N_uS_π and N_uS_o may or may not be real. Both conditions yield some binaural improvement which is somewhat greater than one might

TABLE 8.1

Interaural condition	Relative improvement (in dB, ± .5 dB)
$N_oS_o, N_mS_m, N_uS_m, S_\pi N_\pi$	0
N_uS_π	3
N_uS_o	4
$N_\pi S_m$	6
N_oS_m	9
$N_\pi S_o$	13
N_oS_π	15

expect from simple statistical facilitation. The difference between $N_\pi S_m$ and N_oS_m, or between $N_\pi S_o$ and N_oS_π is undoubtedly real. A number of studies confirmed these differences. The binaural system benefits more from a situation where the noise is the same at both ears, N_o, and the signal antiphasic, than from an unnatural situation such as N_π. There is no situation without headphones where the waveform of a broadband masker, such as noise, is exactly inverted at the opposite ear. Any delay caused by a difference in path length will shift the phase at some frequencies more than others. The N_π condition, however, implies all frequencies are inverted.

Effects of Signal Parameter

In this section and the next we will briefly review some of the signal and noise parameters that affect the size of the binaural masking level difference. We focus on only the most important and thoroughly studied parameters to provide empirical background for theoretical accounts of the phenomenon, which close the chapter.

Signal frequency. The first parameter of the signal to receive careful experimental scrutiny was frequency. In his first study of the masking level difference, Hirsh (1948a) systematically varied the frequency of the signal and found what everyone since has confirmed: the binaural effect decreases as the signal frequency is increased. If the size of the MLD is computed by comparing N_oS_o with N_oS_π, the effect is about 15 dB at low frequencies, decreases to about 6 dB at 1,000 Hz, and reaches a final asymtotic value of about 3 dB at approximately 1,500 Hz. Even above 1,500 Hz the value stays at about 3 dB, a fact now confirmed by half a dozen investigators. The general decrease in the size of effect with frequency is very reminiscent of the apparent loss of the timing cue in the localization of low-frequency sinusoids or the effects of high-pass filtering on the localization of transient signals. It points strongly to the importance of timing information from the two ears. At low frequencies the earlier data also indicated a decrease in the size of the MLD. Later, more carefully controlled studies suggested that in a sufficiently high noise level the MLD remained at about 15 dB, even at signal frequencies as low as 150 Hz (Dolan, 1968).

Signal phase. The other obvious parameter of the signal is the interaural phase. Consider a situation in which the noise is in phase at the two ears, N_0. As we change from S_0 to S_π we are changing the signal phase by 180°. But what of the intermediate values? Again, Hirsh investigated this variable in his earliest study. Jeffress and his collaborators studied this variable later with considerable care at a number of frequencies. The function relating the effects of signal phase is illustrated in Figure 8.8 (Colburn & Durlach, 1965; Jeffress, Blodgett, & Deatherage, 1952, 1962).

Signal duration. Finally, we might briefly mention the effects of signal duration. To a good first approximation, it seems to matter little. The exception is when the signal duration is less than 10 msec, and here, surprisingly, the binaural effects are somewhat larger, although by only a decibel or so (Blodgett, Jeffress, & Taylor, 1958; Green, 1966; McFadden & Pulliam, 1971).

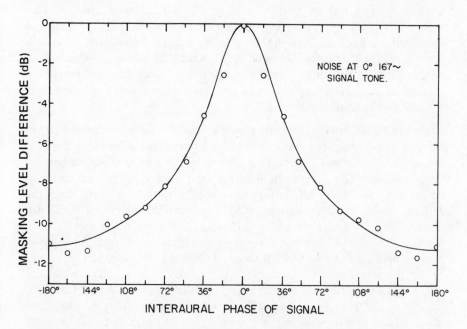

FIG. 8.8 Size of the masking level difference as a function of interaural phase of the 167-Hz signal. The noise is in phase at the two ears. At 0°, the condition is S_0N_0, while at ± 180° the condition is $S_\pi N_0$. (From Jeffress *et al.*, 1962, p. 1124.)

Effects of Noise Parameters

Noise level. As we pointed out earlier in describing results with low-frequency sinusoids, the overall noise level affects the size of the masking level difference. Generally, larger binaural effects occur when the external noise is larger. This is because the internal noise is only partially correlated. The uncorrelated part decreases the correlation in the effective stimulus at the two ears. A large external noise overrides the effects of uncorrelated internal noise. In fact, some systematic measurements of the interaural correlation of the noise at the two ears have been made using three noise sources. One source is led to both ears. Two other independent sources are added in differing amounts to the common source to vary the correlation. The size of the MLD changes consistently with interaural correlation (Robinson & Jeffress, 1963). Wilbanks and Whitmore (1968) have studied the effects at a variety of frequencies. They present a simple equation that fits all data points and requires only one (frequency-dependent) parameter.

In addition to the overall level, we can systematically vary the noise level in the nonsignal ear in a $S_m N_o$ condition. What relative level of noise produces the largest binaural effect? As one might expect, the best detection occurs when the levels in the two ears are equal. A number of studies, however, have demonstrated that sizable binaural effects occur even when the noise in the nonsignal ear differs by ± 10 dB from the noise in the signal ear (Blodgett, Jeffress, & Whitworth, 1962; Dolan & Robinson, 1967; Egan, 1965; Hirsh, 1948a; McFadden, 1968; Weston & Miller, 1965). For differences greater than this amount the binaural advantage gradually diminishes, but some effect is noted when the noise is barely audible in the nonsignal ear.

Interaural time delay. If a noise source is moved from a location directly in front of an observer to one side or the other, then a time delay occurs between the waveforms reaching the two ears. This delay can also be interpreted at any single frequency as a phase shift. Since the velocity of sound is the same for all frequencies, the phase shift is proportional to frequency. An early study by Jeffress, Blodgett, and Deatherage (1952) concerned the effect of a time delay of the noise on the masking-level difference. The signal was a 500-Hz tone. Starting with an $S_o N_o$ condition, the noise was gradually delayed. An improvement in detection of about 10 dB occurred when the noise was delayed 1 msec, or half the period of the 500-Hz signal. As the delay increased, the detectability of the signal decreased and reached a level essentially equal to the original $S_o N_o$ condition. Continuing the delay still further, the detectability of the signal improved and another maximum of somewhat smaller size, about 8 dB, occurred at 3-msec delay. In general, the results of these and other studies at different signal frequencies are local maxima of detectability at half period of the signal and local minima at full periods with the difference between maxima and minima diminishing as delay increases.

Since the width of the head corresponds to a maximum delay between the two ears of about 660 μsec, most of these data are obtained at values of delay that are "unrealistic." The local maxima at the longer delays are understandable, however, if interpreted in terms of the correlation of the noise at the two ears. This correlation coefficient is frequency-dependent because the delay causes a phase shift that is linear with frequency. Thus, a 1-msec delay corresponds to a phase shift of π at 500 Hz ($\frac{1}{2}$ 2π or essentially N_π) but a somewhat smaller phase shift at 400 Hz [(1/2.5) 2π or $N_{\pi - \epsilon}$] and a somewhat longer one at 600 Hz [(1/1.667) 2π or $N_{\pi + \epsilon}$]. If the delay is 5 msec the phase shift is again 5π at 500 Hz, (again antiphasic, N_π) but 4π at 400 Hz (or N_0) and 6π (or N_0) at 600 Hz. In general, the correlation coefficient computed over some small band of frequencies near the frequency of the signal will oscillate with delay much as the data suggest.[3]

The preceding summary has covered a very voluminous literature. Reviews are constantly appearing. Two recent ones are by Green and Yost (1976) and by N. I. Durlach (1972). These reviews should be consulted for further details concerning the phenomenon and how various parameters affect the result.

Now that at least some of the empirical results are clear, let us consider two broad classes of theories offered to account for the results. Although their appearances are quite different, further analyses reveal many similarities.

DETECTION THEORIES

The first class of theories is relatively abstract and mathematical. These theories characterize the auditory system as performing certain operations or calculations on the waveforms at the two ears. They then derive how the detectability of the signal depends on the various signal parameters, such as signal frequency, interaural phase or interaural noise level, and so on. These theories need not specify the correspondence between physiological mechanisms and the assumed processing. They are formal theories; it is "as if" the binaural system worked according to their assumption. Their objective is to predict a great variety of data with relatively few assumptions. Even if the theories are totally incorrect in the various hypothesized mechanisms, their success would provide a convenient mnemonic device for a body of data. These models should be evaluated for simplicity and for the number of free parameters they use in generating their predictions.

The first example is Durlach's equalization and cancellation theory (1963). He pointed out that many binaural masking results can be predicted from simply assuming that it was possible to add or subtract the output of the two ears.

---

[3] For some other comments on "unrealistic" delays obtained in some neurophysiological studies of binaural hearing, McFadden's (1973) comments are recommended.

Stated more formally, he assumed that the binaural system can perform simple linear operations of addition or subtraction after the outputs of the two ears are suitably scaled in magnitude. The assumption of a scaling operation is necessary because we know that the noise level at the two ears does not have to be equal to create a large binaural advantage. Figure 8.9 presents the essentials of the theory. The waveform in each ear passes through a filter—the critical band—and then through a variable gain amplifier to scale the output for maximum cancellation. The two channels are then combined, either being subtracted $(L - R)$ or added $(L + R)$ in the cancellation device. The decision device operates so that the masked threshold is inversely proportional to the signal-to-noise ratio, that is, the ratio of signal power to noise power at the input to the detection device. The ability to switch from a binaural to either monaural channel is assumed because the signal-to-noise ratio in either ear alone might be better than that provided by the binaural processor. In this case only the monaural information would be used by the decision device.

Consider how the system provides better binaural signal-to-noise ratio in a typical condition such as $S_\pi N_0$. In this case the cancellation device would subtract the outputs of the two ears, after suitable scaling. Since the signal is out of phase at the two ears, it doubles after subtraction. The noise, on the other hand, will be reduced to zero. What then limits the detectability of the signal? The theory assumes there are small errors in timing and scaling. These errors prevent even identical noise waveforms at the two ears from exactly canceling.

The assumption of a timing error makes the cancellation process frequency-dependent. A timing error plays no role as long as it is small compared with the period of the signal. However, as the frequency of the signal increases, the effect of timing error becomes appreciable. Eventually, as the period of the signal nears the size of timing error, practically no binaural advantage accrues from using the cancellation device. At this point detection of the signal should be no better than either ear alone.

By the same token, we must expect better and better cancellation at lower and lower frequencies; but this is not the case. Thus, in addition to the timing error, the model assumes some scaling error. The model has only these two parameters, the size of the scaling and timing errors. Remarkably the model can predict most of the binaural results using only these two parameters. The standard deviation of the scaling error is .25 for a unit input and a timing error of $T = 150$ μsec. Neither value is unreasonable in terms of general auditory abilities. One can center a click with an error of about 25 μsec, and although this is a factor of five less than 150 μsec, one must probably use a number of different critical bands in the centering task. Similarly, one can detect a change in intensity of about 1 or 2 dB, which corresponds to amplitude changes of about .12 to .26.

A general criticism of the model is that it is entirely abstract and bears no obvious relation to the physiological mechanisms involved in binaural systems. This criticism raises many interesting philosophical questions such as what is a

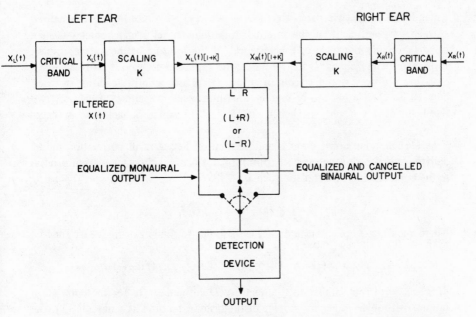

FIG. 8.9 Durlach's equalization and cancellation model. The operations of the model are indicated by the boxes. The detection device will select either ear or the binaural interaction to maximize the signal's detectability.

theory supposed to do, other than explain a body of data in an economic and simple way. But leaving these issues aside, let us turn to a new theory of binaural interaction being investigated by Durlach's collaborator, Colburn (1974), which is much more "physiological" in character. In Colburn's theory the exact form of neurophysiological interaction is specified. We will postpone further discussion of this theory until we have completed a description of the other theories. In many respects the Colburn model is closely related to some suggestions made by Jeffress (1948).

A second binaural detection model is the correlation model of Osman (1971). This model is a natural extension of an energy detection model for monaural detection. It assumes that decisions about the presence or absence of a signal are based on a decision statistic, D, given by

$$D = A \int_0^T x_L{}^2(t)dt + B \int_0^T x_R{}^2(t) + C \int_0^T x_L(t)x_R(t)\,dt,$$

where $x_i(t)$ represents the filtered waveform associated with either ear, after the addition of internal noise, and A, B, and C are appropriately chosen constants. In an $S_\pi N_0$ condition, A and B would be nearly zero and C would be given most weight; in $S_m N_m$ the constant associated with the proper ear A or B would be given most weight and other constants would be near zero. Osman's model also depends on only two parameters. One is ρ $(-1 < \rho < +1)$, the normalized correlation coefficient of the internal noise. The other is a parameter Osman calls R, roughly the ratio of the variances of the internal to the external noise. Both parameters change with frequency in a systematic way. At a fixed signal frequency, however, the effects of interaural phase, amplitude ratio, or interaural noise correlation can be predicted with reasonable accuracy using only two fixed values for ρ and R (Osman, 1971, 1973; Osman, Schacknow, & Tzuo, 1973).

As Osman points out, there is a close relation between his correlation model and the equalization and cancellation model. Consider the cancellation process as the computation of a statistic such as

$$Z = \int_0^T [ax_L(t) \pm bx_R(t)]^2 ,$$

where a and b are constants and $x_i(t)$ is the input to the left or right ear. Then

$$Z = a^2 \int_0^T x_L{}^2(t) + b^2 \int_0^T x_R{}^2(t) \pm 2ab \int_0^T x_L(t)x_R(t)\,dt.$$

This is a form very similar to the quantity D defined above for the correlation model. Although there are several distinguishing features (Osman, 1971), the predictions of the two models are often virtually identical.

LATERALIZATION THEORY

The generic term "lateralization" characterizes a number of specific theories that have evolved since the binaural masking level difference was originally discovered. The specific theories differ in detail and emphasis, but all agree that the increased detectability observed in these binaural experiments arises because mechanisms, like those used in localization, lateralize the noise and signal in different places. The original models emphasized temporal cues. The signal has different interaural temporal properties than the noise. These differences are assumed to account for its improved detectability. The formal statement of the model was first made by Webster (1951) and was considerably elaborated by Jeffress, Blodgett, Sandel, and Wood (1956). Jeffress' (1972) basic assumption is that the binaural improvement in detection occurs because the addition of the signal to the noise causes a relative change in the time that the waveforms reach the two ears. To understand this model we must first recall that a sinusoid can be represented by a rotating vector. The instantaneous amplitude of the sinusoid is the projection of this vector on the vertical axis. The frequency of the sinusoid is determined by the angular velocity of rotation. The phase of the sinusoid is given by the orientation of the vector with the line of projection at time zero (see Figure 1.4, Chapter 1). In some narrow band of frequencies, noise can also be represented by a vector, but there are differences between a vector representing a sinusoid and a vector representing noise. A sinusoidal vector has constant amplitude and angular velocity. A noise vector changes both in amplitude and velocity. The rate of change of these quantities depends on the bandwidth of the noise. The central assumption of these binaural theories is the treatment of noise as a slowly changing sinusoidal process. The noise waveform at any instant is represented by a vector of fixed length, as in Figure 8.10. For the N_0 condition, except for errors in processing, the interaural phase of the noise should be zero. Since the waveform arrives at the same time at the two ears, the binaural image should be lateralized near the center of the head. Next, consider the results of adding a signal, say, to one ear, since this is the simplest case. This causes the resultant vector representing the waveform in that ear to move relative to the vector for the opposite ear, as indicated in Figure 8.10. The parameter ϕ is the phase angle between the signal and the instantaneous phase of the noise, and the relative amplitude of S and N in the figure are the relative amplitudes of noise and signal, respectively. The effect of adding a signal to the noise at one ear produces a phase change between the signal-plus-noise vector in that ear and the noise vector in the other ear. Adding the signal thus changes the interaural phase or interaural time, and this is the cue for detection. For example, by adding a signal to the noise the resultant is moved $10°$, that is, $\theta = 10°$. If the signal frequency is about 360 Hz, then a change of $1/36$ of a period, or about 77 μsec, has been produced between the two ears.

This interaural time difference calculated from the interaural phase angle θ is the crucial variable according to these theories. One would like to calculate its average value exactly. The value of θ depends on the amplitude of the vectors N and S and the value of ϕ. The amplitude of the signal S is straightforward. The amplitude of the noise vector is more complicated. Its average value grows with noise level, in fact, it is proportional to the root-mean-squared (rms) value of the noise.[4] It is also dependent, however, on the assumed bandwidth of the auditory filter or critical band. The phase angle ϕ between S and N should be a random variable with all possible values of ϕ equally likely. Thus, the value of θ will be a random variable with some distribution of possible values, depending on N, S, and ϕ. Henning (1973) has worked out mathematical expressions, and the relevant distributions can be computed to make specific predictions for this model. Although Webster (1951) has made some strong simplifying assumptions, for example, the average value of $\phi = 90°$, the predictions of this model have not been compared with data in as much detail as either Durlach's or Osman's models.

An appealing aspect of this general approach is that it has been embedded in a physiological model for the mechanism that detects these time differences (Jeffress, 1948). This idea is illustrated in Figure 8.11. First, as the two sides of the figure indicate, the incoming sound is filtered by critical bands. The output

[4] For a definition of rms, see Chapter 2.

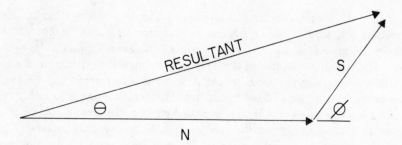

FIG. 8.10 Vector diagram illustrating how adding a signal S added at angle ϕ to noise component produces a phase change θ. The resulting interaural phase cue, θ, or its temporal equivalent, is the basis of detection in this lateralization model.

of the filter feeds a hypothetical axon extending into the brain stem. In some central network the axons send off collaterals that converge on cells along with collaterals from the axons coming from the corresponding filter in the other ear. Each axon carries an impulse caused by the acoustic input from the respective ear. If the anatomy and impulse velocity are suitably arranged, the cell at which these two impulses converge simultaneously will indicate whether the waveform in the left or right ear occurred first. The higher-order neuron represented by a circle in the middle of the figure detects this coincidence. If the waveforms are in phase at the two ears, then neural bursts will be initiated at roughly the same time. If the delays (that is, propagation velocities) are similar for the two sides, the neurons located near the center of the diagram would be stimulated. If the waveform is delayed in the right ear the burst will start later and coincidence will move toward the left side of the diagram. Thus, the place of coincidence codes interaural delay. Licklider (1959) has elaborated an extension of this general coincidence model. In fact, this general idea is the basis for Colburn's recent theory. This physiological model and the lateralization model of Webster and Jeffress suggest a strong link between mechanisms for localizing a sound and lateralization cues responsible for the masking level difference.

Several studies have explored the link between the MLD and the process of lateralization (Hafter, Bourbon, Blocker, & Tucker, 1969). Among the more ingenious experiments is one by Hafter, Carrier, and Stephan (1973) in which the masking level differences for individual subjects were predicted from the subject's lateralization responses. The first part of the experiment consisted of teaching the subjects to map, with a simple scale, the apparent location of the sound image. One end of the scale represented the left ear, the other end of the scale the right ear, and the center values the middle of the head. If $S_m N_o$ is compared with $S_o N_o$, then the lateralization judgment tends to distribute about center in the $S_o N_o$ condition and clusters toward the side containing the signal in the $S_m N_o$ condition. From these responses a computer calculates the likelihood ratio of each lateralization judgment and tabulates the distribution of the particular likelihood ratio, given the two hypotheses ($S_o N_o$ and $S_m N_o$). Using a

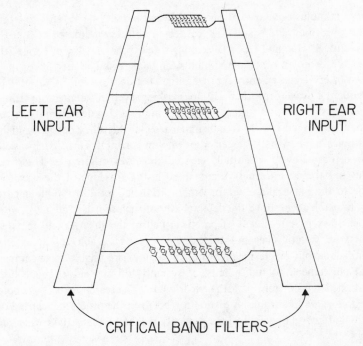

FIG. 8.11 An illustration of Jeffress' hypothesis concerning the physiological mechanism responsible for the interaural time cue. The signal is first filtered by critical bands and initiates neural impulses that travel on the fibers extending toward the opposite ear. Each fiber sends off collaterals to a cell body, indicated by a small circle. If the signal is delayed to the left ear, the finite velocity of neural transmission will cause the impulses generated in each ear to arrive simultaneously at a cell body located on the left side of the diagram.

theorem of signal detection theory, the computer predicts the percentage of correct responses the subject should achieve in the binaural masking task, in which he must detect the signal in one of two temporal intervals. For at least four of the five subjects, the percentage of correct detections was successfully predicted from the lateralization judgments with an accuracy of about ±1 dB. These and other similar experiments provide support for the thesis that binaural masking phenomena and the lateralization phenomenon are simply different manifestations of similar, if not identical, processes. The change in locus of the lateralized image is, of course, clearest in the $S_m N_o$ condition. The lateralized image in the S_π condition is not at either ear but somehow different in form from the S_o or N_o image. Adherents of lateralization theory would still maintain that the detection cues and lateralization changes are intimately related.

An apparent exception to this relation between lateralization and binaural masking level differences are waveforms having energy only in the high-frequency regions (above 2,000 Hz). Such stimuli, either narrow bands of noise centered at high frequencies or amplitude-modulated sinusoids, can be lateralized if the stimulus is delayed at one of the ears. In fact, the abilities to lateralize a 300-Hz pure tone and a 3,900-Hz carrier amplitude modulated at 300 Hz are nearly identical (Henning, 1974). Henning showed that a delay of about 70 μsec in either the complex or simple stimulus can be detected about 75% of the time in a two-interval forced-choice procedure. Despite this ability to lateralize a high-frequency waveform there is no masking-level difference: inverting the envelope of the complex signal does not improve its detectability in noise. Wightman and Green (1971) found similar results when they delayed a high-pass filtered pulse train by half the period of the fundamental. This signal was clearly lateralized but showed essentially no masking-level difference. These results indicate that timing information contained in the envelope of the waveform is available to the binaural system for lateralization and localization judgments but it is not available to improve the detectability of such signals in noise.

This paradox is reminiscent of practically all of the theories and facts in the binaural area. Certain cues and modes of processing are able to explain certain facts and data, but single mechanisms or theories are unable to encompass all binaural phenomena. A multiplicity of systems and cues are probably used in localization, lateralization, or MLD experiments. The search for a single comprehensive theory will continue. A distinction between the processing carried out at the high- and low-frequency regions probably will be fundamental to any general theory.

REFERENCES

Babkoff, H., Sutton, S., & Barris, M. Binaural interaction of transient: Interaural time and intensity asymmetry. *Journal of the Acoustical Society of America*, 1973, *53*, 1028–1036.

Batteau, D.W. The role of the Pinna in Human Localization. *Proceedings of the Royal Society* (London), Ser. B., 1967, *168*, 158–180.

Blodgett, H.C., Jeffress, L.A., & Taylor, R.W. Relation of masked threshold to signal-duration for various interaural phase-combinations. *American Journal of Psychology*, 1958, *71*, 283–290.

Blodgett, H.C., Jeffress, L.A., & Whitworth, R.H. Effect of noise at one ear on the masked threshold for tone at the other. *Journal of the Acoustical Society of America*, 1962, *34*, 979–981.

Colburn, H.S. *Theory of binaural interaction based on auditory-nerve data II, detection of tones in noise.* Unpublished manuscript (1974).

Colburn, H.S., & Durlach, N.I. Time-intensity relations in binaural unmasking. *Journal of the Acoustical Society of America*, 1965, *38*, 93–103.

Diercks, K.J., & Jeffress, L.A. Interaural phase and the absolute threshold for tone. *Journal of the Acoustical Society of America*, 1962, *34*, 981–984.

Dolan, T.R. Effects of masker spectrum level on masking-level differences at low signal frequencies. *Journal of the Acoustical Society of America*, 1968, *44*, 1507–1512.

Dolan, T.R., & Robinson, D.E. An explanation of masking-level differences that result from interaural intensive disparities of noise. *Journal of the Acoustical Society of America*, 1967, *42*, 977–981.

Durlach, N.I. Equalization and cancellation theory of binaural masking-level differences. *Journal of the Acoustical Society of America*, 1963, *35*, 1206–1218.

Durlach, N.I. Binaural signal detection: Equalization and cancellation theory. In J.V. Tobias (Ed.), *Foundations of modern auditory theory*. Vol. II. New York: Academic Press, 1972.

Egan, J.P. Masking-level differences as a function of interaural disparities in intensity of signal and of noise. *Journal of the Acoustical Society of America*, 1965, *38*, 1043–1049.

Feddersen, W.E., Sandel, T.T., Teas, D.C., & Jeffress, L.A. Localization of high-frequency tones. *Journal of the Acoustical Society of America*, 1957, *29*, 988–991.

Gardner, M.B., & Gardner, R.S. Problem of localization in the median plane: effect of pinnae cavity occlusion. *Journal of the Acoustical Society of America*, 1973, *53*, 400–408.

Green, D.M. Interaural phase effects in the masking of signals of different duration. *Journal of the Acoustical Society of America*, 1966, *39*, 720–724.

Green, D.M., & Yost, W.A., Binaural analysis. In W. Keidel & D. Neff (Eds.), *Handbook of sensory physiology*. Berlin, Hiedelberg, and New York: Springer-Verlag, 1976.

Hafter, E.R., Bourbon, W.T., Blocker, A.S., & Tucker, A. Direct comparison between lateralization and detection under conditions of antiphasic masking. *Journal of the Acoustical Society of America*, 1969, *46*, 1452–1457.

Hafter, E.R., & Carrier, S.C. Binaural interaction in low-frequency stimuli: The inability to trade time and intensity completely. *Journal of the Acoustical Society of America*, 1972, *51*, 1852–1862.

Hafter, E.R., Carrier, S.C., & Stephan, F.K. Direct comparison of lateralization and the MLD for monaural signals in gated noise. *Journal of the Acoustical Society of America*, 1973, *53*, 1553–1559.

Hafter, E.R., & Jeffress, L.A. Two-image lateralization of tones and clicks. *Journal of the Acoustical Society of America*, 1968, *44*, 563–569.

Harris, G.G. Binaural interactions of impulsive stimuli and pure tones. *Journal of the Acoustical Society of America*, 1960, *32*, 685–692.

Henning, G.B. Effect of interaural phase and frequency on amplitude discrimination. *Journal of the Acoustical Society of America*, 1973, *54*, 1160–1178.

Henning, G.B. Lateralization and the binaural masking-level difference. *Journal of the Acoustical Society of America*, 1974, *55*, 1259–1262.

Hirsh, I.J. The influence of interaural phase on interaural summation and inhibition. *Journal of the Acoustical Society of America*, 1948, *20*, 536–544.   (a)

Hirsh, I.J. Binaural summation and interaural inhibition as a function of the level of the masking noise. *American Journal of Psychology*, 1948, *56*, 205–213.   (b)

Jeffress, L.A. A place theory of sound localization. *Journal of Comparative and Physiological Psychology*, 1948, *41*, 35–39.

Jeffress, L.A. Binaural signal detection: Vector theory. In J.V. Tobias (Ed.), *Foundations of modern auditory theory*. Vol. II. New York: Academic Press, 1972.

Jeffress, L.A., Blodgett, H.C., & Deatherage, B.H. The masking of tones by white noise as a function of the interaural phases of both components. *Journal of the Acoustical Society of America*, 1952, *24*, 523–527.

Jeffress, L.A., Blodgett, H.C., & Deatherage, B.H. Masking and interaural phase, II. 167 cycles. *Journal of the Acoustical Society of America*, 1962, *34*, 1124–1126.

Jeffress, L.A., Blodgett, H.C., Sandel, T.T., & Wood, C.L., III, Masking of tonal signals. *Journal of the Acoustical Society of America*, 1956, *28*, 416–426.

Licklider, J.C.R. The influence of interaural phase relations upon the masking of speech by white noise. *Journal of the Acoustical Society of America*, 1948, *20*, 150–159.

Licklider, J.C.R. Three auditory theories. In E.S. Koch (Ed.), *Psychology: A study of a science*. Vol. 1. New York, Toronto, and London: McGraw-Hill, 1959.

McFadden, D. Masking-level differences determined with and without interaural disparities in masker intensity. *Journal of the Acoustical Society of America*, 1968, *44*, 212–223.

McFadden, D. Precedence effects and auditory cells with long characteristic delays. *Journal of the Acoustical Society of America*, 1973, *54*, 528–530.

McFadden, D., & Pulliam, K.A. Lateralization and detection of noise-masked tones of different durations. *Journal of the Acoustical Society of America*, 1971, *49*, 1191–1194.

Mills, A.W. On the minimum audible angle. *Journal of the Acoustical Society of America*, 1958, *30*, 237–246.

Mills, A.W. Lateralization of high-frequency tones. *Journal of the Acoustical Society of America*, 1960, *32*, 132–134.

Osman, E. A correlation model of binaural masking level differences. *Journal of the Acoustical Society of America*, 1971, *50*, 1494–1511.

Osman, E., Schacknow, P.N., & Tzuo, P.L. Psychometric functions and a correlation model of binaural detection. *Perception and Psychophysics*, 1973, *14*, 371–374.

Osman, E. Correlation model of binaural detection: interaural amplitude ratio and phase variation for signal. *Journal of the Acoustical Society of America*, 1973, *54*, 386–389.

Osman, E., Tzuo, H-Y., & Tzuo, P.L. Theoretical analysis of detection of monaural signals as a function of interaural noise correlation and signal frequency. *Journal of the Acoustical Society of America*, 1975, *57*, 939–942.

Rayleigh, Lord. On our perception of sound direction. *Philosophical Magazine*, 1907, *13*, 214–232.

Robinson, D.E., & Jeffress, L.A. Effect of varying the interaural noise correlation on the detectability of tonal signals. *Journal of the Acoustical Society of America*, 1963, *35*, 1947–1952.

Roffler, S.K., & Butler, R.A. Factors that influence the localization of sound in the vertical plane. *Journal of the Acoustical Society of America*, 1968, *43*, 1255–1259.

Sandel, T.T., Teas, D.C., Feddersen, W.E., & Jeffress, L.A. Localization of sound from single and paired sources. *Journal of the Acoustical Society of America*, 1955, *27*, 842–852.

Stevens, S.S., & Newman, E.B. The localization of actual sources of sound. *American Journal of Psychology*, 1936, *48*, 297–306.

Tobias, J.V., & Schubert, E.D. Effective onset duration of auditory stimuli. *Journal of the Acoustical Society of America*, 1959, *31*, 1595–1605.

von Békésy, G. *Experiments in hearing*. (E.G. Wever, Ed. and trans.) New York: McGraw-Hill, 1960.

Wallach, H., Newman, E.B., & Rosenzweig, M.R. The precedence effect in sound localization. *American Journal of Psychology*, 1949, *62*, 315–336.

Webster, F.A. The influence of interaural phase on masked thresholds: I. The role of interaural time-deviation. *Journal of the Acoustical Society of America*, 1951, *23*, 452–461.

Weston, P.B., & Miller, J.D. Use of noise to eliminate one ear from masking experiments. *Journal of the Acoustical Society of America*, 1965, *37*, 638–646.

Whitworth, R.H., & Jeffress, L.A. Time versus intensity in the localization of tone. *Journal of the Acoustical Society of America*, 1961, *33*, 925–929.

Wightman, F.L., & Green, D.M. The case of the missing MLD. *Journal of the Acoustical Society of America*, 1971, *49*, 102(A).

Wilbanks, W.A., & Whitmore, J.K. Detection of monaural signals as a function of interaural noise correlation and signal frequency. *Journal of the Acoustical Society of America*, 1968, *43*, 785–797.

Woodworth, R.S. *Experimental psychology*. New York: Holt, 1938.

Yost, W.A., Wightman, F.L., & Green, D.M. Lateralization of filtered clicks. *Journal of the Acoustical Society of America*, 1971, *50*, 1526–1531.

Zwislocki, J., & Feldman, R.S. Just noticeable differences in dichotic phase. *Journal of the Acoustical Society of America*, 1956, *28*, 860–864.

9
Nonlinear Distortion

INTRODUCTION

For the most part we have dealt with linear phenomena. Starting with the wave equation, the concept of linearity and the principle of superposition have been stressed. This emphasis stems from the fact that one can predict the behavior of a linear system in all circumstances. If a system is nonlinear, then we may be able to predict its behavior under some limited set of circumstances, but we often cannot predict how it will behave in general. We stress linearity not because most auditory processes are linear but because linear processes are simple. As Dallos (1973) has stated, "Not, however, until relatively recently did the basic premise begin to permeate our corporate thinking that *life is very nonlinear* [p. 391]." If we add the comment that nonlinear life is also very frightening, because the response is often unpredictable, then we will begin to have a fair appraisal of current thinking.

To appreciate some of the complexities of a nonlinear system we will begin with its general character. This can most easily be accomplished by reviewing what we mean by "linearity." Next, we progress to a few very simple forms of nonlinearity before pointing out the range of nonlinear systems in general.

The basic feature of a linear system is superposition. The response to two different inputs, A plus B, is simply the response to A alone plus the response to B alone. (For a more precise definition and discussion, review the relevant section of Chapter 1.) In contrast, the set of nonlinear systems is almost impossible to classify or characterize because it is so complex and large. The mathematics of nonlinear systems is very complicated. Such systems may defy complete analysis. No matter how many signals we have used to probe the system, some new input signal may produce some unexpected output. Often there is simply no way to generalize about the response of a nonlinear system to different inputs. Nonlinear systems are often unique, and each has particular quirks and characteristics of its own.

NONLINEARITY IN AUDITION

Nonlinear distortion has played an important role in the topic of pitch perception. Von Helmholtz (1863) argued that the transmission of the sound wave from air to the receptor elements must involve nonlinear elements. Thus, as reviewed in Chapter 7, distortion products, particularly difference frequencies, would be present at the receptor surface. Consider, for example, a complex tone comprised of different frequencies such as 1,000, 1,200, 1,400, 1,600 Hz, and so on. Such a complex would produce an apparent pitch of 200 because of the common simple difference frequency of 200 Hz that would arise from almost any nonlinearity in the ear. This is probably the most prominent and best-known nonlinear argument in all auditory theory. Even though it is probably incorrect, at least in an explanation of the pitch of complex tones it still historically represents an important stage in the study of the pitch of complex sounds. At very high intensity levels, of course, the difference tone would occur, but it is relatively unimportant at sound pressure levels below $80 - 90$-dB SPL. At higher levels the difference tone is relatively small, probably $20 - 50$ dB less intense than the tones from which it arises.

Although the simple difference tones are usually small, other combination tones probably play important roles in masking, pitch perception, and other auditory phenomena. Recent years have seen a considerable emphasis on one particular combination tone, the so-called cubic difference tone, $2F_1 - F_2$. If we produce 1,000 and 1,200 Hz, then another component is also heard, namely, 800 Hz $[2(1,000 \text{ Hz}) - 1,200 \text{ Hz}]$. This distortion product is evident, can be measured psychoacoustically with fair accuracy, and displays some quite unusual and interesting properties.

A third and more general reason for considering nonlinear phenomena is to provide the necessary caution and prudence one needs in interpreting linear arguments. Often, in the enthusiasm generated by understanding some nearly linear processes, one may generalize the results of an investigation beyond reasonable bounds. The generality of the linear approach often leads to an expansiveness that extends the analysis well beyond the restricted range of the original investigation. It is important in these circumstances to understand in detail the assumptions of the analysis and especially the range of applicability, so that one may not be too surprised when some unexpected results occur.

No issue of scientific strategy causes more heated debate or division than the topic of linearity. On the one hand there are those who admit that nonlinearities do occur but still wish to extend linear analysis as far as possible. This produces a theory or analysis of great scope and generality. On the other hand there are those who note that a great deal of the world is nonlinear and therefore they mistrust very general global arguments. They know that while many complicated phenomena may appear linear, important nonlinearities often prevent the sweeping generality of the linear analysis from applying. Those who pursue linear explanation do so not because they believe that most systems are inherently linear, but because they prefer a testable and concrete hypothesis to ignorance. Those who emphasize nonlinear mechanisms admit that the processes are often difficult to understand but argue that truth is more important than an ill-founded premise, even though the knowledge is of very limited scope. There is little hope of reconciling these two different views: one is practical and pragmatic, the other pure and correct. Whatever one's position, a rudimentary understanding of some basic nonlinear phenomena is essential.

DESCRIPTION OF NONLINEAR SYSTEMS

As we remarked earlier, there is no complete description of nonlinear systems. We will discuss only those that possess amplitude nonlinearity. Furthermore, this amplitude nonlinearity will be such that the output is a single-valued function of the input. From this restricted class, we are excluding nonlinearities with memory. In such systems the current output depends in some nonlinear manner on the past history of inputs.

A common example of nonlinearity involves a differential equation in which the cube of the displacement appears along with the ordinary displacement and acceleration. The solution, at least for a restricted set of parameter values, is a sinusoid response at the fundamental frequency with some third harmonic distortion. But a more startling aspect of the behavior of this system is how the output amplitude is triple valued near a point that resembles the resonant frequency of the system (see Figure 9.1). Near this pseudoresonance the system has only two stable values. The output will be either relatively low if approached from the lower frequencies, or relatively high if approached from the higher frequencies. The amplitude response is discontinuous if the frequency is either increased or decreased through the point of pseudoresonance. Fortunately, no one has suggested that such a system has an analog to any auditory process, but its very existence reminds us that strange things happen in the realm of nonlinear systems.

Classic Power Series Nonlinearity

Another classic introduction to nonlinear systems is the power series approach which we introduced briefly in the chapter on pitch perception. The system, F, has no memory. The present output depends only on the present input, and thus the input–output relation is a single-valued function relating instantaneous

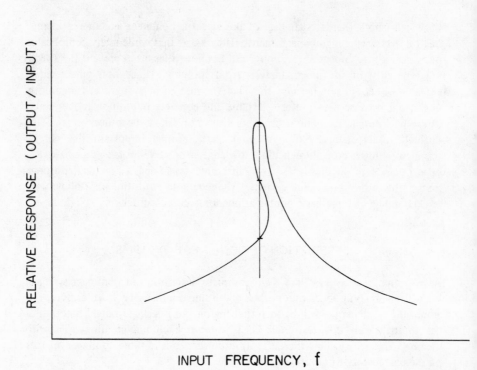

FIG. 9.1 The response as a function of frequency of a nonlinear filter. The relative output to a constant input level depends on whether the input frequency is increasing or decreasing near the apparent resonance frequency.

output to instantaneous input. If F is continuous in the sense that its derivatives exist for any particular value of the input, then one can express F as a power series. The instantaneous output, y, at any particular instance is a linear combination of x, x^2, x^3, x^4, and so forth. Equation (9.1) states such an expansion explicitly:

$$y = F(x) = a_0 + a_1 x^1 + a_2 x^2 + a_3 x^3 + \cdots . \tag{9.1}$$

The values of the constant terms, a_i, are related to the derivatives of the function F near the point along x at which we choose to make the expansion. If we make the expansion near the origin, then the coefficients of the various terms are simply those of a Maclaurin series given by the derivative of the function at the origin. Thus, in Eq. (9.1),

$$a_0 = f(0), \quad a_1 = f'(0), \quad a_2 = f''(0)/2!, \quad a_n = f^n(0)/n!$$

where $f^n(0)$ is the nth derivative of y with respect to x evaluated at 0, and $n!$ is n factorial, that is, $n! = n(n-1)(n-2) \cdots 2 \cdot 1$.

As was pointed out earlier, if we now introduce a sinusoid as an input to such a system, each term or x with power greater than one produces harmonics of the input frequency. Thus, for example, the x^2 term produces an output at twice the input frequency, and so on. Hence, a common way to study auditory distortion is to explore the distortion products present with either single input frequencies or with combinations of sinusoids. The frequencies and magnitude of these distortion products give us estimates of a_1, a_2, a_3, and so on. Before discussing this approach in more detail, we need a more general discussion of distortion phenomena.

Nonpower Series Distortion

Most functions are continuous and their derivatives exist. Systems that exist in the real world do not change abruptly. Thus, we tend to think of distortion in terms of the power series approach. But power series approximation are not always valid and we should emphasize that other nonlinear systems behave in quite different ways. Consider the following example: The function relating input and output is given by the following rule:

$$y = x, \quad x \geqslant 0,$$
$$y = 0, \quad x < 0. \tag{9.2}$$

This device is an ideal half-wave rectifier, but real rectifiers behave very similarly. Figure 9.2 shows this equation graphically. It is a reasonably well-behaved function in the sense that once the input x is greater than zero the output is a smooth, and continuous, and even linear function of the input. The apparent simplicity of this function is deceptive. It is impossible to develop a general power series expansion for this function near the origin because derivatives at the origin do not exist. Thus, there is no Maclaurin expansion and no power series that will uniformly approach the value of the function near the origin.

This fact is more than a mathematical technicality. To show how differently this function behaves from that represented by a power series, consider the behavior of such a system when the input is a sinusoid. The output of an ideal rectifier is only the positive part of the sinusoid with zero elsewhere (see Figure 9.2). Since the output is periodic, we can represent the output as a Fourier series:[1]

$$x(t) = -A \cos wt,$$

[1] The use of a cosine input simplifies the derivation of the output expression. Obviously, if we were to time-shift the input by a certain amount the output would be shifted by the same amount. Thus, if the input were phase-shifted then the phases of the output components would change, but not their magnitude.

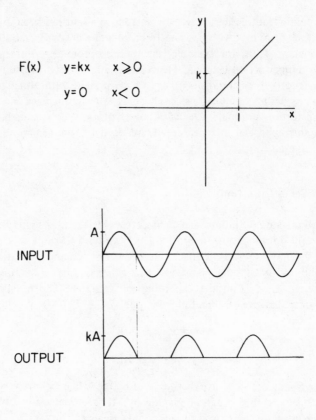

$$F(x) \quad y=kx \quad x \geqslant 0$$
$$\quad\quad\quad y=0 \quad x < 0$$

INPUT

OUTPUT

FIG. 9.2 The input-output function of an ideal half wave rectifier (a). The input and output of that device to a sinusoidal stimulus (b).

and

$$y(t) = \frac{A}{\pi} - \frac{A}{2} \cos wt - \frac{2A}{\pi} \sum_{n \text{ even}} \frac{(-1)^{n/2} \cos nwt}{(n+1)(n-1)}. \tag{9.3}$$

Two principal output components are the dc term, A/π, and the fundamental $\cos wt$, having amplitude $A/2$. The higher harmonics decrease as $1/n^2$. The second harmonic is down $4/3\pi$ (7.4 dB) compared with the fundamental, and the fourth harmonic is down $4/15\pi$ (21.4 dB).

The basic difference between this sort of nonlinearity and the nonlinearity of a power series can be observed by simply doubling the amplitude of the input waveform. In the case of a power series, we would observe a nonlinear growth in the distortion products. This is because they arise from either the quadratic, cubic, or quartic terms and hence increase as the square, cube, or fourth power of the magnitude of the fundamental. For the ideal half-wave rectifier, increasing the input simply increases each output component by the same relative amount (see Eq. 9.3). This mathematical result is easily understood from Figure 9.2. Imagine what would happen if we doubled the input amplitude. Obviously, the half-waves at the output would double in amplitude as well. This linear behavior arises from the fact that the input and output are linear if the input is positive.

There is something fundamentally different between the ideal rectifier and the nonlinearity encountered in a power series expansion. In one case, the classic nonlinearity, the growth of the amplitude is disproportionate to the growth of the input. For the ideal half-wave rectifier, the growth of any output component is linear with the growth of the input. Thus, one important feature to ascertain about nonlinearity devices is how the distortion products behave with changes in the amplitude of the input. We shall see that in hearing distortion products may be of either type.

The Method of Best Beats

The preceding discussion demonstrates that the study of the distortion components provides important information about the nature and character of nonlinearity. If several sinusoids or combination of sinusoids were presented to a nonlinear system and the various components present at the output measured, one might be able to deduce the form of the nonlinearity. But in audition, it is not obvious how to measure the magnitude of the output components. One cannot simply ask the observer how loud a particular component sounds, both because such judgments would be highly variable and because that component is heard in the presence of other components that might mask or otherwise interfere with the judged loudness. The technique usually used to study the magnitude of distortion components therefore is the *method of beats*.

Consider two sinusoids that differ in frequency by a few cycles. If they are audible and approximately equal in amplitude, then beats will be heard: a periodic waxing and waning of the loudness of the sound occurs. The rate of beating will equal the difference in frequency of the two sinusoids. If the amplitudes of the two sinusoids are unequal, then there is less apparent fluctuation in loudness. Finally, if the amplitude of one sinusoid is diminished sufficiently, the more intense sinusoid masks it completely and no loudness variation is discerned. The fact that the strength of beats is greatest when the amplitudes are equal is the key point in the method of best beats.

Consider a pair of sinusoids, say at 2,000 and 2,300 Hz. We call these the *primary* tones. The difference frequency is 300 Hz, and at intense sound pressure levels the subject will report he hears a tone in the region of 300 Hz. As we raise and lower the levels of the primary stimuli, the relative loudness of this 300-Hz tone appears to vary. But how can we measure the apparent amplitude of the 300-Hz tone with some precision? One way is to introduce a probe tone with a frequency near that of the difference tone, say 302 Hz. As we raise and lower the level of this probe tone, the strength of the 2-Hz beat also changes. We might therefore adjust the amplitude of the probe tone until best beats occur and then assume that the 300-Hz distortion component has the same amplitude as the probe tone.

Although the preceding argument has a certain plausibility, there are many serious objections to it. A careful analysis of the temporal waveform produced by adding the probe tone to the two primary tones provides the most serious objection to the best-beat argument. The criticism is similar to the objections expressed against a resonance theory of pitch by temporal theorists. Basically, one can explain the fluctuation in loudness by temporal properties of the waveform. Starting from the observation that best beats occur when the amplitude of the two sinusoids is equal, the temporal theorist would argue that two sinusoids of equal intensity produce the most fluctuation in the envelope of the resultant. Consider the temporal waveforms representing beats between two sine waves. If the frequencies of the sine waves are 1,000 and 1,002 Hz, then the resulting wave can be viewed as a single sinusoid of frequency 1,001 Hz, multiplied by a slowly changing sinusoid. The slow-changing sinusoid or envelope has a frequency equal to the difference frequency or Hz. The maximum and minimum value of the resultant are (see Chapter 10): maximum = $a + b$, minimum = $a - b$, where a and b are the amplitudes of the original sinusoids. Obviously, the ratio of minimum to maximum is largest where the two amplitudes are equal, hence the clearest and most salient beating sensation.

Similarly, the temporal theorist would argue that the perception of beats in the case of the probe tone method may have little to do with distortion product but may simply reflect a fluctuation in the envelope of the entire stimulus. If one takes two sinusoids of quite different amplitudes, the resulting waveform is essentially that of the large amplitude signal. As the amplitude of the weaker component is increased one notices a small fluctuation in the peak amplitude of the larger sinusoid. This fluctuation has a rate equal to the difference frequency, as we will show in Chapter 10. According to the temporal theories, this fluctuation is responsible for the perception of best beats.

One might well ask the temporal theorist how the envelope is abstracted. The easiest way is to subject the waveform to a nonlinearity and then filter to reject all but the lowest beat component. The temporal theorist would admit this argument but reply that such arguments show the absurdity of the place position. The perception of slow auditory events such as 1 or 2 beats per second hardly requires one to assume a nonlinearity. If so, then one might expect all temporal phenomena to be treated in this way. The noise of a plane growing to a maximum as it approaches and then declining as it departs must be an example of auditory nonlinearity.

Thus, although in principle the method of best beats should provide a procedure for assessing the amplitude of a distortion product, the method itself is subject to such criticism as to almost make it useless as an experimental technique. We should note historically that the best beats was used by Wegel and Lane (1924) and the temporal critique was advanced by Timmer and Firestone (1937). For a more recent interchange on this issue, see Lawrence and Yantis (1956, 1957) and the replies by Meyer (1957) and Chocholle and Legouix (1957). A more recent method is now widely used and seems to avoid most of the criticisms leveled at the method of best beats.

The Cancellation Method

The essential problem in the method of best beats is not the phenomenon itself but the interpretation of that phenomenon. Does the presence or absence of the beating sensation indicate the level of the distortion product or does it simply reflect the perception of fluctuations in the envelope of a complex stimulus? Zwicker (1955) introduced a new method, called the cancellation method, which avoids many if not all problems associated with the method of best beats. To illustrate the technique, return to the example of two primary stimuli at 2,000 and 2,300 Hz. A cancellation tone at the difference frequency of 300 Hz is phase-locked to these two stimuli. The apparatus permits control of both the phase and the amplitude of the 300-Hz component. As a distortion product becomes evident, we try to cancel it by varying the phase and the amplitude of the 300-Hz component. A fourth sinusoid is also used as a probe stimulus and may have a frequency of 302 Hz, as with the method of best beats. But the probe stimulus in this case is not used to determine best beats. It is simply used to make sure that the cancellation is complete. Therefore, after we have canceled the tones to the best of our ability by varying the phase and amplitude of the 300-Hz component, we introduce the probe stimulus at 302 Hz and determine if any beats are present. If a two-cycle beat is present, we infer that there is still some residual distortion at 300 Hz and again adjust the amplitude and phase of the 300-Hz tone in an attempt to cancel this component. Thus, in the final adjustment, when we introduce the 302-Hz probe tone, we hear no beats whatsoever. At this point we are confident that cancellation has taken place. We know both the phase and amplitude of the cancellation tone. Therefore, we infer that the two primaries at 2,000 and 2,300 Hz produce a distortion product that has the same amplitude and is exactly $180°$ out of phase with the 300-Hz cancellation tone.

Thus far, no major criticisms of the cancellation method have surfaced. As long as the distortion product is well above threshold, the accuracy should be very good. If the distortion component is near threshold, then the technique is insensitive because a variety of amplitudes (very small) and phases for the cancellation tone can make the distortion production inaudible. The precision of the method is very poor at low intensity values. It would also be nice to have another precise method of measuring the amplitude and phase of the distortion product so as to cross check the cancellation method. As yet, no general method has been devised.

Results Using the Cancellation Method

Since Zwicker's introduction of the cancellation method, a number of studies have measured the amount of auditory nonlinearity under a variety of stimulus conditions. One of the best studies is that of Goldstein (1967). His results have been replicated a number of times and his basic generalizations have been supported by later research. Goldstein measured both the simple difference tone $(f_1 - f_2)$ and the so-called cubic combination tone $(2f_1 - f_2)$. Because the latter is much larger it is more interesting. Let us first summarize the results of measuring the distortion products. We first will simply list a number of the most salient properties of the combination tones and later comment on what these properties mean after their description is complete.

Properties of Cancellation

The simple difference tone $(f_1 - f_2)$ and the cubic difference tone $(2f_1 - f_2)$ are the most widely studied. We will also comment briefly on higher order distortion products.

The following descriptions implicitly accept that the cancellation tone is a measure of the internally generated combination tone. Thus, a phrase such as "the level of the combination tone" means "the level of the cancellation tone." The phase of the combination tone should be read as the phase of the cancellation tone plus 180°.

Properties of Cancellation Measurements of $f_1 - f_2$

1. The level of the cancellation tone is nearly independent of the frequency separation of the primaries. With $f_1 = 2,000$ Hz and f_2 adjusted to vary the difference tone from 200 to 800 Hz, the level of the cancellation tone changes only about 5 dB. (A change of about 200 Hz for $2f_1 - f_2$ causes a change in level of about 50 dB for the cancellation tone for all values of f_1.)

2. If f_1 is larger than 1,000 Hz, the cancellation tone is about 50 dB down when the levels of the primaries are about 70 to 90 dB. The change in level of the cancellation tone is approximately 15 dB to 20 dB for a 10-dB drop in the level of the primaries.

3. If f_1 is less than 1,000 Hz, then, as Hall has shown, the combination tone may be within 10 dB of the primary, and the level of the combination tone depends on the f_1/f_2 ratio being larger for smaller frequency separation of f_1 and f_2.

Properties of the Cancellation Measurements of $2f_1 - f_2$

1. At any level for the primaries, the level of the combination tone strongly depends on the frequency separation of the two primary components. If $f_1/f_2 = 1.2$, the cancellation tone is only 20 dB below the level of the primaries. As f_1/f_2 increases, the level of the distortion decreases and is 40–60 dB below the level of the primaries for a ratio of 1.5. The decrease of combination tone level as the f_1/f_2 ratio increases happens for all values of f_1 but is faster for higher frequency complexes. For ratios of f_1/f_2 less than 1.2 the distortion component lies too close to the primaries in frequency to be resolved. For example, at $f_1 = 1,000$ Hz and $f_2/f_1 = 1.1, f_2 = 1,100$ Hz and the distortion product is at 900 Hz.

2. For any f_1/f_2 ratio the level of the distortion product appears to be independent of the level of two equal primaries. Thus, at $f_1/f_2 = 1.2$, the combination tone is about 20 dB below the level of the primaries over a range from 20 dB – 70 dB. This very interesting and important result has been replicated by at least two other independent investigations (Hall, 1972a; Smoorenberg, 1972a).

3. If f_1 is fixed in level and the level of f_2 is varied, the level of the combination tone is proportional to the level of f_2 as long as the level of f_2 is less than the level of f_1; as the level of f_2 exceeds that of f_1 the combination tone decreases in level.

4. The phase of the cancellation tone changes with both the level of the primaries and the difference in frequency of the primaries. If f_1/f_2 is fixed and both are equal in level, then the phase of the cancellation tone changes by about $200°$ as the level of the primaries is varied over a 40-dB range. Similarly, for a fixed level of primaries, changing the frequency difference of the primaries causes a large, systematic change in the phase of the cancellation tone (Goldstein, 1967; Hall, 1972b).

Other Observations

1. Higher order combination tones, that is, $(n + 1)f_1 - nf_2$, with $n > 1$, appear to behave in much the same manner as the cubic combination tone, $n = 1$. They strongly depend on the ratio f_1/f_2 but are about 20 to 30 dB lower in level than the cubic combination tone. Some sort of interactive process could produce these higher order distortions. For example, 600 Hz, which is $3f_1 - 2f_2$, if $f_1 = 1,000$ Hz and $f_2 = 1,200$ Hz, might also be created by the cubic interaction of 800 $(2f_1 - f_2)$ and 1,000. Goldstein found, however, that loudness of the hertz tone is unaffected by cancellation at 800 Hz. He does, however, report that the amplitude of the 600-Hz combination tone was affected by cancellation at 800 Hz, as was the phase of 600 Hz.

2. Smoorenberg (1974) presented evidence from forward and backward masking experiments that suggest the time course of the nonlinearity is nearly instantaneous. It does not appear to be neural in origin, but appears mechanical in nature.

Implications of the Cancellation Measurements

The strong dependence of the apparent size of the cubic combination tone ($2f_1 - f_2$) on the ratio of f_1/f_2 points to a cochlear origin for the site of the nonlinearity. If the nonlinearity were in the middle ear, then it would be hard to explain why frequency difference of the primaries should affect the apparent amount of the nonlinearity. But if the nonlinearity occurs in the motion of the basilar membrane or in the fluids driving the membrane, then the sound has already undergone some frequency analysis. Only components near each other in frequency will have the opportunity to interact. Hence, the level of the combination tone should vary with the ratio of the two primary frequencies. By this same criterion the simple difference tone, $f_1 - f_2$, probably has a different origin, at least for higher frequencies. For lower frequencies, $f_1 < 1,500$ Hz, Hall's data show the same kind of dependence of apparent distortion amplitude with f_1/f_2 ratio as with the cubic combination tone.

The proportional change in the apparent size of the distortion product with changes in the level of the primaries definitely points to something other than classic power law distortion. Such a model may be basically correct for the simple difference tone $f_1 - f_2$, but it is definitely inadequate to account for the cubic combination tone. Goldstein (1967) uses the phrase "essential nonlinearity" to describe the fact, not a hypothesis, that "the relative level of the cubic combination tone is almost independent of the stimulus level [p. 687]." He introduces an equation which in effect normalizes the distortion terms in a power series expansion by the peak value of the stimulus. Others, for example, Smoorenberg (1972b), argue that the results force us to abandon the notion of any essentially linear system with some small nonlinear elements. Given Smoorenberg's result of the forward and backward masking experiment, there is little evidence of a dynamic nonlinearity. Thus, he advocates looking at a static nonlinearity such as that implicit in a power series expansion. Smoorenberg points out that a simple way to understand the apparent linear behavior of the cubic combination tone is to suppose that there is no significant linear component in the static transfer function. Suppose, for example, that the transfer contains no linear term but is simply

$$y = ax^3.$$

Now, if two frequencies, f_1 and f_2, are introduced, a variety of components occur at the output, including $2f_1 - f_2$. By adjusting the amplitude and phase of a third component at that frequency, cancellation can be achieved. Thus, the energy at $2f_1 - f_2$ is made zero, since we cannot hear a beat when we introduce another component near that frequency. Suppose we summarize that condition by writing the following equation:

$$\left\{ A_1 \cos 2\pi f_1 t + A_2 \cos 2\pi f_2 t + A_3 \cos 2\pi [(2f_1 - f_2) t + \theta] \right\}^3 = 0$$

at $(2f_1 - f_2)$ for some A_3 and θ. By this we mean that there is some amplitude A_3 and phase θ for the cubic combination tone such that when it is added to the other two components no energy appears at $2f_1 - f_2$. In general, such an amplitude and phase will exist because the first two components produce a component at $2f_1 - f_2$. We can then find an amplitude and phase for the cancellation tone that will null this energy. Now what will happen when we raise the levels of the primaries, A_1 and A_2? Since there is no energy at the frequency $2f_1 - f_2$, we can multiply each component within the brackets by the same constant and leave the results unaffected. Thus, the relative sizes of A_3, A_1, and A_2 will remain the same. The size of the cancellation tone will therefore vary linearly with the level of the primaries.

This is quite unlike the usual assumption made with the general power series expansion. In the classic power series approach, one assumes that the linear term predominates at low sound levels. When the primaries are at a high level such that an appreciable distortion component results, the cancellation tone is much smaller than the primaries. It can therefore be treated as if it were only affected by the linear term of the series. The cancellation condition is assumed to be of the following kind:

$$g(A_1 \cos 2\pi f_1 t + A_2 \cos 2\pi f_2 t) - A_3 \sin 2\pi[(2f_1 - f_2)t + \theta] = 0$$

at $2f_1 - f_2$ for some A_3 and θ.

The basic difference then is whether one assumes the cancellation tone is greatly affected by the nonlinearity or whether, as the last equation assumes, it can be treated as essentially linear. Smoorenberg investigated the "essential" nonlinearity assumption and derived many interesting predictions about the form of the cancellation results. In general, his analyses provide a simple and parsimonious interpretation of the cancellation experiment and seriously challenge the classic power series approach.

To close our discussion of distortion phenomena, let us consider two areas where nonlinearity may provide important insights. The first is pure tone masking where combination tones may explain certain anomalies of the masking pattern; the second is two-tone inhibition effects observed in eighth nerve recordings.

PURE TONE MASKING

Anomalies in the pure tone masking pattern appeared in Wegel and Lane's (1924) original study. If the masker is fixed in frequency and the threshold of the signal is measured at highest frequencies, in the region 1.2 to 1.6 times the masker frequency, then certain dips and irregularities occur in the masking pattern. Small's (1959) data show these irregularities quite clearly.

At first, the irregularities were noted at the harmonics of the masker, where clear beats could be heard (Wegel & Lane, 1924). Some of these were due to harmonic distortion introduced by the ear, but at least in some of the early studies the equipment itself caused some harmonic distortion. In recent times, these irregularities have also been noticed at frequency locations that could not reflect simple quadratic distortion. Greenwood (1971), in a lengthy series of studies, has definitely isolated the cause of these irregularities. Basically, Greenwood's explanation is that for signals above the frequency of the masker, the masker and signal interact to generate a cubic difference tone. This distortion component lies below the frequency of the masker and hence is detected. To demonstrate this, one can place a band of low-level masking noise in the frequency region just below the masking frequency. This procedure markedly alters the masking pattern (see Figure 9.3). The bottom masking pattern of the graph (marked T. Alone) is produced by the 2,000-Hz tone alone. The graph shows the threshold produced by this masker on a number of different signal frequencies. Maximum masking occurs near 2,000 Hz and a noticeable notch is present at about 2,500 Hz. A low-pass noise in the region below 2,000 Hz removes this notch. As the spectrum level (dB/Hz) of the noise is increased, the main effect (see Figure 9.3, points 15 or 25) is the expected increased masking on the signal frequencies below 2,000 Hz. What adds considerable credence to Greenwood's hypothesis is that addition of this low-frequency energy affects the high-frequency part of the masking pattern by removing the notch.

Greenwood (1971) has presented many similar demonstrations to illustrate this basic point. There seems little doubt that the notch arises because the 2,000-Hz masker and the 2,500-Hz signal produce a cubic combination component $(2f_1 - f_2)$ at about 1,500 Hz. The detection of this distortion component is the reason the threshold is low in the region of the 2,500-Hz signal. Noise that obscures the 1,500-Hz component elevates the threshold for the 2,500-Hz signal and hence eliminates the notch. In later papers Greenwood has explored other implications of this hypothesis and has used this technique to estimate the level of various combination tones.

Thus, the previous example has provided one illustration where nonlinear analysis allowed us to understand an important and perplexing result. As our second example of nonlinear analysis, we consider the apparent inhibition in the discharge patterns of VIIIth nerve fibers caused by two sinusoids.

TWO-TONE INHIBITION

Sachs and Kiang (1968) have presented the most comprehensive evidence for two-tone inhibition. To understand their experiment, recall that every auditory fiber has a characteristic frequency to which it is most sensitive. Suppose we drive the fiber by presenting a tone at the characteristic frequency. We adjust the

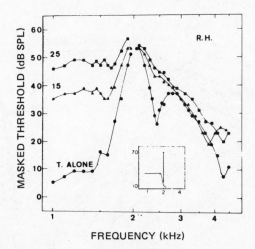

FIG. 9.3 The masked threshold value of a sinusoidal signal as a function of frequency for several masking conditions. The curve marked *T* alone is the masking produced by a 2,000-Hz sinusoid at 70 dB SPL. Note the pronounced notch in the region of 2,500 Hz. The masking curves marked 15 and 25 are obtained with low pass noise added to the sinusoidal masker of 15- or 25-dB spectrum level. The addition of the noise changes the low-frequency thresholds, of course, but also eliminates the notch at 2,500 Hz. (From Greenwood, 1971, p. 512.)

intensity of that tone so that the fiber responds a little faster than its spontaneous rate. Next, we present another tone, called the sweep tone, and study how the level and frequency of the sweep tone affects the discharge rate of the fiber. Frequencies of the sweep tone near the characteristic frequency cause little change in the discharge rate. However, if the frequency of the sweep tone is set a little away from the characteristic frequency of the fiber, a decrease in the base rate of firing results. This effect is called "inhibition" by Sachs and Kiang. The inhibitory regions are the cross-hatched areas of Figure 9.4.

Sachs and Kiang found such inhibitory response areas in every one of the more than 300 fibers they sampled in their study. While others have found similar results, Sachs and Kiang's data still remain the most comprehensive picture of this phenomenon. The word "inhibition" may suggest some direct neural interaction, but no such interaction is directly observed. Inhibition is simply the name for some decrease (say 20%) in the base rate of activity. This decrease in the discharge rate might result from a number of different mechanisms and be totally unrelated to the direct neural interaction which is called inhibition in other contexts. One hypothesis used to explain two-tone inhibition is Pfeiffer's nonlinear model (1970).

Pfeiffer's model is essentially an extension of an earlier suggestion by Engebretson and Eldredge (1968). Basically, the model assumes two filters with a nonlinear element coupling the two filter stages. The nonlinearity assumed is

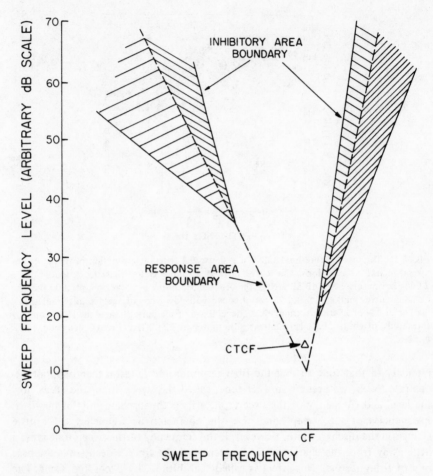

FIG. 9.4 Idealized inhibitory and excitatory response area of an auditory unit. The dotted line shows the usual tuning curve associated with the fiber in response to a sinusoidal signal. The response to a continuous tone set in level near the peak of the tuning curve (denoted CTCF) is then monitored while another, second, tone is intermittently presented at several different frequencies. The shaded portions represent those frequency–intensity combinations of the second tone that cause a decrease in the response of the fiber. (From Sachs & Kiang, 1968, p. 1127.)

nearly a cube root law. The output, $f(x)$, is related to the instantaneous input x as

$$f(x) = kx^{1/3} .$$

Pfeiffer shows that if two sinusoids drive such a device, the output amplitude changes nonlinearly with the ratio of the amplitude of the two components. The amplitude of the output of the nonlinear device actually is smaller when two

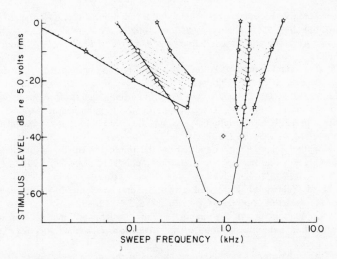

FIG. 9.5 A nonlinear electronic model attempting to mimic the results shown in Figure 9.4. The shaded area represents those combinations of frequency and intensity of a second signal that, when added to a primary signal of 1000 Hz at −40 dB re 5 V, produce a decrease in the total output of the electronic model. (From Pfeiffer, 1970, p. 1376.)

sinusoids rather than a single sinusoid are used as input. In particular, the ratio of amplitudes of the two input sinusoids determines the exact size of the output signal. Certain combinations of inputs can actually suppress the output. The special frequencies combinations that produce suppression are indicated in Figure 9.5. Their resemblance to the eighth nerve data is striking.

Pfeiffer demonstrates this similarity with a model in which he measures the voltage at the output state for certain combinations of input frequencies. We cannot say that Pfeiffer's nonlinear model is widely accepted. There is still considerable uncertainty about the exact mechanisms involved in eighth nerve excitation and considerable difference of opinion on many of the basic issues. Nevertheless, Pfeiffer's interpretation provides an interesting and novel way of viewing a set of complicated results.

Thus we see once more an important application of nonlinear analysis to auditory function. Like the notches in pure tone masking patterns, the eighth nerve results are clearly inexplicable from a linear point of view but may have a relatively simple interpretation in a nonlinear model.

REFERENCES

Chocolle, R., & Legouix, J.P. On the inadequacy of the method of beats as a measure of aural harmonics. *Journal of the Acoustical Society of America*, 1957, *29*, 749–750.
Dallos, P. *The auditory periphery.* New York and London: Academic Press, 1973.

Engebretson, A.M., & Eldredge, D.H. Model for the non-linear characteristics of cochlear potentials. *Journal of the Acoustical Society of America*, 1968, *44*, 548–554.

Goldstein, J.L. Auditory non-linearity. *Journal of the Acoustical Society of America*, 1967, *41*, 676–689.

Greenwood, D.D. Aural combination tones and auditory masking. *Journal of the Acoustical Society of America*, 1971, *50*, 502–543.

von Helmholtz, H.L.F. *Die Lehre von den tenepfindungen als physiologische grundlage fur die theorie der musik.* New York: Dover, 1954. (Originally published in 1863.)

Hall, J.L. Auditory distortion products f_2-f_1 and $2f_1-f_2$. *Journal of the Acoustical Society of America*, 1972, *51*, 1863–1871. (a)

Hall, J.L. Monaural phase effect: Cancellation and reinforcement of distortion products f_2-f_1 and $2f_1-f_2$. *Journal of the Acoustical Society of America*, 1972, *51*, 1872–1881. (b)

Lawrence, M., & Yantis, P.J. Onset and growth of aural harmonics in the overloaded ear. *Journal of the Acoustical Society of America*, 1956, *28*, 852–858.

Lawrence, M., & Yantis, P.J. In support of an "inadequate" method for detecting "fictitious" aural harmonics. *Journal of the Acoustical Society of America*, 1957, *29*, 750–751.

Meyer, M.F. Aural harmonics are fictitious. *Journal of the Acoustical Society of America*, 1957, *29*, 749.

Pfeiffer, R.R. A model for two-tone inhibition of single cochlear-nerve fibers. *Journal of the Acoustical Society of America*, 1970, *48*, 1373–1378.

Sachs, M.B., & Kiang, N.Y-S. Two-tone inhibition in auditory nerve fibers. *Journal of the Acoustical Society of America*, 1968, *43*, 1120–1128.

Small, A.M. Pure tone masking. *Journal of the Acoustical Society of America*, 1959, *31*, 1619–1625.

Smoorenberg, G.F. Audibility region of combination tones. *Journal of the Acoustical Society of America*, 1972, *52*, 603–614. (a)

Smoorenberg, G.F. Combination tones and their origin. *Journal of the Acoustical Society of America*, 1972, *52*, 615–632. (b)

Smoorenberg, G.F. On the mechanisms of combination tone generation and lateral inhibition in hearing. In E. Zwicker & E. Terhardt (Eds.), *Facts in hearing.* New York: Springer-Verlag, 1974.

Timmer, J.D., & Firestone, F.A. An investigation of subjective tones by means of the steady tone phase effect. *Journal of the Acoustical Society of America*, 1937, *9*, 24–29.

Wegel, R.L., & Lane, C.E. The auditory masking of one pure tone by another and its probable relation to the dynamics of the inner ear. *Physical Review*, 1924, *23*,(2), 266–285.

Zwicker, E. Der Ungewöhnliche Amplitudengang der Nichtlinearen Verzerrungen des Ohres. *Acustica*, 1955, *5*, 67–74.

10
Discrimination

INTRODUCTION

An obvious question to ask about any sensory system is how much a stimulus can be changed before the system can detect the alteration. The dimensions along which the signal is altered are usually dictated either by theory or by convenience. In the case of auditory stimuli, the sinusoid is a basic and elementary stimulus. It is therefore natural to ask how much a sinusoid might be altered in either intensity or frequency before the observer notices the change. Although these basic discrimination studies were first conducted nearly 50 years ago, and have often been repeated, there is still little agreement on the answers to these questions. The exact form of these relations potentially could provide a great amount of information about how the system operates. The basic discrimination data are of special interest when compared with neurophysiological data. The dynamic range of the auditory sense and how that range is achieved is but one area that has led to the development of interesting and nonobvious psychophysical models. We call this general class of models "excitation-pattern models," and we will spend some time considering their properties. Although these models avoid some of the more obvious paradoxes imposed by the physiological data, the results of some discrimination experiments are difficult to reconcile with any of these theories. Potentially, discrimination experiments are among the most interesting areas in psychoacoustics because the conflicts between the molar and molecular levels are particularly sharp. It is often very difficult to understand how the peripheral mechanisms can produce the data observed at the psychophysical level.

We begin the chapter with psychophysical data concerning the discrimination of a small change in the intensity of a sinusoid.

INTENSITY DISCRIMINATION

The basic problem is simple. We successively present the observer with two sinusoids that differ only in intensity. The frequency of the sinusoids is the same. How large must the difference in the intensity of the sinusoids be for the observer to reliably detect it? A complete answer to this question would involve manipulating two or perhaps three obvious physical parameters and determining the exact procedure to be used in asking the subject to make the discrimination. The two obvious physical parameters are the frequency of the sinusoid and its initial intensity, I. A third but less frequently studied physical variable is duration of the signal. The psychophysical procedures used in determining this "just-detectable" change in intensity are too varied to be summarized simply. Let us illustrate one by beginning historically with the first study of intensity discrimination.

Riesz (1928) studied the discrimination of an intensity change by adding the output of two oscillators of slightly different frequencies and amplitudes. A basic trigonometric identity shows why these data represent a discrimination of a change in amplitude. Given

$$y(t) = a \cos(2\pi mt - \epsilon) + b \cos(2\pi nt - \epsilon'),$$

where $m - n$ is small, $y(t)$ can be written as

$$y(t) = r \cos(2\pi mt - \theta),$$

where

$$r^2 = a^2 + b^2 + 2ab \cos[2\pi(m - n)t + \epsilon' - \epsilon],$$

and θ is a function of a, b, ϵ, and ϵ' (see Rayleigh, 1877, page 23). The amplitude, r, is a maximum when the cosine term is +1 and a minimum when the cosine term is −1. The value of r is then $a + b$ or $a - b$, respectively. The rate of fluctuation in amplitude or the rate of beating equals the difference frequency, $m - n$. Figure 10.1 shows the waveform when $m - n$ is large enough so that several beat cycles are evident.

The rate of beating is important in measuring discrimination of the fluctuation, so Riesz first found the rate of fluctuation to which the ear seemed most

FIG. 10.1 Beats caused by adding two sinusoids of nearly the same frequency. The rate of beating is equal to the difference frequency.

sensitive. He did this at only one frequency, but some informal checks by the author indicate that his result holds over most of the audio range. Riesz found that the ear was most sensitive to fluctuations at about 3 Hz. Thus, whatever frequency of sinusoid Riesz investigated, the difference between the two sinusoids was set to produce a fluctuation in intensity at 3 Hz. One sinusoid was made much weaker than the other. At each frequency the observer adjusted the amplitude of the weaker tone until an audible fluctuation in the intensity of the signal was noticeable. This defined the minimum detectable change in pressure of the sinusoid at that frequency. Riesz took data at a variety of different intensity levels ranging from bare audibility to 100 dB above the threshold. He also explored the frequency range from 35 Hz to 10,000 Hz. An earphone was used to listen to the signal. His data have been widely quoted in secondary sources ever since.

A rough summary of the data is that the just-detectable increment in intensity is roughly equal for all frequencies but shows a slight minimum around 1,000 Hz. The exact value for this just-detectable increment is sometimes quoted in different forms, so let us spend a little time on the details of the measurements.

Let us denote the pressure of the weaker wave by p and the pressure of the stronger wave by $p + \Delta p$. Since pressure squared is proportional to energy, the increment in energy ΔE is

$$\Delta E = (p + \Delta p)^2 - p^2 = 2p\Delta p + (\Delta p)^2 .$$

The increment in energy divided by the base energy, usually referred to as $\Delta I/I$, is

$$\frac{\Delta I}{I} = \frac{\Delta E}{E} = \frac{2p\Delta p + (\Delta p)^2}{p^2} \cong \frac{2\Delta p}{p} \quad \text{for} \ \Delta p \ll p .$$

For large initial p, the value of $\Delta I/I$ is twice the value of $\Delta p/p$. Hence, one must distinguish whether the ratio is given in pressure or energy terms. Riesz's measurements indicate that the increment in energy is about .1 for a 1,000-Hz tone at 60 dB SL. As the tone further increases in intensity to 100 dB the value of energy ratio, $\Delta I/I$, drops to about .06. Another way to express increment data is in terms of ΔI in decibels. This quantity is defined by

$$\Delta I \text{ in dB} = 10 \log(I + \Delta I)/I$$
$$= 10 \log \left(1 + \frac{\Delta I}{I}\right)$$
$$\cong 10 \log \left(1 + \frac{2\Delta p}{p}\right) \quad \text{if} \ \Delta p \ll p.$$

ΔI in dB is simply ten times the logarithm of the ratio of the base level of energy plus increment divided by the base level. Since often $\Delta I/I$ is small, we can use a power series approximation[1] and express ΔI in decibels as follows:

$$10 \log \left(1 + \frac{\Delta I}{I} \right) \cong 4.3429 \frac{\Delta I}{I} \quad \text{for small} \quad \frac{\Delta I}{I}.$$

If $\Delta p/p = .05$, then $\Delta I/I = 0.1025$ and ΔI in decibels is about .4 dB; if $\Delta p/p = .1$, then $\Delta I/I = .210$ and ΔI in decibels is about .8 dB. In working in the laboratory with attenuators, one can easily increase the sound level by 1 dB. This is equivalent to an increase in pressure of about 13%. Such an increment is usually detectable for practically any sound.

Almost 50 years have elapsed since Riesz's original study. No experiments of comparable scope employing so many intensity levels and frequencies have appeared since then, although restricted studies have investigated various specific conditions. Many have involved procedural changes, avoiding the beat technique. Often two separate and distinct presentation intervals are used so that one can manipulate the duration of the signals to be compared and the interval that separates them. The results of these experiments are varied and sometimes discrepant. Historically the next study using the most careful psychophysical techniques is that of Harris (1963). The main experimental question was the relation of $\Delta I/I$ to I. In recent years this relationship has received a great deal of attention, both experimental and theoretical.

Figure 10.2 summarizes data from several experiments investigating how $\Delta I/I$ varies with I. The frequency of the sinusoid was 1,000 Hz in all cases. The ratio $\Delta I/I$ is large for small values of I and decreases as I is increased. Harris (1963, p. 14) (open squares in Figure 10.2) used the same technique that Riesz (1928) used in his initial study, and the trend in the data is very similar. Harris' other data (1963, p. 7) do not follow the general trend of the other results. In that study, the signals were two .5-sec pulses of a sinusoid that differed in amplitude. The interval between the two signals was about .5 sec. However, this cannot explain the discrepancy from other studies since two other experiments also used a two-alternative procedure and presented the signal in two separate intervals. Further, McGill and Goldberg (1968) used highly practiced subjects, they presented a signal once every 4 or 5 sec, and requested the subject to indicate whether it was the standard, I, or the standard plus the increment, $\Delta I + I$. Despite this rather unorthodox procedure, their data agree with the majority of other data and showed a clear decline in the value of ΔI as a function of I.

Were Weber's law exactly true, the ratio $\Delta I/I$ would be constant and independent of I. This relationship would appear in Figure 10.2 as a horizontal line (zero slope). The data show a systematic departure from this law. McGill and Goldberg have summarized this as the so-called "near miss to Weber's law." This "near miss" is of considerable theoretical interest since the exact form of the function

---

[1] $\ln(1 + x) = x - x^2/2 + x^3/3$ for $-1 < x < 1$. Hence, for small x, $\ln(1 + x) = x$ or since $\log y = \log e \ln y = .43429 \ln y$; thus, $\log(1 + x) \cong .43429x$.

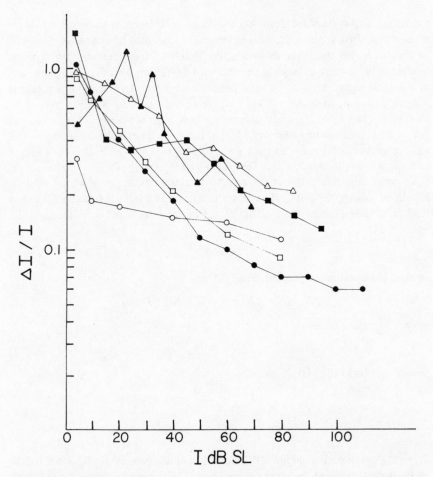

FIG. 10.2 Summary of several studies of the discrimination of a difference in amplitude of two sinusoids as a function of intensity: (●) Reisz (1928); (○) Harris (1963); (□) Harris (1963); (▲) McGill and Goldberg (1968); (△) Campbell and Lasky (1967); (■) Luce and Green (1974). The signal frequency was 1,000 Hz in all cases. (From Luce & Green, 1974, p. 1559.)

should reveal something about a fundamental process of discrimination, the discrimination of change in intensity.

It is easy to construct from probabilistic consideration a number of models that depart fairly dramatically from Weber's law. Probably the simplest one assumes that each intensity establishes some sort of Poisson-like process of neural pulses. Because the process is Poisson, the variance in the number of counts is proportional to the total number of counts. Thus, if 100 counts occur, the variance would be 100 or the standard deviation would be 10. If 10,000 counts occur the standard deviation would be 100. In order to detect reliably a change in intensity, the increment in the count rate must be large enough not to be confused with the inherent variability. Therefore the increment in the count rate must be at least as large as the standard deviation, which is the square root of the total count. If N is the total count number and ΔN the increment that is reliably detected, then $\Delta N = kN^{1/2}$, where k, the detecting criterion, should be about one. The value k merely determines how large we demand the increment ΔN to be compared to variability ($N^{1/2}$). If we are extremely conservative and wish to make no false alarms then we set $k = 3$ or 4 or even 5. If we are willing to make some false alarm, about 16%, then we may set $k = 1$.

We must now relate the count rate to the stimulus to see what the relation should be among the physical variables measured at some constant performance level. The easiest assumption is that N, the count rate, is proportional to I, the intensity. If

$$N = cI, \tag{10.1}$$

where c is a constant of proportionality, then

$$\Delta N = (N + \Delta N) - N \propto (I + \Delta I) - I = \Delta I. \tag{10.2}$$

By our detection criterion

$$\Delta N = N^{1/2}, \tag{10.3}$$

using Eqs. (10.1) and (10.2), we have

$$\Delta I = c^{1/2} I^{1/2}$$

$$\frac{\Delta I}{I} = c^{1/2} I^{-1/2}.$$

Thus, in a graph such as Figure 10.2, $\Delta I/I$ should decrease by about one-third for each 10 dB increment in I (the square root of 10 is approximately 3—on log-log coordinates the slope should be $-1/2$). Since the data do not follow such a rule, an alternative hypothesis must be suggested. McGill and Goldberg assumed a nonlinear relation between N and I that differs from Eq. (10.1). They assume

$$N = cI^p,$$

where p is a fraction such as .2 or .3 and c is a scale constant. Then the bulk of data shown in Figure 10.2 are very nearly predicted.

The mathematics is straightforward. We assume, as before, that a reliable increment demands

$$\Delta N = N^{1/2}.$$

The mapping between neural counts and intensity is

$$N = cI^p \text{ or } N + \Delta N = c(I + \Delta I)^p, \tag{10.4}$$

where c is a proportionality constant. Thus, using the binomial approximation

$$\frac{N + \Delta N}{N} = (1 + \Delta I/I)^p \cong 1 + p\frac{\Delta I}{I}. \tag{10.5}$$

Hence

$$\Delta N = pN\frac{\Delta I}{I}, \tag{10.6}$$

and, using Eq. (10.3),

$$N^{-1/2} = p\frac{\Delta I}{I}. \tag{10.7}$$

Our mapping law (Eq. 10.4) says

$$\frac{\Delta I}{I} = \frac{1}{pc^{1/2}} I^{-p/2}, \tag{10.8}$$

$$\Delta I = \frac{1}{pc^{1/2}} I^{(1-p/2)}. \tag{10.9}$$

The slope of the line in Figure 10.2 is about $-.15$, hence $p \cong .30$. This result agrees with the direct scaling of loudness (see Chapter 11).

Alternative suggestions have also been made to account for the improvement in relative detection as a function of I. One of the more interesting is that of Viemeister (1972) who starts with the assumption that Weber's law is true, that is, $\Delta I/I = k$. He accounts for the relative decrease in $\Delta I/I$ with I in the following way. Suppose the ear generates, because of small nonlinearities, an amplitude distortion that can be expressed in a power series having a linear term, a squared term, a cubic term, and so forth. (We discuss this general type of model in Chapter 7.) As the intensity of the signal increases, the effective level of these higher harmonics increases. Viemeister supposes that the observer listens for a change in intensity on the basis of the higher harmonics rather than the signal frequency itself. To see how this might be the case, consider a change of 1 dB in intensity from say, 50 to 51 dB. At the second harmonic of this frequency, the initial level might be, say, 20 dB. But the increment increases as the square of the base signal and will be 2 dB, a change from 20 to 22 dB. Thus, if the subject hears the second harmonic the relative change in intensity is actually greater at that frequency than at the fundamental. Similarly, at even higher levels, the third harmonic becomes detectable and because the third harmonic grows as the third power of the fundamental, a change of 1 dB at the fundamental implies a 3-dB change at the third harmonic. At higher signal levels discriminability of a slight change in intensity becomes relatively better because this nonlinearity causes the higher harmonics to grow more rapidly than the fundamental. As Viemeister observed in his study, not only can this theory account for the data shown in Figure 10.2, but it suggests an interesting additional experiment.

Suppose we obscure the higher harmonics of the tone by asking that the subject discriminate a change in intensity at 1,000 Hz in the presence of a high-frequency noise extending from 1,500 Hz and above. Such a noise should presumably mask the distortion product generated by the 1,000-Hz tone and thus Weber's law should hold for this condition. This is exactly what Viemeister observed.

Several other studies have now questioned this general model on several grounds (Moore & Raab, 1974; Penner, Leshowitz, Cudahy, & Ricard, 1974). While sufficient data are still not available, it seems clear that Viemeister's initial hypothesis is probably too simple. Nevertheless all results agree that if one surrounds the signal with a noise masker then Weber's law is almost exactly true. This indicates that in general the classic data are not based simply upon a change in intensity at the signal frequency but upon some overall change in the pattern of mechanical excitation produced on the basilar membrane or upon some change in the total pattern of neural excitation. We will pursue this general line of thought in more detail later. Let us turn for a moment to an equally puzzling area, the discrimination of a change in frequency.

FREQUENCY DISCRIMINATION

If intensity discrimination data are occasionally discrepant, then frequency discrimination data are chaotic. The basic problem is again quite simple. We have a certain tone at a given frequency and another tone at the same intensity but a slightly different frequency. We wish to know the minimum change in frequency that the observer needs to reliably detect a discrepancy between the two tones. Once more, the original experiment was not conducted by presenting two signals separated in time, but rather with a continuous sound that was slowly varied in frequency. This was the procedure in Shower and Biddulph's classic study (1931). The rate of change of frequency was about 3 Hz. The actual time course of the change between the two frequencies was cyclical with about twice as much time spent at either frequency than in making a gradual transition from one frequency to the other. This generates a rather complicated spectrum. Were the change from one frequency to another sinusoidal, then we would have simple FM modulation. An FM spectrum contains a large number of line components. Only two or three are prominent if the rate of change between the two frequencies is slow relative to the extent of the change, as it was in Shower and Biddolph's experiment. Once more, the classic data are still the best available in terms of the range of frequencies and intensities studied. The intensity was varied from 0 to 90 dB SL at 1,000 Hz and frequencies from 31 to 12,000 Hz were used. The general trend in the data is easy to describe. The quantity Δf, the just-detectable change in frequency, diminishes as intensity is increased. The ratio of $\Delta f/f$ is large at low frequencies and diminishes to a constant value of about .003 at frequencies of 500 Hz and above. One encounters a number of problems in trying to compare these data with other determinations of the just-noticeable change in frequency.

As with intensity discrimination, several procedures have been used to study this basic auditory parameter. Some studies employed brief presentation intervals that allowed the subjects to compare two bursts of the sinusoids differing only in frequency. Others have used the method of adjustment in which the subject adjusts the frequency of a continuous sinusoid so that he can just discriminate it from the base or standard frequency. Unfortunately, in major respects the data are widely discrepant. The absolute value sometimes differs by as much as a factor of 10 from one study to another. Furthermore, such basic questions as whether frequency discrimination changes with intensity are still not yet clearly resolved, nor are the reasons for the discrepancies across experiments understood.

Figure 10.3 shows a summary from three papers. While the absolute level of discriminability might change somewhat depending upon the method used, this factor alone can hardly account for the different shapes of the various functions. Clearly, there are some factors that are not well understood in this area. Their elucidation will probably greatly assist our understanding of basic psychoacoustic processes.

One serious error in the classic data has been revealed by Henning (1966). At very high frequencies, say 4,000 Hz and above, the wavelength of sound approximates the acoustic resonances of the ear channel, especially when measured under earphones. Thus, as the sound stimulus is changed, standing waves and other interference phenomena rather drastically alter the sound pressure level developed at the eardrum (Shaw, 1966). Consequently, a small change in frequency can produce a relatively large change in intensity. At high frequencies these changes of intensity are sufficient cues for detecting a change in frequency. In short, at these frequencies the subjects in the classic experiments may have discriminated between two sinusoids differing in frequency on the basis of changes in apparent loudness. Henning was the first to realize this potential source of difficulty and he demonstrated its existence by randomizing the intensity of the sinusoids. His subjects listened to a standard sinusoid of a fixed intensity and frequency. The comparison stimulus was another sinusoid of different frequency but it also differed in intensity from the standard. If the intensity of the comparison stimulus is randomized over about a 10-dB range, then the value for Δf may increase by as much as an order of magnitude at high frequencies. At lower frequencies, below 2,000 Hz, randomizing intensity produces no change in Δf. The results are very close to those of Stucker (1908), who avoided any loudness cues by using a Galton whistle. The intensity of the whistle was not controlled and probably varied over a considerable range in the experiment.

While this will explain discrepancies at high frequencies, there is still no adequate explanation of the many discrepancies that appear even at low frequen-

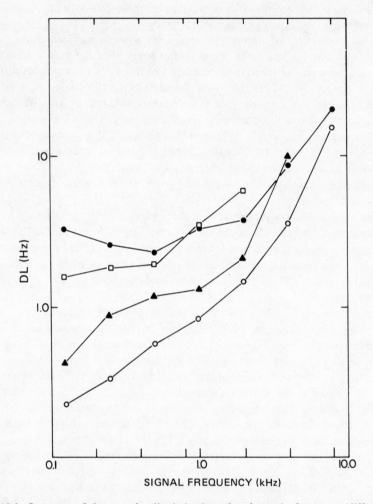

FIG. 10.3 Summary of data on the discrimination of a change in frequency (difference limen) as a function of frequency. The level of the signal is approximately the same in all studies: (△) Harris (1952), 30 dB SL; (○) Nordmark (1968), 45 dB SL; (□) abrupt variation and (●) sinusoidal variation in Shower and Biddulph (1931), 40 and 50 dB SL.

cies. Those who have worked in this area are impressed by the large individual differences among subjects. The sensitivity to a change in frequency varies greatly from one subject to the next. Certainly the variability among subjects in frequency discrimination is much larger than those encountered in intensity discrimination. The character of the differences among subjects in frequency discrimination is of a peculiar kind. While many subjects, both musically trained and untrained, might hear a 2-Hz change at 1,000 Hz, some subjects may require 20 Hz or more. Such subjects are quickly identified and their data never appear in published studies. In existing data, then, the subjects are preselected to some degree. Still, the amount of variability is impressive.

In summary, the data on frequency discrimination are varied. At high frequencies the change in loudness as a function of frequency has led to spurious values of Δf. At the lower frequencies the different procedures have produced data that differ by a factor of 3 or more. There are large individual differences in this ability and that may contribute in part to discrepancies among different studies. Some would claim that most of this difference depends on whether modulation is used as opposed to comparing two pulsed sinusoids. Just why this procedural factor is important has not been explained.

Let us now leave the psychoacoustic data and turn to what we know on the physiological level concerning the discrimination of a change in intensity. The physiological data raise sharp problems for the interpretation of psychoacoustic data. We are forced to think more in terms of patterns of excitation coming over several parallel fibers or channels rather than simply the discharge rate in a single fiber or channel.

CODING INTENSITY AT THE PERIPHERAL LEVEL

A persistent question in the study of the auditory system concerns the input–output function for intensity. Suppose we have an isolated fiber and have determined its best frequency. Suppose also we measure the rate at which the fiber fires as a function of intensity. These so-called rate functions were measured in Galambos and Davis' (1943) original studies of single auditory nerve potentials. The exact way in which the frequency of discharge changes with intensity of the tone differs somewhat from one fiber to the next. Nevertheless, certain general properties appear. At the lowest intensity levels we find a low constant rate—the spontaneous activity of the nerve fiber. An increase in intensity generally increases the frequency of firing. Occasionally, a slight decrease in frequency occurs, as shown in the phase-locked period histograms presented earlier in Chapter 5. Eventually, however, the rate increases as intensity is increased. Then, after an increase of 20–40 dB in intensity, the fiber reaches its maximum firing rate. A further increase in the intensity of the signal generally does not increase the frequency of firing and, in fact, may lead to a gradual or even sudden decline in the rate. The striking fact is that a change in intensity of only 20–40 dB is all that is needed to move the fiber from a spontaneous to a maximum rate of firing. The effective dynamic range of an individual fiber is about 30 dB. Granted that individual rate functions are sometimes quite complicated, the majority of fibers seem to obey the general properties listed above.[2] If we accept this description, how can normal hearing achieve an effective range of 100 to 120 dB?

One obvious answer is to assume that although each element has a limited dynamic range, the thresholds of these elements are distributed over the intensity scale. In combination, then, the fibers span the larger range. In simplest form, one would assume that one fiber covers the range from 0 to 30 dB SPL, the next fiber from 30 to 60 dB SPL, the third 60 to 90 dB, and the fourth fiber the last range from 90 to 120 dB. This simple and attractive idea gained some initial support from the earliest recordings from individual fibers. One could simply take available data on the threshold at the best frequency for a fiber and form the distribution of such thresholds at any single frequency. Unfortunately, this often required comparisons across different animals which might contribute to differences in sensitivity due to the different physiological states of the animals during recordings. The distribution of thresholds, at, say, a characteristic frequency of about 1,000 Hz over a group of 12 cats yielded a large range of thresholds, apparently about 60 dB (see Figure 10.4).

In contrast, however, the data obtained within a single animal gave a very small distribution of thresholds for all fibers having similar characteristic frequencies. At nearly similar characteristic frequencies, little variation occurs in the thresholds for those fibers. Certainly the range is less than 10 dB (see Figure 10.4b, c).

In more detailed work, Kiang (1968) later confirmed the second impression. Figure 10.5 shows the plot of threshold against characteristic frequency for a large population of fibers in single animals. Threshold intensity, that is, the frequency and intensity to which the particular fiber is most sensitive, is about the same for all fibers having similar characteristic frequencies. Therefore, the idea seems definitely wrong that the threshold for the fibers is staggered so as to encompass a large dynamic range. Rather, the rule for physiological data is very simple. Once you know the characteristic frequency of the fiber you also know its threshold value to within ± 10 dB.

There are, however, some doubts about the absolute validity of this rule. First there is the recent study of Sachs and Abbas mentioned earlier. In addition there are some anatomic considerations that raise some questions. From an anatomic

---

[2] About the time this was written the article by Sachs and Abbas (1974) appeared which contains the most detailed study of rate function presently available. They find the rate function to be of a form

$$ r = \frac{d^P}{\theta + d^P} , $$

where d is the displacement of the membrane, P is a constant, and θ is the threshold value of the fiber. For large θ, $r \propto d^P$, whereas for small θ, $r \approx 1.0$. Thus the dynamic range of the fiber is related to its threshold value. Sachs and Abbas find a somewhat larger range of threshold values than Kiang (1968) reports—see the later sections of this chapter. As of this writing there is no clear reason for these discrepancies.

viewpoint, it appears that the outer hair cells should have quite different thresholds than the inner hair cells. We reviewed this point in Chapter 3 where it was observed that the basilar membrane was hinged near the inner hair cell. The shear forces generated on the outer hair cells should therefore be considerably greater than those present at the inner hair cells. Therefore, the outer hair cells might be somewhat more sensitive. While this expectation appears to be reasonable on anatomic and mechanical grounds. no electrophysiological evidence supports it. Technical difficulties may prevent us from seeing this difference, however. In the first place, only about 1 in 20 fibers would be connected to the outer hair cell if one selected at random from the eighth nerve bundle. It is also possible that fibers from the outer hair cells are somewhat smaller in diameter. If this is true, it would be a further bias against their selection. Although there is no report of two groups of differential sensitive fibers, Pfeiffer and Kim (1972) have reported two distinct populations of fibers recorded in the cat in response to acoustic click stimuli. The relative frequency is about 10 to 1 for the two populations. Population I, as they call it, shows a compound histogram to a click stimulus similar to that illustrated in Figure 5.20, Chapter 5. The most distinctive feature of these fibers is that the total number of peaks in the click histogram is largely independent of stimulus level. For Population II fibers, the histogram is often asymmetric, showing more tendency to fire on a condensation rather than a rarefaction wave. Also the total number of peaks observed in the click histogram is a strong function of click intensity. We have no information to indicate the thresholds of these two fiber classes are different. Nor do we have information concerning their response to sinusoidal stimuli. Our information in this area is limited and highly speculative.

To return to the main theme, the general picture from studies of threshold of individual fibers is that at any single frequency the dynamic range and sensitivities of the fibers are all quite similar. Thus, we are faced with the original paradox—how does a system whose individual elements respond over a limited range code intensity over $100-120$ dB?

One way to avoid this dilemma is to appeal to the pattern of excitation produced by peripheral fibers. Assume we have a sinusoidal signal of a given frequency and that we slowly increase the intensity, starting well below the threshold. First, we would begin to excite those fibers having the characteristic frequency of the sinusoid. Figure 10.4b, c shows the remarkable selectivity of the fibers to its characteristic frequency. As we increase the intensity of the sinusoid, these sensitive fibers rapidly saturate and are soon firing at their maximum rate. However, because of the nature of the tuning curves, continued increase in the intensity of the sinusoid will make other fibers active. At intensities of 70, 80, or 90 dB SPL the threshold of many fibers with different characteristic frequencies will become activated. The argument then is simply that changes in the intensity of the sinusoid produce two effects. One is to increase the rate at which the sensitive fibers respond. The second is to change

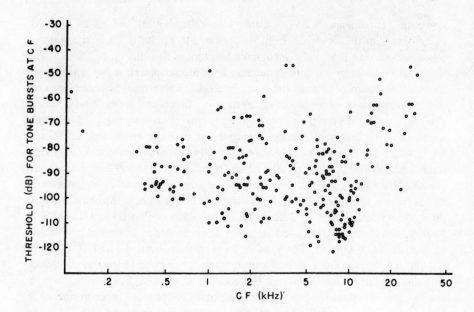

FIG. 10.4a

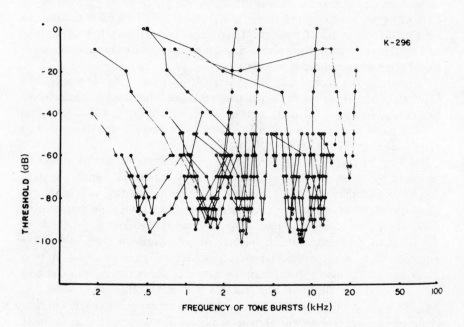

FIG. 10.4b

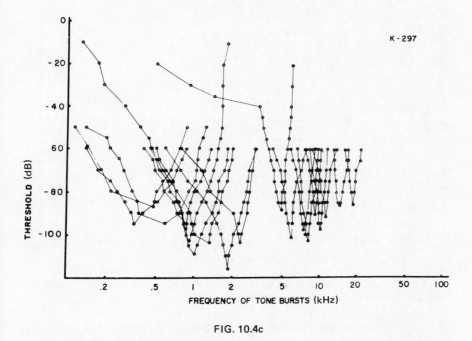

FIG. 10.4c

FIG. 10.4 (a) Threshold at characteristic frequency for a number of units from 12 cats: Note the scatter in level at any frequency region. (b and c) Tuning curves from two different cats; $K = 296$ in (b), $K = 297$ in (c). Note the thresholds at the tip of the tuning curve are nearly the same for fibers with similar characteristic frequency. Undoubtedly some of scatter in (a) arises because the individual cats were in somewhat different physiological condition during recording sessions. (From Kiang, 1965, pp. 87 and 91, Figs. 7.4, 7.5 and 7.8.)

the excitation pattern, that is, the range or number of fibers that respond to this frequency. The next section considers these so-called "excitation" models in somewhat greater detail.

EXCITATION MODELS

Any place theory faces the problem of explaining how the spatial distribution of cochlear activity associated with a sinusoidal stimulus elicits the percept of a single pitch. Grey's "principle of maximum stimulation" is an example of an early concern with how a broad spatial pattern was coded into pitch (Wilkinson & Gray, 1924). Similarly, modern investigators are concerned with how changes in these patterns, caused by a change in intensity or frequency, are detected.

The best way to understand the general class of models called "excitation models" is to return to the concept of the response area of an auditory neuron.

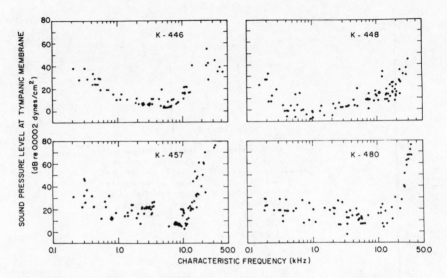

FIG. 10.5 Threshold at the tip of the tuning curve as a function of characteristic frequency for four different cats. (From Kiang, 1968, p. 11.)

This is a plot of the rate at which the fiber fires as a function of frequency for various sound pressure levels. Figure 10.6 shows some typical data from peripheral auditory fibers, collected by the Wisconsin group. The activity of a fiber, as can be seen from the figure, is heavily dependent upon both intensity and frequency of the sinusoidal input. For low sound intensities, a noticeable change in rate occurs for a very restricted set of frequencies. But at higher intensities this same fiber is responsive to a large range of frequencies. For example, at around 80–90 dB SPL, the fiber is near its maximum responsiveness for more than an octave range in frequency.

Each graph represents essentially the activity present at a single place along the cochlear partition. We know from anatomic considerations discussed in Chapter 4 that the activity displayed in Figure 10.6 probably comes from a single hair cell. The activity may be influenced by adjacent hair cells and perhaps even by some of the outer hair cells. But evidence is against this and we will consider this response to represent essentially the activity at a single point along the basilar membrane. To understand the essential arguments of excitation models we next must imagine the pattern of firings or excitation of the auditory system, were we able to view an entire array of fibers simultaneously. Consider a plot of activity or excitation as a function of place along the membrane. Figure 10.6, a recording from the cochlear nucleus, shows what happens at any single place. Because of the strict relation between place and frequency, we may infer what happens as a function of distance along an entire array of such fibers. The essential concept is that no interaction occurs among adjacent fibers. While the assumption is easy to state, it is very difficult to evaluate. Clearly, it is not true

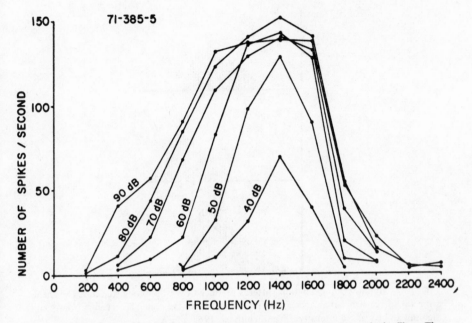

FIG. 10.6 Rate of neural discharge as a function of frequency for a single fiber. The parameter of the curve is the intensity of the 5-sec signal. As the intensity increases, more and more frequencies are capable of eliciting activity in the fiber. (After Rose *et al.*, 1974.)

in detail, for we cannot use the principle of superposition to explain the response of the peripheral fibers. There is interaction in the sense of the period histograms being different as we change the relative intensity of sinusoidal inputs. Even the frequency of discharge shows unpredictable changes as we introduce additional stimuli while tracing out a tuning curve for a single fiber (see the section "Two-Tone Inhibition," Chapter 9). But in one sense, such demonstrations may be irrelevant to the essential information transmitted about the acoustic stimulus. Until we break the acoustic code and know exactly how to interpret the auditory records, we can neither affirm nor deny the assumption of superposition.

If we then consider the distribution of activity as a function of distance along the basilar membrane we can construct the sorts of patterns seen in Figure 10.7. This diagram, taken from Whitfield (1967), is a hypothesis about what happens to an array of fibers when we either change the frequency of stimulation, as from (a) to (b) in the figure, or the intensity of the stimulus, as from (a) to (c). In essence, the rule is that changes in the frequency of stimulation shift the pattern in space, whereas changes in intensity raise or lower the amount of excitation.

Let us now recall the limited dynamic range of the individual fibers. At reasonably high intensities, that is, 40 or 50 dB above the threshold for

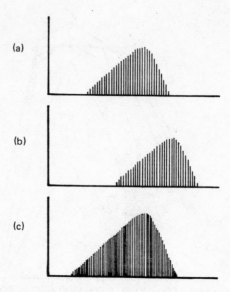

(a)

(b)

(c)

FIG. 10.7 Hypothetical excitation patterns produced by a pure tone stimulus. The change from (a) to (b) signifies an increase in the frequency of the tone. The change from A to C signifies an increase in intensity. (From Whitfield, 1967, p. 67.)

individual fibers, the fibers are often saturated. Thus, at this level and above, the excitation pattern cannot change along the vertical dimension. The fibers are already responding at their maximum rate and increasing the intensity of the stimulus will not affect this maximum. How then can further changes in intensity be appreciated? The answer is that changes in intensity must be coded by changes in the spread of excitation, that is, the number of neural fibers active when the sound is applied. This leads to the schematic diagram in Figure 10.8. The first panel of the figure shows the excitation produced by a sinusoid of moderate intensity. The second and third panels illustrate the presumed changes in pattern with increases in the frequency of the signal (Figure 10.8b) or in intensity (Figure 10.8c). Since the fiber's threshold is near 0 dB at an intensity of 70 dB, most of the fibers are saturated. In the figure, all fibers between the points a and b are assumed to be at their maximum rate. Changing the frequency of the input merely displaces the pattern to a new location (see Figure 10.8b). Now the saturated region extends from point c to point d. To the left or right of the saturated regions, the excitation diminishes as a function of distance along the array of fibers. These latter fibers are tuned to quite different characteristic frequencies and respond less vigorously (see Figure 10.6). The decrease in excitation is drawn differently on the two sides merely to emphasize that it need not be the same. We know comparatively little about the exact shape of these edges. Figure 10.8c illustrates the presumed change in the excitation pattern as we increase the intensity of the signal while leaving the frequency the same as in

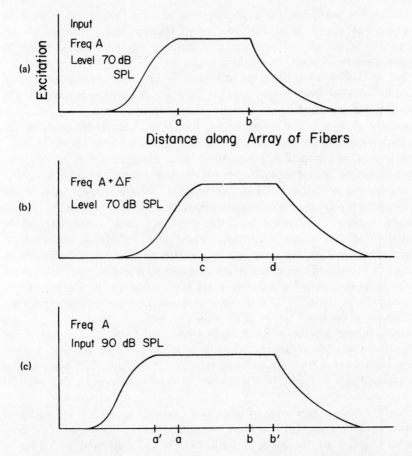

FIG. 10.8 Hypothetical patterns of excitation produced by a pure tone. Because of the high intensity of the tone, many of the fibers are saturated, for example, *a* to *b* in pattern (a). A change in frequency of the tone displaces the pattern (b), whereas a change in intensity spreads the pattern (c). If half of the pattern were obscured, then changes in intensity and frequency would produce similar effects.

Figure 10.8a. Here the essential change in the pattern is to increase the saturated region. In this instance the region involving fully saturated fibers runs from a' to b'. According to excitation models then, frequency is discriminated by a displacement of the original pattern whereas intensity is discriminated by an increase in the breadth of the pattern.

Several people have suggested models of this general type to account for frequency or intensity discrimination—Schuknecht (1960), Siebert (1968), Whitfield (1967), and Zwicker (1960). None of their ideas are identical and details of their theories differ from the simple account presented here. The preceding discussion has abstracted the basic principles of their theories while omitting some essential details. In what follows, we will take up some problems confronting models of this kind. To see how any particular theorist avoids some of the pitfalls, one must consult the original sources.

The first point to note about this view of excitation is that changes in intensity, at least from levels 10 to 20 dB above the saturation limits of the fibers, do not depend upon changes in activity at the point of maximum sensitivity along the basilar membrane. Rather changes in the edges of the excitation distribution code such a change. The new edges of saturation move from a to a' and b to b' in Figure 10.8c. This change in edge is probably the most important change in excitation for discriminating a change in intensity. The change in excitation at the signal frequency, corresponding roughly to the midpoint between a and b in Figure 10.8a, is unimportant because the fiber is already saturated. Therefore, increasing the input does little to change the excitation at that point. What does change are the sides or edges of the excitation pattern. In the same way, a change in frequency is also signaled by change in the excitation pattern. Again the edges move, but this time both move in the same direction. On a very abstract level, changes in intensity cause the edges of the excitation pattern to move in opposite directions, whereas changes in frequencies cause movements in the same direction.

This argument suggests some immediate empirical tests. For example, if one side of the excitation pattern were obscured, then confusion should occur between changes in the frequency and intensity of the tone. If either the right- or left-hand side of Figure 10.8 is covered, changes in intensity are very similar to changes in frequency.

One important exaggeration of this idea appears in Figure 10.8. The pattern is drawn so that a change in frequency or a change in intensity produces the same shaped edges. Thus, the forms of both the left- and right-hand side of Figure 10.8b and c are identical. The edge of the pattern is the same shape whether generated by change in frequency or intensity. This would be true only under the most extraordinary circumstances. In particular, the key issue is to see exactly how the rate function changes with intensity. From this one can deduce how a change in either frequency or intensity will produce differences in rate. These changes would in turn influence the exact shapes of the edges of the excitation pattern. In Siebert's model, for example, there are exact equations to describe the assumed form of the excitation functions. They would be quite different if one changed the intensity or the frequency, since the equations relating rate to frequency and sound intensity are not similar. Also Siebert's model has no saturation in the sense of that expressed in Figure 10.8. The excitation continues to increase as one increases the sound pressure level, although high intensities cause comparatively little change in rate. Therefore, details of the assumptions of the theories are extremely important. Nevertheless, the general idea should be clear. If the edges of the excitation patterns convey the crucial information about the stimulus, then the auditory system could confuse changes of frequency and intensity.

Another problem for the excitation models is the difficulty of accounting for an intensity discrimination in the change of sinusoidal signal presented in a wideband noise. Wideband noise contains energy at all frequencies. Such a stimulus should make it difficult to infer the exact shape and location of the edges of the excitation pattern. Therefore, the discrimination of a change in an amplitude of a sine wave would become increasingly difficult, since the noise would blur the edges. It should be particularly difficult if the sine wave is presented in a noise containing a notch so that on either side of the signal there is more noise energy than signal energy. In this case, one would expect the excitation pattern edges to be completely obscure and because the nerve is nearly saturated, intensity discrimination should be virtually impossible. This is not the case and some modification to the general model must be made to avoid this problem.

An equally dramatic case concerns the discrimination of an increment in the intensity of a noise stimulus. This is such an interesting case and the data are so clear that we will discuss it in detail.

DISCRIMINATION OF A NOISE INCREMENT IN NOISE

The excitation pattern caused by noise should have no edges since noise contains all frequencies. The average frequency of firing or excitation pattern should be roughly the same at all locations. If one then increases the intensity of the noise slightly, how does the excitation pattern change? Since the shape does not change it can only increase slightly in height. The discharge rate of the fibers must increase as the excitation in each place along the basilar membrane increases. But because these discharge rates are limited at high intensities, the just noticeable increment, ΔI, would grow larger and larger at high intensities. Figure 10.9, taken from Miller (1947), shows the just-noticeable increment in intensity of a wideband noise. Over a range of nearly 100 dB, this increment is a linear function of the base intensity. Weber's law ($\Delta I/I = k$) is almost exactly true except near the absolute threshold of hearing. But for most of the curve, a range of nearly 90 dB, one need increase the noise by about 2% for the increment to be just detectable. How is this linearity possible with elements whose discharge rate is such a nonlinear function of intensity, particularly if these elements all have nearly similar thresholds? Two recent studies have provided us with more neurophysiological information. Ruggero (1973) has studied how discharge rate varies for narrow bands of noise at different intensities. The rate functions for sinusoids at the characteristic frequency of the fiber or narrow (200-Hz wide) noise bands with that same center frequency are nearly identical. The rate function is S shaped but the dynamic range of the sample of

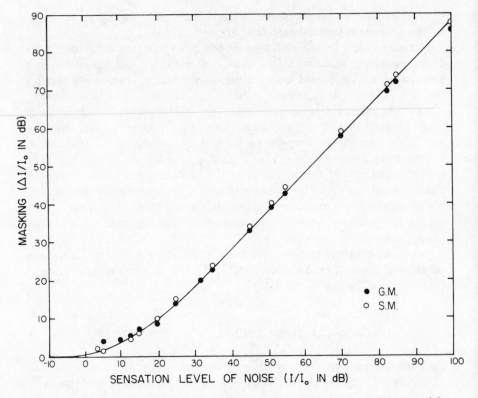

FIG. 10.9   The just noticeable increment in the intensity of a noise, ΔI, as a function of the intensity of the noise, I. The solid straight line represents the relation $\Delta I/I = k$, or Weber's law. (From Miller, 1947, p. 615.)

fibers presented shows a 40–60-dB dynamic range. Probably the most interesting result is how the discharge rate varies with the bandwidth of the noise stimulus. For all fibers studied the rate first increases for bandwidth up to 200 to 400 Hz and then decreases for larger bandwidths. Such a result strongly implies an interaction among adjacent fibers similar to the two-tone interactions mentioned earlier. Greenwood and Goldberg (1970) studied cells in the cochlear nucleus. They also observed a nonmonotonic relation between the discharge rate and the bandwidth of a noise stimulus similar to Ruggero's result. In cochlear nucleus the discharge rate as a function of intensity is often nonmonotonic. One unit, for example, has a rate of 10 spikes/sec at 20 dB, increases to 70 spikes/sec at 50 dB, and then decreases to 8 spikes/sec at 90 dB. Other units have monotonic rate function but show relatively limited dynamic ranges, about 20 to 40 dB. It appears that there are strong interactions among adjacent units. A greater understanding of this interaction will probably help us to understand how intensity is coded.

But one can hardly use this interaction alone to avoid the problems posed by noise detection results. The noise has equal energy at all frequencies, and the amount of mutual interaction should be nearly constant or at least reciprocal over the entire intensity range. Yet, over this 90-dB range, the just-detectable increment intensity, ΔI, is simply a constant proportion of the original intensity, I.

THEORIES OF FREQUENCY DISCRIMINATION

We have concentrated most heavily in this chapter on theories of intensity discrimination. This emphasis reflects the status of the field. Theoretical work in pitch concentrates mainly on pitch perception, and theories of frequency discrimination are not very far advanced. Obviously there are two main approaches to explaining frequency discrimination. One can follow the excitation pattern theories and argue that frequency discrimination is based on the detection of a shift in the excitation pattern. This is the traditional place analysis. A second approach argues that frequency discrimination is based on a detection of a change in the interarrival times between neural events. This is the traditional temporal analysis. Neither theoretical position has been presented in much detail. Few theories are developed to an extent that they predict how Δf will vary with f, or any of the other obvious physical parameters such as intensity or duration of the signals.

An exception is Siebert (1970) who has presented a very interesting analysis of optimum and near optimum use of information as encompassed in his model of the auditory system. This model involves a first stage of filtering and some Poisson channels whose discharge rates are monotonic with stimulus intensity. Taking the entire aggregate of time that spike occurs over all channels, Siebert estimates how large a change in frequency is needed for reliable detection to occur, assuming the optimum processing of the "auditory" data. He concludes on two grounds that the observer is not making optimum use of the timing information: first, because the predicted value of Δf is too low, $\Delta f - .01$ instead of $\Delta f = 2$. Second, the variation of Δf with intensity, duration, and frequency is different for model and human observer. Unfortunately this failure implies only that the observer is not using temporal information in an optimum fashion; it does not imply that the temporal information is ignored. Luce and Green (1974) present a nonoptimum, temporal model of frequency discrimination. They manage to find parameters for the model that fit the data with reasonable accuracy. Unfortunately they cannot clearly reject an alternative model of a different kind. It appears that a variety of different models might do just as well.

On the empirical side there is little hard information. Henning and Psotka (1969) have measured $\Delta I/I$ and Henning (1970) has measured $\Delta f/f$ as a function of signal duration. The change of these functions with signal duration is quite different at the three frequencies studied. This result is disquieting to pattern models in general. The model presumes that discrimination of a change in intensity or frequency is based on a change in the locus of excitation. Detection of this change should then depend in similar ways on variation in other variables such as duration. Obviously the variation with duration need not be identical for intensity and frequency discrimination, but a complete theory must explain how the differences arise and why the differences should depend on frequency. One is inclined to think that a theory assuming completely different processes for the two discrimination tasks might have an easier time explaining the differences.

REFERENCES

Campbell, R.A., & Lasky, E.Z. Masker level and sinusoidal signal detection. *Journal of the Acoustical Society of America*, 1967, *42*, 972–976.

Galambos, R., & Davis, H. The response of single auditory-nerve fibers to acoustic stimulation. *Journal of Neurophysiology*, 1943, *6*, 39–57.

Greenwood, D.D., & Goldberg, J.M. Response of neurons in the cochlear nuclei to variations in noise bandwidth and to tone-noise combinations. *Journal of the Acoustical Society of America*, 1970, *47*, 1022–1040.

Harris, J.D. Pitch discrimination. *Journal of the Acoustical Society of America*, 1952, *24*, 750–755.

Harris, J.D. Loudness discrimination. *Journal of Speech and Hearing Disorders*, 1963, (Monograph Supplement II.)

Henning, G.B. Frequency discrimination of random-amplitude tones. *Journal of the Acoustical Society of America*, 1966, *39*, 336–339.

Henning, G.B. A comparison of the effects of signal duration on frequency and amplitude discrimination. In R. Plomp & G.F. Smoorenburg (Eds.), *Frequency analysis and periodicity detection in hearing.* Leiden: A. W. Sijthoff, 1970.

Henning, G.B., & Psotka, J. Effect of duration on amplitude discrimination in noise. *Journal of the Acoustical Society of America*, 1969, *45*, 1008–1013.

Kiang, N.Y-S. A survey of recent developments in the study of auditory physiology. *Annals of Otology, Rhinology, and Laryngology*, 1968, *77*, 1–20.

Kiang, N.Y-S. *Discharge patterns of single fibers in the cat's auditory nerve.* Research Monograph 35, Cambridge, Massachusetts: MIT Press, 1965. 154 pages.

Luce, R.D., & Green, D.M. Neural coding and psychophysical discrimination data. *Journal of the Acoustical Society of America*, 1974, *56*, 1554–1564.

McGill, W.J., & Goldberg, J.P. Pure-tone intensity discrimination and energy detection. *Journal of the Acoustical Society of America*, 1968, *44*, 576–581.

Miller, G.A. Sensitivity to changes in the intensity of white noise and its relation to masking and loudness. *Journal of the Acoustical Society of America*, 1947, *19*, 609–619.

Moore, B.C.J., & Raab, D.H. Pure-tone intensity discrimination: Some experiments relating to the "near-miss" to Weber's law. *Journal of the Acoustical Society of America*, 1974, *55*, 1049–1054.

Nordmark, J.O. Mechanisms of frequency discrimination. *Journal of the Acoustical Society of America*, 1968, *44*, 1553–1540.

Penner, M.J., Leshowitz, B., Cudahy, E., & Ricard, C. Intensity discrimination for pulsed sinusoids of various frequencies. *Perception and Psychophysics*, 1974, *15*, 568–570.

Pfeiffer, R.R., & Kim, D.O. Response patterns of single cochlear nerve fibers to click stimuli: Descriptions for cat. *Journal of the Acoustical Society of America*, 1972, *52*, 1669–1677.

Rayleigh, Baron, & Strutt, J.W. *Theory of sound* Vol. 1. New York: Dover, 1945. (Originally published, 1877.)

Riesz, R.R. Differential sensitivity of the ear for pure tones. *Phys. Rev.* 1928, *31*, 867–875.

Rose, J.E., Kitzes, L.M., Gibson, M.M., & Hind, J.E. Observations on phase-sensitive neurons of anteroventral cochlear nucleus of cat: Nonlinearity of cochlear output. *Journal of Neurophysiology*, 1974, *37*, 218–253.

Ruggero, M.A. Response to noise of auditory nerve fibers in the squirrel monkey. *Journal of Neurophysiology*, 1973, *36*, 569–587.

Sachs, M.B., & Abbas, P.J. Rate versus level functions for auditory-nerve fibers in cats: Tone-burst stimuli. *Journal of the Acoustical Society of America*, 1974, *56*, 1835–1847.

Schuknecht, H.F. Neuroanatomical correlates of auditory sensitivity and pitch discrimination in the cat. In G.L. Rasmussen & W.F. Windle (Eds.), *Neural mechanisms of the auditory and vestibalar system*. Springfield, Ill.: Charles C Thomas, 1960.

Shaw, E.A.G. Earcanal pressure generated by circumaural and supraaural earphones. *Journal of the Acoustical Society of America*, 1966, *39*, 471–479.

Shower, E.G., & Biddulph, R. Differential pitch sensitivity of the ear. *Journal of the Acoustical Society of America*, 1931, *3*, 275–287.

Siebert, W.M. Stimulus transformations in the peripheral auditory system. In P.A. Kolers & M. Eden (Eds.), *Recognizing patterns*. Cambridge, Mass.: MIT Press, 1968.

Siebert, W.M. Frequency discrimination in the auditory system: place or periodicity mechanism. *Proceedings of the Institute of Electrical and Electronics Engineers*, 1970, *58*, 723–730.

Stucker, H. Über die Untershiedsenpfindlichkeit für Tonhöhen. *Z. Sinnephysiol*, 1908, *42*, 392–408.

Viemeister, N.F. Intensity discrimination of pulsed sinusoids: The effects of filtered noise. *Journal of the Acoustical Society of America*, 1972, *51*, 1265–1269.

Whitfield, I.C. *The auditory pathway*. London: Arnold, 1967.

Wilkinson, G. & Gray, A.A. *The mechanism of the cochlea*. London: Macmillan, 1924.

Zwicker, E. Ein Verfahren zur Berechnung der Lautstarke. *Acustica*, 1960, *10*, Akustishe Beihefte 1, 304–308.

11
Loudness

INTRODUCTION

Loudness is an obvious characteristic of all sounds and has an enormous range. Sounds are faint or blaring, barely audible or nearly deafening, weak or strong. One can distinguish the loudness of two sounds that differ in intensity by only 1 dB (a difference of about 25% in intensity), and this sensitivity is true over a range of 10^{12} W. How loudness varies with intensity is a basic problem in understanding the mechanisms of hearing. For this reason loudness has always been a central area in auditory research. It also is a central topic in psychophysics, the discipline concerned with the relations between physical and psychological attributes.

Although the general reasons for studying loudness are clear, one should recognize that there are two distinct and different motives for investigating loudness. First there is the practical motive. Obviously very loud sound can damage hearing, as is discussed in Chapter 13. Less intense sounds can be loud enough to be annoying or a nuisance, even if they do not damage hearing. We would like some scale of magnitude by which we could calculate the loudness of any sound. Ideally, a single number should represent the loudness of the sound. If two sounds had different loudness numbers, then the one of greater magnitude should sound the louder. Such a scale would be of great practical value. If it appeared to have general validity, then very shortly we could use the scale to set maximum allowable loudness levels. The levels would apply to sources, such as vehicles or equipment, and in certain areas, such as our living room or back yard. Some limits already exist, for example, most countries have regulations concerning the noise produced by airplanes on takeoff and landings. In the United States the Federal Aviation Agency requires that all new aircraft must first be tested to determine if they are below certain maximum noise limits. The Environmental Protection Agency (EPA) is presently developing regulations that will set limits on the sound levels produced by various machines and appliances. Modern society threatens to grow constantly louder, and a reasonable limit should be set on the auditory stimulation to which our ears are subjected.

Setting reasonable limits, however, is a complex problem. Loudness is but one of many factors that must be considered. Noise exposure near a runway of a modern airport is one good example. Loudness is not the only variable that influences public reactions. The number of flights, the time of day or season, the fear of a plane crashing, and a host of other factors all influence popular reaction. This is an area of subtlety and of considerable economic consequence. The disputes that arise are both vigorous and lengthy.

A second, more theoretical, motivation for the study of loudness is simply to understand how that aspect of auditory experience is encoded. How does loudness grow as we change the intensity of certain simple sounds such as sine waves or noise? How do combinations of different sounds influence or change the experience of loudness? Here the issues are somewhat removed from practical concerns but disagreements are no less intense.

METHODOLOGICAL CONSIDERATIONS

The methods and procedures used to investigate loudness are somewhat different from those used for many other areas covered in this book. For example, the methods differ in fundamental ways from those used to study discrimination capacity. Discrimination tasks involve clearly right and wrong answers. Two stimuli or more are compared and judged either the same or different. Sometimes the difference is very small and the subject cannot consistently discriminate the difference. Nonetheless, we expect his discrimination to co-vary appropriately with the difference in the physical stimulus. If we increase the physical difference between two stimuli, we expect better discrimination. If we obtained data where better discrimination occurred with decreasing stimulus differences, then we would search for errors in the procedure used. Similarly, among normal subjects, we usually anticipate a large degree of agreement. Even if subjects are not exactly alike, we can expect them to follow a regular ordering—the more sensitive subject being consistently better over repeated measurements.

Loudness judgments are subjective; loudness is a psychological dimension, not a physical one, and judgments of loudness will have considerably more variability than will measurements of intensity discrimination. Of course for simple stimuli such as sinusoids or broad-band noises the judged loudness will order almost perfectly with stimulus intensity. But ratings of loudness over different stimuli produce varied responses. Even comparing the loudness of sinusoids of two different frequencies or durations produces considerable variability. One subject might judge sound A louder than sound B, whereas another subject might make the reverse judgment. Fundamentally, there is no reason to say that the first subject is right and the second subject is wrong. Differences in past experience or attitude are usually assumed to account for these discrepancies. But in the last analysis there is no correct answer. Both subjects are simply evaluating the stimulus along the dimension of loudness as they appreciate it. One can quantify the amount of discrepancy between observers by allowing them to attenuate the louder sound until it equals the weaker one. In certain cases, for example, in the judgment of transient stimuli of different durations, two subjects may differ by as much as 25 dB. Such discrepancies among normal subjects are inconceivable in discrimination data.

Because of these large individual differences, judgments by single subjects are infrequently cited. Loudness data are usually means or medians over a large number of observers. As our understanding of psychophysics increases, we will undoubtedly begin to control and even eliminate the factors that lead to these individual discrepancies. At present, we must accept these rather sizable individual differences and simply obtain data from enough observers to cancel idiosyncratic differences.

PROCEDURES AND GOALS

The objective in measuring loudness is to attach a number to any possible sound which will represent its loudness. Obviously sounds vary in many different ways, and temporal variation is one. Let us restrict our discussion to steady sounds, sounds that do not fluctuate in intensity. The sound of a motor, a relatively steady noise, a complex of sinusoids, or a single sinusoid are examples. We want a way to calculate the loudness of such a sound from its physical measurement. Imagine that we have a spectral analysis of the sound so that we know its intensity as a function of frequency. From that spectrum we want to derive a single number—the loudness of the sound. Note the spectrum provides a nearly complete description of the sound, since we have ruled out temporal changes.

Given this objective, several subproblems must be solved to achieve it. To make these issues concrete, suppose we want to determine which of two sounds, A or B, is louder. Their spectra are shown in Figure 11.1. Each sound has two components whose frequency and intensity are given in the figure. Were only the 1,000-Hz component present, we would think B should be louder than A because B has 10 dB more energy at that frequency. There are immediate complications, however, since the low-frequency components of the two sounds and their intensities are different and in the opposite direction. At least three problems must be solved.

1. How do we equate loudness over different frequencies? Given a pure tone at different frequencies how does the loudness vary with frequency? The ear is

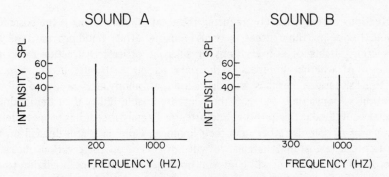

·FIG. 11.1 Spectra of two sounds whose loudness we wish to evaluate. Each sound has two components; the low-frequency component of *A* is more intense than that of *B*, whereas at the higher frequency the reverse is true.

not equally sensitive to energy at all frequencies. Some frequencies are so high as to be inaudible at any intensity. We need some contours or weights to help us calculate a loudness value at all intensities and frequencies.

2. How does loudness grow with intensity? Even if we have solved the first problem, we must know how loudness grows with intensity in order to compare sounds of different spectral distributions. For example, suppose that we knew that 200 Hz at 60 dB was exactly three times as loud as 300 Hz at 50 dB. Then the relative loudness at sound *A* and *B* would depend in part on how loudness changes at 1,000 Hz in going from 40 to 50 dB. It would also depend on our third factor.

3. How do we combine loudness over different frequencies? This is a complicated question since the answer may depend on the frequencies involved. The masking results discussed earlier show that if a sound has two components near each other in frequency but that differ in amplitude, then one component may completely obscure the other (see Chapter 6). This is not the case for our example. The components are separated enough in frequency and sufficiently close in intensity so that masking effects can be ignored. But generally, and especially for continuous spectra such as noise, masking presents a vexing problem in calculating loudness.

These questions form the central empirical problems that have received the most experimental effort. Several others should be mentioned. We have explicitly excluded from our present discussion the important issue of how to treat sounds that vary in time. If temporal variation is allowed, it is easy to think of examples where two or more sources can be recognized as distinctive. Is the combined loudness of the several sources equal to the sum of the individual loudnesses or should it be computed simply from the combined spectrum? Do fluctuating sounds of the same total energy sound louder than steady sounds? If so, then perhaps one could raise the background level of noise and obscure the fluctuations entirely, thereby reducing the total loudness. This is the basic idea behind "noise perfume" that is used in many office buildings to mask the distracting effects of conversations in adjacent offices. Distraction raises the question of whether loudness is the only relevant attribute in question. In practical situations perhaps the distraction or annoyance produced by the intrusion of unwanted sounds is the relevant variable rather than the loudness. Several people take this position and attempt to construct scales to measure the annoyance of sounds rather than their loudness. Opinion is still divided on the merits of these distinctions and we will not review all these various measures here. Later, however, we will comment briefly on one of them in relation to the traditional loudness measures.

Finally, we must also discuss how the spectrum of a sound is measured. Although we have assumed that the spectrum is known, in practice it must be measured. To measure a spectrum we employ a filter of some width and center frequency. Until now we have described noise as having a spectral density—the power in a 1-Hz band. In fact, practical noise sources are rarely measured with 1-Hz filters. Commonly an octave filter, a one-third octave filter, or occasionally a one-tenth octave filter is used. The center frequencies of these filters are conventionally set at certain values. Table 11.1 gives the recommended center frequencies. As the table makes clear, there are three one-third octave bands within an octave band. The center frequency, f_c, of a filter is half way between the upper, f_u, and lower, f_l, cutoffs on a logarithmic frequency scale

$$\log f_c = \tfrac{1}{2} \log f_l + \tfrac{1}{2} \log f_u,$$

$$f_c^2 = f_l f_u.$$

For an octave band $f_u = 2f_l$,

$$f_c^2 = f_u f_l \quad = 2f_l^2,$$

$$f_c = \sqrt{2} f_l \quad = f_u/\sqrt{2}.$$

EQUAL LOUDNESSES AT DIFFERENT FREQUENCIES

The question of equal loudness contours was one of the earliest raised. In principle its answer involves a simple method. The experimenter selects two different sinusoids or noise bands and the subject adjusts one in level until the loudnesses are equal. Some workers have placed the two sounds in different ears and attempted to obtain an interaural balance. The most common procedure, however, is to present the two sounds in succession and to use both ears in listening. If the frequencies are widely separated, the adjustments of equality may show standard deviations of about 6 to 10 dB. Some of this variability may include systematic errors as well as the usual error of measurement. The exact

TABLE 11.1
Preferred Center Frequencies of Octave and One-Third
Octave Filter

One-third octave	Octave
	16
20	
25	
	31.5
40	
50	
	63
80	
100	
	125
160	
200	
	250
315	
400	
	500
630	
800	
	1,000
1,250	
1,600	
	2,000
2,500	
3,150	
	4,000
5,000	
6,300	
	8,000
10,000	
12,500	
	16,000

outcome of an adjustment task depends on which stimulus is adjusted. This phenomenon is sometimes called a regression effect (Stevens & Greenbaum, 1966) and has been commented upon by many investigators (Scharf, 1959a, b; Zwicker, 1958; Zwicker, Flottorp, & Stevens, 1957). The usual procedure for controlling it interchanges the standard and adjustable stimulus and averages the results. The first to publish equal loudness contours was Fletcher and Munson (1933). Their curves have been widely cited and are well known to most high-fidelity enthusiasts.

Since 1950 at least 12 different laboratories have made at least 25 determinations of equal loudness—noisiness—acceptability contours. The numerous studies were motivated by a strong practical reason. The contour is a key part of any loudness calculation procedure, and various procedures for calculating loudness were being adopted in noise pollution legislation. Although the many different contours have the same general shape, they can differ by as much as 5 dB at some frequencies. These differences might arise from any number of reasons. The instructions to the subjects were different in the various experiments; some subjects were asked to make the sounds equally annoying or acceptable; others to make them equally loud. Some experiments used earphones, others used diffuse fields, and still others free fields. In the recent studies bands of noise were used, sometimes octave, sometimes one-third octave, and sometimes one-tenth octave bands. The number of observers per experiment ranged from 5 to 200.

Stevens (1972) has presented an excellent review of this literature. He presented results averaging over a number of studies. Figure 11.2 shows the means and medians along with Stevens' straight line segments that approximate the combined data.[1] As Stevens (1972) observes: "Further experiments may alter the median or the mean to some extent, but the quantity of data now available is such that it will require a rather ambitious experiment to make more than a modest alteration in the form of the average function [p. 582]."

Despite the convergence of many studies, several other contours are used at present which differ in some way from the contour shown in the figure. Robinson and Whittle (1964) have proposed slightly different contours based on their average of available data. Kryter and Pearsons (1963) used their own contours in their calculation of perceived noise level (PNdB).

The form of the equal loudness contour changes somewhat with level. Above about 40 dB SPL the curves are roughly parallel, at least for frequencies above 500 Hz. At very low sound pressure levels the contour changes more with frequency than the curve shown in Figure 11.2. At the very low levels it resembles the absolute threshold curve (see Chapter 2, Figure 2.1). The behavior of the contour at very low frequencies, less than 100 Hz, is still a matter of considerable dispute. Measurement problems become severe at such long wavelengths and many technical problems beset experiments there. Robinson and Dadson's (1956) measurements probably represent the best available data.

LOUDNESS LEVEL (THE PHON)

The matching operation that defines the equal loudness contours suggests one simple scale of loudness. We take any given sound and adjust a pure tone of some frequency to an intensity that equals the sound in loudness. The level of

---

[1] This contour is taken from Stevens' latest proposal for calculating loudness (Mark VII). The rest of the chapter will discuss features of the Mark VI Stevens (1961) procedure, which is more widely used in practice and has been adopted as an international standard. The equal loudness contour in the Mark VI procedure is very similar to that shown in Figure 11.2.

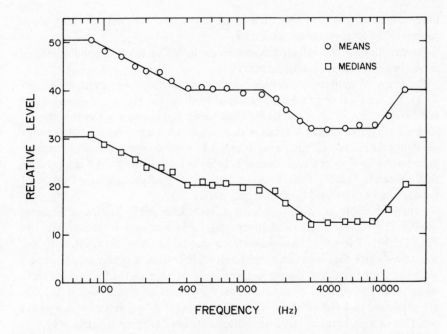

FIG. 11.2 Equal loudness contours as obtained from a number of studies. The circles represent means taken over a number of studies; the triangles represent medians from the same studies. (From Stevens, 1972, p. 582.)

the pure tone in SPL is then a measure of the sound's loudness. A 1,000-Hz sinusoid is used as the standard and its sound pressure level is by definition equivalent to the loudness in *phons* of the given sound. If an electric motor is equal in loudness to a 1,000-Hz tone at 65 dB SPL, then the motor is said to have a loudness of 65 phons. In principle, any steady-state sound can be matched and hence given a loudness level in phons. Presumably if one sound has a loudness of 75 phons, then the latter should sound louder than the former. In fact, to achieve equal loudness one should have to attenuate the latter by 10 dB.

Loudness level in principle solves the problem of constructing a scale of loudness. In practice it may be difficult to match the sound to the standard tone. Also, observers may disagree. In that case, one must assemble a large number of observers and average their judgments to determine the given sound's phon value.

We would like some more convenient procedure to calculate loudness. We should understand the judgment of loudness enough to abstract some general principles that can be incorporated into a calculation procedure. We can then simply measure the spectrum of the sound, apply the calculation procedure, and determine a number that represents the sound's loudness. Of course, once we have calculated the loudness of a given sound, we can test the calculation procedure by employing the phon scale.

Construction of the calculation procedure brings us to our second question: How does loudness grow with intensity?

The essential motivation for this question is revealed in our example (Figure 11.1). We need a scale to represent units of loudness so that we can combine and compare loudnesses across different frequencies and intensities. Construction of such a scale seems simple. We start with a standard loudness, say a 1,000-Hz tone at 40 dB SPL. We call that level 1 unit of loudness and ask the observer to increase the level of the tone until it is twice as loud. If the subject can perform that operation reliably then we have 2 units of loudness and other values of loudness can be obtained by similar procedures.

Actual attempts to construct such a scale have often produced different results. The earliest study of auditory magnitude was done by Richardson and Ross (1930). The subject was presented a standard tone of fixed intensity and was told to give that loudness a numerical value of one. A variety of other tones were then presented and the subject was asked to estimate the loudness of these other tones with respect to the standard. Pure tones in regions of 550 to 1,100 Hz were used and Richardson and Ross concluded that loudness grew as a power function of sound pressure with an average exponent of approximately .44.

Thus if ψ denotes the psychological magnitude, loudness, and p the sound pressure (dynes per square centimeter), then

$$\psi = kp^{.44}, \tag{11.1}$$

where k is a dimensional constant. It is important to note that the value of the exponent depends on the units one uses to express the physical scale. For example, if intensity I (W/cm^2) is used instead of pressure, then since I is proportional to p^2 (see Eq. 1.3, Chapter 1), we can rewrite Eq. 11.1 as

$$\psi = cI^{.22}, \tag{11.2}$$

where c is a different dimensional constant. The exponent of the power law is twice as large when expressed in pressure rather than intensity.

Several different investigations on this same topic were published within a few years of the Richardson and Ross paper. Ham and Parkinson (1932), Laird, Taylor, and Wille (1932), Geiger and Firestone (1933), and Rschevkin and Rabinovitch (1936) all explored how loudness varies with intensity for a variety of stimulus situations. The procedures differed widely. Some involved fractionation procedures, that is, adjusting the loudness to one-half or one-fourth of the standard, as well as judgments of two or four times the standard.

We can compare the various studies by asking how much reduction in level is needed to halve the loudness of a sound. The answers range from 5 to 24 dB, depending on the study one consults and the initial level of the sound. Practically all studies agree that a larger reduction is needed if the initial sound is very intense. A 20-dB reduction may be needed to halve the loudness of a 100-dB sound, but only 10 dB may be needed to halve the loudness of a 50-dB sound. The different studies yield a range of answers, although the subjects within any single study are generally consistent with each other. Stevens (1955) has published a thorough summary of all the available data.

Churcher (1935) summarized the results of the earlier experiments and proposed a simple relation between loudness and sound pressure level. Stevens (1936) used Churcher's summary and suggested that loudness values be called sones. Stevens suggested that the unit of the sone scale be a 1,000-Hz sinusoid heard binaurally at 40 dB above threshold. Since we are assuming an average subject, 40 dB above threshold at 1,000 Hz will nearly be 40 dB SPL, or 40 phons.

In Stevens' review of all previous studies he suggests that the loudness in sones L be related to the loudness level in phons by the following formula:

$$L = 10^{.03P - 1.2}. \tag{11.3}$$

If $P = 40$ dB, then $L = 1$, so the constant 1.2 simply adjusts the unit of the scale.

At any place on the scale, if we increase the level P by 10 dB, then

$$L_2 = 10^{.03 \, (P_1 + 10) - 1.2}, \tag{11.4a}$$

$$L_2 = 10^{.3} \, 10^{.03 P_1 - 1.2}, \tag{11.4b}$$

$$L_2 = 2 \cdot L_1, \tag{11.4c}$$

where L_1 is the initial loudness corresponding to P_1, and L_2 is the increased loudness. Thus to double the loudness means an increase in intensity of 10 dB.

Another important implication of this definition of loudness is that loudness grows as a power function of stimulus intensity I or pressure p. To derive this relation let us take the logarithm of both sides of Eq. (11.3); then

$$\log L = .03P - 1.2. \tag{11.5a}$$

Let us write P in terms of pressure,

$$\log L = .03(20 \log p - 20 \log p_0), \tag{11.5b}$$

where

$$20 \log p_0 = 40 \quad \text{dB SPL,}$$

then

$$L = (p/p_0)^{.6}. \tag{11.5c}$$

Note that lower case p, pressure, is different from capital P, the phon level in dB.

The form of the relation between psychological magnitude and stimulus intensity is a very important topic in the area of sensory psychology ever since the founding of the subject matter.[2]

We may also express Eq. (11.5c) as an intensive relation

$$L = (I/I_0)^{.3} , \qquad (11.6)$$

where I_0 is the reference intensity corresponding to 40 dB SPL.

HOW DO WE COMBINE LOUDNESS OVER DIFFERENT FREQUENCIES?

So far we have reviewed data on equal loudness at different frequencies and how loudness grows with intensity. Given any spectral analysis of the sound, such as

[2] The general name for this area is psychophysics and its main goal is, as the name implies, to relate the physical measurements of the stimulus to corresponding psychological attributes. There are two recent books that provide an excellent introduction to this topic. They are *The New Psychophysics,* by L. E. Marks, and *Psychophysics,* by the late S. S. Stevens. We will attempt no more than a brief diversion to acquaint the reader with some of the history of the problem.

The father of psychophysics was Fechner (1860), who formulated the first psychophysical law, namely, that the magnitude of the sensations varied as the logarithm of the physical stimulus:

$$\psi = k \log (I/I_0).$$

This law, which Fechner "derived" by integrating Weber's law, alleges that equal ratio changes in the stimulus cause equal increments in sensation. Its importance lies in that it represents the first attempt to precisely relate the mental and physical world. Fechner did not claim that loudness could be measured directly; rather he used discrimination data to infer something about psychological magnitude. In recent years others, notably S. S. Stevens, have argued that magnitude is directly observable and have urged direct measurements of sensory magnitude. The subject may be presented with stimuli having different intensities and simply has to give a number proportional to the perceived magnitude of each stimulus. This latter technique is called "direct magnitude estimation" and it enjoys considerable popularity in psychophysics today.

The results of direct magnitude estimation has almost uniformly shown that the numerical estimates generated by the subjects are related to stimulus magnitude according to a power law (such as Eqs. 11.5c or 11.6).

By now more than 30 different sensory continua have been investigated. The results seem to follow a power law where the exponent depends upon particular conditions of the experiment. Many factors influence the exponent besides the continua being judged. For example, the range of the stimuli influences the exponent. The exponent relating loudness to pressure seems to be in the neighborhood of .6, although variations from this value have also been found in specific experiments (Warren, 1970).

For our purposes it is important to note that the Fechnerian scale formed by integrating just-noticeable differences is definitely not the same as the sone scale. In fact, there is a strong nonlinear relation between the two, although both increase monotonically with stimulus intensity. Roughly the sone scale seems to be the 2.2 power of the integrated jnd scale (Stevens, 1936).

in Figure 11.1, we first determine the phon value of that component and from that value determine the sone value. Thus, in terms of our original example, suppose the 200-Hz component of sound A has a loudness of 3.6 sones and a component at 1,000 Hz has a loudness of 1 sone. Similarly for sound B, suppose the 300-Hz component has loudness 1.5 sones and the 1,000-Hz component has loudness 2 sones.[3] What is the numerical value for the loudness of the combination of the two components that comprise each sound? Which is louder, sound A or sound B?

One straightforward approach would simply add the sone values for the two components. A little reflection shows the hazard of this course. Suppose one of the components was much more intense than the other. Then the second component might well be inaudible because of masking. Of course, in the case of two components, the error in neglecting this factor would be small. If the two components were very different in intensity then their sone values would be very different and whether the smaller one was exactly zero or not would change the sum by a very small percentage. In general, however, many components might be inaudible, so the percentage error could be sizable. Masking is too big to be ignored; something must be done to deal with it.

Several solutions have been suggested. Garner (1959), who suggests a different formula for the relation between loudness and intensity, combined loudness as the square root of the sum of the squares of the individual loudnesses, after subtracting a masking correction from each individual loudness. This is essentially a vector combination model. The magnitude of the vector represents the total loudness and the components of the vector the loudness of the individual sounds.

Stevens' method is a little different. To appreciate how it works, let us return to Eq. (11.6), which represents loudness as a function of intensity. Let us use that equation to investigate how loudness grows as we increase sound energy by adding several components of exactly the same kind. If we were to add sinusoidal components we would have to specify their phases, since the total power would depend on the relative phase of the components. Assume, however, that the sounds are incoherent noises. Thus, if we add together two equally intense sounds, we simply produce another sound of twice the initial intensity. Let us simplify Eq. (11.6):

$$L_1 = (I_1)^{.3} , \tag{11.6a}$$

where we have set $I_0 = 1$. Now consider the loudness produced by adding two identical noises together:

$$L_2 = (2I_1)^{.3} = 1.231(I_1)^{.3} = 1.231 \, L_1, \tag{11.7a}$$

$$L_2 = (1 + .231)L_1. \tag{11.7b}$$

---

[3] Approximate values taken from Stevens (1956).

The second form of the equation (11.7b) makes it clear that adding two equally loud sounds amounts to adding one at full loudness value and the second at about one-fourth the value. One way of viewing this is to argue that mutual masking accounts for the failure of perfect addition.

Now suppose we create a third sound by adding three components together:

$$L_3 = (3I_1)^{.3} = 1.390(I_1)^{.3} \cong (1 + .20 + .20)L_1,$$

and if we add four,

$$L_4 = (4I_1)^{.3} = 1.516(I_1)^{.3} \cong (1 + .17 + .17 + .17)L_1.$$

Thus the effect of adding more and more components can be expressed roughly as

$$L_n = L_1 + k(n)\sum_{i=2}^{n} L_i. \tag{11.8}$$

Here n is the total number of components and $k(2) = .23$, $k(3) = 0.20$, $k(4) = .17$. The value of $k(n)$ is roughly as a constant, especially if n is large; for example, $k(10) = .11$ and $k(20) = .0766$, a change of only 30%. Furthermore this approximation really considers only the worst case. Normally the sounds are not all equally loud and the influence of the weaker sounds contributes relatively less. Hence the approximation will be better for unequal components.

Stevens proposes the following formula:

$$L_t = L_m + F\sum_{i \neq m} L_i, \tag{11.9}$$

where L_m is the band of maximum loudness, L_i is the loudness calculated in the various other bands, either octave or one-third bands, and F, a constant, depends on the size of the analysis band. $F = .3$ for octave band analysis and $F = .13$ for one-third octave analysis. Stevens has shown this formula to be a fair approximation for a wide variety of noise stimuli. There are certain limiting cases where the predictions are not correct, but overall, Eq. (11.9) predicts very well.

One point we should make concerns the effects of masking within and across the critical band. Notice that if we compare the effects of doubling the energy in the stimulus by doubling the energy in the same critical band, then from Eq. (11.7b) we increase the loudness .231. If we double the energy by placing the noise in another critical band, then Eq. (11.8) suggests (assuming the two bands are on equal loudness contours) that the increase will be .3. Therefore, spreading the energy to different critical bands actually increases the loudness of the noise. This fact has been verified experimentally many times (Scharf, 1959a; Zwicker, Flottorp, & Stevens, 1957). As one might expect with a masking phenomenon, it is level dependent. At moderate and high intensity levels, spreading the energy to different frequency regions generally increases the loudness. At very low intensity levels, near absolute threshold, and perhaps 20 dB above, the opposite rule applies. Concentrating the energy as much as possible maximizes the detectability and hence the loudness of the signal.

The calculation formula also simply treats the total energy in a band, ignoring its distribution within the band. As long as the band is as small as a critical band (roughly one-third octave), this assumption has been experimentally verified (Scharf, 1959b; Zwicker, Flottorp, & Stevens, 1957).

Summary of Stevens' Calculation Procedure

To summarize the preceding discussion, let us review the steps in calculating the loudness of a given, steady-state sound according to Stevens (1956; also international standard ISO R532, Method A):

1. Determine the total sound pressure level in the various frequency bands, using either an octave or some fraction of an octave band.

2. Convert each band level to the proper number of phons. This is the step that implicitly uses the equal loudness contours.

3. Convert each phon level for each band to the proper number of sones, using Eq. (11.3). This step implicitly assumes that loudness grows as a .3 function of intensity, at least near 1,000 Hz. (Naturally most charts used in practical calculation of loudness would combine Steps 2 and 3 simply relate the SPL at each band to the number of sones.)

4. Combine the sones according to Eq. (11.9), using the value of F appropriate for the analysis band used in Step 1.

In the case of sound A and B (Figure 11.1), we have already determined the sone values for A to be 3.6 and 1.2 sones, while for B the values are 1.5 and 2.0 sones. Assuming the analysis was done using octave bands, then $F = .30$. Therefore the total loudness of A is 3.96 sones and of B 2.45 sones. Rewriting Eq. (11.3) we find

$$P = \frac{\log L + 1.2}{.03} ,$$

where P is the phon value and L is the loudness in sones. Sound B has a phon level of 53 dB, and sound A has a phon level of 59.9 dB. Thus, if one were asked to match the loudness of sound A with a 1,000-Hz tone, the latter should have a level of 59.9 SPL. Sound B should be matched by a 53-dB tone. Note that the loudness of sound A is apparently determined almost entirely by the low-frequency component.

Stevens' method of calculating loudness has provided one illustration of how the three basic questions posed earlier in the chapter can be answered. While his method has been adopted as an international standard, it is not the only one used in the area. The remainder of the chapter will be devoted to alternate methods. We will explain how the alternate procedures proceed and point out where they are frequently used.

ALTERNATE METHODS OF ASSESSING
LOUDNESS OR ANNOYANCE

Perceived Noise Level

Kryter (1970) and Kryter and Pearsons (1963) have been the main advocates of a method of calculating the annoyance produced by the noise of airplanes. The method was developed largely in response to the Port of New York Authority, who had to enforce noise abatement procedures in the area's airports. Noise exposure increased markedly in the late 1950s and early 1960s when jet planes began being used in civilian transportation. Perceived noise level (PNdB), according to Kryter, assesses an aspect of noise magnitude related to, but somewhat different than, loudness. The calculation procedure is identical to Stevens' procedure except Kryter uses equal noisiness contours that are slightly different from the equal loudness contours. The unit of perceived noisiness is the *noy,* which is analogous to the sone. The combination rule is identical to that employed by Stevens. The perceived noise level in dB (PNdB) is analogous to the loudness level (phon).

There are a variety of corrections that can be added to the basic calculation. These include correction for audible pure tone components or whine, for exposure duration, and the like. The perceived noise level is frequently employed in evaluating aircraft noise. It is the basic quantity calculated in the FAA regulations of this nation that certify the acceptability of all planes that land at United States airports.

Zwicker's Calculation Procedure

Zwicker's procedure for calculation of loudness is also an international standard ISO R532, Method B (1958). The system is somewhat different from Stevens', and deserves some discussion. It stems directly from the view that loudness is related to the total excitation produced along the basilar membrane by the sound stimulus. We discussed the general concept of "excitation patterns" earlier (Chapter 6). Zwicker begins by dividing the frequency scale into equal functional units (Barks). Each band is roughly the width of a Frequenzegruppe (see Chapter 6) and is well approximated by one-third octave filter.

The sound pressure level in each of these bands generates a certain amount of excitation or loudness. So far the system is similar to Stevens' except that the form of the equal loudness or sone scales may be slightly different. What is unique about Zwicker's procedure is the manner in which the loudnesses from the different bands are combined. Here the concept of excitation patterns is utilized. A nomograph is provided with frequency along the abscissa and loudness along the ordinate. A series of dotted lines indicates the upward spread of masking. To calculate the total loudness one first enters the loudness associated with each band and then extends this loudness to the upper bands according to these dotted lines. In effect a level of 90 dB in the one-third octave band at 1,000 Hz produces excitation equivalent to 85 dB in the 1,250-Hz band, and 75 dB in the 1,600-Hz band, and so forth. Only if the level in the next band is sufficient to exceed the level of masking produced by a lower band does that band contribute to the total loudness of the noise. The total loudness is simply the area produced by the observed band levels and after masking is taken into account by extrapolations of these levels to higher frequency bands.

Additional details include the treatment of lower bands where one-third octave filters are wider than the Frequenzegruppe. Different nomographs have been prepared for frontal sound fields and diffuse fields. A meter is available from Hewlett-Packard that makes Zwicker's calculations automatically.

Weighted Sound Level Meter

So far we have discussed calculation procedures that depend on a spectral analysis of the sound. The basic description of the sound is the sound pressure level measured in octave or one-third octave bands. Even the simplest of these systems is complicated. The sound level meter provides an inexpensive means of measuring the approximate loudness of a sound. The first standard on such a meter dates from 1936.[4] Basically, the meter is a pressure-sensitive device calibrated in decibels. The pressure as sensed by the microphone is filtered, that is, the pressure at different frequencies is weighted and the total rms pressure computed. The dial of the meter is calibrated so that a 1,000-Hz sinusoid at 40 dB SPL will read 40 dB on the sound level meter. Most commercially available meters have three filters or frequency weights, A, B, and C. Two of the three filters were originally chosen to approximate the equal loudness contours at high levels, B, and at low levels, A. The third, the C, weight, is essentially flat over the range from 30 to 10,000 Hz.

The A weight is the most interesting because it is so widely used. Figure 11.3 shows the A frequency weights. The A weights were originally chosen to approximate the 40-dB phon level; the response is down 30 dB at 50 Hz and essentially this is a high-pass filter. It has 0-dB gain at 1,000 Hz, 1.3-dB gain at 2,500 Hz, and is only 2.5 dB down at 10,000 Hz.

Compared with Stevens' loudness calculations, a sound level meter employs some equal loudness contour and then simply combines the loudness values over

---

[4] See report of McCurdy Committee, *Journal of the Acoustical Society of America*, 1936, *8*, 147–152. For a more modern description, see Peterson and Gross (1972).

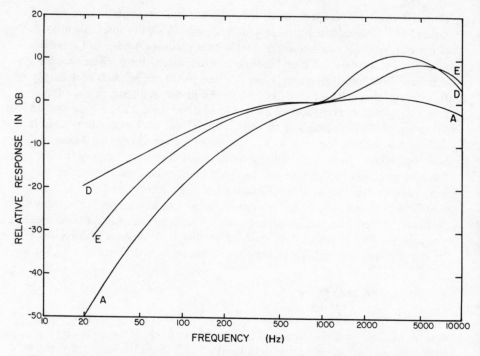

FIG. 11.3 Frequency weighting function used in *A, D,* and *E* level meters. All scales give relatively little weight to lower frequency and have a broad maximum in the 2,000–5,000 Hz region, consistent with the general features of the equal loudness contours, see Figure 11.2.

frequency, ignoring both the effects of masking and any nonlinear relation between loudness and intensity. Despite these gross approximations the A weighted sound level is of great practical value. For most practical noise sources, for example, aircraft, vehicle traffic, or construction machinery, sound level A correlates very highly with results from more complicated procedures. For these sources the *A* weighted sound level values are about 12 dB slower than Stevens' loudness level and about 14 dB lower than perceived noise level.

A weighted sound level has been adopted by the Environmental Protection Agency as their principal measure of noise level and hence as their scale for noise pollution control. Even if it correlated poorly with subjective response, and all the available evidence suggests the opposite, its simplicity would recommend it highly as a practical and convenient means of assessing the subjective magnitude of sounds.

Because of convenience, other procedures have also proposed frequency weights that might be employed in the sound level meter. Kryter's *D* weights are included in Figure 11.3 along with the *A* weights.

OTHER MEASURES OF SUBJECTIVE RESPONSE TO NOISE

The past 20 years have witnessed a tremendous concern and interest in environmental matters. Noise as one of the pollutants has received its share of attention. Because of the many different sources that create noise and because the exposure to the noise occurs in many different ways, different scales for evaluating noise have arisen. Many classifications of these different measures are possible. A principal class that we have ignored involves the temporal variable and tries to get at an integrated or composite exposure, one that combines the magnitude of the source with its duration.

The mere listing of these different measures would require several pages. Schultz (1972) has written a small book explaining most of the measures and illustrating their uses. It is hoped that the trend toward proliferation of measures has peaked and future developments will lead to consensus about few. The four measures described here, loudness level, perceived noise, Zwicker's method, and A weighted sound level, are the principal measures used in this country.

REFERENCES

Churcher, B.G. A loudness scale for industrial noise measurements. *Journal of the Acoustical Society of America*, 1935, *6*, 216–226.

Fechner, G.T. Available in English translation as *Elements of psychophysics.* Vol. I (English translation.) New York: Holt, Rinehart and Winston, 1860. (Originally published as *Elemente der Psychophysik,* 1860.)

Fletcher, H., & Munson, W.A. Loudness, its definition, measurement and calculation. *Journal of the Acoustical Society of America*, 1933, *5*, 82–108.

Garner, W.R. On the lambda loudness function, masking, and the loudness of multicomponent tones. *Journal of the Acoustical Society of America*, 1959, *31*, 602–607.

Geiger, P.H., & Firestone, F.A. The estimation of fractional loudness. *Journal of the Acoustical Society of America*, 1933, *5*, 25–30.

Ham, L.B., & Parkinson, J.S. Loudness and intensity relations. *Journal of the Acoustical Society of America*, 1932, *3*, 511–534.

Kryter, K.D., & Pearsons, K.S. Some effects of spectral content and duration on perceived noise level. *Journal of the Acoustical Society of America*, 1963, *35*, 866–883.

Kryter, K.D. *The effects of noise on man.* New York: Academic Press, 1970.

Laird, D.A., Taylor, E., & Wille, H.H., Jr. The apparent reduction in loudness. *Journal of the Acoustical Society of America*, 1932, *3*, 393–401.

Peterson, A.P.G., & Gross, E.E. *Handbook of noise measurement* (7th ed.). Concord, Mass.: General Radio Corporation, 1972.

Richardson, L.F., & Ross, J.S. Loudness and telephone current. *Journal of General Psychology*, 1930, *3*, 288–306.

Robinson, D.W., & Dadson, R.S. A re-determination of the equal-loudness relations for pure tones. *British Journal of Applied Physics*, 1956, *7*, 166–181.

Robinson, D.W., & Whittle, L.S. The loudness of octave-bands of noise. *Acustica*, 1964, *14*, 24–35.

Rschevkin, S.N., & Rabinovitch, A.V. Sur le Probleme de L'estimation Quantitative de La Force d'un Son. *Revue d'Acoustique,* 1936, *5,* 183–200.

Scharf, B. Critical bands and the loudness of complex sounds near threshold. *Journal of the Acoustical Society of America,* 1959, *31,* 365–370. (a)

Scharf, B. Loudness of complex sounds as a function of the number of components. *Journal of the Acoustical Society of America,* 1959, *31,* 783–785. (b)

Schultz, T.J. *Community noise ratings.* London: Applied Science Pub., 1972.

Stevens, S.S. A scale for the measurement of a psychological magnitude: loudness. *Psychological Review,* 1936, *43,* 405–416.

Stevens, S.S. The measurement of loudness. *Journal of the Acoustical Society of America,* 1955, *27,* 815–829.

Stevens, S.S. Calculation of the loudness of complex noise. *Journal of the Acoustical Society of America,* 1956, *28,* 807–832.

Stevens, S.S. Procedure for calculating loudness: Mark VI. *Journal of the Acoustical Society of America,* 1961, *33,* 1577–1585.

Stevens, S.S. Perceived level of noise by mark VII and decibels E. *Journal of the Acoustical Society of America,* 1972, *51,* 575–601.

Stevens, S.S., & Greenbaum, H.B. Regression effect in psychophysical judgment. *Perception and Psychophysics,* 1966, *1,* 439–446.

Warren, R.M. Elimination of biases in loudness judgments for tones. *Journal of the Acoustical Society of America,* 1970, *48,* 1397–1403.

Zwicker, E. Über psychologische and methodische Grundlagen der Lautheit. *Acustica,* 1958, Akustishe Beihefte 1, 237–258.

Zwicker, E., Flottorp, G., & Stevens, S.S. Critical band width in loudness summation. *Journal of the Acoustical Society of America,* 1957, *29,* 548–557.

12
Speech Perception

INTRODUCTION

For humans the most important auditory function is the comprehension of speech. Verbal communication is important in virtually all aspects of our existence. Whether or not man is unique in utilizing this communication depends on how one defines speech or language, but certainly his use of this skill is without peer. Speech allows information to be transmitted at a high rate and is remarkably resistant to interference from other sounds. The intelligibility of the speech waveform is remarkably robust, being impervious to a variety of physical transformations.

To most of us speech is immediate and obvious. Our decoding of speech is so simple and direct that we scarcely consider the act. Yet even a minimum of reflection should convince us that it is a very complex skill. As a physical stimulus, speech is a sound wave containing frequencies between 50 and 4,000 Hz and intensities in the range of 30 to 80 DB SPL. There are many ways to describe the speech waveform. Whatever the description it is a remarkably variable stimulus. Despite this variety we can usually understand a wide range of speakers—people of various ages, both sexes, and quite different regional backgrounds. Only the most extreme dialect or regionalism interferes with our understanding of the speech of other English-speaking people. This variability makes speech one of the most intriguing of perceptual stimuli. Clearly there are some invariances if one is to correctly perceive a word such as "cat" despite the many changes in the physical stimuli. We begin our description of speech with the pressure waveform. To describe that waveform it is easiest to consider the process of speech production.

SPEECH PRODUCTION

The basic elements of the production process are an energy source, some acoustic cavities, and some articulators, so the size and shape of these cavities can be modified. A schematic view of the speech process is presented in Figure 12.1.

The energy for speech derives from pressure produced by the diaphragm on the lungs. This pressure forces air out of the lungs up the trachea and into the pharynx, or throat cavity. At the top of the trachea is a structure of considerable importance in speech production, the larynx. Within the larynx is a sort of cartilaginous frame containing two important ligaments and some muscle. These ligaments form the vocal cords or vocal folds. If they are forced into vibration by the passage of air from the lungs, then a so-called "voiced" sound is produced like the sound of "a" in *father*, the "e" in *meet*, or the "ou" in *foul*. Sounds produced without the vibration of the vocal cords are by definition "voiceless," such as the "p" in *pet* or the "s" in *some*. In either case the air from the lungs passes through the larynx into the cavities formed by the mouth and nose. These cavities act as resonators and influence the sound in several ways. At the back and top of the mouth is the soft palate or velum. If open, the velum allows air to

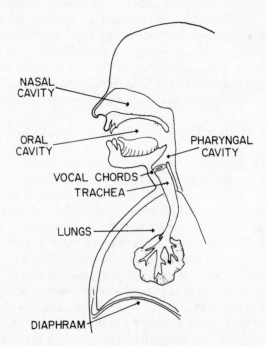

FIG. 12.1 Major anatomical components of speech production system. (From Potter *et al.*, 1947, p. 32.)

pass into the nasal cavity producing a nasal quality that one can hear if one says "singing." If the velum is closed and the air flow is forced into the mouth, then several structures, such as the lips and tongue, can influence the sound's quality. These elements, sometimes called articulators, can assume many different positions and thereby alter the acoustic parameters of the resonant cavities. The entire system can best be understood if we consider an acoustic analog of its parts designed to mimic the essential acoustic properties of the physiological system. Figure 12.2 is one such analog.

As shown in the figure, the essential acoustic components for producing a speechlike sound are a volume of trapped air and several cavities. Pressure on the lungs forces air through a tube and past the vocal cords into an acoustic filter or cavity representing the pharynx. Leaving, the pharynx air is forced out through two more cavities—one is the mouth, the other the nose. The simple flap connected to the shunt branch of the nasal cavity mimics the velum and determines the relative amount of air leaving by the nose or the mouth. A good

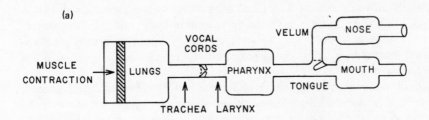

(a)

MUSCLE
CONTRACTION

LUNGS

VOCAL
CORDS

TRACHEA   LARYNX

PHARYNX

TONGUE

VELUM

NOSE

MOUTH

FUNCTIONAL ANALOG OF VOCAL TRACT

(b)

NOISE
SOURCE

PULSE
SOURCE

FILTER
1

FILTER
2

FILTER
3

FILTER
4

ADDER

ELECTRICAL ANALOG OF VOCAL TRACT

FIG. 12.2 (a) Functional analog of speech production system. (b) Electrical analog of speech production system.

analog of the acoustic filtering produced by the cavities of the pharynx, mouth, and nose is obtained by passing air through simple cylindrical pipes. The inner walls of these pipes must be constructed of a material that produces some loss of energy as air flows through the pipes.

Sound is a rapid change in pressure so that even rapid breathing produces change in air pressure in the 2- or 3-Hz range. Audible sound results when the air passage is constricted in some way, producing a rapid change in air pressure. An example is the turbulence produced by constricting the tongue against the teeth in the "hiss" sound. The turbulent waveform contains many components, such as white noise. The configuration of the vocal tract varies its resonant properties and influences the resulting spectrum. This filtering action is apparent if one compares the sounds produced by the "th" in "thin" and the "s" in "see." In the first case the tongue is forward and more of a constriction is produced. Other kinds of turbulent sounds can be produced, for example, by vibrating the lips against the teeth as in the "f" in "for" or by simply opening the tract and forcing air through quickly as in the "h" sound in "he." All of these sounds are called fricatives because of their mode of production. There are also sounds of a slightly different quality such as the "p" sound in "pay" and the "k" sound in "key." These are called stop consonants and are produced by actually constricting the tract momentarily, letting pressure build up and then releasing it in one sudden burst.

All of the preceding sounds involve some sort of turbulence. The pressure waveform is noiselike and the resulting spectrum depends on the filtering produced by the various cavities at the time of production. Another way to cause a rapid variation in pressure is to vibrate the vocal cords. A periodic pressure wave is then produced. The fundamental of this wave is about 75–100 Hz for men and 150–200 Hz for women. It is rich in overtones and the filtering action of the pharynx, mouth, and nose alter the harmonic content of this wave.

If the vocal cords are vibrating, then by definition, a *voiced* sound is produced. If the cords are not vibrating, allowing air to steam up through the larynx, then by definition, the sound is *voiceless.*

Depending on exactly how the sound is produced we can develop a classificatory scheme that would contain two main groups: (1) vowels, and (2) consonants. The following subgroups fall in the main consonant grouping: (a) fricatives, (b) stops, (c) nasals, (d) glides and semivowels, and (e) diphthongs and affricatives. For vowels the cords are vibrating and the rest of the vocal tract is relatively open. For consonants the cords may or may not be vibrating and the tract is more constricted.

Vowels all involve a voicing quality. The fricatives can be broken into two classes—voiced and unvoiced. Similarly, the stop consonants can be either voiced or unvoiced. The nasals are all voiced. The glides are defined in terms of a dynamic movement of the vocal tract toward the vowel sound that follows the glide, and the diphthong is some combination of basic vowels where one starts at one vowel position and ends at the other. For example, the acoustic elements in the word "father" could be described in terms of production as (1) a voiceless fricative ["f" as in "for"] (2) an open voiced sound, the "a," (3) another voiceless fricative ["th" as in "thin"] , and so forth. Such a description is in fact the principle underlying phonetic spelling. Each phoneme represents a distinctive vocal gesture within the language and the string of phonemes represents the word. The transcriptions are a reasonably precise method of specifying the sound of a word. Phonemic descriptions are widely used in dictionaries. The method can be used by someone unfamiliar with the word to reconstruct the correct pronunciation.

Phonetic spelling is unsatisfactory as an acoustic description, however. If we look at the acoustic wave in detail, then we do not see the elementary sounds spliced together in a way that a simple phonemic transcription process might imply. The phonetic description leaves the matter of transition from one phoneme to the next up to the speaker. His good sense, along with the physical limitation on the movements of his mouth and tongue, supply the transition information. In the speech waveform, the transition from one elementary phoneme to another seems to be as important as the elements themselves. This fact can be demonstrated by splicing some basic sounds together to construct a word. If, for example, one tries to make a simple sound like "cat" by taking a "c" sound from one word and the "a" sound from another word and the "t" sound from a third word, the spliced composite is simply unintelligible. The composite has some of the right elements. There are transients at the beginning and end of the utterance and some vowel in the middle. But our spliced utterance is not a word—certainly not "cat." This simple exercise demonstrates that the transitions are extremely important. These transitions arise and are distinct because of inertia in the vocal production mechanism. The tongue cannot move instantly, nor can the shape of the mouth change from one form to another without appreciable delays. These delays are an inherent part of the speech process when we try to articulate a phonetic transcription. Phonetic descriptions are useful because the production apparatus has its own built-in constraints. But from an acoustic point of view, the phonemic description is inadequate.

The motor aspects of speech may be summarized as follows. In English there are probably 30–40 basic sounds (phonemes) which are useful in trying to provide a phonetic description of the speech sound. Combinations of these elements specify a word and these combinations when executed by a talker are sufficient to produce a recognizable version of the correct word. The phonemic elements cannot be regarded as sufficient acoustic specifications, since the elements change with context and the transitions from one element to the next are nearly as important as the elements themselves.

Let us temporarily leave the motor aspects of speech production and consider the speech pressure waveform. The waveform can best be understood by considering another analog, an electrical one, this time in place of the mechanical one.

PRESSURE WAVEFORM OF SPEECH

In Figure 12.2b we show a simple electrical analog of the speech signal. Two sources of energy are used. One, a noise source, produces the voiceless sound, the other, a pulse train, produces a voiced sound. The source of energy, whether noise or a pulse train, excites a series of filters, each a simple resonant circuit. These filters correspond to the various cavities in the pharynx, mouth, and nose. They filter the spectral energy developed by the source. The output of these filters is added to produce the final output. Because the excitatory energy goes through each filter in parallel, this arrangement is called a "parallel synthesizer." The vocal output could equally well be mimicked by passing the signal through successive filters arranged in series to provide a "series synthesizer." Although there are some technical differences between the two, for the purposes of exposition the parallel synthesizer is easier to understand.

For a vowel sound, Figure 12.3 shows both the pressure wave and the spectrum that such a synthesizer produces. The source in this case is the pulse train and the periodic sequence of brief pulses has a spectrum rich in harmonics. The fundamental is the repetition rate of the pulse train, $1/T$, and energy is present at all harmonics of the fundamental. The various filters modify the pressure wave as shown in Figure 12.3b and c, left. These operations produce peaks or "formants" at certain frequencies in the spectrum (see Figure 12.3b and c, right). The center frequency of the first filter corresponds to the first formant frequency. The center frequency of the second filter corresponds to the second formant frequency, and so on. The formant frequencies reflect the resonant properties of the vocal tract for the given vowel. As the shape of the mouth changes in uttering the various vowels, these formant frequencies change. Only two filters are shown in Figure 12.3. The last row (Figure 12.3d) shows the total output of the synthesizer, which represents the combination of the two filters. The combined time waveform (left part of figure) is simply the instantaneous sum of the two filter responses. The combined spectrum (right part of figure) is roughly the sum of the two filter spectrums. It is not exactly the sum since the combination depends on the amplitude and phase of the constituents. For example, if two individual components are 180° out of phase, the combined component is their difference in amplitude. Only the amplitude is illustrated in the figure.

In this electrical analog the important parameters are (1) whether or not the source is a pulse train (voiced) or a broadband noise excitation (voiceless); (2) the center frequencies of the formant frequency of the various formant filters, f_1, f_2, f_3, and f_4; and (3) the bandwidth of the various filters, that is, the exact

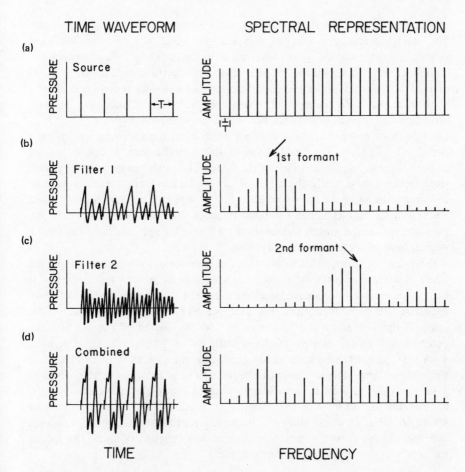

FIG. 12.3 Temporal and spectral representation of the electrical analog, see Figure 12.2b, in the production of a vowel with fundamental $1/T$.

resonant characteristics of the filters. In the case of simple resonant filters, two parameters, the bandwidth and center frequency, determine the entire filter shape. Thus for simple filters the entire speech spectrum could be specified in terms of about 10 parameters. Such a synthesizer would make tolerably good single utterances. The quality of its continuous discourse would depend on how well the transitions were made from one set of parameter values to the next. As we pointed out earlier, these transitions are probably as important as the steady-state values. Such a synthesizer, while perhaps being intelligible, would produce speech having a definite "mechanical" quality. Part of the mechanical quality is related to the form and regularity of the pulse train. Studies have been conducted to investigate how the form of the periodic excitation affects the perceived quality of the synthesizer; see, for example, Rosenberg (1971).

Thus far, we have emphasized the spectral representation of the speech sound. The electrical analog should make it easy to match the pressure waveform produced by the various speech utterances. In the case of a voiceless sound, the waveform, of course, will be irregular since noise is the basic excitation. However, the frequency regions predominant in the voiceless sounds will depend upon the center frequency and tuning of the filters. Hence, the pressure waveform is irregular or random but might contain more high-frequency than low-frequency energy. In the case of a voiced sound the waveform repeats itself periodically in time. The exact shape of this periodic wave is determined by center frequency and bandwidth of the filters. The fundamental frequency for a given talker will be nearly the same for all vowels. The fundamental frequencies determine the pitch of the voice. Men, as a group, tend to have lower pitched voices (about 100 Hz) than do women (about 200 Hz). There is, of course, variation within the groups so that some men have high-pitched voices and some women have relatively low-pitched voices.

There are difficulties with either the time waveform or the spectrum (Figure 12.3) as a representation of the speech waveform. The time representation is cumbersome since once a vowel is encountered the same periodic waveform may appear for 10 or 20 repetitions. For example, a vowel segment may last for 200 msec. If the fundamental of the voice is 200 Hz (period of 5 msec) then the entire vowel would consist of 40 repetitions of nearly the same periodic waveform. Similarly, the spectral representation is awkward since it relates to a single time frame. The spectrum can be thought of as a Fourier series analysis of a brief waveform that is periodically repeated. Once the waveform changes, another analysis must be derived. Some combination of the two representations would be ideal. It would show the frequency content of the speech waveform and also display how the spectrum changes as a function of time. The speech spectrograph was developed for this purpose.

SPEECH SPECTROGRAM

A sound spectrogram of the utterance, "this is a sound spectrogram" is displayed in Figure 12.4. Spectrographic representations contain a considerable amount of information and appear complicated at first glance. But they are easily interpreted after some practice. First, note the coordinates of the spectrogram. Along the ordinate is the frequency scale. The scale is linear and ranges from about 0 to 7,000 Hz. Along the abscissa is time in seconds. The entire utterance lasts about 2 sec. The shading in the graph represents the intensity of energy at that point in the time–frequency plane. The dark bar occurring at about .9 sec between 2,000 and 3,000 Hz therefore indicates a considerable amount of energy at that frequency region at that point in time.

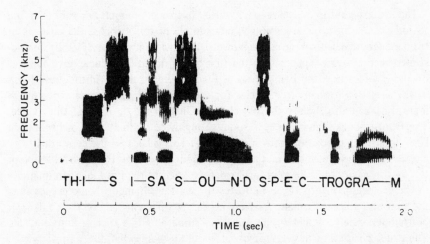

FIG. 12.4   A sound spectrogram of the utterance, "This is a sound spectrogram." The dark regions represent concentration of energy at that frequency–time locus. (From Stevens & House, 1972, p. 4.)

To relate the spectrogram to our previous discussion, let us begin with the last vowel in the word "spectrogram " The first formant is evident as the dark bar having a frequency of approximately 500 Hz. A second formant is evident at about 1,200 Hz. Compare the spectrogram with the spectral representation shown in Figure 12.3 (right). The spectrogram is essentially a series of spectra oriented along the vertical axis with time running along the horizontal axis. There are vertical striations running throughout certain portions of the spectrogram, especially during the vowels. These striations represent the period of the voice. There are about 10 in each one-tenth of a second, for a fundamental frequency of about 100 Hz. As an example of an unvoiced segment of the spectrogram, consider the "s" part of the word "this." Here we see broadband energy at a high frequency, predominantly 3,000 Hz and above. It is also clear that most of the dark marking occurs when a vowel sound is uttered. There is comparatively little energy present in the consonants. For example, the consonants in "spectrogram" contain practically no energy at all.

The sound spectrogram was devised by Koenig, Dunn, and Lacey (1946) and was first used extensively in an attempt to teach profoundly deaf children to speak (Potter, Kopp, & Green, 1947). Speech of deaf children is often poor in quality since they obtain little or no auditory feedback to correct or modify their utterances. Therefore, Potter and his associates hoped to use the spectrogram to provide the missing feedback and thereby instruct deaf children about their utterances and how they should be produced. Regrettably, the experiment was of only limited success.

The spectrogram is, however, widely used in speech research as a tool in trying to understand speech perception. One example of this effort is the analysis of formant frequencies for different vowels. Peterson and Barney (1952) demonstrated in their classic paper that the first two formant frequencies give a means of identifying the vowel being spoken. Figure 12.5a is a plot of the mean locus of the first two formant frequencies for the various English words. Not surprisingly, one can also specify the vowels according to the position of the tongue. The front-to-back dimension corresponds roughly to f_1; the height of the tongue from low to high position corresponds to f_2. This is because the combined filter characteristics of the vocal tract are determined, in part, by the size and shape of the mouth cavity and these, in turn, can be related to the prominent frequencies in the spectrum. Figure 12.5b indicates the scatter obtained when one measures the first and second formant frequencies for 76 different talkers. Each talker, if plotted separately, would produce a locus something like that in Figure 12.5a. The exact position of the various vowels would be somewhat different, however, and hence there would be scatter, indicated by areas in Figure 12.5b. The second formant frequency is plotted on logarithmic coordinates in Figure 12.5b in order to encompass all the data.

INTENSITY OF SPEECH

We have briefly commented on the asymmetry in power or energy between vowels and consonants. Let us consider in more detail this intensive aspect of speech production. Then we will take up the topic of understanding or recognition of the speech signal, how it is affected by various maskers, and how various distortions affect its intelligibility.

The average power radiated by a talker, calculated over long periods of talking, including pauses, is about 10–20 microwatts (μW).[1] If the pauses are excluded in the averaging, the total energy increases about a factor of 2, indicating that the effective duty cycle of speech is approximately 50%. When the talker raises his voice and attempts to speak as loud as possible, the total wattage increases to approximately 1,000 μW. Thus the usable dynamic range of the voice from a normal level to a shout is about 20 dB. Naturally, one can also drop the level of one's voice to a very faint whisper. This faint whisper might be as low as .001 μW or about 40 dB below the normal voice level. If one measures the energy produced by various types of sounds such as vowels and consonants, then one

---

[1] At 1 m from a talker an average speech level is about 60–70 dB SPL. Recall that 0 dB SPL corresponds to 10^{-16} W/cm². A level of 60 dB is then 10^{-10} W/cm² and assuming this intensity is uniformly distributed over a sphere of radius 100 cm (an area of approximately 10^5 cm²) we calculate the source as approximately 10^{-5} W or 10 μW. These assumptions are rough but come close to measured values (Dunn & Farnsworth, 1939).

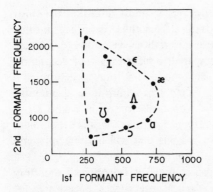
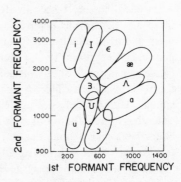

FIG. 12.5 First and second frequency regions for various vowels over a large number of talkers: (a) The regions containing the bulk of data for each vowel. Note some regions overlap and logarithmic scales are needed to contain variation over talkers. (b) The centers of gravity for the different regions. (From Peterson & Barney, 1952, p. 182.)

would notice a vast asymmetry between the two classes of speech utterance. The vowels would average about 20 to 25 μW, and a vowel such as "a" in father is one of the strongest and might measure about 35 μW. In contrast, consonant sounds are extremely weak. The "t" and "d" sounds or the "f" and "v" sounds might be as low as .1–.05 μW. Thus, the average power difference between a consonant and a vowel is between a factor of 200 and 500 or 23–27 dB.

The long-term energy present in the speech sound as a function of frequency is of some interest. Dunn and White (1940) measured the spectral distribution of energy in speech. Their measurements indicated that the most energy in an octave band was centered in the region of about 300 Hz.[2] The energy present in higher octave bands declined by about 10 dB per octave. The average was roughly the same for women as well as men. The vast majority of speech energy was contained below 1,000 Hz.

ARTICULATION TESTS

We have reviewed how speech is produced and how it can be represented as a physical stimulus. The next question is how speech is perceived. What are the invariants of the speech waveform? What aspects of the speech waveform are critical in carrying information? To answer these questions we can modify the speech waveform in various ways and determine how these modifications affect our perception of the speech.

[2] An octave band is a region of frequency such that the high-frequency cut is a factor of 2 larger than the low-frequency cut (see Chapter 11).

Before discussing these modifications, however, we must note that the study of speech perception involves methods different from those described in other parts of this book. In other sections the typical methods were those of discrimination or detection. Two stimuli were compared to see if they were discriminable, or some small signal was added to a background condition to determine if the signal was detectable. Speech perception involves a multitude of potential stimuli. The task is basically identifying the correct alternative in a large set of potential stimuli. In terms of a stimulus—response matrix, there are n stimulus alternatives and n potential responses. For reasons that will become apparent, this identification task was called an "articulation test."

Modern research in speech reception began at the Bell Telephone Laboratory in Harvey Fletcher's group. The primary practical interest was in assessing the quality of various telephone communication systems. Further developments of these and other methods occurred at the Psychoacoustic Laboratory at Harvard during World War II. The primary practical interest was how to improve communication in noisy environments such as tanks and airplanes. In general, the goal was to evaluate communication systems and, in particular, how clearly these systems transmitted the speech signal. These tests became known as "articulation tests." In the simplest articulation test a talker speaks a group of words over some communication system. The listener attempts to record what the talker said. The score on the articulation test is simply the percentage of words correctly received by the listener. Needless to say, a number of variables affect the score on an articulation test. One important class of variables involves the listener's familiarity with the utterances that may be transmitted during the test. In some cases, nonsense syllables are used. If so, the training of the subject is extremely important. In an attempt to avoid some of the variability due to training, different test batteries have been devised over the years that incorporated different features and were useful for different purposes. Egan (1948) gives an excellent review of many of these underlying problems. He selected several sets of monosyllabic words. Each list is roughly of the same difficulty and unusual or infrequent words are avoided. In each list of 50 words, phonemes occurred with approximately the same frequency as they occur in the English language. These so-called PB (phonetically balanced) word lists have been widely used in articulation testing.

The familiarity of the words, which can roughly be measured by counting their raw frequency of occurrence in the English language, profoundly affects intelligibility. As Howes (1957) demonstrated, the signal-to-noise ratio at which the word is correctly heard changes as much as 15 dB depending on the frequency of occurrence of the word in the English language. This frequency effect also affects the threshold of PB words. Subjects must therefore have some experience with the lists before testing is begun. Intelligibility also depends on the context offered, for example, by imbedding the word in some meaningful sentence. Some extensive tests have measured the intelligibility of different material under a variety of different conditions (French & Steinberg, 1947; Miller, Heise, & Lichten, 1951).

Finally, we should mention a class of words that are often used because they have roughly similar intelligibility. These are two syllable words with equal stress on both syllables. They are called *spondees* and examples are: baseball, doorstep, mousetrap, and sidewalk. Standard spondee lists have been developed. Spondees are few in number so that it is fairly easy to teach the entire list to a group of listeners.

Because of the commercial importance of evaluating different speech communication systems, and because of the expense involved in actually testing each system, elaborate calculation procedures have been developed to predict the intelligibility of the communication system from physical measurements alone. We will not attempt to review this extensive enterprise here. A brief description may be found in Beranek (1954) and a detailed description in French and Steinberg (1947). The development of this prediction scheme has led to a great deal of research concerning intelligibility testing. We will review some of this research in the following section.

MASKING

A low-frequency tone produces considerably more masking of speech than a high-frequency tone of the same energy. This result is consistent with the asymmetry in masking patterns described in the earlier chapter. If wide-band noise is used as a masker, then the important variable is the signal-to-noise ratio. As Fletcher (1929) and Hawkins and Stevens (1950) showed, once the noise level exceeds a certain low value, intelligibility depends only on signal-to-noise ratio. Thus changes in the noise background of, say 30 dB, can be completely overcome by increasing the level of the speech equally. This same fact is evident if one considers the intelligibility of speech with and without earplugs. Since the earplugs attenuate the noise as much as the signal, the intelligibility of the speech is largely unaffected, as long as the original amplitude of the speech is sufficiently great.

Speech may, of course, be rendered unintelligible in various ways besides masking. Systematic distortions of the speech waveform have been studied extensively in an attempt to determine those aspects of speech that are critically important in successful communication systems. We know that the pressure waveform can be modified considerably with practically no change in intelligibility. Drastic alterations of the pressure wave occur when speech is heard at different points in a reverberant room. Therefore the pressure wave is not the invariant quantity. But reflection changes the phase spectrum and leaves the short-term amplitude spectra, which is displayed in the speech spectrogram, largely unaltered. Preserving the amplitude spectrum therefore seems to be important for speech intelligibility. Let us consider this possibility more closely. We will discuss three distortions: (1) changes in the frequency distribution (filtering the speech waveform); (2) changes in the amplitude of the pressure waveform; and (3) changes in the temporal pattern of the speech waveform.

Frequency transformation. A change in the frequency distribution occurs by filtering out certain portions of the speech waveform and preventing the energy in these regions from reaching the listener's ear. We hear this kind of transformation whenever we listen on the telephone, which passes only frequencies in the range between 300 and 3,000 Hz. Thus the 7,000-Hz range of the speech spectrogram is not needed because intelligibility remains excellent if we throw away the upper 4,000 Hz. French and Steinberg (1947) were the first to present systematic measures of speech intelligibility under a variety of filtering and gain conditions. They presented the speech waveform at a fairly high level and filtered out either the low or the high side of the spectrum. The results taken from French and Steinberg are given in Figure 12.6. The graph displays the percent of the syllable articulation as a function of the high-pass or low-pass frequency cutoff. The curves cross at a value of approximately 1,900 Hz. If the only information one has is therefore either above or below 1,900 Hz, the intelligibility of the speech (syllables) is roughly equal and approximately 70% of that obtained with the full speech spectrum.

As we mentioned previously, the vast majority of energy lies in the region of about 300 Hz. Less than 2% of the total energy in the speech waveform lies above 1,900 Hz. Despite this lack of energy, frequencies above 1,900 Hz

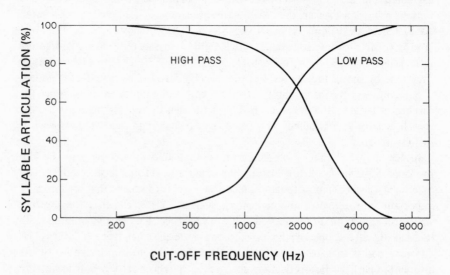

CUT-OFF FREQUENCY (Hz)

FIG. 12.6 Percentage of correct syllable identification as a function of high- and low-frequency cutoff of filtered speech. (From French & Steinberg, 1947, p. 102.)

apparently contain as many cues to the identity of syllables as do the lower frequencies.

Amplitude transformation. Modifying the amplitude of the speech waveform usually has comparatively little effect on intelligibility. This is because many amplitude transformations leave the spectrum largely intact. Clipping the top of the speech waveform introduces extraneous high-frequency energy which is not a very effective masker. Consider, for example, speech which is essentially a square wave having only one positive and one negative value of pressure. The transition between the two values occurs at the zero crossings of the original waveform. This waveform (called infinitely clipped speech) is nearly as intelligible as normal speech. The voice of the talker is readily evident; although the speech sounds peculiar, because of a distinct high-frequency whine, its intelligibility is not markedly affected (Licklider, 1946).

Temporal factors in speech. Speech perception involves a high rate of information processing. Temporal transformations of the waveform may provide some insight into how these processes work. What are the natural durations of units of the speech stream? How does the ear bridge the silent gaps between utterances that are so apparent in the spectrographic representation? These are some of the questions underlying studies of temporal transformation of speech.

The earliest systematic treatment of the topic was Miller and Licklider's (1950) study of interrupted speech. They measured the intelligibility of PB word lists when the speech wave itself was interrupted or periodically masked by noise. The effects of periodic interruption are shown in Figure 12.7. The speech wave was turned on and off periodically at different duty cycles (shown as a parameter in the figure). The results of temporal interruption are complicated and suggest the influences of several different mechanisms. We will explore this result in some detail, first because the two extremes of the function are understandable on purely physical grounds. What is of substantive interest for speech perception is the middle part of the figure.

The results for very slow rates of interruption are easily understood. When the rate of interruption is very slow, then duty cycle determines intelligibility. If the words are present once every hour, with a 50% duty cycle, then half the words are heard.

The right-hand part of the graph shows that for all duty cycles intelligibility approaches 100%. To understand this phenomenon, consider the curves for a duty cycle of 50%. Denote the original speech wave as $s(t)$ and the interrupting or modulating wave as $c(t)$. The interrupted speech $s'(t)$ wave is a product of $c(t)$ and $s(t)$, that is,

$$s'(t) = c(t) \cdot s(t).$$

Therefore, $c(t) = 1$ when the wave is on and $c(t) = 0$ when the wave is off. For a 50% duty cycle, $c(t)$ is a simple square wave, alternating between 1 and 0 at some rate of interruption f_i. This square wave can easily be expanded in a Fourier series,

$$c(t) = \frac{1}{2} + \frac{2}{\pi} \sum_{n=1,3,5} \frac{1}{n} \sin 2\pi f_i n t,$$

where $n = 1, 3, 5$. Thus, $c(t)$ contains only odd harmonics and their successive amplitudes diminish as $1/n$.

The speech wave $s(t)$ for any brief period also has Fourier representation which will be of the form

$$s(t) = \sum_n (a_n \sin 2\pi f_n t + b_n \cos 2\pi f_n t).$$

Consider how one component of that speech wave is affected by the interruption, that is, by the multiplication by $c(t)$. Take a sine component of amplitude a_s and frequency f_s,

$$y(t) = (a_s \sin 2\pi f_s t)c(t),$$

$$y(t) = (a_s \sin 2\pi f_s t)\left[\frac{1}{2} + \frac{2}{\pi} \sum_{n=1,3,5} \frac{1}{n} \sin 2\pi f_i n t\right],$$

$$y(t) = \frac{1}{2} a_s \sin 2\pi f_s t + a_s \frac{2}{\pi} \sum_{n=1,3,5} \frac{1}{n} (\sin 2\pi f_i n t) \sin 2\pi f_s t,$$

$$y(t) = \frac{1}{2} a_s \sin 2\pi f_s t + a_s \frac{2}{\pi} \sum_{n=1,3,5} \frac{1}{n} \cos 2\pi (nf_i - f_s)t$$

$$+ a_s \frac{2}{\pi} \sum_{n=1,3,5} \frac{1}{n} \cos 2\pi (nf_i + f_s)t.$$

Thus, as f_i increases, components such as $nf_i - f_s$ and $nf_i + f_s$ fall outside the audible range, and only the first term in the final equation remains. This component retains its original frequency but the switching has reduced its amplitude by one half. This same argument applies to all sinusoidal and cosinusoidal components. Hence at high rates of switching, the audio part of the modified speech wave is transmitted at a reduced amplitude but with components located at the same frequencies as in the original wave.

Pursuing this same argument with different duty cycles yields the same conclusions. The amount of amplitude reduction depends on the duty cycle, as one might expect. At high switching rates the audio components of the original speech wave are only attenuated but not altered in frequency.

The two extremes of the figure are easily understood on purely physical grounds. What explains the irregular behavior of the intelligibility functions in the region of 10–100 interruptions per second? The local plateau in the region of 10–100 interruptions per second and the clear decline around 100 interruptions per second may indicate the important temporal characteristics of speech.

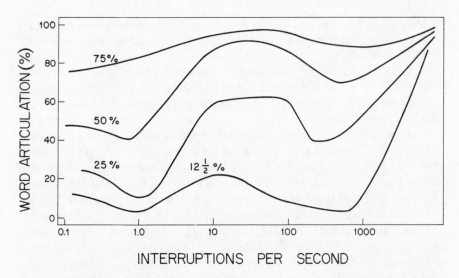

FIG. 12.7 Percentage of correct word identification as a function of the interruption rate for the speech. The parameter is the duty cycle (12.5% is 1 part on to 7 parts off). (From Miller & Licklider, 1950, p. 169.)

Historically, the next important development in this area was due to Cherry and Taylor (1954). Instead of interrupting the speech waveform, they alternated the waveform between the subject's two ears. The left ear of the subject received half of the message and the right ear received the other half. The results of this manipulation were striking. Intelligibility deteriorated severely at alternation rates of about 3 per second. Cherry and Taylor interpreted this result as a measure of the time it takes "attention" to switch between two ears. Since minimum intelligibility occurred at about 3 alternations per second, this was estimated as the switching time. Slower rates of alternation would allow the attention mechanism to switch between the two ears. At faster rates the subject could listen to a single ear, since at the higher rates the silent interval is short enough to be bridged and the intelligibility preserved even with a single ear.

Despite Cherry and Taylor's emphasis on an attention mechanism, their own data showed similar declines in intelligibility when the speech was simply interrupted at one ear. Huggins (1964) pursued this problem with careful replication and analysis of the Cherry and Taylor results. His data agreed with the original observations. Alternation of continuous speech between the two ears at a rate of about 3 per second considerably reduced the intelligibility of speech. Huggins concluded, however, that this loss of intelligibility occurs because the speech reaches the listener's ears in segments. This segmentation presents the cues in the speech waveform in an unusuable form. Alternation does not significantly reduce intelligibility except by preventing adjacent segments of the speech waveform from running together. Huggins also concluded that the critical rate of alternation is probably closely related to the duration of syllables in the speech of the talker.

Most of Huggins' earlier work involved either an interruption or alternation of the speech waveform at approximately a 50% duty cycle. In his latest research he has employed a procedure of segmenting the speech by inserting silent intervals in continuous speech. Segmented speech differs from interrupted speech in that no speech material is missing, it is simply separated by silent intervals. By fixing the speech-to-silence ratio at several values and by varying the silent interval, Huggins has measured the intelligibility of segmented speech under a variety of conditions. The results indicate that the critical silent interval is about 60 – 120 msec. If the silent interval exceeds that range then intelligibility is adversely affected. If the silence lasts less than 60 msec, almost perfect intelligibility is possible if the speech portion is long enough. Given a silent interval of about 200 msec, intelligibility is a monotonic increasing function of the duration of the speech segment with 50% intelligibility occurring near a value of 60 msec. Huggins shows how to predict the effects of interruption very nicely by a simple probabilistic model involving two independent factors—the speech interval and the silent interval. Too long a silent interval or too short a speech segment yields low intelligibility. The study of the temporal factors affecting intelligibility therefore seems to have converged on the following conclusion: a natural time segment for speech is in the range from 50 to 100 msec. Successive speech segments must follow one another with a gap less than 60 – 120 msec in order to preserve intelligibility.

SPEECH RECOGNITION

We now turn to the problem of speech recognition. From the viewpoint of hearing, the ultimate question is how speech is perceived. What are the elements of speech? What acoustic cues signify these elements? If the elements depend upon their context, how can we describe these complex interrelationships and catalog the modifications that may occur? A great deal has been written on this topic over the past two decades. Significant changes in our thinking about speech perception have occurred in this period. Unhappily, a completely satisfactory theory of speech perception still does not exist. The ultimate test of a theory of speech perception would be to build a mechanical device that would accept the acoustic waveform and transcribe it, as if taking dictation. Work on this project dates back to the mid-1930s. Although optimistic engineers proclaim that success is just around the corner, we are still waiting for a speech transcriber. One reason for the delay is that mechanical transcription involves fundamental problems of pattern recognition.

Speech recognition is a problem no different in form from any other kind of pattern recognition. The basic ingredients are the same. We have a set of objects that we wish to map into a smaller subset of types. In visual form recognition, the objects might be geometric drawings. The types might be simple categories such as circles, squares, triangles, and so on. In general, for each type there is a variety of objects all of which may differ from one another. All are, however, exemplars of a given type. These various representatives of the type are sometimes called "tokens." The essential problem is the complexity of the token. To appreciate this problem, consider the question of recognizing handwritten characters. In addition to the style of letter, the size of the character or its orientation may vary widely. Despite this diversity, most people have little difficulty recognizing the letter "a." Building a machine to emulate this ability has proved beyond our present technology. Character recognizers are possible, but they usually succeed by severely restricting the tokens allowed to represent the given type. Thus banks can machine-read the number printed on your check, but the characters are standardized and appear at a fixed location on the paper.

The objects or tokens of speech perception are the speech waveforms. The question of what constitutes a type is still moot. Initially, the phoneme seemed to be the type since transcription in phonemic characters allows one to infer correctly the word being spoken. But a great deal of disagreement arises exactly at this point. In fact, no machine can yet recognize spoken utterances of more than a few words over more than a few talkers. This small success is gained from restricting the token class considerably. Recognition of speech depends on several factors.

Context

Redundancy. Contextual cues play an important role in speech recognition. There are various kinds of contextual rules and we will do no more than mention the different classes here. First, there is the redundancy provided by the topic of the conversation itself. It is unlikely that the word "anteaters" will arise in a conversation about sailboat racing. Next there is a syntactic redundancy—the boy expected a (blank). It is probable that the (blank) is a noun. Finally there is the combined redundancy of meaning and structure. The sentence, "The girl was sailing in a lovely red boat on the quiet (blank)" is an example of this kind of context. The (blank) could be several things: water, pond, lake. The point is that the acoustic cues leading to a choice of these alternatives are far different from those utilized in discriminating "lake" or "pond" or "water" from a wider set of alternatives. Hearing another person's name when first introduced is often difficult simply because the alternative set is so large. The effect of contextual redundancy is obviously very strong in understanding everyday speech and probably will be an important aspect of any mechanical speech recognizer.

Character of the speaker.   Another kind of context not widely appreciated is the character of the speaker's voice. Plots of the f_1, f_2 formant space show considerable variation among talkers. Head sizes are different and the head cavities vary considerably in shape, so the formant frequencies of vowels differ considerably from one person to the next. Although every individual speaking vowels will place the f_1, f_2 frequencies generally as indicated in Figure 12.5a, it is usually impossible to decode any one vowel until something is known about the formants of other vowels as spoken by that particular speaker. The problem is analogous to listening to a speaker with a strong accent. Some sample of his speech is needed to begin to appreciate how he says certain words and thus how to understand his utterances. Probably the most dramatic experiment illustrating this effect is that of Ladefoged and Broadbent (1957). They measured the perception of a target word that followed a carrier phrase. The carrier phrase had the characteristics of one talker and the target word was sampled from another. A speech synthesizer actually generated the sentences, but its programming followed either one talker's parameter values or another's. Broadbent and Ladefoged showed that the same target word would be heard as a different word, depending upon the carrier phrase that preceded it. It is comparatively easy to recognize different talkers. Mechanical procedures for recognizing different speakers seem to be much advanced over those used to recognize what different speakers say. Thus context aids in our ability to understand speech in two general ways. First there is the effect of redundancy; second, there is the context provided by the nature and character of the talker's individual speech parameters.

Unit of Speech

The heart of the problem of speech perception is to identify the speech unit. We discussed the phonemic unit and its descriptive use in specifying a speech sound. Transcriptions in the dictionary illustrate the usefulness and importance of this speech unit. The problem with the phonemic unit, however, is that its exact acoustic specification depends strongly upon context. The acoustic correlates of a given phoneme depend strongly upon the preceding and following text. The problem is nicely summarized by Stevens and Halle (1967): "We are thus faced with the difficulty that, though on the one hand speech can be described in very satisfactory fashion in terms of segments and features, the latter do not seem to be directly present in the observable speech event [p. 90]." This basic fact, which has become clearer in the last ten years or so, poses a serious problem for developing a satisfactory model of speech perception. Transitional clues represent the inertial constraints of the production system and contain important information concerning the speech utterance. These transitional cues have been stressed by workers at the Haskins Laboratory. Their general position is summarized in the motor theory of speech perception. As Liberman, Cooper, Shankweiler, and Studdert-Kennedy (1967) have stated: "The acoustic cues for successive phonemics are intermixed in the sound stream to such an extent that the definable segments of sound do not correspond to segments at the phonemic level [p. 432]." They conclude from this observation that there is "a marked lack of correspondence between sound and the perceived phoneme."

Thus speech perception requires a technique to break through the bewildering complexity of content and to emerge with a phonemic transcription of the correct word. Cole and Scott (1974), in a recent review, advance the theory that there are essentially three types of cues to speech. One set is essentially invariant, another transitional, and finally, they argue, the envelope of the speech waveform helps to integrate syllables into higher order units such as words and phrases.

Whether or not they are correct, the topic remains an intriguing one. Clearly speech is perceived, even by small children. Yet our understanding of the fundamentals of this process, while elaborate and detailed, has still not managed to penetrate the essential problems. Research on the topic has been extensive and the advances in the last two decades have been impressive. But we still cannot take the speech waveform as recorded mechanically, even by a sound spectrogram, and transcribe without error what we could easily write if we listened. A solution to this problem would reveal the basic invariances in the speech process.

REFERENCES

Beranek, L.L. *Acoustics.* New York: McGraw-Hill, 1954.

Cherry, E.C., & Taylor, W.K. Some further experiments upon the recognition of speech, with one and with two ears. *Journal of the Acoustical Society of America,* 1954, *26,* 554–559.

Cole, R.A., & Scott, B. Toward a theory of speech perception. *Psychological Review,* 1974, *81,* 348–374.

Dunn, H.K., & Farnsworth, D.W. Exploration of pressure field around the human head during speech. *Journal of the Acoustical Society of America,* 1939, *10,* 184–199.

Dunn, H.K., & White, S.D. Statistical measurements on conversational speech. *Journal of the Acoustical Society of America,* 1940, *11,* 278–288.

Egan, J.P. Articulation testing methods. *Laryngoscope,* 1948, *58,* 955–991.

Fletcher, H. *Speech and hearing in communication* (2nd ed.). 1953, New York: Van Nostrand, 1953. (Originally published, 1929).

French, N.R., & Steinberg, J.C. Factors governing the intelligibility of speech sounds. *Journal of the Acoustical Society of America,* 1947, *19,* 90–119.

Hawkins, J.E., Jr., & Stevens, S.S. The masking of pure tones and of speech by white noise. *Journal of the Acoustical Society of America,* 1950, *22,* 6–13.

Howes, D. On the relation between the intelligibility and frequency of occurrence of English words. *Journal of the Acoustical Society of America,* 1957, *29,* 296–305.

Huggins, A.W.F. Distortion of the temporal pattern of speech: Interruption and alternation. *Journal of the Acoustical Society of America,* 1964, *36,* 1055–1064.

Koenig, W., Dunn, H.K., & Lacy, L.Y. The sound spectograph. *Journal of the Acoustical Society of America,* 1946, *18,* 19–49.

Ladefoged, P., & Broadbent, D.E. Information conveyed by vowels. *Journal of the Acoustical Society of America,* 1957, *29,* 98–104.

Liberman, A.M., Cooper, F.S., Shankweiler, D.P., & Studdert-Kennedy, M. Perception of the speech code. *Psychological Review,* 1967, *74,* 431–461.

Licklider, J.C.R. Effects of amplitude distortion upon the intelligibility of speech. *Journal of the Acoustical Society of America,* 1946, *18,* 429–434.

Miller, G.A., Heise, G.A., & Lichten, W. The intelligibility of speech as a function of the context of the test materials. *Journal of Experimental Psychology,* 1951, *41,* 329–335.

Miller, G.A., & Licklider, J.C.R. The intelligibility of interrupted speech. *Journal of the Acoustical Society of America,* 1950, *22,* 167–173.

Peterson, G.E., & Barney, H.L., Control methods used in a study of the vowels, *Journal of the Acoustical Society of America,* 1952, *24,* 175–185.

Potter, R.K., Kopp, G.A., & Green, H.C. *Visible speech.* New York: Van Nostrand, 1947.

Rosenberg, A.E. Effect of the glottal pulse shape on the quality of natural vowels. *Journal of the Acoustical Society of America,* 1971, *49,* 583–590.

Stevens, K., & Halle, M. Remarks on analysis by synthesis and distinctive features. In W. Wathen-Dunn (Ed.), *Models for the perception of speech and visual form.* Cambridge, Massachusetts: MIT Press, 1967.

Stevens, K.N., & House, A.S. Speech perception. In J. Tobias (Ed.), *Foundations of modern auditory theory.* Vol. II. New York and London: Academic Press, 1972.

13
Hearing Loss

INTRODUCTION

Among the most tragic sensory deficits is hearing loss. "The silent world" is a chilling, but accurate, description of this condition. Hearing disabilities often occur in the later years. The term "presbycusis" refers to the general diminution of hearing acuity with age. For the elderly, the affliction is sad because it breaks communication between the individual and his friends, neighbors, and relatives. Loneliness and isolation are but two of the more obvious results.

For the young, hearing loss is even more tragic because of the far-reaching consequences of this disability. A child with profound hearing loss may never develop the use of normal language. In extreme cases, the outlook is indeed bleak. While the individual may be able to function, and may be fortunate enough to provide a living for himself, the prospect for more outstanding achievement is relatively slim. Although blindness is a far-reaching impairment, there have been blind poets, mathematicians, and musicians of note throughout the ages. No individual with severe hearing loss is likely to achieve eminence if the disability occurs at a very early age and special treatment is not available.

Although this book is primarily about normal auditory functions, a few brief words about hearing loss and its diagnosis are appropriate, since this is such a common affliction and because malfunctions of the sensory system provide some insight into its normal operation. To begin this review, we must start with how hearing is measured, the audiogram.

AUDIOGRAM

As we reviewed in Chapter 2, normal hearing is defined as the average threshold for the normal population at a group of pure tone frequencies. These frequencies are traditionally 250, 500, 1,000, 2,000, and 4,000 Hz. In recent times, there has been an effort to increase the upper frequencies used to test hearing because the early diagnosis of abnormalities at the very high frequencies may be prognostic of later hearing impairment. Audiologists, people who measure hearing, have traditionally used a graph in which 0 dB is defined as the average threshold for young normal adults at each of the audiometric frequencies. A "hearing level" is then the departure from these average thresholds at each of the frequencies. Thus, hearing level is the decibel difference between the individual's threshold at that frequency and the average threshold of the normal population.

A typical audiogram obtained for two different hypothetical patients is shown in Figure 13.1a. Patient A shows a relatively flat loss of about 30 dB at each frequency. To understand exactly what this loss means we have plotted next to the audiogram the actual threshold obtained by Patient A on a graph of log frequency versus sound pressure level. The solid curve at the bottom of Figure 13.1b indicates the threshold values for the normal population. As can be seen at each frequency, Patient A requires about 30 dB more sound intensity in order to hear the sinusoid at the indicated frequency.

Patient B shows quite a different pattern of loss. There is no difference between his hearing and that of normal individuals at the low frequencies. At the high frequencies B requires more intensity than normal individuals and a hearing loss of 32 dB is evident at 4,000 Hz. In Figure 13.1b we have also plotted the actual sound pressure levels required by Patient B to hear the various sinusoidal frequencies. Since ISO threshold at 4 kHz is 9.5 dB SPL, Patient B needs a signal 32 dB more intense, or 41.5 dB SPL at that frequency.

The results obtained by these patients are typical of two different classes of hearing disorders. There are many types of hearing loss and their classification is a complicated area. We will not attempt more than a superficial review here. More comprehensive treatments can be found in *Hearing and Deafness* by Davis and Silverman (1960); *The Measurement of Hearing* by Hirsh (1952); or *Modern Developments in Audiology,* edited by Jerger (1973); as well as the *Journal of Speech and Hearing Research.* Nevertheless, we will explore our two hypothetical patients in more detail and thus illustrate the division of hearing loss into two broad classes, so-called "conductive," and "sensory—neural."

We must realize that the audiogram as plotted in Figure 13.1a and b is an *air-conduction* audiogram The sound was delivered to the ear with some sort of earphone or transducer and hence an airborne sound wave is used to stimulate the sense of hearing. Naturally, the thresholds for the normal population are measured in the same way as those of the patient. A different kind of audiogram is obtained if, instead of using airborne sound, we place a vibrator somewhere on the subject's head, usually slightly in back of the ear itself on the hard bony prominence—the mastoid. This stimulator actually shakes the skull, inducing motion in the fluids of the inner ear. The vibrator can deliver several different frequencies. We thereby obtain an audiogram for *bone conduction.* Again, the

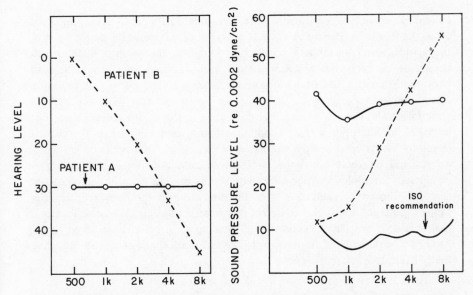

FIG. 13.1 The measured threshold or audiograms of two hypothetical patients: (a) presentation in the form of a typical audiogram—hearing level versus a logarithmic frequency scale; (b) the measured thresholds (SPL) versus logarithm of signal frequency. The International Standards Organization (ISO) values for "normal" threshold is indicated by the solid line near the bottom of the graph.

usual way to evaluate these measurements is with respect to a group of normal individuals. The standardization of the thresholds for bone conduction is not very well advanced. The major difficulty is in specifying the physical stimulus since the effectiveness of the vibrator depends on its placement and the static force or impedance coupling the transducer to the skull. No one has yet determined an entirely satisfactory technique of standardizing the coupling procedure. Each audiology clinic generally develops its own standards and relates patient thresholds to its own local norms.

Differences in hearing level for airborne and bone-conducted tests are diagnostic of the type of hearing impairment. Suppose a patient had a blockage, or a partial occlusion, of the middle ear. He might, for example, have wax in the meatus or fluid in the middle ear. Then his air-conduction hearing might be 20–30 dB poorer than the average of a normal subject, and this loss would be approximately constant at all frequencies. His results would be similar to those shown for Patient A in Figure 13.1. His bone-conduction hearing would be normal, since the energy delivered by the vibrator bypasses the middle ear. On the other hand, suppose Patient B showed a bone-conduction threshold with the same relative loss as the air-conduction thresholds. One would then be disinclined to suppose the difficulty was purely a middle-ear problem. The source of

Patient B's difficulty is probably related to some malfunction occurring at, or after, the hair cells. Patient A's loss is probably of a conductive variety, that is, the acoustic-mechanical path conducting sound to the cochlea is abnormal. Patient B probably has a sensory-neural loss. Although one can distinguish between different types of sensory-neural hearing losses, we will simply lump them into one category.

We might also note in passing that there are a variety of precautions that must be taken in interpreting bone-conductive losses, especially when the patient seems to have a loss in only one ear. For example, if the patient's left ear is normal and his right ear shows a 50-dB air-conductive loss, then the bone-conduction thresholds must be taken with some care. The vibrator will obviously stimulate the entire skull as well as the area close to the measured ear. The subject will therefore be able to detect the sound via the left, good ear. To insure that this does not occur, some sort of masking noise must be delivered to the good ear. Noise is therefore frequently used to mask the contralateral ear while the ipsilateral ear is being measured.

RECRUITMENT

A second test that can be carried out is a test for recruitment, which is especially easy if one ear is normal and the other abnormal.

Suppose both patients, A and B, have a hearing deficiency only in their left ear—their right ears are completely normal. In this case it is possible to introduce airborne sounds to both ears simultaneously and ask the subjects to adjust the two sounds until they are equal in apparent level or loudness. If these tests were carried out, then the following pattern of results might well occur: in Figure 13.2a we have plotted the presumed results from Patient A's two ears. Notice the graph's coordinates are the hearing level in each ear, that is, the relative level of the sound in the two ears compared with "normal" hearing. Since Patient A has a 30-dB loss in the left ear, we would have to increase the sound by about 30-dB more in the left ear than in his right ear for equal loudness. This would be true at all levels of the sound and so his results would appear as indicated by the dotted lines in Figure 13.2a. Along the major diagonal we have indicated the line of equal intensity, that is, the line at which the sound pressure levels in the two ears are identical. Patient A's hearing is 30 dB depressed at all levels, and this result should be the same at all frequencies.

Contrast these results with those obtained by Patient B. Recall that we are assuming his right ear is normal. Patient B's audiogram shows approximately a 20-dB loss at 2,000 Hz (see Figure 13.1). Thus the first point in Figure 13.2b occurs at the coordinates 20, 0. At this intensity the sounds are just audible in each ear. If Patient B shows a phenomenon called "recruitment," then the pattern of results shown by the dotted line in Figure 13.2b will obtain. As we

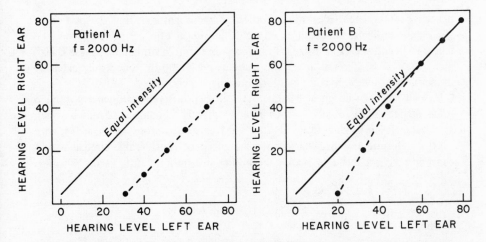

FIG. 13.2 Hypothetical data representing a loudness match between (a) the right ear of the subject, presumed normal, and (b) the left ear. Note at zero hearing level in the right ear the hearing level in the left ear is consistent with the audiograms given earlier, see Figure 13.1. At high intensity equal hearing level (equal intensities) are heard as equally loud for Patient B. This result is called *recruitment*.

increase the absolute sound pressure level, the left ear, the abnormal ear, seems to catch up with the normal ear. At intense sound pressure level, for example, those corresponding to about 60 dB hearing level, the apparent loudness of the sounds in the two ears is the same. Recruitment is this nonlinear growth of loudness with level in the abnormal ear. Generally the sound in the abnormal ears sounds rough or distorted—but the loudness is the same. A recruitment test is helpful in differentiating among types of nerve disorders. Not all sensory-neural losses show recruitment but it is a common phenomenon in many nonconductive losses.

For our hypothetical patients, recruitment was relatively easy to measure because we assumed that one ear was normal and the other abnormal. A loudness balance is easy to make and shows little variability. A more likely circumstance is to have some hearing loss in both ears. In such a case a loudness balance cannot be used to assess recruitment. How then can we test for recruitment? The usual procedure is to have the subject balance two tones of different frequency in the same ear: for example, we might use a tone of 500 Hz and alternate it with one of 4,000 Hz. For the purely conductive loss, the results would again be a straight-line function with a slope of 45° if we plotted the hearing level of the 500-Hz tone against the hearing level of the 4,000-Hz tone. For example, suppose the loss was a 30 dB conductive one, as in Patient A. If we plotted the hearing level of the 500-Hz tone versus the hearing level of the 4,000-Hz tone, we would find the same 30-dB loss at both frequencies and hence the results would fall along the major diagonal. On the other hand, with the nerve-type loss, such as shown in Patient B, we might well find the pattern of results not unlike that shown in Figure 13.2b, except the coordinates would be labeled "hearing level at 500 Hz" along a y axis and "hearing level at 4,000 Hz" along the x axis. If recruitment was present, the 4,000-Hz tone would catch up in loudness to the 500-Hz tone at high intensity levels.

Unfortunately, a loudness balance between two different frequencies is much more difficult and subject to greater error than is a loudness balance between two ears. Recruitment tests of this kind must therefore be regarded with caution. Despite this drawback, they are often of considerable clinical significance in trying to evaluate hearing disabilities and are frequently used.

SPEECH DISCRIMINATION

Although the pure tone audiogram is the principal measure of hearing level, the most important social and practical implication of hearing impairment is the inability to hear speech. Such an impairment causes the individual great hardship. Not only may his normal social existence be impaired, but in some cases, his livelihood may be affected. Individuals with hearing losses as measured by a pure tone audiogram are often tested with speech material.

The use of speech material raises several problems of measurement. Before discussing the problems as they arise in the clinic, let us consider the general problem. First, different words have different energies. As we saw in Chapter 12, the vowels produce the most acoustic energy, while certain consonant sounds, particularly the stop consonants and fricatives, produce a great deal less energy. The difference may be as great at 30 dB. Thus the first problem to be solved is what one means by "the level of the speech material," since each word has a different level as measured in isolation. One way to avoid this problem is to prepare a tape with all of the words spoken with the same vocal effort. A long-term average of the speech material can then be used as the "speech level." Other problems concern the selection of the material to be used as the speech stimuli. Should one use familiar words and phrases or should some of the material include uncommon words and unlikely utterances? A variety of different material exists. The majority contains relatively familiar and common words but each list may have slightly different properties, depending on the particular speech test.

If the words are spoken live, the speaker attempts to maintain the same vocal effort, sometimes monitoring the words as they are produced on a VU meter—the kind of meter used in a broadcast studio to monitor the level of the program material. In any case, the words are presented to the subject either in isolation or at some point in a carrier phrase such as "You will write ——— now." The carrier phrase is also useful since it is helpful in maintaining equal vocal effort. However the speech is presented, consider the typical function one might obtain for speech presented at different intensity levels. At the highest level of speech material, the subject hears all of the words correctly. As the level is decreased, more and more words are missed. For the subject with a hearing loss a different result will occur. If the subject has a purely conductive loss, for example, the 30-dB loss of our Patient A—then one would expect his speech reception function to be exactly like that obtained from a normal patient, except displaced on the intensity scale by about 30 dB. If the normal achieves 50% correct identification of the words at a level of, say, 40 dB SPL for the speech, we would expect Patient A to achieve the same percentage at 70 dB. Similarly, if the normal achieves 90% correct at 50 dB, we would expect Patient A to achieve 90% correct at 80 dB. At every sound level were we to subtract 30 dB from the level obtained by Patient A, we would have a function indistinguishable from that of a normal.

For Patient B this function may be quite different. If Patient B has a certain form of sensory—neural loss, then he will find that as we raise the level of the speech, a point is reached at which the intelligibility does not increase. For example, in the medium to high levels of speech, the subject will report that the words are loud enough but he simply cannot distinguish what word is being spoken. He may also confidently report the wrong word, for example, "fake" instead of "sake." He may, in fact, complain if the level is raised—saying he can hear the words—he just cannot understand them. Thus, the speech reception function may show asymptotic behavior. Patient B might show an asymptotic reception threshold at about 60% correct. No matter how much more we increase the level of the speech, the patient achieves only 60% correct identification of the speech material. This maximum level of intelligibility is an important number to know, especially when we consider prescribing a hearing aid for the subject (Hirsh, 1952, Chapter 5).

A standard procedure in the clinic is to slowly increase the level of the speech material until the patient reports he can just detect the material. This level is designated the speech reception threshold (SRT). One then increases the level 20 dB and scores the number of words the patient can correctly *identify*. Scores less than 90% correct are an indication of a neural-type hearing loss.

HEARING AIDS

Patient A would greatly benefit from a hearing aid if the gain was 30 dB or better. Patient A's aided hearing would then be indistinguishable from normal, assuming the hearing aid produced no distortion and amplified all frequencies equally. For Patient B, it is clear that amplifying the sound by itself is not sufficient. Patient B, no matter what the speech level, will have difficulty distinguishing between certain sounds and therefore a hearing aid can be of only limited value for this individual. Because of Patient B's recruitment the speech may be loud enough; indeed, he might even be annoyed if the sound was amplified still further. Recall that the loudness he perceives at high intensities is essentially normal. His speech reception would be inferior to normals even with a hearing aid.

In order to provide some assistance for the sensory-neural patients, such as Patient B, a variety of modifications of the hearing aid has been utilized. The simplest modification would be to differentially amplify the different frequencies. Thus, at the low frequencies, for example, at 500 Hz where Patient B is essentially normal, no amplification is used. On the other hand, at 4,000 Hz where Patient B appears to be about 30 dB down, one might attempt to amplify the sound by 30 dB. Such a procedure appears reasonable but probably would not make Patient B's speech reception threshold equal to that of a normal. Again, the problem of recruitment arises. The mere fact of recruitment suggests a strong nonlinear element in the hearing process. Trying to overcome these nonlinearities is not easy.

One technique used to aid patients with extreme recruitment is to modify the gain of the hearing aid in such a way as to make it compressive. A compressive device is one whose input–output relation is nonlinear: for example, a change of 10 dB at the input produces only a 5-dB change at the output. The problem with such nonlinear devices is that they may introduce spurious harmonics (see Chapter 7). Practical compressive devices are usually built to change the gain of the linear amplifier, depending upon the average input. But measuring the average input, of course, requires some time before the average can be established. Therefore, there are lags between the momentary amplification and the momentary speech level. Compressors then add peculiarities of their own to the speech waveform, such as brief high-level bursts before very intense vowels or other intense transients that occur after periods of silence.

The selection of a hearing aid is a difficult and complicated problem. In many cases the best advice to an individual is simply to try a number of different hearing aids until one finds one that seems to be particularly effective. Research on hearing aids has probably not been pursued as vigorously as it should. It is hoped that in the next few years more basic information will be forthcoming. This information should allow us both to design more effective hearing aids and to optimize the match of hearing aid to patient.

TUNING FORK TESTS

The preceding section has indicated some of the more standard audiometric tests administered to patients in an attempt to diagnose hearing difficulties. We have particularly stressed the division of the hearing impairment into two broad classes: bone conduction and sensory–neural loss. Many of the readers have had tests of their hearing performed by their own physician using the simple tuning fork. These tests are obviously less elaborate than the audiometric procedures described earlier but they can also be effective in providing at least a tentative diagnosis as to the nature of the impairment. The first common test is called the Rinne test. First, the turning fork is struck and the hilt of the tuning fork is applied to the mastoid of the patient. When the patient reports that he no longer hears the sound, then the fork is immediately held close to the patient's ear. If the patient hears the tone he is said to have a positive Rinne, if he does not hear the tone he is said to have a negative Rinne. The normal patient should hear the tuning fork about twice as long via air as by bone conduction. Thus, a negative Rinne is presumptive of a conductive loss in that ear.

The Schwabach test is very similar to the Rinne except that the comparison is between how long the patient can hear the fork applied to the mastoid and how long the physician can hear the fork in the same environment. If the patient is experiencing a conductive loss then the airborne sounds will be attenuated, making the local environment effectively more quiet. The patient should therefore be able to hear the fork when applied to the mastoid for a longer period of time than the physician.

The Weber test is a comparison of the bone conduction in the patient's two ears. In this case, the hilt of the fork is applied to the center of the patient's forehead and he is asked where the sound appears. If both ears are normal the stimulation will be approximately equal and the sound will be heard in the center of the head. If the patient has a conductive loss in only one ear then the sound will generally be heard at that ear. The rationale for this test is similar to that of the Schwabach test. The ear experiencing the conductive loss has a large signal-to-interference ratio and hence the sound is localized on that side. In the case of the sensory—neural loss, however, the stimulus, even when delivered via bone conduction, has less effect on the abnormal side and hence the sound will be localized at the normal ear.

While these tests are obviously less quantitative than the audiometric procedures described in the preceding section, the essential rationale for the tests and the diagnosis based on them are basically the same as we outlined previously.

This concludes our review of the topic of hearing loss and our brief outline of its types and its measurement. In the remainder of this chapter we would like to take up one of the causes of hearing loss. There are a variety of causes for hearing disabilities, many of which are essentially medical and outside the scope of this book. German measles during the pregnancy of the mother, otosclerosis (a bone disease that affects the inner ear), otitis media (an inflammation of the middle ear that often leads to infections of the inner ear itself), and a host of other diseases are well known in their potential effects on hearing. Hearing loss can also result from ototoxic effects of a drug. Some of the wonder drugs such as streptomycin and neomycin are known to attack the hair cells and profound hearing loss can result from large dosages. Simple aspirin, if taken in large amounts, can cause hearing loss and tinnitus (ringing). The effects of aspirin are apparently reversible. Improvements are noted within 2 or 3 days after withdrawal (see Schuknecht, 1974, Chapter 6).

However, one cause of hearing loss arises from simply being exposed to sound. Repeated exposure to intense noise may produce permanent hearing disability. We shall take up some of the known relations between extreme noise exposure and both permanent and temporary hearing loss. We will also discuss some of the relations between temporary threshold shifts (TTS) and the more permanent changes in hearing, permanent threshold shifts (PTS).

NOISE-INDUCED DEAFNESS

The relationship between noise exposure and hearing loss was made evident by certain extreme occupational groups, particularly the weavers in the textile mills in Scotland and England during the last century. The high level of noise, generated by both machinery and the weaving process itself, produced whole populations of people whose hearing impairments were so obvious that measurements were hardly necessary. But quantitative evaluations of these effects date only from the 1930s. The initial data were simply samplings of the hearing level of a large group of people engaged in some occupation. These studies confirmed earlier impressions and for the last 40 years we tried to collect evidence and data that are sufficient for predictive purposes. Recently, criteria have been set up, commonly called damage risk criteria. These criteria establish upper limits of noise exposure. If observed, these limits should protect a given proportion of the population from a certain level of hearing loss. Evidence is still not as clear-cut as one would desire, especially for unusual or intermittent exposure conditions.

A host of very difficult questions remains largely unanswered in this field and new data are constantly being sought. One can predict with reasonable accuracy the average amount of hearing loss one can expect for a continuous 8-hr per day exposure over a long period of time such as 5, 10, or 15 years. But if the exposure is not continuous, then predictions become uncertain. What are the effects of short interruptions of the noise exposure, for example: "noise breaks" of various durations? How does the exact frequency composition of the noise influence the amount of hearing loss? Is it effective to rotate the worker through a variety of different noises, of somewhat different quantity and quality, to minimize the hearing loss experienced over the entire group? Are some people more sensitive to noise exposure than others? These questions illustrate where our knowledge is limited. To understand why we have difficulty obtaining sure answers to these questions, consider the problem of gaining knowledge in this field.

Retrospective Studies

The most common source of information on noise-induced hearing loss is the retrospective study. This kind of study, as the name implies, simply involves the measurement of the present hearing level of a large group of people. Owing to their occupation, residency, or some other characteristic, one has reasonable confidence about the noise exposure of these people during some past period of time. One then tries to relate the presumed noise exposure that has occurred in the past to the present level of hearing. Ideally one can describe a functional relationship between noise exposure and present hearing level. If such a relationship can be established and the variability over the group of subjects exposed is tolerably small, then the major objective of a retrospective study has been met.

Often the variability is not small. Even within a group of subjects experiencing what are presumably similar noise exposures, the amount of hearing loss varies considerably from one subject to the next. Many factors contribute to this variability. The first and most obvious is that the noise exposure may indeed be quite varied from one subject to the next even within a single occupation. Second, even if the effects of exposure were to produce exactly the same amount of change in hearing level, the final hearing level may show a large range because the initial levels were quite different. Generally we have no way of knowing the initial hearing level of each subject. Finally, there may be a variety of other effects, for example, general health, that are indirectly involved in the hearing loss suffered by some members of the group. On occasion these can be ascertained and controlled, but the degree of control is usually not very great.

In a retrospective study, even if the relationship between noise exposure and hearing loss is reasonably tidy, there remains a host of problems. Can one infer a causal relation between the noise exposure and the apparent hearing loss? The vulnerability of a retrospective study is that one can usually argue for some other factor being responsible for the relationship. It might be argued that people differ in their susceptibility to noise exposure just as they differ in their susceptibility to other illnesses. Those with high susceptibility simply leave the industry and therefore a biased population remains—one that shows less average loss than would occur in a normal (unbiased) population. Often extreme noise exposure is accompanied by a variety of other unusual conditions. In the steel industry, for example, the high noise levels are invariably accompanied by high levels of toxic chemicals in the air. Perhaps these chemicals indirectly affect hearing. If this were the case, then studies in such industries would find more loss than would occur in a normal population without the chemical exposure. Whatever the results, one can usually imagine plausible arguments that make the obtained results suspect in one direction or another. These posthoc explanations, while relatively farfetched from a scientific point of view, often exert considerable influence on a policy level.

Prospective Study

This kind of objection to retrospective studies can be partially corrected with the use of a prospective study. In the prospective study, as the name implies, we first select a group of people and then follow their hearing level as a function of time. The major advantage of this type of study is a secure baseline from which changes in hearing can be detected. Also, because the people have been identified in advance, their noise exposure can be more carefully monitored and measured. The major practical difficulty with such studies is that they are extremely expensive and inefficient. There will be an inevitable attrition in the number of subjects due to employment in a different industry, for example. One must therefore start with a very large number of subjects. If the loss is too great, one may suspect selective factors such as those mentioned as criticism of retrospective studies.

Finally, there is the moral or ethical problem that arises if the study is extremely successful. For example, if the noise seems to be creating a noticeable impairment in hearing, then it is the responsibility of the researcher to bring this to the attention of the people in authority. If the change is large enough they will probably modify the noise exposure, and thus restrict the range of exposure, thereby hampering the ability of the study to find clear relationships.

In short, the accumulation of reliable and valuable data in a field setting is very difficult.

Animal Studies

For the reasons just mentioned, animals are often used in studies of hearing loss due to noise exposure. The use of animals has a number of advantages other than humanitarian ones. First of all, the noise exposure can usually be more accurately controlled and measured. Naturally the study is invariably a prospective one and furthermore one can obtain a histological examination of the animal's ear, postmortem. For these reasons a large number of animal studies have been conducted and the histological changes have been correlated with the physical parameters of the exposure.

If animals are used, the histological preparation is usually inspected to see the extent and kind of hair cell damage that has occurred because of the exposure to high noise. Damage is often manifest by the loss of hair cells in the exposed animals. One common measure of damage is simply to count the number of missing or damaged hair cells as a function along the basilar membrane.

One can also construct a scale of injury to the cochlea using a light microscope (Covell, 1963). Grade 1, for example, indicates no discernible change; Grade 3 includes moderate to severe changes in the supporting cell and hair cell injury of slight degree is apparent; Grade 5 implies hair cells have been lifted from the basilar membrane. The correlation between PTS at a frequency corresponding to the place of injury is remarkably close in a sample of 34 cats subjected to a variety of partially deafening noise exposures (Miller, Watson, & Covell, 1963).

Summary of Permanent Threshold Shift
Due to High Exposure to Noise

As a result of all the preceding types of evidence, the following rough generalizations concerning permanent threshold shift can be stated:

1. Noise levels in excess of 85 dBA for an 8-hour period are likely to cause some permanent threshold shift. The greater the intensity of the noise, the more damage to hearing will result (Ward, 1974).

2. The hearing loss increases with longer exposure duration. For industrial noise of the 8-hr-per-day variety at low frequencies, it appears that the amount of loss increases gradually over a 30-year period, while at the high frequencies, particularly 4 kHz, the greatest amount of loss occurs in the first 10 to 15 years (Nixon & Glorig, 1961; Taylor, Pearson, Mair, & Burns, 1965).

3. We seem particularly vulnerable to noise in the high-frequency range, especially between 2,000 and 4,000 Hz (Burns, 1968; Davis, 1960).

One might expect a simple relationship to hold between the energy spectrum of the noise exposure and the amount of PTS measured over frequency. After all, the sound does undergo a filtering operation in delivering its energy to various places along the membrane. The results are far from clear. The issue is discussed often in the literature but few firm conclusions can be drawn. Perhaps part of the problem is the fact that the growth of noise-induced PTS seems to differ at the high and low frequencies (Nixon & Glorig, 1961; Taylor *et al.*, 1965). Any relation between exposure spectrum and frequency of greatest PTS may depend on how long after exposure the loss is assessed.

Faced with some of the difficulties of interpreting the data on permanent threshold shift, a fourth source of data has been used in an attempt to formulate a more specific criteria for exposures that occur from intermittent exposure and to assess how recovery occurs during escape from the exposure. This source of data is temporary threshold shifts (TTS).

Temporary Threshold Shifts

A temporary threshold shift (TTS) is an elevation of threshold caused by exposure to some sound (called an adapting stimulus) that disappears within, say, 16 hours of the exposure. These threshold shifts have been studied extensively, because they permit one to investigate details of the physical parameters of exposure in a manner that is impossible using permanent threshold shift data.

The main motivation for studying temporary threshold shifts is the insight that such studies may provide concerning the process of permanent threshold shift (PTS). A wide range of stimulus parameters has been used in the exposure condition, and their immediate effects, as well as the course of recovery, are known to a fair degree of accuracy. Unfortunately, the growth of TTS seems to be subject to an almost bewildering variety of stimulus parameters. Recovery from TTS, on the other hand, seems to be dependent on fewer stimulus parameters and hence we will begin our discussion with the recovery phase.

Recovery from Temporary Threshold Shifts

An attractive first hypothesis concerning the recovery from a temporary shift in threshold due to noise exposure is that recovery depends only upon the amount of temporary threshold shift and not how that amount was produced. Such an hypothesis appears to be too simple when speaking of the recovery in the first two minutes after an exposure to noise. The very short-term recovery appears to be quite complicated, indeed the recovery curves may be nonmonotonic as a function of time (Hirsh & Ward, 1952). But Ward, Glorig, and Sklar (1959b) have pointed out that if temporary threshold shift is measured approximately 2 min after noise exposure, then the course of recovery appears regular and seems to reflect a single slow process. In particular they show that the time course for recovery appears to be independent of exposure conditions as long as the TTS is approximately the same, two minutes after exposure. Figure 13.3 shows their result for recovery of 4 kHz at three different exposure conditions. The amount of recovery measured in decibels is a logarithmic function of recovery time. Indeed, most recovery curves show this simple relation—decibel recovery is proportional to log time. The exact form of the curve is still somewhat in doubt, for there is some uncertainty about the total recovery time; that is, the exact time at which TTS goes to zero may depend somewhat on the initial TTS.

Given the previous consideration, it should be obvious why we so often measure the temporary threshold shift only after some fixed period of recovery, for example, 2 min. Let us now review some of the factors that influence the amount of TTS.

Intensity

The intensity of the noise exposure is obviously an important determinant of the amount of TTS. If the sound level is low, there is essentially no threshold shift produced. Only if the exposure exceeds some critical or minimum value will TTS result. Once that minimum value is exceeded, the increase in threshold shift is roughly proportional to the amount in decibels that the exposure level exceeds this minimum level (Ward, Glorig, & Sklar, 1959a). For an octave band of noise, for example, a level of about 80 dB overall is needed to produce any temporary threshold shift. At higher levels, 95 dB exposure for 50 min produces about 15 dB threshold shift, and 105 dB for 50 min produces a TTS of about 30 dB. The exact way intensity affects the TTS will depend upon the nature of the exposure, for example, whether the noise is narrow- or wideband, or the

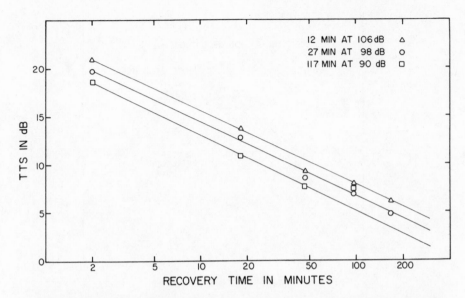

FIG. 13.3 Measurement of temporary threshold shift (TTS) as a function of recovery time for three different exposure conditions. The similarity of the recovery curves, despite the differences in either exposure time or level, supports the hypothesis that recovery depends only on the amount of TTS produced shortly after the exposure. (From Ward *et al.*, 1959b, p. 601.)

fatiguing sound is a pure tone. For all stimuli tested, the amount of TTS is a monotonic function of the level of exposure, as one might expect.

Frequency of the Adapting Stimulus

First of all we must consider the amount of TTS produced by narrowband stimuli. Data are still ambiguous on this question. A safe generalization is that the higher the frequency, up to at least 4–8 kHz, the greater will be the TTS (Ward, 1963). Thus an octave band of noise at a lower frequency will produce relatively less temporary threshold shift than will the same exposure at a higher frequency.

Next we might consider the amount of TTS produced at different frequencies by a narrowband exposure. The results are relatively uniform and consistent. Figure 13.4, taken from Ward (1962), illustrates the general character of the result. Here we see an exposure with an octave band of noise in the range 1,200 to 2,400 Hz and also exposure by a very narrow bandmasker having the same center frequency. The exposure was 1 hour in duration at 105 dB SPL. The test frequencies are shown along the abscissa; the amount of TTS measured 20 min after exposure is shown along the ordinate. For both exposures the maximum threshold shift occurs somewhat less than an octave above the center frequency

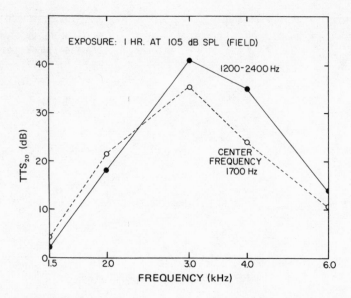

FIG. 13.4 Typical threshold shift as a function of frequency produced by exposure to a narrow band stimulus. The curves are for exposure to an octave band 1,200–2,400 Hz and for a very narrow band of noise having a center frequency of 1,700 Hz. Note that the maximum TTS is produced at a frequency higher than the frequency of exposure stimulus. (From Ward, 1962, p. 1611.)

of the exposure. As Ward and others have shown, the same result holds for sinusoidal maskers. Why the maximum temporary threshold shift should be displaced from the frequency of maximum exposure is not altogether clear. It is presumably related to the mechanics of the cochlea, but a more specific statement cannot be made at this time.

The figure also illustrates that an octave band of noise and a sinusoid produce roughly the same amount of TTS if the total energy is the same. Miller (1958) found the amount of TTS produced by a broad-band masker could be reasonably well predicted by assuming the "critical band" (see Chapter 6) was about 2.7 times wider than the width estimated from masking experiments. The rough rule that the TTS critical band is an octave wide must be qualified in some respects, however, for example, the arousal of the middle-ear reflex is somewhat different for tone and noise and also varies with frequency and level (Ward, 1962).

Duration

As one would expect, TTS increases with increased duration of exposure. In general, the relation appears to be logarithmic, that is, the amount of TTS increases in proportion to the logarithm of the duration of the exposure. The exact constant of proportionality will depend upon a variety of other factors, such as the level of exposure, the frequency of the fatiguing stimulus, and other temporal factors, including the on—off ratio. For a more detailed discussion of this parameter, the most quantitative work is that of Ward, Glorig, and Sklar (1958, 1959c). This concludes our discussion of the physical factors influencing TTS. Before closing let us review one other item which is of some practical importance.

TEMPORARY THRESHOLD SHIFT AND HEARING LEVEL

An important question in the topic of permanent threshold shift is how a given noise exposure will affect people who have already suffered some loss in auditory sensitivity. For example, suppose we have a 40-year-old man who has, for some reason or another, suffered 50 dB of 4-kHz hearing loss. Suppose he and another 40-year-old, with essentially normal hearing, work in the same job under identical conditions. The noise exposure on the job is such that we would expect a 30-dB threshold shift in the normal individual over a period of ten years. What threshold shift should we expect from the individual who goes into this situation with a 50-dB hearing loss?

There are two possible arguments that lead to diametrically opposed conclusions. One is that the individual with the 50-dB loss will be less affected by the noise exposure and hence will suffer less additional loss in the course of ten years on the job. This would certainly be true if the 50-dB loss were conductive, since then, in effect, the exposure on the job would be 50 dB less for that individual. If, on the other hand, the 50-dB loss were sensory-neural in origin, then the amount of energy delivered to the cochlea would be identical for both the normal and the hearing-impaired individual.

Another line of argument is that the individual with the 50-dB loss, assuming that it is not conductive, has already demonstrated a certain susceptibility to noise injury and in fact has a partially damaged cochlea. Given a normal cochlea and a partially damaged one, 10 years of the same exposure might be expected to produce a larger than normal decrement in the susceptible ear.

Obviously both arguments are nonnumerical. It is understandably difficult to secure precise information from field studies on this question. For this reason the study by Ward (1963) concerning the amount of *temporary* threshold shift experienced by an individual with the various amounts of hearing loss is extremely critical. Figure 13.5 shows the result of this experiment. The sample contained 81 workers and their TTS was measured 9 min after a day's work. The exposure was a high level of broadband noise. As one can see, at all three frequencies those workers with essentially no hearing loss, 0-dB hearing level, suffered the most threshold shift. Those who initially had a substantial amount of initial hearing loss suffered less TTS. However, in all cases, if one added the

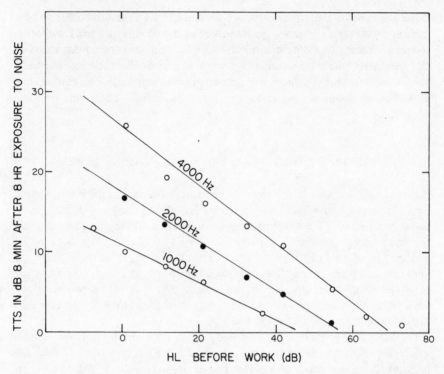

FIG. 13.5 The TTS measured shortly after 8-hr exposure on the job as a function of hearing level (HL) measured before work. The TTS is shown at three frequencies. (From Ward, 1963, p. 272.)

permanent hearing loss to the temporary threshold shift, the total hearing loss is greater for the impaired individual than the normal. In terms of a change in the hearing level, the normal's hearing level changes more, due to the 8 hr on the job. It is a peculiar fact that a noisy environment acts as a kind of leveler to reduce the difference in hearing level between individuals with hearing impairments and those that are initially normal.

SUMMARY

The chapter has covered the topic of hearing loss, its measurement and diagnosis. In addition, the major cause of hearing loss was reviewed; the exposure to high levels of noise. There are two general types of hearing abnormality, conductive and nerve types. The prominent features of each type of loss were discussed in terms of air- and bone-conduction tests, recruitment tests, and speech discrimination tests. Finally, some simple tests administered with tuning forks were described and their rationale explained.

The effects of prolonged exposure to intense noise was described. Permanent threshold shifts were discussed and the major methods of obtaining data on the topic were examined. Some generalizations concerning exposure and permanent threshold shift were presented. Finally, the phenomenon of temporary threshold shift (TTS) was discussed. Both the course of recovery from TTS and its generation were reviewed.

REFERENCES

Burns, W. *Noise and man.* London: John Murray, 1968.

Covell, W.P. Histological findings. In J.D. Miller, C.S. Watson, & W.P. Covell (Eds.), *Deafening effects of noise on the cat. Acta-Oto Laryngologica,* supplement 176, 1963.

Davis, H. In H. Davis & S.R. Silverman (Eds.), *Hearing and deafness.* New York: Holt, Rinehart & Winston, 1960. Pp. 104–107.

Davis, H., & Silverman, S.R. *Hearing and deafness.* New York: Holt, Rinehart & Winston, 1960.

Hirsh, I.J. *The measurement of hearing.* New York, Toronto, and London: McGraw-Hill, 1952.

Hirsh, I.J., & Ward, W.D. Recovery of the auditory threshold after strong acoustic stimulation. *Journal of the Acoustical Society of America,* 1952, **24**, 131–141.

Jerger, J. (Ed.), *Modern developments in audiology* (2nd ed.) New York and London: Academic Press, 1973.

Miller, J.D. Temporary threshold shift and masking for noise of uniform spectrum level. *Journal of the Acoustical Society of America,* 1958, **30**, 517–522.

Miller, J.D., Watson, C.S., & Covell, W.P. *Deafening effects of noise on the cat. Acta Oto-Laryngologica,* supplement 176, 1963.

Nixon, J.C., & Glorig, A. Noise-induced permanent threshold shift at 2000 cps and 4000 cps. *Journal of the Acoustical Society of America,* 1961, **33**, 904–908.

Schuknecht, H.F. *Pathology of the ear.* Cambridge, Massachusetts: Harvard University Press, 1974.

Taylor, W., Pearson, J., Mair, A., & Burns, W. Study of noise and hearing in jute weaving. *Journal of the Acoustical Society of America,* 1965, **38**, 113–120.

Ward, W.D. Damage-risk criteria for line spectra. *Journal of the Acoustical Society of America,* 1962, **34**, 1610–1619.

Ward, W.D. Auditory fatigue and masking. In J. Jerger (Ed.), *Modern developments in audiology.* New York, London: Academic Press, 1963.

Ward, W.D. Noise levels are not noise exposures! *Proceedings of the Noisexpo, National Noise and Vibration Control Conference,* Chicago, Illinois, June 4, 5, 6, 1974.

Ward, W.D., Glorig, A., & Sklar, D.L. Dependence of temporary threshold shift at 4 kc on intensity and time. *Journal of the Acoustical Society of America,* 1958, **30**, 944–954.

Ward, W.D., Glorig, A., & Sklar, D.L. Temporary threshold shift from octave-band noise: Applications to damage-risk criteria. *Journal of the Acoustical Society of America,* 1959, **31**, 522–528. (a)

Ward, W.D., Glorig, A., & Sklar, D.L. Relation between recovery from temporary threshold shift and duration of exposure. *Journal of the Acoustical Society of America,* 1959, **31**, 600–602. (b)

Ward, W.D., Glorig, A., & Sklar, D.L. Temporary threshold shift produced by intermittent exposure to noise. *Journal of the Acoustical Society of America,* 1959, **31**, 791–794. (c)

ANSWERS TO QUESTIONS IN APPENDIX III

1a. 10 dB
1b. $\sqrt{10}$
2. 20 dB, +20 dB or −20 dB, 100
3. 40 dB, 10, 10, 100
4. 12 dB
5. 34 dB = 40 dB − 6 dB
6. 74 dB
7. 194 dB
8. −40 dB
9. −134 dB

Indices

Author Index

The numbers in *italics* refer to pages on which the complete references are listed.

Subject Index

PARIS PASTRY CLUB

Served by Fanny Zanotti

150 g (5 oz) kneading
100 g (3½ oz) piping
120 g (4 oz) whipping
100 g (3½ oz) drinking
2 teaspoons talking
a fat pinch of laughter
a pinch of crushed delight

A COLLECTION OF CAKES, TARTS, PASTRIES
AND OTHER INDULGENT RECIPES

hardie grant books
MELBOURNE · LONDON

PARIS PASTRY CLUB

CONTENTS

I DON'T KNOW for sure when it all started. Perhaps on that early morning of an endless Paris summer, where stars felt like projectors on my dreams.

I pushed the door to the empty pâtisserie and walked down the stairs of what would become a home of some kind. A home where aprons are tightly knotted and tea towels never far from your fingers. A home where *'chaud!'* (hot!) is the only spoken word and pastries get made all day. All night too.

Yes, from that very first step, I knew I'd never look back. This is where I belonged. And like a never-ending story, this is where I stayed. One pâtisserie after the other. One restaurant at a time, it would grow on me; it would make me grow up. As a girl, as a chef.

And yet, just like there is a hidden world behind puddles after a summer storm, there is also one behind the stainless-steel counters that we clean restlessly.

It's a world where the little stories matter. The big ones too, in fact. That kiss you can't wait to tell your best-friend about. That beach you can never – oh no, ever – forget. That road-trip you took with the fog as the only horizon.

It's about imperfections. And glitter on my nails.

It's about falling in love; and baking at two in the morning, or in the afternoon. Breaking up, and crying. Chocolate cake will happen. And flour in our hair too.

Because that's what we do.

I grew up in France and no matter how clichéd this might be, I learnt how to bake with my *grand-mère*, her mother *mémé* and my mother. We would talk about what we were going to make over a breakfast made of baguette slices toasted until just so, butter from the neighbour and strawberry jam that my grandfather used to can every year around that time when bushes are more berries than leaves.

We rode our bicycles to the city centre, along a road – more of a path, really – where trees were paper-cut into the sky, clouds in the shape of waves and waves in the shape of clouds. With a basketful of fruits, we headed back home, where all the flour, sugar and eggs in the world would be waiting for us in the larder.

This was the one door in the kitchen that meant the most to me. I could spend mornings in there, looking at all the products, neatly aligned on shelves. There were pots and pans, cake tins too. And more canning jars than I could count.

I remember the tea towels. Mostly red and blue. White of course too, but only to dry the dishes. And I might have never admitted this to my *grand-mère*, but every year, as I packed my suitcase en route for the city, I would sneak one or two of them. It goes without saying that I still have them, twenty – or so – years later. Still as worn out, but nothing could ever match what they represent. Much more than just cloths, they're a reflection of my dreams.

But I digress. And really, that's sort of ok. Because, when we were in that kitchen, we sure digressed.

And somehow, without us even noticing, we forgot the difference between baking and life.

Ever since, I've chosen to keep on forgetting.

INTRODUCTION

INGREDIENTS

NOTES ON …

No matter how much I love a treasure hunt for obscure ingredients, this book is not about that. Most of the ingredients I use here are easy to find, and you'll probably already have them in your cupboards. And just as I like having only square containers in my fridge, all labelled with the same felt-tip pen, I'm sort of a girl of habit when it comes to ingredients too. However I can't stress enough that it's ok to substitute. It might work, it might not work, but hey, that's the way we create recipes. So go wild… or not!

CREAM

I'm in love with French cream. It has 35 per cent milk fats, which makes it very versatile: mousse, Chantilly, custards, soft caramels …

And of course, when I moved to London, it felt like I was leaving the love of my life behind. Luckily, I've found that whipping cream makes a suitable replacement. It's slightly richer, but works beautifully in all of my recipes.

I don't, however, recommend using double cream, unless specified, as its simply too heavy for pâtisserie with its 50 per cent fat content.

BUTTER

Unless otherwise noted, all butter is unsalted. I like to use French butter – as we say in French *'Chassez le naturel, il reviendra au galop!'* (literally, 'You might brush your spirit off, it will come back galloping!').

Not only because it's French, mind you, but also because it tends to have slightly less moisture than other butters. However, you can use any high-quality butter and will still have perfect results.

CHOCOLATE

I usually like to specify the cacao content of chocolate in my recipes: for dark it's most likely 70 per cent and for milk, I'm addicted to Valrhona's wonderful 40 per cent Jivara. But this is not a book about chocolate confectionary, so please just use these as a guideline. It won't make a dramatic difference to most of the recipes.

EGGS

Eggs can range between 40–70 grams (1½–2½ ounces) each, which can make a dramatic difference in most recipes. While I always weigh eggs at the restaurant, I'm partial to the no-fuss quality of home pâtisserie-ing. I use medium-sized eggs of around 50 grams (2 ounces) each. And for best results, you should too!

SALT

Even more than French fleur de sel, I've fallen in love with the large and delicate flakes from Maldon.

I'm especially fond of their crunch and the fact they won't dissolve easily in doughs, creating happy bundles of saltiness throughout cookies and shortbreads. If using regular table salt, reduce the quantities by half to achieve the same balance of flavours.

VANILLA

I mostly use fresh vanilla pods because I love their flavour and also, because I'm lucky enough to have plenty stashed in my fridge.

I have a fondness for both Madagascar and Tahiti pods, which have very different flavours. Bourbon vanilla, from Madagascar, is the very essence of the vanilla of my childhood; while Tahitian beans have a more distinct floral note to them. I like to combine them to create my perfect vanilla flavour. Alternatively, you could substitute one teaspoon of vanilla extract for each vanilla pod. Or use a tea-spoon of vanilla paste. I tend to keep used vanilla pods – cleaned under running water, then hung until dry – as they make the best vanilla sugar.

ICE-CREAMS

While you can stock milk powder from pretty much any supermarket, dehydrated glucose can be a bit tricky to come across. It's a very fine sugar that has a slightly less sweetening power than regular caster (super fine) sugar. Using these sugars will increase the dry matter of the ice-cream mix without affecting the sweetness of the finished products. The brand I use is Louis François and they come in neat old-fashioned – white and red – one-kilogram (2-pound-3-ounce) tubs. When it comes to stabilisers, there are two different kinds: one for ice-creams, and one for sorbets. You don't have to use them, but they do come in pretty handy for making the perfect texture.

EQUIPMENT

I'm very fond of minimalism. And not only because my kitchen is as big as a shoe box. As a pastry chef, I have collected many utensils over the years, but back in the day I remember asking my dad to cut a pipe in half to make a bûche de Noël mould. And I can only encourage you to do the same. No rolling pin? Please, hand me the empty wine bottle! However, I must admit, your life will be easier with the must-haves I've listed below.

PYREX BOWL, MANY OF THEM

Two things take the most time in pâtisserie: weighing out all of the ingredients (which I can only recommend to do all at once before starting the recipe) and washing dishes (which I can only recommend to do all at once after the mess has been made and you don't recognise your kitchen anymore).

Having plenty of heatproof glass bowls in different sizes will make those two key-steps a dream. And since you won't run out of bowls, you won't have to do the dishes during baking.

SMALL UTENSILS

Metal whisks, wooden spoons, a good rolling pin, a set of round cutters, a Microplane grater, a few rubber spatulas (otherwise known

as 'Maryse' in the kitchen world), palette knives in different sizes, and you're good to go.

If you decide to go for silicone moulds, make sure to buy them in professional shops as they will last longer and are less likely to break or give baked goods a plastic flavour.

CAKE/
TART TINS

When it comes to regular tins, I'm genuinely fond of heatproof glass that makes it so easy to check if your tart or cake is baked underneath. But non-stick tins are great too.

If you don't have the size called for in the recipes, don't make it stop you. Simply use a size smaller, taking cake not to overfill the tin. And keep in mind that two-thirds full always seem to work!

When it comes to specialty tins, I'm using a few in this book, but all of them are easy to find. Think baba moulds, a madeleine pan ...

METAL RINGS

Metal rings are my life. I'm not joking. I think I might have more rings than pairs of shoes.

Round rings usually come into different heights. For tarts, I go for the 2 cm (¾ in) high rings, and for entremets, 4–6 cm (1½–2⅓ in) is perfect.

At times, I'll even bake cakes using them as they make for the prettiest straight edges ever.

In this book, I've tried to limit their use as they're quite expensive, and I guess you're probably not as besotted as I am.

You'll need a 20 cm (8 in) ring for desserts like the the Fraisier (page 94); a 22 cm (9½ in) ring for the Triple Chocolate Mousse Cake (page 102) or the Peach Melba Charlotte (page 144); a 24 cm (9½ in) ring for the Lemon Meringue Tart (page 98); and four 6 cm- (2¾ in-) wide rings for the Coulants au Chocolate (page 36).

If you don't have the right size, once again, it's more than ok. As my grandmother used to say, 'If there is no solution, there is no problem.'

A PROBE

You'll need it for caramels and mousses, sugar syrups ... I like the old-school ones, but an electronic probe is perhaps easier to store.

A BLOWTORCH

From the caramelisation of Crème Brûlée (page 62) to the unmoulding of frozen entremets, a little blowtorch is a favourite of mine. And for the record, it's totally fine to go for your dad's one. Yes, that very same one he uses to burn things-that-are-not-food. Not that I've ever done it ... Sure.

SCALES

Scales are an absolute must in every kitchen. Home or professional. I might have said this book is not about perfection and tweezer-plating, but pastry without precision will end up in a disaster. Most likely, of the messy kind!

That's why all the recipes in this book call for measuring in grams, including the liquids. To make it easy for you, when it's ok to be a little bit rough, I've also included some measurements in teaspoons (5 ml) and tablespoons (15 ml).

But, yes, back to scales! Once you've started weighing out everything, it will feel like a breeze. You can thank me later, just run to the closest shop and get yourself some digital scales. I bought mine for 5 euros and they've been following me for years now.

**SILPATS OR
SILICONE MATS**

Although they can easily be replaced by baking paper, they are wonderful to bake shortbreads and other dough as they diffuse the heat so much more evenly than baking paper.

MIXERS

You don't have to invest in a stand-mixer, although I do believe it will change your life! With the paddle attachment it is super easy to make shortbread or cake batters; use the hook for brioche or other sweet doughs and the whisk for whipping up cream and egg whites.

An electric hand-held beater also does a fine job for these whisking and beating tasks, while a stick blender is perfect for emulsifying or puréeing.

ACETATE

Acetate is thin sheets of plastic used to support cream filling or butter cream. While I use it on a daily basis to make entremets, I know that acetate can be a bit tough to come across and is fairly expensive if you're not planning on using three metres a day.

In this book, there are a couple of recipes that call for acetate but you could always replace it with a strip of baking paper. It might wrinkle slightly with humidity, but works just fine. You can also make-your-own-ish by layering clingfilm (six layers), making sure to chase any air bubbles and then cutting it into strips using a sharp knife.

OVENS

I've always been amazed by how much ovens vary. In fact, I've been known to bake macarons at various temperatures – ranging from 145°C (293°F) to 180°C (356°F) – depending on the oven I'm using.

All of the recipes in this book have been tested in my home fan-assisted oven – and if you knew my oven, you'd be pouring me a glass of crisp white wine right now – but if there is one thing I can't predict it is the temperature of yours. This is why I strongly recommend you use an oven thermometer. It's super cheap and it'll help you to understand how your oven works.

And if your oven doesn't have a fan, please remember to increase the baking temperatures by 20°C (70°F).

NOTES ON ...

LEMON & BLUEBERRY
MADELEINES

VANILLA ICE-CREAM
WITH OLIVE OIL

SPICY
NOUGATINE

ORANGE &
YOGHURT CAKES

BABAS AU
GIN & TONIC

CRÊPES AU BEURRE
NOISETTE

MY FAVOURITE
CHOCOLATE MOUSSE

(EVERYTHING A GIRL NEEDS TO KNOW)

THERE ARE ONLY so many things I know.

Getting lost, of the make-believe kind, in the Marais; the beauty of sunsets pretending to be rainbows.

Watching – and, more importantly, hearing – waves crash into the sand. And then see them disappear with the low tide, the sun sparkling in cloudy puddles the water has left behind. The flavour of vanilla ice-cream when our fingers still tasted of the ocean. The miniature merry-go-round of sand fleas jumping from one sandcastle to another. My *grand-mère* making madeleines and cakes, and clafoutis too. And me, sat on the kitchen counter.

Yes, I learnt how to bake during the summers I spent with my grandmother. On the weekends, she would knead butter into flour and add water. And tarts would be made throughout the week. Apricots and plums, golden and plump with sun. And on Wednesdays she would teach me how to make waffles. With beer in the batter.

Nowadays her words still sound like music to me. We discuss what we're going to bake over a breakfast of French coffee and thick slices of baguette toasted until barely warm and spread with salted butter and honey. For lunch, she cracks open a few almonds (the ones in the green shells) with a hammer.

And then the oven gets turned on and we laugh and we try to make the cakes we dreamed about.

Yes, there are only so many things I know. For the unknown, I rely on magic and wishful thinking.

And my *grand-mère*. She's the most beautiful person in my world. And when we bake together magic happens. Or perhaps it's the boxed rosé wine we sip as soon as the clock hits five o'clock.

CHAPTER 1

MAKING PLUMP MADELEINES

THE SECRET TO PLUMP MADELEINES IS
HEAT SHOCK. I CHILL MY BATTER FOR
AT LEAST 3 HOURS (2 ARE OK-ISH TOO, SO
GO AHEAD, I'LL CLOSE MY EYES AND
PRETEND NOTHING EVER HAPPENED) OR
UP TO 3 DAYS. AND I PREHEAT MY OVEN
TO 220°C (430°F) FOR A GOOD 30 MINUTES
BEFORE REDUCING TO 180°C
(350°F) TO BAKE THEM.

LEMON & BLUEBERRY MADELEINES

Makes 24 madeleines

80 g (2¾ oz) butter, really soft
100 g (3½ oz) caster (superfine) sugar
2 eggs
zest from 2 lemons
a pinch of sea salt
100 g (3½ oz) plain (all-purpose) flour
½ teaspoon baking powder
(baking soda)
a punnet of blueberries

Taking a tray of madeleines from the oven feels like pressing the shutter of a Polaroid camera. Boom, instant gratification.

The batter is made in advance – up to 3 days – because it makes for plump little cakes with the fat domes we've all come to love. And by the time you bake them, you've forgotten the effort you put into making the batter. Effort is somewhat misleading though. Eggs and sugar get whisked together until fluffy. And flour gets folded. The only tricky step is to incorporate the butter without deflating the batter. But I've come up with a little trick to make that stage easier after the commis-of-my-life tried to turn madeleines into pancakes: the butter is creamed with a tablespoon of sugar until very soft and light. It's then mixed with a part of the batter before getting folded back into the rest. Ever so gently.

Cream the butter with a tablespoon of the sugar. Whisk the remaining sugar with the eggs, lemon zest and the pinch of salt in a separate bowl until light and fluffy.

Gently fold in the flour and baking powder until just combined.

Scoop out a third of the batter into the butter and mix vigorously. Transfer into the remaining batter and fold in very gently.

Scrape the batter into a plastic piping bag and chill for at least 3 hours (or up to 3 days).

Preheat the oven to 220°C (430°F). Butter and flour a madeleine pan.

Snip a small 8 mm (⅓ in) hole from the tip of the piping bag and pipe the batter three-quarters of the way up the prepared moulds. Stick two blueberries in each madeleine. Reduce the oven temperature to 180°C (350°F) and bake for 14 minutes or until the edges are a deep-golden brown and the domes are just beginning to brown.

Remove from the oven and leave to cool for a few minutes in the pan, then turn out onto a wire rack.

VANILLA ICE-CREAM WITH OLIVE OIL

Makes 2 litres

FOR THE ICE-CREAM
850 g (1 pint/12¾ fl oz) whole milk
175 g (6 oz) whipping cream
80 g (2¾ oz) skimmed milk powder
3 Tahitian vanilla pods
3 Madagascan vanilla pods
120 g (4 oz) caster (superfine) sugar
80 g (2¾ oz) dehydrated glucose
6 g (⅛ oz) ice-cream stabiliser

TO SERVE
extra-virgin olive oil
a sprinkle of sea salt
Spicy Nougatine (page 19)

Not unlike the memory of licking melted ice-cream off my fingers made salty with the ocean, this has become a summer favourite over the years.

It is more of an idea, rather than a recipe. In fact, you could use store-bought ice-cream or make your own. However I would strongly advise you to try this one which is so loaded with vanilla seeds it's almost grey.

Pour the milk, cream and milk powder into a large saucepan. Slice open the vanilla pods and scrape the seeds into the milk, then roughly chop the pods into 5 mm (¼ in) long segments and add to these milk as well.

Set the pan over a medium heat and stir with a whisk every now and then until the temperature reaches 50°C (120°F) – use a probe to measure it. In the meantime, place all of the remaining ingredients in a bowl and whisk really well to combine.

When the milk reaches temperature, slowly add the powders, whisking as you go, and bring to a rolling boil.

Remove from the heat and blitz using a stick-blender for 3 minutes.

Pour into a plastic container, lay clingfilm over the top so it touches the surface (to prevent a skin forming) and chill for at least 5 hours or, even better, overnight.

Once chilled, strain the ice-cream mixture through a fine-mesh sieve and churn according to the instructions of your ice-cream maker.

Scrape the ice-cream into a 1 litre (34 fl oz) plastic container and cover with a piece of baking parchment the size of your container and freeze for a couple of hours before serving.

Scoop into small bowls or serving glasses and drizzle with olive oil. Top with a pinch of sea salt and a sprinkle of crushed nougatine.

MAKING A SUGAR SYRUP

WHEN MAKING A SUGAR SYRUP,
I ALWAYS PUT THE WATER IN THE PAN FIRST
TO PREVENT THE SUGAR FROM CLUMPING
TOGETHER AND POSSIBLY CARAMELISING.
GLUCOSE, WHICH CAN BE FOUND IN MOST
SUPERMARKET BAKING AISLES,
PREVENTS THE SUGAR FROM CRYSTALLISING
AND MAKES FOR AN EASIER-TO-WORK-WITH
SYRUP. TO SCOOP OUT GLUCOSE FROM
A JAR, JUST WET YOUR HANDS WITH
COLD WATER AND DIG IN. THE WATER
WILL STOP THE GLUCOSE STICKING
TO YOUR FINGERS, WHICH TRUST ME,
IS A GOOD THING!

SPICY NOUGATINE

Makes 1 small slab

150 g (5 oz) blanched almonds
100 g (3½ oz) water
120 g (4 oz) caster (superfine) sugar
100 g (3½ oz) liquid glucose
2 teaspoons sea salt
a fat pinch of cayenne pepper
a fat pinch of smoked paprika
a pinch of crushed chilli pepper
20 g (¾ oz) butter, cubed

I love nougatine so much that I might have dipped my finger in caramel when my great-grandma, *Mémé*, was making some, or that's how the story goes.

She would toast almonds just until light golden and deeply aromatic, then mix them into a light amber caramel made creamy with a touch of butter. Of course, a fat pinch of fleur de sel was added. And the giant slab was left to cool down before being broken into bite-size pieces.

Nougatine will keep well for up to a fortnight in an airtight container. And please, don't take after me – be super-careful with the hot caramel!

Preheat the oven to 160°C (320°F). Spread the almonds in a single layer onto a baking tray lined with baking parchment and bake for 15 minutes, giving them a good shake every now and then, until golden-brown and aromatic. Set aside while you get on with the caramel.

Before you start, have two Silpats (or two large pieces of baking parchment) and a rolling pin ready on a flat work surface.

Bring the water, sugar, glucose and salt to the boil in a large pan over high heat, stirring as you go. The syrup tends to boil over when it reaches 100°C (210°F) so make sure you use a larger pan than you'd think.

Cook the syrup until the temperature reaches 165°C (330°F) or it is a light-amber colour, then add the spices and whisk in the butter, one cube at a time. When the butter has melted and is emulsified with the caramel, tip in the roasted almonds and stir quickly to coat them evenly.

Pour the coated almonds onto one of the Silpats, cover with the other and roll so that the almonds are all in a single layer. Allow to cool completely, then gently lift off the top Silpat and break the nougatine into pieces, or roughly chop using a large knife.

ORANGE & YOGHURT CAKES

Makes 8 small cakes

8 oranges
200 g (7 oz) plain (all-purpose) flour
½ tablespoon baking powder
(baking soda)
a pinch of salt
120 g (4 oz) yoghurt
3 eggs
175 g (6 oz) caster (superfine) sugar
zest of 2 oranges
60 g (2 oz) butter, melted
30 g caster (superfine) sugar,
for the orange syrup

This is the cake of my childhood, of Sunday mornings at the beach and Wednesday afternoon *goûters* (snacks) at home. My mum used to make it every week. At times I would help her too – in fact, the only recipe she has is a drawing I made with felt-tip pens and a not-so-steady hand.

In those days, we wouldn't weigh anything but would measure the flour, sugar and butter using the empty yoghurt pot. And we'd bake the cake in a large tin.

You could do the same and bake it in a large cake tin, generously buttered and lined with baking paper, but I have a soft spot for plump little oranges filled with the crumbly and melt-in-your-mouth cake, just like the oranges *givrées* (frozen oranges) my grandmother would make for birthdays. To make one large cake, bake at 180°C (350°F) for 35–40 minutes.

Preheat the oven to 180°C (350°F).

Wash and dry the oranges. Slice off the tops, scoop out the flesh using a metal spoon and set aside in a bowl. Arrange the empty oranges sitting cut-side-up on a muffin tray.

Combine all the ingredients in a large bowl and mix well until smooth.

Divide the batter between the prepared oranges until each is two-thirds full and bake for 25–30 minutes or until golden-brown and a skewer inserted into the centre of each cake comes out clean.

Strain the orange flesh through a fine-mesh sieve over a jug, squeezing as you go to extract as much juice as possible.

Place the juice and extra caster sugar in a small pan and bring to the boil over medium heat. Simmer for 10–15 minutes or until reduced by half; set aside until needed.

When the cakes are still warm from the oven, drench each with a little of the hot orange syrup.

PARIS PASTRY CLUB

BABAS AU GIN & TONIC

Serves 4

FOR THE BABAS
250 g (9 oz) plain (all-purpose) flour
½ teaspoon of sea salt
20 g (¾ oz) honey
10 g (½ oz) fresh yeast (or 1 teaspoon instant)
5 eggs, beaten together
70 g (2½ oz) butter, softened

FOR THE RASPBERRY CONSOMMÉ
500 g (1 lb 2 oz) raspberries
50 g (2 oz) caster (superfine) sugar

FOR THE RASPBERRY GIN AND TONIC SYRUP
300 g (10½ oz) water
500 g (1 lb 2 oz) caster (superfine) sugar
300 g (10½ oz) Raspberry Consommé (see above)
200 g (7 oz) tonic
200 g (7 oz) gin

FOR THE ROSE CHANTILLY CREAM
400 g (14 oz) whipping cream
40 g (1½ oz) icing (confectioner's) sugar
seeds from 1 Tahitian vanilla pod
1 teaspoon rose extract

watermelon and fresh raspberries, to serve

I always joke that my mum can only make three perfect desserts: vanilla pudding popsicles (which I remember eating one hot summer day of garage sales and neon tropeziennes sandals); upside-down pineapple cakes (which were always eaten first on my childhood birthdays); and baba au rhum. Her recipe has never failed me and, despite a few tweaks here and there, it's always the one I use at home or in the restaurant kitchen.

She would serve hers as a giant savarin, soaked with more rum than you

Start by making the babas. Using a stand-mixer fitted with the paddle attachment, mix the flour, salt, honey, yeast and half the eggs on a slow speed until it forms a rough dough. Add the remaining eggs, a little at a time, kneading on medium speed until incorporated. Crank up the speed to high and knead for 10 minutes, or until the dough detaches from the edges of the bowl. Reduce the speed to low and add the butter, a little chunk at a time, until the dough is smooth and satiny.

Cover the bowl with clingfilm and leave to rise for around an hour until doubled in size. While the babas are proving, make the syrup.

First make the consommé – place the raspberries and caster sugar into a large bowl set over a pan of simmering water and cook on low heat for an hour, stirring now and then. Transfer to a sieve lined with muslin cloth and drain without pushing. Discard the raspberries and keep the juices.

Bring the water and sugar to the boil in a large pan to dissolve the

think you could handle and a big fluffy pile of whipped cream in the centre. In the summer, berries would always be folded into the cream with their juices. Perhaps this is why I like to serve mine (in the traditional bouchon shape) with a light raspberry syrup and a lot of gin and tonic, inside and on the side.

sugar. Take off the heat, add the consommé and when the syrup reaches 60°C (140°F), add the tonic and the gin. (You can make the syrup in advance and reheat when ready to soak the babas.)

Back to the babas ... Butter 12 dariole moulds and preheat the oven to 195°C (375°F). Quickly mix the dough using a wooden spoon to deflate it then tip into a piping bag fitted with a large plain nozzle. Pipe 40 g (1½ oz) into each mould and leave to rise until the dough almost reaches the top of the moulds.

Bake for 15–20 minutes, until deep-brown and fragrant. Leave the babas to cool down slightly before turning out. You can freeze them for later or use them straight away.

Use your syrup straight away when it is at 60°C (140°F) or reheat to this temperature if you have made it in advance. Place the babas in the hot syrup and soak for 1 hour, flipping them around every 15 minutes.

Remove the babas from the syrup using a slotted spoon and leave to cool on a wire-rack set over a baking tray. Chill, covered with clingfilm, in the fridge for at least 30 minutes and up to a day.

When you're ready to serve, make the rose chantilly cream: whisk all the ingredients together until firm peaks form.

Lay out 4 soup plates, place a baba in each, arrange some fresh raspberries and watermelon cubes around and generously drizzle with the cold gin and tonic syrup. Finish with a fat dollop of the cream.

CRÊPES AU BEURRE NOISETTE

Makes 12 x 25 cm (10 in) crêpes

FOR THE BEURRE NOISETTE
100 g (3½ oz) butter, cubed

FOR THE CRÊPES
500 g (1 lb 2 oz) whole milk
2 eggs
2 egg yolks
seeds from 2 vanilla pods
200 g (7 oz) plain (all-purpose) flour
70 g (2½ oz) icing (confectioner's) sugar
vegetable oil, for cooking

Crêpes are a Friday night tradition in our house. My dad, who used to own a crêperie, is always in charge and he makes the best savoury crêpes you could dream of.

When dessert-time comes, I'll jump in to make my very own favourite. The batter is delicate and light it has the intense flavour of vanilla and subtle hints of nuttiness from the beurre noisette.

These crêpes are a delight on their own, but you could serve them with a topping of your choice. To keep them warm while you cook, layer them on a plate set over a pan of simmering water and cover loosely with foil.

Start by making the beurre noisette. Melt the butter in a small pan over a medium heat. Once melted, keep cooking until the butter becomes a deep-golden colour and starts to smell nutty (this takes around 1–2 minutes). Leave to cool for a few minutes, then pour into a small bowl, making sure to keep most of the browned milk solids in the bottom of the pan. Keep in the fridge for up to a week.

Mix the milk, eggs, egg yolks and vanilla seeds together in a jug. In a large bowl, mix the flour and icing sugar. Slowly pour the liquids over the dry ingredients, whisking constantly, then mix in 70 g (2½ oz) of the melted beurre noisette. Pass the batter through a fine-mesh sieve to make sure there are no lumps.

Leave the batter to sit at room temperature, covered with a clean kitchen cloth, for at least 30 minutes or, even better, for 2 hours or overnight (in which case, keep it in the fridge).

When you are ready to cook the crêpes, heat a lightly oiled non-stick frying pan over high heat. Pour the batter onto the pan, using approximately one-third of a cup for each crêpe. Tilt the pan in a circular motion so that the batter coats the surface evenly.

Cook the crêpe for about 2 minutes, until the edges start to brown and curl slightly. Loosen with a palette knife, flip over and cook the other side for a minute. Serve hot.

PERFECT WHIPPED CREAM

1. TEN MINUTES BEFORE YOU START, PLACE A BOWL AND THE WHISK IN THE FREEZER TO CHILL. CREAM DEFINITELY WHIPS FASTER AND IN A MORE STABLE WAY IF EVERYTHING AROUND IT IS SUPER-COLD.

2. IF YOU'RE WHIPPING CREAM FOR A MOUSSE, WHIP IT UNTIL IT JUST STARTS TO GET TO THE SOFT PEAK STAGE. IT MIGHT LOOK UNDER-WHIPPED TO YOU BUT, TRUST ME, THE JUST-WHIPPED TEXTURE MAKES FOR THE SOFTEST FLUFFIEST MOUSSE. IN FACT, CREAM HAS THE MOST AIR IN WHEN IT FORMS SOFT PEAKS. UNDER-WHIPPING IT EVER SO SLIGHTLY ENSURES THAT WHEN YOU INCORPORATE IT, THE CREAM WON'T BECOME OVERWORKED AND LOSE TOO MUCH AIR.

3. YOU CAN MOST DEFINITELY WHIP CREAM AHEAD OF TIME – UP TO AN HOUR BEFORE YOU PLAN TO USE IT. SIMPLY GIVE IT ANOTHER ONE-MINUTE WHISKING BEFORE YOU DO SO.

4. CHANTILLY IS CREAM WHIPPED WITH SUGAR AND A LITTLE VANILLA TO STIFF PEAKS. I USUALLY USE 10 G (½ OZ) ICING SUGAR PER 100 G (3½ OZ) CREAM.

MY FAVOURITE CHOCOLATE MOUSSE

Serves 4

75 g (2½ oz) 70% dark chocolate
25 g (1 oz) 40% milk chocolate
150 g (5 oz) whipping cream
25 g (1 oz) caster (superfine) sugar
25 g (1 oz) water
2 egg yolks

This chocolate mousse is incredibly light. It sort of melts on your tongue the way candyfloss does. And clouds too. It might sound a bit tricky with three different components, but really can be assembled in a matter of minutes.

Once the mousse is made, it will still look a little runny, but don't worry, it will set as it cools down into a pillow of chocolate.

Melt both chocolates in a large heatproof bowl set over a pan of simmering water. In the meantime, whip the cream to soft peaks and set aside in the fridge (see box opposite).

Once the chocolate is melted, keep it warm over the pan of hot water off the heat while you make a sabayon. Bring the sugar and water to the boil in a small pan. Quickly whisk the egg yolks together in a bowl using either an electric beater or a stand-mixer fitted with the whisk attachment. Pour the piping-hot syrup over them a little at a time, whisking constantly. Once all the syrup is incorporated, whisk for 3–4 minutes, or until thick and holding soft peaks.

Now that all the elements are ready, use a balloon whisk to mix half the whipped cream into the melted chocolate until smooth and shiny. Still using the whisk, fold in the remaining cream. When the white streaks just start to disappear, add the sabayon and incorporate gently, starting from the centre of the bowl and going up the side, turning the bowl clockwise as you do so.

At this point, the mousse should look almost even in colour. Switch to a spatula and give it a few more stirs. Divide between 4 small bowls or martini glasses and chill in the fridge for at least 4 hours.

SOME THINGS ARE BOUND TO HAPPEN

(LIKE CHOCOLATE CAKE ON A RAINY DAY)

I'M NOT QUITE sure when I fell in love with rain. Wellington-boot trips to the boulangerie, jumping into every puddle we saw. Walks through a forest we didn't know, getting lost and drenched, with an old wooden basket filled with mushrooms we'd picked as our only refuge. Hours spent by a lighthouse, unsure whether the mist that covered our faces came from the ocean or the clouds. Long drives on the motorway to the music of raindrops and thunder and windscreen wipers.

On afternoons at the farm eating brioche and drinking never-ending cups of tea, we'd milk cows and collect eggs like treasures hidden in hay. The milk got boiled until pasteurised; the eggs were cracked and mixed with flour and yeast.

On rainy days, nothing will stop me from wandering into the wild. Hair tangled by branches, cheeks blushed from the cold wind and my sweater soaked by raining trees, I step back into my house with the restless soul of an adventurer, only to find the one-of-a-kind comfort that comes with storms. A comfort that smells of earth and moss, and makes kettles whistle and blankets wrap around you ever so tightly.

And like a merry-go-round, a rainy day will always feel the same, yet always be unique.

PARIS PASTRY CLUB

CHAPTER 2

CARAMEL CIDER-POACHED PEARS

Serves 4

350 g (12 oz) caster (superfine) sugar
60 g (2 oz) butter, cubed
350 g (12 oz) pear cider
500 g (17½ oz) water
2 cinnamon sticks
zest of 1 orange
1 vanilla pod, with its seeds
4 small pears, peeled

I like to make these poached pears in the morning with plenty of time to cook them into tender bites and, perhaps, read a book with a side of wool blanket and some sort of caffeinated drink.

It seems to me that cooled-down poached pears and ever-so-slightly-too-hot Sticky Toffee Pudding (page 50) are kindred spirits. Of the opposite kind. Just like that boy you had a crush on in high school. But to be fair, they also make a decent dessert or *goûter* (snack), when still warm in their juices and placed whole on a plate, with a good measure of vanilla ice-cream. (Because, let's face it, everything sort of tastes better à la mode.)

Put the sugar in a large pan set over medium heat and stir continuously until it starts to melt. The sugar might clump together – don't worry, just keep stirring. I find a whisk does a marvellous job on caramels as the sugar will eventually melt when it reaches the right temperature. As you keep stirring, the sugar will slowly turn into liquid gold. Who said making caramel was hard?

When it reaches a deep amber tint, remove from the heat and carefully add the butter, a couple of cubes at a time, stirring with the whisk after each addition.

Add the pear cider and water – it will splash and spit so make sure you back away for a few seconds before slowly stirring as it bubbles away. Place back over a medium heat and bring to the boil to dissolve any bits of caramel that might have seized.

Add the cinnamon sticks, orange zest, vanilla pod and seeds and the pears. Cover with a cartouche – a piece of baking paper cut to the diameter of your pan, with a small hole in the centre to let the steam escape (see page 154).

Simmer over low heat for 20 minutes or until you can insert a knife into the pears without any resistance.

The pears will keep for a week chilled in their poaching liquid. To reheat, simply put them back in a pan over a low heat until the butter melts and the liquid starts to bubble around the edges.

ULTIMATE MILK CHOCOLATE CHIP COOKIES

Makes 36–40 cookies

180 g (6⅓ oz) butter, soft
260 g (9¼ oz) light brown sugar
80 g (3 oz) caster (superfine) sugar
seeds from 1 vanilla pod
2 eggs
200 g (7 oz) plain (all-purpose) flour
200 g (7 oz) strong flour
1 teaspoon baking powder (baking powder)
1 heaped teaspoon sea salt
150 g (5 oz) milk chocolate,
chopped into small chunks
a little extra sea salt, for sprinkling

I think that eating the perfect chocolate chip cookie, still warm from the oven, feels like kissing (of the French kind). With no other reason than kissing being one of my favourite pastimes, I like to have ready-to-bake cookie dough stashed away in my freezer.

This recipe will make 4 logs of dough, each yielding 8–10 cookies.

I usually make a batch and keep one log in the fridge overnight to firm up and bake the next day, while the remaining logs go straight to the freezer for fun at a later date.

If you are using a stand-mixer, fit the paddle attachment and cream the butter and sugars. Add the vanilla seeds and the eggs, one at a time, beating well after each addition. Alternatively mix by hand with a wooden spoon.

Mix in the flours, baking powder and salt until just combined. Add the chocolate chunks and knead briefly in the bowl with your hand until there are no more floury patches.

Divide the dough into 4 and turn out a portion onto the centre of a large sheet of baking parchment. Fold the paper in half (like a closed book), then using the flat side a plastic scraper and holding both ends of the baking paper, push the dough into a tight log. You should have enough dough to make 4 x 5 cm (2 in) wide logs. Wrap each log in clingfilm and chill overnight or freeze for up to 3 months.

When you crave some cookies, simply take out one log from the freezer and leave at room temperature to thaw for around 10 minutes, or in the fridge for a few days. Preheat the oven to 180°C (350°F) and simply cut the log into 1.5 cm (½ in) thick slices, arrange on a baking sheet lined with baking paper and sprinkle with a little extra sea salt.

Bake for 10–12 minutes, depending on how well-done you like your cookies. Leave to cool for 5 minutes before lifting the cookies onto a plate using a palette knife.

STICKY TOFFEE PUDDING

Serves 8

FOR THE CAKE
260 g (9 oz) water
150 g (5 oz) stoned dates
150 g (5 oz) plain (all-purpose) flour
1½ teaspoons baking powder (baking soda)
1 teaspoon bicarbonate of soda
150 g (5 oz) dark brown sugar
50 g (1¾ oz) butter, at room temperature
2 eggs

FOR THE SAUCE
400 g (14 oz) whipping cream
80 g (3 oz) demerara sugar
25 g (1 oz) dark brown sugar

This is perhaps my favourite cake of all time. It's moist and slightly chewy, and it tastes like holidays in a chalet with a glowing fireplace and mulled wine bubbling away on the stove. I make it almost every week during winter months as it keeps beautifully in the fridge and warms to that just-out-of-the-oven feel with just a few seconds in the microwave.

It is delicious served with Caramel Cider-Poached Pears (page 47) and/or some vanilla ice-cream. When it comes to the toffee sauce, it could not be easier to make. Cream and sugars are cooked together until they resemble flowing melted gold. And possibly taste like it too – almost nutty and definitely delicious.

Preheat the oven to 160°C (320°F). Butter and line a 20 cm (8 in) cake tin with baking parchment.

Bring the water to the boil in a small saucepan, take off the heat and add the stoned dates. Soak for a few minutes.

Combine the flour, baking powder and baking soda in a small bowl and set aside. Blitz the dates using a hand-blender until smooth.

Cream the sugar and butter in a large bowl, either with a wooden spoon or electric beaters. Add the eggs, one at a time, beating well after each addition. Then add the puréed dates and mix until combined. Fold in the dry ingredients until you have a smooth mixture.

Pour the mixture into the prepared tin and bake for 45 minutes, or until a skewer inserted in the centre of the cake comes out clean.

While the cake is cooking make the toffee sauce. Bring the cream and sugars to the boil in a pan over high heat, stirring every now and then. Lower the heat and simmer for 10 minutes or until you can see the bottom of the pan as you stir with a spatula and the sauce coats the back of a cold metal spoon.

Serve straight away or leave to cool down in a plastic container and keep refrigerated for up to a week. It will thicken a lot as it cools down, but simply reheat a small quantity in a pan over low heat until piping hot.

SPICY CHOCOLATE POTS-DE-CRÈME

Serves 4

240 g (9 oz) whipping cream
100 g (3½ oz) whole milk
3 star anis
2 cardamom pods, crushed
1 teaspoon hot chilli powder
¼ teaspoon ground cinnamon
1 vanilla pod, with its seeds
4 egg yolks
20 g (¾ oz) caster (superfine) sugar
90 g (3 oz) dark chocolate, finely chopped

When the sky looks like it's been bruised and thunder roars, I love to make hot chocolate. Rich and warm with spices, it makes rainy days the best you could ever hope for. I also like to turn my favourite spicy hot chocolate recipe into lush pots-de-crème just by adding four egg yolks and baking for a few minutes in the oven.

Preheat the oven to 150°C (300°F) and boil a kettle of water.

Pour the cream and milk into a saucepan, add the spices, scraped vanilla pod and its seeds and bring to the boil. When the cream mixture boils, remove from the heat, cover with a lid and leave to infuse for 15 minutes.

Whisk the egg yolks and sugar in a bowl. Strain the cream through a fine-mesh sieve onto the egg mixture, stirring as you do so. Add the chocolate and mix with a rubber spatula until melted.

Divide the mixture between 4 small ramekins arranged in a deep baking tray. Pour in enough hot water from the kettle so it reaches halfway up the sides of the ramekins. Bake for 25 minutes until just set and still slightly wobbly in the centre.

Carefully lift the ramekins from the water bath and cool at room temperature for a few minutes before refrigerating. Chill for 2 hours, or overnight, before serving.

CHOCOLATE
-ME-
CAKE

GOUGÈRES,
WITH A SIDE OF
RED WINE

CRÈME BRÛLÉE
FOR ONE

ROAST
GARLIC BREAD

BETTER-THAN-
BROWNIES COOKIES

BANANA-SPLIT(ISH)
SUNDAE

ONE-BOWL
TIRAMISU

WHEN WE FIRST met he was wearing a sweater made of the softest bright-red wool and his hair was the colour of charcoal. His eyes too. That night we kissed on stairs made of stones. By a theatre door. Under raindrops that looked like shooting stars by the glow of a lamp post.

And then, one day, he was gone, leaving a hole in the shape of an empty bed in my life. A bed which would become my fortress for the weeks to come. I would wear that sweater he once loved. Too tired to eat, I would doze into dreams I wished would last forever.

Dreams made of days at the beach, and gin and tonic we sipped through the same straw. Crab-hunting and late-night bonfires by the sea; road trips through the mountains where the clouds blanketed everything around us and it seemed like we were on an island. But mostly dreams made of nights spent in the deserted streets of a Paris under the snow.

Then I would wake up to a cold empty room wishing for more, hoping for more. Hoping for a miracle really. We were strangers again, with an unfinished cup of coffee on the bedside table as the only proof that it wasn't always so cold in this house. I couldn't see through my tears. I felt like I didn't belong anywhere. And I thought I could never fall in love again. But you can only stay underwater for so long. Or so he'd told me, one day when the sea sparkled and the sun burnt, and the fish were an aquatic rainbow.

Yes, you can only stay underwater for so long.

CHAPTER 3

CHOCOLATE -ME- CAKE

Makes 10 slices

FOR THE CAKE
200 g (7 oz) plain (all-purpose) flour
½ teaspoon bicarbonate of soda
50 g (1¾ oz) cocoa powder
275 g (10 oz) caster (superfine) sugar
a pinch of sea salt
175 g (6 oz) butter
2 eggs
175 g (6 oz) 70% dark chocolate, melted
80 g (3 oz) double cream
125 g (4 oz) boiling water

FOR THE SYRUP
1 teaspoon cocoa powder
125 g (4 oz) water
100 g (3½ oz) caster (superfine) sugar

FOR THE TOPPING
25 g (1 oz) dark chocolate, grated

This cake is part of a routine made of paper tissues and drunken phone calls I wish I could forget. And for it we have to thank Nigella Lawson – the one person who turned those sleepless nights into a chocolate cloud, one slice at a time. In fact, it's the one thing I always make after a break-up and I'm not the only one. My best friend 'A' is fond of it too. Off the record, when she craves – or more accurately, needs – chocolate, she's been known to bake it in a massive cassoulet pot. This recipe makes more cake than you could eat in one go. So make it, bake it, eat half of it, freeze the rest (already sliced) and feel better.

Preheat the oven to 170°C (340°F). Generously butter a 1 litre (2 lb) loaf tin or a 24 cm (10 in) cake tin and line with baking parchment, making sure to leave a collar above the rim.

Mix all the cake ingredients (except the boiling water) in a bowl with a wooden spoon until you have a smooth mixture. Slowly incorporate the boiling water, then pour the batter into the prepared tin.

Depending on the size of your tin you might have a bit extra. Just bake this alongside the monster cake in a little bowl. Bake for 50–60 minutes, or until a skewer inserted into the centre of the cake comes out clean.

Bring the syrup ingredients to the boil in a small saucepan and boil for approximately 5 minutes until thickened.

When the syrup is ready, pierce the cake a few times using a skewer or a long match and pour the syrup as evenly as possible over the cake. Let the cake cool down in its tin before turning out (using the excess baking paper as handles) and transferring to a serving plate

Sprinkle with grated chocolate and slice away.

GOUGÈRES, WITH A SIDE OF RED WINE

Serves 4

125 g (4 oz) whole milk
50 g (1¾ oz) butter
2 teaspoons ground paprika
1 teaspoon chilli flakes
1 teaspoon sea salt
75 g (2½ oz) plain (all-purpose) flour
2 eggs
1 egg, beaten for eggwash
60 g (2 oz) Gruyère, Parmesan, mature Cheddar,
or any other hard cheese, grated

Gougères are my favourite comfort food. Gooey pockets of cheese begging to be eaten with fingers and a large glass of red wine. I've called this a dinner many many times. I make the choux paste to the sound of my favourite music, and while the gougères are baking, red wine gets poured. These are always eaten, still piping hot, with a book in one hand and a glass in the other.

Preheat the oven to 250°C (480°F) and lightly butter a baking tray.

Bring the milk, butter, spices and salt to a rolling boil in a saucepan over low heat (the butter needs to be fully melted before the milk boils). Take the pan off the heat, add the flour all at once and stir well until combined. Return to the heat and mix with a wooden spoon until a thin crust appears at the bottom of the pan. This shows that the dough is dry enough. It should not be sticky.

Transfer the dough to a large bowl and leave to cool for 2–3 minutes. Add the eggs, one at a time, mixing with the wooden spoon after each addition until fully incorporated.

Fold in half of the grated cheese while still warm and transfer the dough to a piping bag fitted with a 12 mm (½ in) nozzle.

Pipe the gougères in lines onto the baking tray and brush with eggwash, making sure to smooth the tops. Dip a fork into the eggwash and score the top of each choux. Sprinkle with the remaining grated cheese.

Turn off the oven and bake for 15 minutes or until the choux are puffed but still light in colour. Turn the oven back on to 180°C (350°F), with the oven door held slightly open with the handle of a wooden spoon, and bake for a further 10–15 minutes or until golden-brown.

Remove from the oven and cool for a few minutes. Transfer to a serving plate and eat your way through your favourite TV series with a side of red wine.

PIPING CHOUX

HOLD YOUR PIPING BAG 2 CM (¾ IN)
FROM THE TRAY AT AN ANGLE. PIPE
UNTIL YOU HAVE A DOLLOP ROUGHLY
3 CM (1 IN) WIDE, THEN STOP
SQUEEZING AND QUICKLY 'CUT'
THE DOUGH BY MOVING
IN A SMALL CLOCKWISE CIRCLE.
PIPE A LINE OF DOLLOPS, THEN PIPE
THE SECOND LINE A FEW CENTIMETRES
BELOW AND BETWEEN THE
PREVIOUSLY-PIPED CHOUX IN A
QUINCONCE (STAGGERED) FASHION.

CRÈME BRÛLÉE FOR ONE

Serves 1

100 g (3½ oz) whipping cream
seeds from ½ vanilla pod
2 egg yolks
1 tablespoon caster (superfine) sugar
demerara sugar, extra, to caramelise

There is not much to say about crème brûlée that hasn't already been said. It's creamy, it's delicious, it's understated. Even more so, in fact, when it's turned into a lonesome pleasure. One ramekin. One spoon. One crisp caramelised crust. I can't promise it will change your life. But I can tell you for sure that it will make you feel better.

Preheat the oven to 150°C (300°F). Boil a kettle of water.

Bring the cream and vanilla seeds to the boil in a small pan over a medium heat.

Whisk the egg yolks and caster sugar together in a small bowl. When the milk has boiled, slowly pour it over the egg mixture, whisking as you go. Scoop off any froth with a large spoon and pour the mixture into a small ramekin.

Place the ramekin in a deep baking tray and pour in hot water so it comes halfway up the sides of the ramekin. Bake for 40 minutes, or until set yet still very slightly wobbly in the centre.

Carefully lift the ramekin from the water-bath and leave to cool at room temperature for a few minutes. Chill for 2 hours or overnight. Sprinkle with a thin coating of demerara sugar and burn with a blow torch or place under a hot grill for a few minutes until the sugar turns into caramel.

Crack the caramel crust with a spoon and feel happy.

PARIS PASTRY CLUB

ROAST GARLIC BREAD

Makes 1 loaf of bread

FOR THE DOUGH STARTER
100 g (3½ oz) strong flour
120 g (4 oz) water
10 g (½ oz) fresh yeast
(or 1 teaspoon dried yeast)

FOR THE ROAST GARLIC
2 garlic heads
3 tablespoons extra-virgin olive oil

FOR THE BREAD
50 g (1¾ oz) water
2 tablespoons extra-virgin olive oil
1 teaspoon sea salt
150 g (5 oz) strong flour
extra-virgin olive oil, extra

One of my favourite dinners, of the eat-alone kind, is a bowlful of potatoes, pan-fried until golden and crispy, with plenty of garlic and a sprinkle of salt. Yes, plenty of garlic, more than any boy could take. Even a French one.

At times, I like to turn my garlic addiction into bread. Not only because I find the process of making bread almost magic – kneading a rough dough into a smooth ball, watching it grow like a bubbly monster, smelling its wonderful aromas as it bakes – but also because I can't resist the doughy pockets that burst with roast garlic cloves. It promises all kinds of magic, especially with a bowl of soup or a simple *œuf à la coque* (boiled egg).

Combine the flour, water and yeast in a large bowl to make the starter for the dough. Cover with a clean kitchen cloth and leave to prove for 2 hours.

Preheat the oven to 200°C (400°F). Cut the tops off the garlic heads and drizzle with the olive oil. Wrap each head in foil and bake for around 30 minutes.

Leave to cool, then squeeze the cloves from the heads trying not to break them too much. Set aside while you get on with the bread.

Whisk the water, olive oil and salt into the starter mix. Add the flour and mix until just combined. Turn out onto a clean, lightly oiled surface and knead for 6–8 minutes until smooth. Cover with a clean kitchen cloth and leave to rest for 30 minutes.

Generously oil a large baking tray and stretch the dough into a 15 x 20 cm (6 x 8 in) rectangle. Sprinkle the garlic cloves on the right-hand side. Fold in half widthways, pressing down to seal the ends. Prove for 1 hour. Stretch again into a 15 x 20 cm (6 x 8 in) rectangle and prove for another hour. Preheat the oven to 250°C (480°F).

Sprinkle a little water over the dough and bake for 30 minutes or until golden-brown. Allow to cool a little before eating.

BETTER-THAN-BROWNIES COOKIES

Makes 12 cookies

100 g (3½ oz) dark chocolate,
chopped into chunks
1 tablespoon butter
90 g (3 oz) plain (all-purpose) flour
¼ teaspoon baking powder
¼ teaspoon sea salt
1 egg
75 g (2½ oz) light brown sugar

These cookies have been a favourite for years now. Chewy and chocolatey they will remind you of brownies (in a cookie kind of way, that is). I love to munch on them while they are still warm or serve them sandwiched with ice-cream. Trust me, they'll make your fingers and your mouth happy.

Preheat the oven to 170°C (340°F) and line a baking sheet with baking parchment.

Stir the chocolate and butter in a large heatproof bowl set over simmering water until melted. Set aside to cool down slightly while you get on with the rest.

Combine the flour, baking powder and salt in a bowl.

Beat the egg and sugar in a separate bowl for 5 minutes or until light and fluffy, then gently fold into the melted chocolate. Working quickly, tip the flour mixture in and mix well with a wooden spoon.

The dough will feel quite sticky and soft but you should be able to roll it with your hands into walnut-sized balls and arrange them on the prepared baking sheet.

Bake for 10 minutes. The cookies should still be soft and their tops will be cracked. Leave to cool on the baking sheet for a few minutes before transferring to a serving plate.

BANANA-SPLIT(ISH) SUNDAE

Serves 2

FOR THE FUDGE SAUCE
200 g (7 oz) double cream
50 g (1¾ oz) unsalted butter
125 g (4 oz) dark muscovado sugar
1 teaspoon cocoa powder
¾ teaspoon sea salt
75 g (2½ oz) 40% milk chocolate

2 bananas, skin-on
4 scoops of Vanilla Ice-cream, shop-bought
or homemade (page 17)
6 Better-Than-Brownies Cookies (page 67)

My super-decadent treat is to layer some Better-Than-Brownies Cookies (page 67) in a tall glass with caramelised banana, vanilla ice-cream and an insane chocolate fudge sauce.

The perfect break-up cure!

Preheat the oven to 180°C (350°F).

Start with the fudge sauce: bring the cream, butter, dark muscovado sugar, cocoa powder and salt to the boil in a small pan.

Pour over the chocolate in a large bowl and stir well with a spatula until everything is fully combined. Set aside to cool down slightly at room temperature until ready to use.

While the sauce is cooling, make the black bananas. Just arrange the bananas on a baking tray lined with foil and poke a few holes through the skin using a small knife. Bake in the pre-heated oven for 15 minutes or until black and juices come out from the holes. Allow to cool for a little while, taking care not to burn your fingers when you peel them.

In tall glasses, layer the vanilla ice-cream, baked banana and cookies. Top with a generous amount of milk chocolate fudge sauce.

ONE-BOWL TIRAMISU

Serves 1

1 heaped tablespoon caster (superfine) sugar
1 egg yolk
100 g (3½ oz) mascarpone
6–8 Biscuits Cuilliéres (page 114)
or store-bought sponge fingers
a cup of strong coffee
70% dark chocolate, for topping

This is my little selfish pleasure. One big fat bowl of mascarpone mousse with the occasional coffee-drenched biscuit.

The mousse is rich and creamy with egg yolk and, of course, mascarpone. And really, when I think about its name, I believe it could not have borne its name better. It means 'pick me up', and this bowl will indeed pick you up. This recipe can easily be doubled/tripled/you name it for a crowd and looks absolutely darling in small glasses.

Whisk the sugar and egg yolk with a hand-held mixer for 3–4 minutes or until thick and doubled in size.

Add the mascarpone, a tablespoon at a time, beating well – for at least for a minute – after each addition. Chill in the fridge while you get on with the layering action.

Soak the biscuits in the strong coffee and place three at the bottom of a bowl. Cover with half the mascarpone cream. Top with more soaked biscuits and spread with more cream. Grate some dark chocolate on top and chill the tiramisu for an hour or two. Dig in with the largest spoon you can find.

BREAKFASTS OF KINGS

I WOKE UP with a hangover of the bloody mary/gin and tonic/champagne kind. Oh, and to a man who had no problem whatsoever sleeping in an upside-down, inside-out bed.

Men are always hungry in the morning. And no matter how delicate I felt, this one would never wake up if it wasn't for the scent of an *à-la-minute* breakfast. I craved some food too – food that would make me remember things the alcohol made blurry. And just like a firecracker lit in the middle of the summer, or the one we felt that night, I realised not everything can be forgotten. Some things can only be felt.

Things like his hand in my hair and how we would forget the world as the short walk to my flat turned into a real-life board-game. We were the prizes. It was fun. He was fun. Perhaps we were a little funny together; not unlike a pair of mismatched socks. Wild blond hair and out-of-control brunette curls.

Yes, I was going to make him the best breakfast he'd ever eaten. And more. And really, what I thought right there, right then, was to start with the more. Pancakes would come later.

PARIS PASTRY CLUB

CHAPTER 4

WAFFLES (THE QUICK KIND)

Makes 8–12 large waffles

100 g (3¼ oz) butter
125 g (4½ oz) whole milk
seeds from 1 vanilla pod
120 g (4¼ oz) plain (all-purpose) flour
3 egg whites
60 g (2 oz) caster (superfine) sugar

I could have given you the recipe my grandmother makes, with yeast and a touch of beer, but who'd want to wait 3 hours for waffles? These are quick to make and even quicker to eat.

If there is a reason good enough to dust off your old waffle iron, then this is it. Don't look any further; your life will have a new meaning.

Preheat your waffle iron.

Place the butter, milk and vanilla seeds in a small pan, and cook over low heat until the butter is just melted. Transfer to a jug, and allow to cool down slightly. It shouldn't feel too warm to the touch.

Place the flour in a large bowl and slowly pour the milk over it, whisking as you go.

In another bowl, whisk the egg whites until foamy, then add the sugar – a little at a time – until the meringue is thick and glossy. Scoop half into the batter and whisk in to loosen the mixture, then gently fold in the rest.

Ladle the batter onto the hot iron and cook for 4–6 minutes, or until the waffles are golden-brown.

Transfer to a wire rack while you cook the rest of the batter.

WHISKING EGG WHITES

WHISKING EGG WHITES IS ONE OF
THE FIRST THINGS YOU LEARN HOW TO DO,
AND YET I OFTEN FIND THAT PEOPLE ARE
DOING IT THE WRONG WAY.
YOU SHOULD ALWAYS START
WHISKING YOUR WHITES AT SLOW SPEED,
WHICH CREATES SMALL,
EVEN AIR BUBBLES THAT WILL BE
MUCH MORE STABLE.

CROISSANT PAIN-PERDU

Serves 2

2 croissants
2 eggs
3 tablespoons caster (superfine) sugar,
plus extra for cooking
80 g (3 oz) whole milk
30 g (1 oz) whipping cream
butter, for cooking

The best thing to eat after a wild night and, trust me, I don't know a single guy on this planet who'd refuse them. A crème-brûlée-like French toast with the buttery flavour of croissant and a crisp caramel crust.

Just one tiny thing – be careful. I know it's the morning-ish (and 2 pm does qualify here), but there is a tiny bit of caramel here and the last thing you want is to burn your fingers. So please, do yourself a favour – use a spatula to flip the French toast around.

Slice the croissants in half lengthwise.

Mix the eggs and caster sugar in a bowl with a whisk until combined. Add the milk and cream and mix until just smooth.

Transfer this eggy mix to a large container and arrange the slices of croissants cut-side-down and allow to soak for a minute. Flip around and soak for a further minute.

Melt a knob of butter until foamy in a hot pan set over medium heat. Fry the croissant halves, cut-side down, 1 or 2 at a time for a minute. Flip with a palette knife and sprinkle generously with caster sugar.

Cook for a minute then turn over and fry for a further minute to let the sugar caramelise. It sounds like a lot of flipping, but trust me, it barely takes 3 minutes and makes for the crispiest crust ever.

CORNBREAD PANCAKES

Makes 6 fat pancakes

130 g (4½ oz) plain (all-purpose) flour
½ tablespoon baking powder (baking soda)
1 heaped teaspoon sea salt
a pinch of ground cumin
130 g (4½ oz) whole milk
1 egg
juice of 1 lime
200 g (7 oz) corn kernels
(from 2 medium corncobs)
3 spring onions (scallions), sliced
1 chilli pepper, thinly sliced
2 heaped tablespoons chopped
coriander (cilantro)

I didn't grow up on cornbread but cornbread grew on me. It might have been because of that guy with deep-blue eyes and the cutest American accent ever. He would make me peanut butter and honey sandwiches, and halve strawberries into salads.

One morning, as I was still deep inside my dreams, he went to the kitchen and pan-fried a whole lot of cornbread pancakes. That very morning, after too many pancakes than I'd like to admit, I told him those three words of the loving kind. This is his recipe and, trust me, you'll fall in love with it too.

I like to serve mine with a salsa made of crushed avocado and chopped tomatoes, drizzled with lots of lemon juice and sprinkled with sea salt, sliced chilli peppers and lots of fresh coriander.

Combine the flour, baking powder, salt, cumin, milk, egg, and lime juice in a large bowl. Add the corn kernels, spring onions, chilli and coriander and give it a good stir.

Heat a non-stick pan over low heat and ladle the batter (roughly one-third of a cup) into the hot pan and cook for about 1 minute until the bottom of the pancake is golden-brown. Flip the pancake over with a palette knife and cook for a further minute. Transfer to a plate and keep on cooking pancakes until all the batter has been used up.

BREAKFAST COOKIES (SORT OF)

Makes 12 cookie-sized pancakes

2 eggs, separated
120 g (4¼ oz) plain yoghurt
60 g (2 oz) whole milk
60 g (2 oz) light brown sugar
1 tablespoon vanilla extract
½ teaspoon sea salt
120 g (4¼ oz) plain (all-purpose) flour
50 g (1¾ oz) 70% dark chocolate,
chopped into chunks
50 g (1¾ oz) 40% milk chocolate,
chopped into chunks
1 teaspoon baking powder (baking soda)
butter, for frying

CHOPPING CHOCOLATE

NEXT TIME YOU CHOP CHOCOLATE, TRY TO DO IT WITH A SERRATED KNIFE. SO MUCH EASIER!

These are not your everyday pancakes. They are pockets of melting chocolate and light brown sugar.

If you ever make them, please drop a fat knob of butter in your pan and leave it to turn golden brown. It will give these breakfast 'cookies' the best flavour ever.

Combine the egg yolks, yoghurt, milk, sugar, vanilla extract and salt in a large bowl.

Whisk the egg whites in a separate bowl until they form soft peaks. Scoop one-third of the egg whites onto the yoghurt mixture and whisk in to loosen the batter, then gently fold in the remaining egg whites. Add the flour, chocolate chunks and baking powder and mix until just combined.

Heat a knob of butter in a non-stick pan over a high heat until brown and foamy. Reduce the heat, ladle in the batter – roughly a quarter of a cup – onto the hot pan and cook for about 2 minutes until the bottom of the pancake is golden-brown. Flip the pancake over with a palette knife and cook for a further minute. Transfer to a plate and keep on cooking pancakes until all the batter has been used. Eat with your fingers, with a glass of ice-cold milk.

PARIS PASTRY CLUB

CHAPTER 4

CARROT CAKE PANCAKES

Makes 10–12 pancakes

FOR THE CREAM CHEESE 'FROSTING'
100 g (3½ oz) cream cheese
3 tablespoons yoghurt
1 tablespoon light brown sugar
1 teaspoon vanilla extract

FOR THE PANCAKES
100 g (3½ oz) cream cheese
80 g (2¾ oz) whole milk
2 eggs, separated
3 tablespoons light brown sugar
1 teaspoon vanilla extract
90 g (3 oz) plain (all-purpose) flour
1 teaspoon baking powder
(baking soda)
½ teaspoon ground cinnamon
160 g (5½ oz) carrots, finely grated
(approx 4 small carrots)

These pancakes are perfect for those mornings when you want a breakfast celebration. I made them for the very first time for my boyfriend's birthday. That day, we had pancakes in bed – with all the trimmings, candles and kisses included – lunch in a fancy restaurant, and chocolate cake with glasses of champagne for dinner.

I like to serve them with a one-minute 'frosting', but they're great with maple syrup or honey too. And when it comes to the carrots, they need to be grated super-finely. I use Microplane grater, which does a fantastic job.

Start by making the frosting. Whisk all of the ingredients in a bowl until smooth and chill until needed.

Combine the cream cheese, milk, egg yolks, sugar and vanilla extract in a large bowl. Add the flour, baking powder and cinnamon and mix until smooth.

In a separate bowl, whisk the egg whites until they hold soft peaks. Gently fold into the pancake mix along with the carrots.

Heat a non-stick pan over low heat. Ladle the batter – roughly a quarter of a cup – into the hot pan and cook for about 2 minutes until the bottom of the pancake is golden-brown. Flip the pancake over with a palette knife and cook for a further minute. Transfer to a plate and keep on cooking pancakes until all the batter's been used up.

Serve with a generous dollop of frosting.

RICOTTA & HONEY DOUGHNUTS

Makes 30–40 bite-sized doughnuts

125 g (4 oz) whole milk
50 g (2¾ oz) butter
1 teaspoon sea salt
75 g (2½ oz) plain (all-purpose) flour
2 eggs
100 g (3½ oz) ricotta cheese
1 tablespoon honey

vegetable oil, for deep-frying
runny honey, to serve
toasted pinenuts, to serve (optional)

You can call them doughnuts or fritters, but to me, these will always be *beignets* (pronounced 'bay-nee-yeah'). They are made from a simple pâte à choux with just a touch of honey and lots of ricotta. Thick yoghurt works like a charm too, if that's all you have in your fridge. All you'll need is a generous drizzle of honey and perhaps a small handful of pinenuts, toasted in a frying pan until just golden, and a fun breakfast made of sticky fingers will happen.

To make a choux paste, bring the milk, butter, and salt to a rolling boil in a saucepan over a low heat – you want the butter to be fully melted before the milk boils. Take the pan off the heat and add the flour all in one go, mixing well until combined.

Return the pan to the heat and stir with a wooden spoon until a thin crust appears at the bottom of the pan. This shows that the dough is dry enough – it should not be sticky.

Transfer the paste to a large bowl and leave to cool for 2–3 minutes. While still warm, fold in the ricotta and honey. Scrape the mixture into a piping bag fitted with a 20 mm (¾ in) nozzle.

Heat the vegetable oil in a deep saucepan to 160°C (320°F).

Start piping the dough into the oil, snipping off 1 cm (½ in) pieces as you go with scissors. Cut 6 or 7 at a time and please be careful not to burn yourself. Fry for around 6 minutes, flipping the balls halfway through, until they are deep brown.

Use a slotted spoon to transfer the fried doughnuts to a plate lined with a few layers of kitchen paper and repeat with the remaining dough.

Serve on a large plate and drizzle with plenty of runny honey. A scattering of toasted pinenuts on top makes a wonderful addition.

SWEET CHILLI BRUFFINS

Makes 12

350 g (12 oz) plain (all-purpose) flour
2½ teaspoons baking powder (baking soda)
a good grind of black pepper
a fat pinch of sea salt
180 g (6⅓ oz) Gruyère, grated
250 g (8¾ oz) milk
50 g (2¾ oz) sweet chilli sauce
1 egg
130 g (4½ oz) baby spinach leaves
4 spring onions (scallions), finely sliced
2 chilli peppers, finely chopped
1 fat garlic clove

These bruffins (bread muffins, call them cheesy, that's okay by me, in all accounts) are my secret hangover trick. Not so secret anymore, though, as I've made them countless times for friends after a dinner-turned-party kind of night. There is nothing special here – spring onions and garlic, big fat handfuls of spinach and Gruyère, and a healthy dash of sweet chilli sauce – and yet they're always a hit.

You should know they also make a killer side dish for dinners made of old-school TV series and piping hot soup in the winter.

Preheat the oven to 170°C (340°F).

Stir the flour, baking powder, pepper, salt and Gruyère together in a large bowl.

Whisk the milk, sweet chilli sauce and egg in a separate bowl, then pour onto the flour mixture using a wooden spoon to fold together.

Add the spinach, spring onions, chopped chilli peppers and grated garlic – the batter will be quite thick so I like to use my hands to do this. Divide the mixture into 12 muffin cases and bake for 35 minutes. Remove the muffins from the tin and allow to cool slightly on a rack.

FRAISIER

LEMON
MERINGUE TART

TRIPLE CHOCOLATE
MOUSSE CAKE

PISTACHIO &
CHERRY CAKE

BROWN SUGAR
CHEESECAKE WITH
SUGARED NUTS

PEACH MELBA
CHARLOTTE

ALMOST-INSTANT
CHOCOLATE
FONDANT CAKE

CHERRY
CLAFOUTIS

(FOR GLITTERY DAYS AND BALMY NIGHTS)

THERE IS THE upside-down pineapple cake with shiny, almost-golden, pineapple slices and cherries of the fake-red kind. There are the vanilla pudding lollipops and the candy necklaces. And balloons too. In the shape of a rainbow. Yes, birthdays used to mean all of that.

As I grew up, the juice I used to drink at my birthday parties turned into champagne, and the butterfly make-up into cat's eyes eyeliner. I put on my favourite sundress, the one that floats when I spin. Because that is what you should do – dance and spin and jump and fall and kiss. And your head should turn, not unlike it does when you're tipsy.

We drink beers as the sun goes down. And tequila when fireflies rush around us. We lie in the grass. And laugh, and maybe even cry a little. But that's ok, because a birthday should be a party like no other. With stories told and my favourite faces that remind me what it feels like to laugh until your cheeks hurt.

With glitter in the swimming pool and on (as well as in) our eyes. Perhaps on that cake sitting on the table too. A cake that glows with candles. A cake we eat with our fingers as soon as it gets cut into slices. A cake that tastes like a dream.

CHAPTER 5

FRAISIER

Serves 8–10

FOR THE SPONGE
3 eggs
75 g (2½ oz) caster (superfine) sugar
75 g (2½ oz) plain (all-purpose) flour, sieved

FOR THE SYRUP
250 g (9 oz) water
175 g (6 oz) caster (superfine) sugar

FOR THE CRÈME PÂTISSIÈRE
500 g (1 lb 2 oz) whole milk
3 vanilla pods, with their seeds
4 egg yolks
125 g (4 oz) caster (superfine) sugar
50 g (2¾ oz) cornflour (cornstarch)

FOR THE CRÈME MOUSSELINE
150 g (5 oz) butter, at room temperature
1 batch of Crème Pâtissière (quantities above)
icing (confectioner's) sugar, to dust

500 g (1 lb 2 oz) strawberries,
washed and halved

A fraisier can either mean garden strawberries or a gorgeous entremet (dessert cake). And while I've tried growing a potager many times with varying success, my fraisier entremet is always a hit.

At home, we used to eat it for Sunday lunch after a roast chicken of some sorts, as soon as the first strawberries would make the farmers market stands glow like red gemstones. And, of course, for my birthday, which happily falls at the beginning of May – at the very start of my favourite season.

Making a fraiser is not complicated. You have to start with the crème pâtissière and the génoise sponge, which

Preheat the oven to 180°C (350°F). Line a baking tray with baking parchment and place a 20 cm (8 in) metal ring on it.

First make the sponge. Combine the eggs and caster sugar with a whisk in a heatproof bowl. Set it over a pan of simmering water and gently whisk the egg mixture until it feels hot to the touch; it should be around 50°C (120°F), but I like to use my little finger to test it instead of a probe. If you feel some heat after a few seconds then it's ready.

Remove the bowl from the heat and whisk vigorously for 3 minutes. Or transfer to a stand-mixer and beat on a high speed. Then reduce the speed and keep whisking until the mixture has cooled down. It should form a thick glossy mass with millions of tiny air bubbles.

Fold in the flour and stop mixing as soon as you've got rid of any lumps. The batter should still be somewhat firm and hold soft peaks.

Scrape the batter into the prepared ring and bake for 18–20 minutes or until the cake springs back to the touch. Leave to cool completely, then run a small paring knife carefully around the edge of the cake and lift off the ring. Set aside while you make the other components or tightly wrap in

both need to cool down for quite some time. Once the sponge is baked and cold it is unmoulded by running a small sharp knife around the edges of the metal ring. This step can be quite tricky but is nothing to be afraid of. Just go for it and a stunning fraisier will only be a few minutes away!

clingfilm and freeze for up to a month.

Now make the syrup: simply place the water and sugar in a pan, and bring to the boil. Allow to cool down and store in the fridge in an airtight container for up to a week.

To make the crème pâtissière (you can do this up to 3 days ahead), bring the milk and vanilla pods and seeds to a rolling boil in a medium pan set over moderate heat.

In a separate bowl, whisk the egg yolks and sugar to prevent the egg yolks from clumping. Add the cornflour and mix well until combined. When the milk has boiled, remove from the heat and pour a third of it over the egg mixture, whisking as you do so. This step is key when making crème pâtissière as it loosens the egg yolks but also tempers them, avoiding any lumps.

Pour all of the egg mixture back into the remaining milk in the pan, return to the heat and cook slowly, whisking at all times, until it starts to thicken and boil.

Once it has bubbled for a few minutes, transfer to a plastic container and lay clingfilm over the surface to avoid the formation of a skin. Chill in the fridge for at least 4 hours before using.

When you are ready to assemble your fraisier, place a 20 cm (8 in) metal ring onto a serving plate and line it with a strip of 6 cm (2¹⁄₃ in) wide acetate (or a strip of baking paper 65 x 6 cm/25½ x 2¹⁄₃ in).

Slice the génoise sponge in half with a large bread knife and place the top half of the sponge in the bottom of the ring with its cut-side up. Brush generously with syrup. Arrange strawberries around the edge, taking care to use even-sized fruit. Set aside while you make the crème mousseline.

Cream the butter until light and fluffy. Add 600 g (1 lb 5 oz) of crème pâtissière, one third at a time, beating well after each addition. Once all of the crème pâtissière has been added, whisk for 5 minutes. The mousseline should be firm and glossy.

If the butter has seized a little, simply place the bowl on top of a pan of simmering water for a few seconds before beating for a minute or two. Repeat until all the butter has disappeared and you're left with a gorgeously thick crème mousseline.

Spoon a third of the mousseline over the sponge and use a palette knife to spread it over the cake and the strawberries around the sides. Arrange a layer of halved strawberries over the mousseline, then pour the remaining crème mousseline over, smoothing the top with your palette knife. Top with the second half of sponge, cut-side down, and press gently and evenly to sandwich it all together. Brush generously with syrup.

Chill for at least 4 hours and for up to 1 day.

Carefully lift off the ring and delicately peel the rhodoid or parchment from the side of the cake. Serve dusted with icing sugar.

FOLDING

IN COOKERY TERMS, THIS USUALLY
MEANS TO COMBINE TWO MIXTURES
WITHOUT DEFLATING THE BATTER.
THIS CAN BE DONE WITH EITHER
A WHISK OR A RUBBER SPATULA.
I FIND THE WHISK TO
BE THE QUICKER METHOD, BUT CAN
ONLY ADVISE YOU TO MASTER FOLDING
USING A SPATULA BEFORE MOVING
ON TO THE WHISK.
THE CORRECT MOVEMENT IS
TO START IN THE CENTRE OF THE BOWL –
THIS IS SOMETHING I INSIST
ON A LOT, ASK ANY OF MY COMMIS –
THEN GO UP THE SIDE OF THE BOWL
AND TURN IT COUNTER-CLOCKWISE
AS YOU DO SO. STOP FOLDING
AS SOON AS THE STREAKS/TRACES
DISAPPEAR AS YOU DO NOT WANT
TO OVERMIX AND LOSE AIR.

LEMON MERINGUE TART

Serves 10–12

FOR THE LEMON SHORTBREAD
100 g (3½ oz) butter, diced
40 g (1½ oz) icing (confectioner's) sugar
1 egg yolk from a hard-boiled egg,
finely grated
zest of 2 lemons
100 g (3½ oz) plain (all-purpose) flour
2 tablespoons cornflour (cornstarch)
½ teaspoon sea salt

FOR THE LEMON CURD
200 g (7 oz) caster (superfine)sugar
finely grated zest of 3 lemons
4 large eggs
180 g (6⅓ oz) freshly squeezed lemon juice
(from 4–5 lemons)
300 g (10½ oz) unsalted butter,
at room temperature, cubed

FOR THE LEMON SPONGE
120 g (4¼ oz) ground almonds
80 g (2¾ oz) caster (supefine) sugar
2 eggs
1 egg yolk
2 tablespoons cornflour (cornstarch)
zest and juice of 1 lemon

FOR THE ITALIAN MERINGUE
2 egg whites
185 g (6⅓ oz) caster (superfine) sugar
5 g (¼ oz) dehydrated egg whites (optional)
50 g (2¾ oz) water

This tart is one of my sister's favourite desserts. One day, when I was still in Paris working for Pierre Hermé, I told her how good his lemon curd was. And as soon as I landed back in the south of France, guess what she asked me to make?

Since that day, I've been making lemon meringue tarts by the dozen. At times for the restaurant, most of the time for my sister, and each time using Pierre Hermé's lemon curd (or crémeux citron).

Yes, it's that good. Creamy to the point of no return, it melts in your mouth with the perfume of freshly squeezed lemons.

The base is not a pastry tart case, as you might have thought, but a crumbly shortbread base which makes for the perfect balance of creamy and crunchy.

First make the shortbread. Cream the butter, icing sugar, egg yolk and lemon zest for a few minutes. Add the flours and salt, and mix until the dough just comes together.

Roll out the dough between 2 sheets of baking paper until it's around 4 mm (¼ in) thick. Chill in the fridge for at least 30 minutes, or for up to 3 days.

To make the lemon curd, rub the sugar and lemon zest together between your fingers in a large heatproof bowl until it is moist and aromatic. Whisk in the eggs followed by the lemon juice.

Set the bowl over a pan of simmering water, stirring constantly with a spatula. Cook the lemon cream until it reaches 85°C (185°F). It will take a long time, so turn on the radio and stir away for around 20–30 minutes. As soon as it reaches temperature, remove the curd from the heat and allow to cool down to 60°C (140°F). Gradually incorporate the butter, whisking well after each addition.

When all the butter has been added, blitz the lemon curd using an immersion blender for 8–10 minutes. It might sound long, but it will give the cream a too-smooth-to-be-true texture.

Pour the curd into a container, lay clingfilm over the surface and refrigerate overnight, or for up to 3 days.

On the day you're planning to serve your tart, preheat the oven to 160°C (320°F) and generously butter a 24 cm (9½ in) metal ring.

Lift the shortbread onto a baking tray, remove the top piece of paper and bake for 18–24 minutes or until golden-brown. Remove from the oven and immediately press the tart ring onto the shortbread to cut through. Leave to cool slightly, then trim the excess shortbread, leaving the tart ring in place.

While the shortbread base is cooling down, make the lemon sponge. Mix all the ingredients, except the lemon juice, in a large bowl until smooth. Transfer to a piping bag fitted with a 9 mm (½ in) nozzle and pipe onto the shortbread in a spiral shape, starting from the centre and spiralling outwards to the edge.

Bake for 8 minutes, then cool down completely and gently lift the ring off. Using 2 palette knives, transfer the tart to a large plate. It will be very crumbly and fragile so take care.

Scrape the lemon cream into a plastic piping bag fitted with a 10 mm (½ in) nozzle and pipe the lemon curd on the shortbread in a spiral, as with the sponge, but this time leave a 1 cm (½ in) rim around the edge. Chill while you make the meringue.

Whisk the egg whites with a pinch of salt in a stand-mixer on a slow speed until foamy, then add 35 g (1¼ oz) of the sugar, gradually increasing the speed until the mix holds soft peaks. Reduce the speed while you make the syrup.

Heat the water and remaining sugar to 115°C (240°F) in a small pan over a medium heat.

With the mixer still on slow to medium speed, pour the boiling syrup down the sides of the bowl to mix with the egg whites. Increase the speed and whisk until the bowl no longer feels hot to the touch.

Scrape the meringue into a plastic piping bag fitted with a 15 mm (⅔ in) nozzle and pipe on top of the lemon curd. Smooth into curls and peaks with a small palette knife.

Gently caramelise the meringue with a blowtorch.

The lemon tart will keep for a day in the fridge but is definitely best eaten on the day it's made.

TRIPLE CHOCOLATE MOUSSE CAKE

Serves 10–12 people

FOR THE SPONGE
120 g (4¼ oz) dark chocolate
60 g (2 oz) butter
2 eggs
100 g (3½ oz) caster (superfine) sugar
1 teaspoon ground almonds

FOR THE MOUSSES
550 g (1 lb 3 oz) whipping cream

FOR THE CRÈME ANGLAISE
270 g (10 oz) whole milk
6 egg yolks
60 g (2 oz) caster (superfine) sugar

FOR THE DARK CHOCOLATE MOUSSE
1⅓ gelatine leaves
⅓ batch Crème Anglaise (quantities above)
80 g (2¾ oz) 70% dark chocolate,
chopped into chunks
150 g (5 oz) chilled whipped cream
(see above)

FOR THE MILK CHOCOLATE MOUSSE
1½ gelatine leaves
⅓ batch crème Anglaise (quantities above)
80 g (2¾ oz) 40% milk chocolate,
chopped into chunks
190 g (6¾ oz) chilled whipped cream
(see above)

FOR THE WHITE CHOCOLATE MOUSSE
2 gelatine leaves
⅓ batch Crème Anglaise (quantities above)
80 g (2¾ oz) white chocolate,
chopped into chunks
190 g (6¾ oz) chilled whipped cream
(see above)

TO SERVE
100 g (3½ oz) 70% dark chocolate,
finely grated

SOAKED GELATINE IN 3 EASY STEPS

1. ALWAYS USE ICE-COLD WATER.
2. PLACE THE GELATINE LEAVES
ONE BY ONE INTO THE WATER AND NOT
THE OTHER WAY AROUND (OR YOU MIGHT
HEAR THE ECHO OF MY VOICE SAYING
'NOOOOOOO'!).
3. CHILL THE CONTAINER IN THE FRIDGE
UNTIL YOU'RE READY TO USE
THE SOAKED LEAVES. THEY USUALLY
TAKE AROUND 5 MINUTES
TO SOFTEN BUT 20 MINUTES
IS THE OPTIMUM TIME TO MAXIMISE
THEIR GELLING PROPERTIES.

Preheat the oven to 170°C (340°F). Line a baking tray with baking parchment.

First make the sponge. Melt the chocolate and butter in a heatproof bowl set over a pan of simmering water and set aside.

Whisk the eggs and sugar until light and fluffy. Add the ground almonds, then gently fold in the melted chocolate using a rubber spatula. Pour the batter onto the prepared baking tray and spread into a 1 cm (½ in) thick rectangle.

Bake for 8 minutes. Allow to cool down on a wire rack, then freeze for at least 1 hour well wrapped in clingfilm.

Once frozen, remove from the freezer and gently peel off the baking paper. Press a 22 cm (9½ in) metal ring onto the sponge to cut through it. Place the metal ring onto a baking sheet lined with baking paper and line the ring with a strip of rhodoid (or strips of baking parchment). Arrange the sponge disk in the bottom and place back in the freezer.

Now make the mousses. Start by whisking the whipping cream to soft peaks and keep it in the fridge while you make the crème anglaise. This way you'll have a supply of ready-whipped cream to add to each mousse.

The method is the same for each mousse. Place each type of chopped chocolate in a large bowl and set aside.

Soak the gelatine leaves in 3 separate bowls of ice-cold water (see page 103) while you make the crème anglaise.

Bring the milk to the boil in a small pan. Combine the egg yolks and sugar in a bowl and when the milk has boiled, slowly pour it over the egg mixture, whisking as you go. Pour the mixture back into the pan and cook over a low heat until the anglaise thickens enough to coat the back of a spoon or the temperature reaches 80°C (175°F) on a probe.

Pour the hot crème anglaise onto the chocolate and whisk until smooth and shiny.

Squeeze out each portion of gelatine leaves and add to the 3 different chocolate crème anglaise mixtures. Stir until incorporated.

From this point, continue to make each mousse one by one. Start with the dark chocolate crème, and keep the other two set over barely simmering water to ensure they stay warm (at around 36°C/97°F).

Measure out 150 g (5 oz) of the chilled whipped cream and gently fold into the dark chocolate crème using a whisk. When the mousse seems smooth, finish folding with a spatula then scrape it onto the frozen sponge in the prepared ring. Tap the tray gently on a work surface to even out the surface. Return to the freezer for at least 30 minutes before continuing.

Make the milk chocolate mousse, as above, then pour into the ring and freeze for 30 minutes. Finally, make the white chocolate mousse, pour into the ring and freeze for at least 2 hours or up to a month.

A few hours before you wish to serve, remove the cake from the freezer.

This is a classical entremet (dessert cake) that looks stunning with its many layers and grated chocolate topping. It's a darling choice for birthdays as it's so easy to make and will please your favourite chocoholics.

A flourless chocolate sponge is topped with three different kinds of chocolate mousse, and each mousse takes barely more than ten minutes to come together. The longest step is the chilling time. And the great thing is that you can make it way ahead of the big day as it will keep in the freezer for up to a month.

Gently lift off the metal ring and carefully peel away the rhodoid (or baking paper). Transfer to a serving plate and leave in the fridge to thaw for at least 4 hours. (If made ahead of time, you will need to thaw in the fridge overnight.)

Before serving, sprinkle with grated chocolate.

PARIS PASTRY CLUB

CHAPTER 5

PISTACHIO & CHERRY CAKE

Serves 10

FOR THE WHITE CHOCOLATE
AND CINNAMON MOUSSE
2 gelatine leaves
150 g (5 oz) whole milk
⅛ teaspoon ground cinnamon
2 egg yolks
1 tablespoon caster (superfine) sugar
230 g (8 oz) white chocolate, melted
200 g (7 oz) whipping cream,
whipped to soft peaks

FOR THE PISTACHIO DACQUOIS
6 egg whites
200 g (7 oz) caster (superfine) sugar
240 g (9 oz) ground almonds
190 g (6 oz) icing (confectioner's) sugar, sieved
4 tablespoons plain (all-purpose) flour
90 g (3 oz) unsalted roasted pistachios,
roughly chopped

FOR THE TOPPING
icing (confectioner's) sugar, for dusting
400 g (14 oz) cherries, pitted
40 g (1½ oz) blanched pistachios, chopped

These are my favourite flavours for this cake. With a hint of cinnamon in the white chocolate mousse it really is the perfect combination. It also works well with many other summer fruits. Try peaches or apricots or even a combination of berries.

The base cake is a dacquois. Egg whites are whipped with a little sugar, then almonds and icing sugar are folded in just so.

Soak the gelatine leaves in ice-cold water.

Make a crème anglaise: bring the milk and cinnamon to the boil in a small pan over a medium heat.

Mix the egg yolks and sugar together in a bowl. When the milk has boiled, slowly pour onto the eggs, whisking as you do so. Return to the pan and cook over low heat, stirring with a spatula, until the anglaise reaches 80°C (175°F) or coats the back of a metal spoon.

Squeeze out the gelatine leaves, add to the anglaise and stir to combine.

Pour onto the melted white chocolate and whisk well. Leave to cool to 30°C (85°F), it should feel barely warm to the touch.

Stir a third of the whipped cream into the crème to loosen the mixture. Then gently fold in the rest of the cream, first using a whisk and switching to a spatula at the end. Transfer the mousse to a plastic piping bag, seal the end and chill for at least 3 hours.

In the meantime, make the pistachio dacquois. Preheat the oven to 180°C (350°F). Butter and line a 24 cm (10 in) metal ring with a strip of baking parchment and set on a lined baking tray.

Whisk the egg whites until they hold soft peaks, then add the sugar, a third at a time, whisking well after each addition. Keep on whisking for 5 minutes, until the meringue is stiff and the sugar has dissolved.

Mix the ground almonds, icing sugar and flour in a separate bowl, then tip the dry ingredients onto the meringue and fold very gently until just combined.

Scrape the batter into a plastic piping bag fitted with a 15 mm (½ in) nozzle.

Pipe the dacquois into the prepared metal ring starting from the centre and spiralling out until you reach the edges. Now pipe a circle of 14–16 golf ball-sized around the edge of the dacquois.

Sprinkle generously with the chopped pistachios, then bake for 30 minutes, or until evenly golden-brown.

Leave to cool completely on a wire rack. Lift off the ring, then carefully peel the paper away from the sides and bottom. Transfer to a large plate and set aside.

To assemble the cake, dust the rim of the dacquois with icing sugar. Cut the tip off the chocolate mousse piping bag and fit inside another piping bag fitted with a 10 mm (½ in) nozzle.

Pipe a layer of mousse onto the dacquois. Arrange the cherries on top and scatter with pistachios. If you have any leftover mousse, you can always dollop or quenelle some on top of the cherries for an instant celebration effect.

Chill in the fridge for up to 6 hours and serve.

QUENELLE ME CRAZY?

A QUENELLE IS A RUGBY-BALL SHAPE
(THE CLOSEST I COULD FIND) THAT IS
USUALLY MADE USING ONE OR TWO SPOONS.
WHEN TALKING ABOUT QUENELLES,
MOST PEOPLE REFER TO ICE-CREAM,
BUT YOU CAN ALSO QUENELLE MOUSSES,
AS I DO HERE.
JUST MAKE SURE TO DIP YOUR SPOON IN
HOT WATER BEFORE YOU DO SO AS IT MAKES
IT MUCH EASIER AND NEATER.

BROWN SUGAR CHEESECAKE WITH SUGARED NUTS

Serves 8–10

FOR THE BASE
30 g (1 oz) ground hazelnuts
150 g (5 oz) digestive biscuits
90 g (3 oz) butter, melted

FOR THE CHEESECAKE
450 g (1 lb) cream cheese
50 g (1¾ oz) caster (superfine) sugar
60 g (2 oz) dark brown sugar
1 egg
1 egg yolk
170 g (6 oz) double (thick) cream

FOR THE SUGARED NUTS
300 g (10½ oz) nuts (walnuts, pecans, almonds,
hazelnuts, macadamia, cashew)
200 g (7 oz) caster (superfine) sugar
40 g (1½ oz) water
a fat pinch of sea salt

This cheesecake is perfect for those birthdays made of early nights and jokes by the fireplace. In fact, I made it for the very first time for my mum's birthday, which falls at the end of October. We were in an old house in the north of Italy with nothing else to do other than pick chestnuts and hazelnuts that we'd roast on the fire at night and burn our fingers on the shells as we cracked them open.

I remember wrapping an old tin in plenty of layers of foil. And mixing eggs with cream cheese, wondering why the egg yolks always seem brighter in Italy. I remember roasting a handful of nuts and coating them in a crunchy sugar.

Preheat the oven to 100°C (215°F). Line a 22 cm (9½ in) springform pan with baking parchment and wrap in 2 layers of foil.

Spread the hazelnuts in a single layer onto a baking tray lined with baking paper and bake for 8 minutes, giving them a good shake every now and then, until golden-brown and aromatic. Set aside.

Put the digestive biscuits into a plastic bag and bash them with a rolling pin until they turn into fine crumbs. Mix in a bowl with the melted butter. Add the ground hazelnuts to the crumbs, mixing until it forms a thick paste.

Scrape into the springform pan and spread out to form an even layer, smoothing the top with the back of a spoon. Chill while you get on with the cheesecake mix.

Work the cream cheese for a minute or two in a large bowl until it is smooth and no longer lumpy. Add the sugars and eggs and mix well. Gently fold in the double cream until just combined. Pour onto the biscuit base and sit the pan in a deep baking tray. Pour in hot water from a kettle

so that it reaches halfway up the sides of the pan.

Bake for 1 hour or until firm to the touch and the edges start to turn golden-brown. Turn off the oven, open the oven door and let the cheesecake to cool inside for another hour. Transfer to a wire rack and leave until it reaches room temperature. Then chill for at least 4 hours or, preferably, overnight.

On the day you're planning to serve the cheesecake, make the sugared nuts.

Preheat the oven to 170°C (340°F).

Line a baking tray with baking paper and sprinkle the nuts on. Bake for 10 minutes, or until golden. Leave to cool slightly while you make the sugar syrup.

Place the sugar, water and salt in a large pan and cook over medium heat until it just starts to caramelize in the centre of the pan. Off the heat, stir in the nuts with a wooden spoon and keep stirring until the syrup forms a sugary crust around the nuts. Transfer to a bowl and allow to cool completely.

Spoon the sugared nuts over the cold cheesecake and leave to set at room temperature. Do not refrigerate the cheesecake at this point as it will make the sugared nuts sticky.

PEACH MELBA CHARLOTTE

Serves 10–12

FOR THE POACHED PEACHES
8 ripe yellow peaches
1 kg (2 lb 3 oz) water
450 g (1 lb) caster (superfine) sugar
10 mint leaves

FOR THE RASPBERRY PURÉE
1 kg (2 lb 3 oz) raspberries
100 g (3½ oz) icing (confectioner's) sugar

FOR THE BISCUIT CUILLÈRE
5 eggs, separated
150 g (5 oz) caster (superfine) sugar
150 g (5 oz) plain (all-purpose) flour, sieved
50 g (1¾ oz) icing (confectioner's) sugar,
to decorate

FOR THE RASPBERRY MOUSSE
9 gelatine leaves
400 g (14 oz) Raspberry Purée (recipe above)
160 g (5½ oz) caster (superfine) sugar
400 g (14 oz) whipping cream

TO SERVE
250 g (9 oz) raspberries

I have wonderful memories of my childhood summer holidays. A happy mess packed into our camping-car; cat and dog included. We would stop in the wild and make a barbecue. In the afternoons we would explore little villages and their café terraces.

One summer, the only ice cream I would have would be pêche melba. Three scoops of vanilla ice-cream, of the almost-melted kind, marbled

Bring a large pan of water to the boil and fill a bowl with cold water and ice cubes.

Halve the peaches and remove the stones. When the water is boiling, plunge in the fruits for 15 seconds then remove using a slotted spoon and immediately place into the iced water bowl for a few minutes. Gently peel the skin away from the peach cheeks and keep in cold water until needed.

In the meantime, make a syrup. Bring the water, sugar and mint leaves to the boil in a medium pan.

Put the peach halves in the boiling syrup, cover with a cartouche (page 154), and simmer for 5 minutes. Remove from the heat and cool down at room temperature, then chill in the fridge.

with a tangy raspberry coulis; a yellow peach, poached to perfection; all happily topped with fresh raspberries, practically begging to be eaten with fingers. More than one of these coupes glacées tinted my lips and fingers pink that summer.

Nowadays, I don't often eat pêche melba. But every summer, it has become a tradition for me to make a Charlotte with the flavours of my childhood favourite.

While the peaches are chilling, make the raspberry purée. Blitz the raspberries and icing sugar in a blender for 5 minutes, then pass through a fine-mesh sieve. You should get around 500 g (1 lb 2 oz) of purée. Cover the surface with clingfilm and chill in the fridge until needed.

Line a small baking tray that can fit in your freezer with baking paper and place a 20 cm (8 in) metal ring on top.

Once the peaches have cooled down, chop 6 halves into cubes and mix with 100 g (3½ oz) of the raspberry purée. Spread this into the prepared ring, covering the base. Freeze for at least 4 hours or overnight.

When the peach ring is frozen make the biscuit cuillère. Preheat the oven to 170°C (340°F).

Cut 2 large pieces of baking paper and draw one 18 cm (7 in) wide circle on one and three 8 x 30 cm (3 x 12 in) rectangles on the other, spacing them by at least 4 cm. Place the papers upside-down on 2 baking trays and set aside until needed.

Whisk the egg yolks and half the sugar in a large bowl for 5 minutes or until light and fluffy. In another bowl, whisk the egg whites until frothy, then add the remaining sugar – whisking as you do so – in small batches, and whisk to stiff peaks.

Add one third of the meringue to the egg yolks and stir with a spatula to loosen the mixture. Then gently fold in the remaining meringue until just combined.

Add the flour and fold in until there are no more lumps.

Scrape the mixture into a piping bag fitted with a 10 mm (½ in) nozzle and pipe four dots underneath each corner of each piece of baking paper to stick the paper to the prepared trays.

Pipe a spiral of mixture inside the drawn circle, starting from the centre and spiralling out. This will form the base of your charlotte.

On the second tray, fill each drawn rectangle with 8-cm (3-in) long piped 'fingers' to create 3 solid biscuit 'strips'. These strips will join together to line the tin and form the outer wall of the charlotte. Pipe at a 45° angle, with the fingers touching, and aligning them to the edges of the drawn rectangles.

Dust the circle and the 3 strips with icing sugar. Leave for 10 minutes, then dust again and bake for 12 minutes, or until golden-brown and springy to the touch. Leave to cool completely. When cold, invert all the cooled biscuits onto a clean, dry work surface and peel off the baking paper.

To assemble the charlotte, place a 22 cm (9½ in) metal ring on a large plate. Position the biscuit circle in the base of the metal ring.

Use a sharp knife to straighten the short ends of each of the biscuit strips. Now trim along the long edges, if necessary, so that each strip will be the same height, when positioned in the metal ring.

Lift one of the strips into the ring, with the sugared side facing out,

and nestle it to fit snugly against the side of the ring. Arrange another biscuit strip inside the ring so that they join snugly. Roughly measure the length of the remaining gap and trim the third biscuit so that it is just slightly longer. Ease it into the gap so that you form a tight-fitting biscuit border around the inside of the ring. Set aside while you make the mousse.

Soak the gelatine leaves in ice-cold water for about 20 minutes.

Pour 400 g (14 oz) of the chilled raspberry purée into a large bowl.

Put the remaining purée and sugar in a pan, and cook over a low heat until the sugar is melted. Squeeze the gelatine leaves and add to the hot purée. Stir until just dissolved.

Pour onto the cold raspberry purée, whisking as you do so. Allow to cool slightly.

Whip the cream to soft peaks in a large cold bowl. Scoop a third of the whipped cream into the purée and whisk it in to loosen the mixture. Gently fold in the remaining whipped cream, at first with a whisk, then with a spatula, until just combined. Pour half into the biscuit-lined ring.

Take the frozen peach ring out of the freezer, remove the metal ring and peel off the paper. Gently sit the peach ring on the raspberry mousse. Top with the remaining mousse, leaving a 1 cm (½ in) gap on top.

Loosely cover with clingfilm and chill in the fridge for at least 6 hours or overnight.

When you are ready to serve, gently remove the ring, then arrange the raspberries and remaining peach halves, cut into quarters, on top of the mousse. Serve cold on its own or with a big scoop of vanilla ice-cream.

ALMOST-INSTANT CHOCOLATE FONDANT CAKE

Serves 12

100 g (3½ oz) 70% dark chocolate,
chopped into chunks
120 g (4¼ oz) butter, cubed
4 eggs
200 g (7 oz) caster (superfine) sugar
60 g (2 oz) plain (all-purpose) flour

When it is hard to find time to make a cake – and really, a birthday can't be without a cake – this fondant cake is here for you. It takes less than an hour from start to finish.

In my notebook, I've called it 'perfect chocolate cake'. And it is, trust me. A crisp, almost brittle, crust and a rich and dark crumb.

It's also pretty great for random days when chocolate is needed. Just saying …

Preheat the oven to 170°C (340°F) and generously butter a 20 cm (8 in) cake tin.

Melt the chocolate and butter together in a pan over a low heat, stirring every now and then with a spatula.

Whisk the eggs and sugar in a heatproof bowl set over a pan of simmering water for a few minutes. The aim is to bring the mixture to slightly above room temperature.

Remove from the heat, pour the chocolate over the egg mixture and fold in with a spatula.

Sprinkle the flour in and gently incorporate it until just smooth.

Pour the batter into the prepared tin and bake for 20–25 minutes until just set in the centre. Allow to cool slightly. Cut into wedges and serve with ice-cream – big fat scoops – and as many candles as you can fit.

CHERRY CLAFOUTIS

Serves 10

200 g (7 oz) plain (all-purpose) flour
120 g (4 oz) caster (superfine) sugar
a pinch of salt
3 eggs
80 g (2¾ oz) butter, melted
400 g (14 oz) whole milk
500 g (1 lb 2 oz) cherries, pitted

I can't talk about this dish without an anything-but-subtle hint of delight in my voice. It is one of my favourite recipes ever. As you must have guessed from its name, it comes from my grandmother. An incredibly smooth batter enfolds pieces of slightly sour cherries. I usually make it on the very first days of June when the cherries turn into bright-red jewels waiting to be picked.

It's a bit of a bore to pit them and in fact there is a great debate in France whether the cherries used in a clafoutis should be pitted or not. But I use a small paring knife to pit them for easier eating. You could also use other fruits depending on the season. And if you want to know one of my best-kept secrets, finely sliced apples work like a charm in autumn.

I like to eat clafoutis at any time of the day, but it does make a lovely dessert when served with some sharp yoghurt ice-cream or a dollop of crème fraiche.

Preheat the oven to 200°C (400°F) and generously butter a 30 cm (12 in) tart dish.

Combine the flour, sugar and salt in a large bowl. Add the eggs, one at the time, beating well after each addition. When the batter is smooth, mix in the melted butter. Then gradually add the milk, mixing well so no lumps form. If you're not fully confident it is lump-free, strain the batter through a sieve.

Scatter the pitted cherries into the prepared dish and gently pour the batter over. Bake for 30 minutes or until golden and quite firm. It can be slightly wobbly in the centre but a skewer inserted in the middle of the clafoutis should come out clean.

Allow to cool and serve in thick wedges.

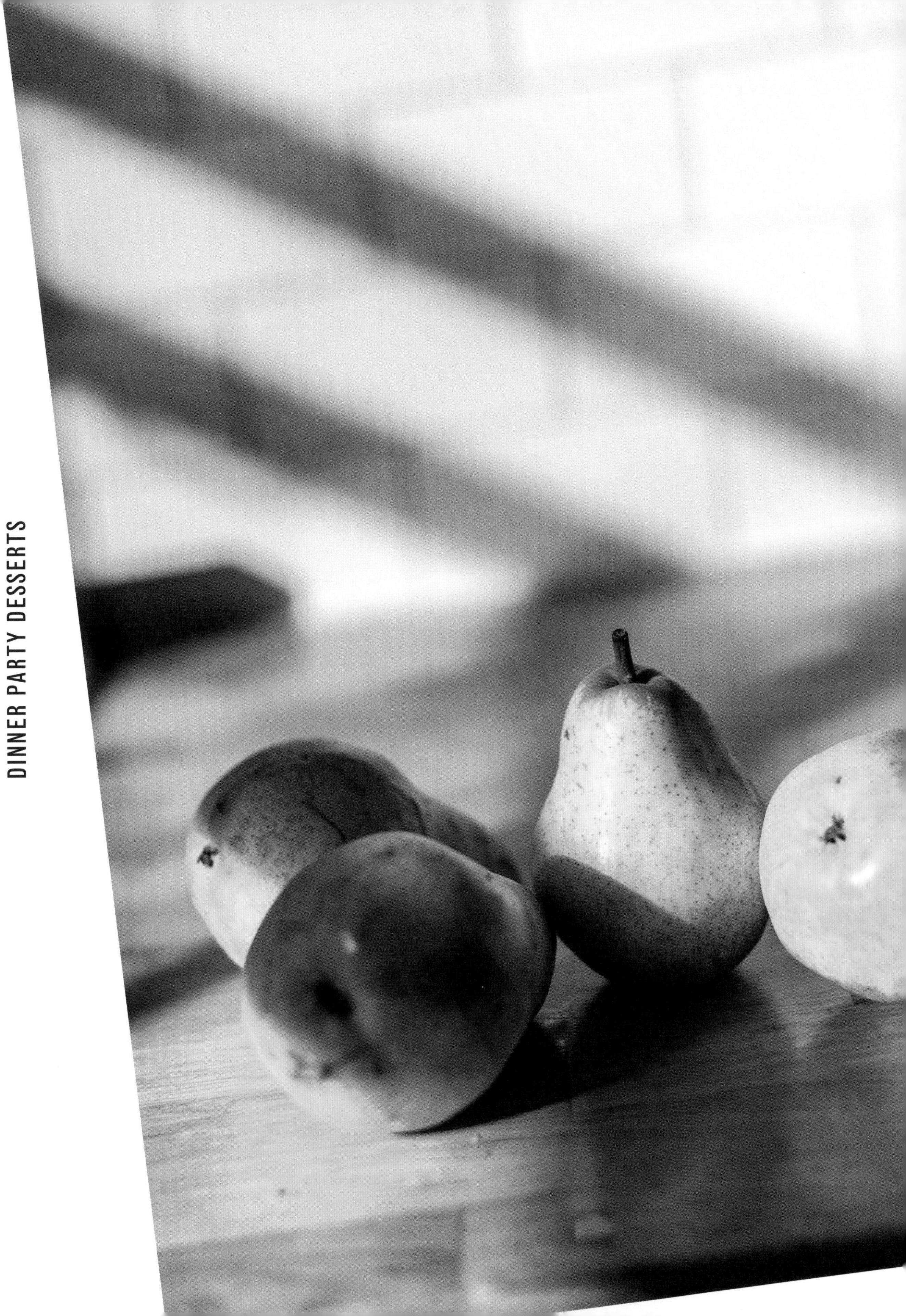

ICED YOGHURT
(NOT UNLIKE A NOUGAT)
WITH MEAD-BAKED PEACH

PISTACHIO NOUGAT

FRESH STRAWBERRIES
À LA PIMM'S & LEMONADE

PUMPKIN PIE, SORT OF

ROASTED FIGS,
VANILLA SPONGE,
GOATS' CHEESE CURD,
OLIVE OIL JELLY

AVOCADO & CHILLI,
HORCHATA FOAM

ELDERFLOWER
SUMMER PUDDING

SALTED CARAMEL
& MILK CHOCOLATE
FLAN PÂTISSIER

(THE PERFECT END TO A PERFECT EVENING)

I HAD FORGOTTEN how it feels to gaze at the Milky Way and get lost in our thoughts; making wishes for every shooting star we see.

I had forgotten how to make a cake batter with a wooden spoon; how to knead without a dough hook; how to bake without a timer, and how to eat with our fingers.

I had forgotten how he makes me smile for no reason other than just being him. And how cold it gets when hours are spent sitting on the steps overlooking the garden, talking about anything – everything, really – with a beer or two and a slice of cake; that's what we do.

We chop and we mix. We fold and we whisk. And when it's all over and our kitchen looks like a flour storage unit and the sink wishes it never existed, we gather around a table.

A table made of upside-down wooden pallets and my favourite tablecloth. The one with embroidered flowers that my great grand-mother cross-stitched years ago now. We have mismatched plates and glasses. And really, that's fine. More than fine, in fact.

Because, the very essence of it all hides behind every dessert you'll put on that table. It's about much more than food. So much more. Always, and for ever, more.

CHAPTER 6

ICED YOGHURT (NOT UNLIKE A NOUGAT) WITH MEAD-BAKED PEACH

Serves 6

FOR THE ICED YOGHURT
60 g (2 oz) caster (superfine) sugar
30 g (1 oz) water
1 egg white
125 g (4½ oz) thick yoghurt
125 g (4½ oz) whipping cream,
whipped to soft peaks

FOR THE MEAD-BAKED PEACHES
6 ripe yellow peaches, halved and stoned
60 g (2 oz) caster (superfine) sugar
2 tablespoons honey
250 g (9 oz) mead

FOR THE HONEYCOMB
150 g (5 oz) caster (superfine) sugar
60 g (2 oz) glucose syrup
30 g (1 oz) honey
30 g (1 oz) water
1 teaspoon bicarbonate of soda

TO SERVE
Pistachio Nougat (page 130), optional

To make the iced yoghurt, first place 6 x 6 cm (2 in) metal rings on a baking tray lined with baking parchment. Line each ring with a strip of rhodoid or baking parchment.

Heat the sugar and water in a small pan set over medium heat to 118°C (245°F). As the syrup reaches the correct temperature, start whisking the egg whites until soft peaks form. When the syrup is ready, slowly pour it into the side of the bowl, to avoid splatters. Keep on whisking on a high speed until firm and glossy and the bowl feels warm-ish to the touch

Whisk the yoghurt in a large bowl to loosen it, then gently fold in the Italian meringue until almost fully incorporated. Add the cream and fold in until combined.

Pour the yoghurt mousse into a piping bag, cut the tip off and pipe the mousse into the prepared rings so that each is around 3 cm (1¼ in) deep. Freeze for at least 5 hours or overnight.

In the meantime, make the honeycomb. Have a baking tray lined with baking paper ready. Place the sugar, glucose syrup, honey and water into a large pan, and cook over low heat until it turns into a light caramel. Off the heat, add the bicarbonate of soda, mixing well using a wooden spoon. Immediately scrape onto the prepared baking tray and allow to cool completely. Then break the slab into pieces and store into an airtight container until needed.

Preheat the oven to 160°C (320°F). Arrange the peaches cut-side up on a baking tray. Sprinkle with the sugar and honey, and drizzle with the mead. Bake for 20 minutes, spooning the juices over the fruits every 4 minutes or so. Transfer the fruits to a plate and keep at room temperature to cool down slightly.

Bring the juices to the boil in a small saucepan over a high heat. Simmer for 6–8 minutes, or until syrupy. Spoon the syrup over the peaches to coat them slightly.

When you are ready to serve, unmould the frozen yoghurts onto a large serving plate. Add the roasted peaches and drizzle some more syrup on the plate. Break the honeycomb into small pieces and scatter over. Add chopped up nougat, if using.

Some things will never – ever – be different. And really, I wouldn't want it any other way.

This dessert is exactly that. A childhood memory of picking peaches in an orchard, more eating than picking to be completely honest.

But when we got home, with a car-trunkful of fruits, the dessert we had for lunch would always be some kind of yoghurt, with honeycomb and juicy peaches.

Perhaps, that's why I like to serve it in a help-yourself-and-get-messy kind of way.

PISTACHIO NOUGAT

Makes 1 slab

icing (confectioner's) sugar, for lining the
baking tray plus extra for dusting

1 egg white
260 g (9 oz) caster (superfine) sugar
125 g (4½ oz) honey
100 g (3½ oz) water
50 g (2¾ oz) glucose syrup
150 g (5 oz) blanched pistachios

Nougat is one of those things that feels scary to make. I mean it involves two hot sugar syrups and it's sticky; but really, your stand-mixer does most of the job.

This very recipe doesn't come from my *grand-mère* as she seems to make it without weighing out anything (oh the many wonders of grandmothers), but from a friend, 'E' who's worked with me for a few years. I remember the first time we made it together, we might have turned the kitchen into an icing sugar coated winter wonderland.

The rest is history. The rest is nougat.

Line a baking tray with baking paper and sprinkle it with a generous amount of icing sugar.

Place the egg white in a stand-mixer and whisk on slow speed until soft peaks form. Add 30 g (1 oz) of the sugar and whisk until stiff. Keep on whisking on slow speed while you get on with the syrups.

In a small pan, cook the honey to 130°C (266°F). In another pan, place the remaining sugar, water and glucose syrup in another pan and cook to 155°C (311°F). With the mixer still on slow to medium speed, pour the boiling honey down the sides of the bowl to mix with the egg white, increase the speed a bit and whisk for a minute or two. When the sugar syrup reaches 155°C (311°F), pour it down the sides of the bowl. Crank up the speed to the maximum and whisk until the bowl just feels slightly warm to the touch. Remove the whisk and add the pistachios, mixing with a wooden spoon as you do so. Immediately scrape the nougat onto the prepared baking tray. Dust with more icing sugar and top with a sheet of baking paper, then roll to a 2 cm thick slab using a rolling pin. Allow to cool down at room temperature for 12 hours, then slice into squares or bars.

FRESH STRAWBERRIES À LA PIMM'S & LEMONADE

Serves 6

FOR THE BASIL PÂTE DE FRUIT
250 g (9 oz) water
185 g (6⅓ oz) caster (superfine) sugar
20 g (¾ oz) basil leaves, blanched in boiling
water and squeezed
50 g (1¾ oz) glucose syrup
9 g (⅓ oz) yellow pectin
15 g (¾ oz) citric acid
15 g (¾ oz) water

FOR THE CRYSTALLISED BASIL LEAVES
1 egg white
granulated sugar, to coat
6 small basil leaves

FOR THE PIMM'S AND LEMONADE SORBET
180 g (6⅓ oz) water
90 g (3 oz) caster sugar
100 g (3½ oz) dehydrated glucose
250 g (9 oz) lemonade
120 g (4¼ oz) Pimm's

FOR THE STRAWBERRY COULIS
900 g (1 lb 13 oz) strawberries
50 g (1¾ oz) icing (confectioner's) sugar

FOR THE CUCUMBER LEMONADE
1 cucumber
500 g (1 lb 2 oz) lemonade
2 fat pinches of xanthan gum

There is French summer. Mornings at the market, with the complusory cup of café au lait; afternoons in the garden, picking strawberries and herbs for dinner.

And then, there is the English summer. One day – two, if you're lucky – that makes you forget about the many shades of grey. Yes, for one day, it's all about laying in the grass and watching clouds go by. Of course, there is that jug of Pimm's and lemonade too. And this dessert is all of this. On a plate.

THE BASIL PÂTE DE FRUIT

Line a baking tray with a large piece of acetate or baking parchment and set aside.

Bring the water and the 25 g (1 oz) of the sugar to the boil in a small pan and pour onto the basil leaves in a blender. Blitz until smooth, then pass through a fine-mesh sieve lined with muslin cloth.

Weigh out 250 g (9 oz) of this juice into a small pan and add the glucose syrup. Combine the remaining sugar and pectin in a bowl and set aside. Cook the basil syrup on a high heat until it reaches 40°C (100°F). Then add the sugar-pectin mix, whisking as you go. Heat to 107°C (225°F) and take off the heat. Mix the citric acid with the water and add to the syrup. Immediately pour the syrup onto the prepared acetate sheet and leave to set at room temperature.

Use a small knife to cut the pâte de fruit into thin long strips and keep on the acetate until ready to use.

THE CRYSTALLISED BASIL LEAVES

Whisk the egg white until just frothy. Spread the sugar in a thin even layer on a baking tray or plate.

Coat the basil leaves, one at a time, with the egg whites, removing any excess with your fingers. Dip into the sugar to cover evenly. Gently place onto a lined baking tray and leave to dry overnight at room temperature.

THE PIMM'S AND LEMONADE SORBET

Bring the water and sugars to the boil. Allow to cool down completely and mix in the Pimm's and the lemonade. Transfer to a plastic container and chill in the fridge for at least 4 hours or overnight. Churn according to your ice-cream machine manufacturer's instructions.

THE STRAWBERRY COULIS

Blitz 500 g (1 lb 2 oz) strawberries and sugar in a blender until smooth. Pass through a fine-mesh sieve and chill in the fridge. An hour before servng, halve the remaining strawberries and mix with 200 g (7 oz) of coulis. Keep at room temperature.

THE CUCUMBER LEMONADE

Slice half the cucumber lengthwise into four 5-mm (¼-in) thick slices, trimming the edges to neat rectangles. Add into 300 g of the lemonade, cover and leave in the fridge for at least 3 hours.

Juice the rest of the cucumber in a juicing machine and mix with the remaining lemonade. Mix in the xanthan gum by hand, taking care not to create too many bubbles. Keep chilled until needed.

TO SERVE

Drop a spoonful of strawberry coulis onto the left-hand side of each dessert plate and drag it across diagonally. Place a small mound of marinated strawberries on the left of the plate.

Dice the soaked cucumber slices into tiny cubes and scatter over the strawberries. Top with a couple of crystallised basil leaves and a strip of basil pâte de fruit.

Form quenelles of Pimm's sorbet and place on the right-hand side of each plate. Drizzle with the thickened cucumber lemonade.

PUMPKIN PIE, SORT OF

Serves 8

FOR THE CINNAMON
WHOLEWHEAT SHORTBREAD
yolk from 1 hard-boiled egg, thinly grated
520 g (1 lb 2¾ oz) butter
180 g (6⅓ oz) icing (confectioner's) sugar
1 teaspoon sea salt
1 teaspoon ground cinnamon
300 g (10½ oz) wholewheat flour
150 g (5 oz) plain (all-purpose) flour
100 g (3½ oz) rolled oats
50 g (1¾ oz) cornflour (cornstarch)

FOR THE CARAMELISED
WHITE CHOCOLATE GANACHE
300 g (10½ oz) white chocolate, chopped
200 g (7 oz) whipping cream

FOR THE PUMPKIN CONFIT
125 g (4 oz) caster (superfine) sugar
1 vanilla pod
1 cinnamon stick
220 g (8 oz) water
1 butternut squash or ½ pumpkin
(around 1 kg/2 lb 3 oz)

FOR THE CREAM CHEESE FOAM
400 g (14 oz) cream cheese
220 g (8 oz) water
120 g (4¼ oz) icing (confectioner's) sugar
seeds of 1 vanilla pod
½ teaspoon sea salt

FOR THE PUMPKIN CURD
300 g (10½ oz) pumpkin flesh, diced
4 egg yolks
2 eggs
60 g (2 oz) muscovado sugar
½ tablespoon ground cinnamon
½ tablespoon vanilla extract
seeds of ½ vanilla pod
2 gelatine leaves
100 g (3½ oz) butter, softened

THE SHORTBREAD

Cream the yolk, butter, sugar, salt and cinnamon in a bowl until light and fluffy. Add the flours and oats and mix until just combined. Spread the mixture between two sheets of baking paper and roll until it is 4 mm (¼ in) thick. Transfer to a baking sheet and freeze for 30 minutes.

Preheat the oven to 150°C (300°F).

Remove the shortbread from the freezer and bake for around 18 minutes or until golden brown. Break into pieces and store in an airtight container when cooled down.

THE CARAMELISED WHITE CHOCOLATE GANACHE

Preheat the oven to 160°C (320°F).

Place the chopped white chocolate onto a baking tray and bake for around 8 minutes, or until golden brown.

In a small pan, bring the whipping cream to the boil. Off the heat, add the caramelised white chocolate, and stir until smooth. Transfer to a small container and chill for a few hours or overnight.

THE PUMPKIN CONFIT

Put the sugar in a pan set over medium heat and cook to a dark, amber-brown caramel. Slice the vanilla pod lengthwise and add to the caramel along with the cinnamon stick. Briefly mix, then tip the water in. The caramel will seize – do not worry. Just keep heating and slowly bring to the boil, then remove from the heat to cool down slightly while you prepare the pumpkin

Preheat the oven to 220°C (430°F).

Peel the squash or pumpkin and use different sizes of Parisian scoops (melon ballers) to scoop out little spheres of the flesh and place into a 20 cm (8 in) cake tin.

Pour the syrup over the balls and bake for an hour, turning and basting regularly. Allow to cool at room temperature and keep covered in the fridge.

THE CREAM CHEESE FOAM

To make the cream cheese foam, whisk all of the ingredients together in a large bowl until smooth, around 1 or 2 minutes. Pass through a fine-mesh sieve and transfer to a nitrogen foam canister. Charge with one cartridge of nitrogen and shake well. Keep in the fridge.

THE PUMPKIN CURD

Preheat the oven to 180°C (350°F). Spread the diced pumpkin flesh onto a baking tray and roast for approximately 30 minutes until tender. Blend the roasted pumpkin in a mixer. Then leave it to cool down slightly.

I remember the first pumpkin pie I ever had. I must have been six or seven, and back then, I didn't realise that this simple tarte would one day make it to a restaurant menu.

And yet, this is a dessert I've made countless times now. When I feel like it, I'll add a pumpkin sorbet. Or replace the sugar in the foam with maple syrup.

I've changed the shortbread recipe pretty much every time too (and trust me, it's a killer with a cup of tea, any day, anytime).

Sometimes I add gels and pulled sugar and all sorts of fancies. Above all I love to accompany it with smooth cream cheese foam. You'll need a nitrogen canister to make this, but I think it's well worth it.

Mix the eggs and egg yolks, sugar, cinnamon, vanilla extract and seeds in a heatproof bowl, and add the pumpkin purée, whisking as you go. Set the bowl over a pan of simmering water and cook the mixture, stirring every now and then, until it reaches 84°C (183°F).

Soak the gelatine in ice-cold water. When the curd is cooked, take the bowl off the heat and add the squeezed gelatine leaves. Add the butter and stir well for 5 minutes. Transfer to a container, cover the surface with clingfilm, and chill for a few hours in the fridge, or until set.

Once the curd has set, whisk to loosen it and scrape into a piping bag fitted with a 12 mm (½ in) nozzle.

TO SERVE

Spoon a dollop of caramelised ganache onto the side of each dessert plate and smear it roughly with a spoon.

Pipe a big mound of pumpkin curd next to the ganache and arrange a few small spheres of confit pumpkin around it. Pipe on the foam – I usually go for a small amount, but you could definitely go wild here without any regrets.

Break the shortbread into bite-sized pieces and scatter here and there. Finally, drizzle a spoonful of the confit pumpkin syrup around the edge of the plate.

PARIS PASTRY CLUB

CHAPTER 6

ROASTED FIGS, VANILLA SPONGE, GOATS' CHEESE CURD, OLIVE OIL JELLY

Serves 4

FOR THE VANILLA SPONGE
20 g (¾ oz) polenta
1 heaped tablespoon plain (all-purpose) flour
55 g (2 oz) ground almonds
½ teaspoon baking powder (baking soda)
2 eggs
75 g (2½ oz) caster (superfine) sugar
seeds of 3 vanilla pods
1 tablespoon vanilla extract
50 g (2¾ oz) olive oil

FOR THE ROASTED FIGS
6 figs, cut in half
80 g (2¾ oz) butter, cut into cubes
honey, to drizzle

FOR THE GOATS' CHEESE CURD
250 g (9 oz) goats' cheese
100 g (3½ oz) whipping cream
70 g (2½ oz) icing (confectioner's) sugar

FOR THE OLIVE OIL JELLY
2 gelatine leaves
50 g (1¾ oz) water
80 g (2¾ oz) caster (superfine) sugar
10 g (½ oz) glucose syrup
100 g (3½ oz) extra-virgin olive oil

FOR THE TOASTED PINE NUTS
125 g (4 oz) pine nuts
1 teaspoon olive oil
1½ teaspoons sea salt

This dessert is more than you could believe. Warm roasted figs on a pillow of fresh goats' cheese curd, with the crunch of pine nuts and my absolute favourite: olive oil jelly bits.

It is a stunner for an autumn dinner party when figs are to be seen everywhere.

THE VANILLA SPONGE

Preheat the oven to 180°C (350°F) and line a 1 litre (34 fl oz) loaf tin with baking paper. In a small bowl, mix the polenta, flour, ground almonds, and baking powder.

In a large bowl, whisk the eggs, caster sugar, vanilla seeds and extract for a minute. Sprinkle with the flour mixture and whisk for another minute.

Take a third of this mix and whisk vigorously with the olive oil, until smooth, then fold back into the batter.

Scrape into the prepared tin and bake for 30–40 minutes or until golden-brown and the point of a knife inserted in the centre of the cake comes out clean. Allow to cool down slightly, then unmould.

THE ROASTED FIGS

Preheat the oven to 180°C (350°F). Arrange the figs, cut-side up on a baking tray and place a small piece of butter onto each. Drizzle with honey and bake for around 18 minutes. Set aside at room temperature.

THE CURD

Whisk all of the ingredients together for around 3 minutes until light and fluffy. Keep refrigerated until needed.

THE OLIVE OIL JELLY

Soak the gelatine leaves in ice-cold water.

Bring the water, sugar and glucose syrup to the boil in a small pan. Squeeze out the gelatine leaves, remove the pan from the heat and whisk in.

Slowly pour in the olive oil, whisking with a hand whisk or an immersion blender as you do so. Pour into a container and chill for at least a couple of hours.

THE TOASTED PINE NUTS

Heat a small frying pan over high heat. Add the pine nuts and cook until fragrant and golden, stirring at all times.

Take off the heat, add the olive oil and the salt, shake well and tip into a bowl to cool down.

TO SERVE

To serve, spoon a big dollop of goats' cheese curd onto the left-hand side of 4 dessert plates and use a spoon to drag it around the edge of the plate. Arrange 3 roasted fig halves on the curd.

Use your fingers – because that's how it should always be – to crumble the cake into rough 4 cm (1½ in) pieces and place 3 pieces and some crumbs onto the plate. Sprinkle with a small handful of pine nuts. Stir the olive oil jelly to loosen it and spoon little dollops here and there.

AVOCADO & CHILLI, HORCHATA FOAM

Serves 4

FOR THE CHOCOLATE ICE-CREAM
400 g (14 oz) whole milk
100 g (3½ oz) whipping cream
125 g (4 oz) caster (superfine) sugar
20 g (¾ oz) dehydrated glucose
20 g (¾ oz) skimmed-milk powder
5 g (¼ oz) ice-cream stabiliser
100 g (3½ oz) 70% dark chocolate
20 g (¾ oz) 100% dark chocolate

FOR THE AVOCADO CURD
2½ gelatine leaves
200 g (7 oz) whole milk
3 egg yolks
50 g (1¾ oz) caster (supefine) sugar
100 g (3½ oz) avocado flesh, roughly chopped

FOR THE CHILLI JAM
100 g (3½ oz) water
50 g (1¾ oz) glucose
1 red chilli, finely sliced
50 g (1¾ oz) caster (superfine) sugar
1 teaspoon jam pectin
a pinch of citric acid,
or a squeeze of lemon juice

FOR THE HORCHATA FOAM
500 g (1 lb 2 oz) whole milk
30 g (1 oz) caster (superfine) sugar
1 stick cinnamon
50 g (1¾ oz) pudding rice
100 g (3½ oz) whipping cream

TO SERVE
rice crispies

At times, desserts are created with no other reason than me being obsessed with some flavours.

This one is. Chocolate, chilli, avocado and horchata, which is my absolute favourite summer drink (think rice milk infused with cinnamon). Horchata originates in Spain, but my mum always used to make bottles of it during the holidays.

I don't have anything to compare it with. If you're after something a little different for when daylight fades into stars over your head, then don't look any further.

THE CHOCOLATE ICE-CREAM

Bring the milk and cream to 40°C (105°F) in a medium pan. In a small bowl, combine the caster sugar, dehydrated glucose, milk powder and stabiliser and sprinkle on the milk, whisking constantly. Bring to the boil, then pour over the chocolate. Stir well and transfer into a plastic container. Cover the surface with clingfilm and chill for at least 4 hours or overnight. Reserve a few tablespoons of the mix to brush on your dessert plates later. Churn the rest according to your ice-cream machine manufacturer's instructions.

THE AVOCADO CURD

Soak the gelatine leaves in ice-cold water.

Bring the milk to the boil in a small pan. Mix the egg yolks and sugar until combined. When the milk has boiled, pour over the egg yolks, whisking as you do so, then transfer back into the pan and cook over low heat until it reaches 80°C (175°F) or the custard coats the back of a spoon.

Transfer to a bowl and add the squeezed gelatine leaves and the avocado flesh. Use a stick-blender to blitz until smooth and pipe into small half-sphere silicone moulds. Freeze overnight, then unmould and keep frozen until ready to use. Defrost an hour or 2 before serving.

THE CHILLI JAM

Place the water, glucose and chill in in a small pan, and bring to the boil over low heat. Turn the heat off and allow to rest for 30 minutes, with a lid on.

Combine the caster sugar and pectin and whisk into the chilli water. Bring to the boil and simmer for 3 minutes.

Off the heat, add the citric acid and transfer in a small jar. Chill for at least 2 hours or overnight.

THE HORCHATA FOAM

Place all of the ingredients except for the cream in a pan and bring to the boil. Reduce the heat, cover, and cook for 20 minutes. Remove the cinnamon stick and blitz in a blender until smooth. Pass through a fine-mesh sieve, add the cream and allow to cool completely. Transfer to a canister. Charge with 2 cartridges of nitrogen and shake well. Keep in the fridge.

TO SERVE

Brush each plate with some of the reserved ice-cream mix. Arrange 2 half-spheres of avocado curd on each plate, together with a quenelle of ice-cream and a few dollops of foam. Dot with chilli jam and sprinkle with rice crispies.

ELDERFLOWER SUMMER PUDDING

Serves 6

FOR THE ELDERFLOWER CORDIAL
1.25 kg (2 lb 12 oz) water
250 g (9 oz) caster (superfine) sugar
500 g (1 lb 2 oz) fresh elderflowers,
stems removed
200 g (7 oz) lemon juice

FOR THE ELDERFLOWER SORBET
280 g (10 oz) water
75 g (2½ oz) glucose syrup
100 g (3½ oz) caster (superfine) sugar
100 g (3½ oz) dehydrated glucose
9 g (⅓ oz) sorbet stabiliser
900 g (2 lb) Elderflower Cordial (recipe above)

FOR THE BERRY COMPOTE
200 g (7 oz) strawberries, halved
160 g (5½ oz) raspberries
120 g (4¼ oz) blackberries
80 g (2¾ oz) blueberries
100 g (3½ oz) Elderflower Cordial (recipe above)
70 g (2½ oz) caster (superfine) sugar
seeds from 1 vanilla pod

FOR THE SOAKING SYRUP
500 g (1 lb 2 oz) strawberries, hulled
50 g (1¾ oz) caster (superfine) sugar

FOR THE BRIOCHE BASE AND CUBES
1 Brioche (page 38)
200 g (7 oz) caster (superfine) sugar

A somewhat French version of the pudding *d'été* (summer pudding) I grew up on. We'd slice brioche and top it with barely cooked berries. At times, it just came with vanilla ice-cream, but then during that one early summer week a year just before elderberry trees start snowing blossoms, we'd make elderflower sorbet. And I think you should too.

THE ELDERFLOWER CORDIAL

Bring the water and sugar to a rolling boil in a large pan. Add the flowers and simmer for 5 minutes. Take off the heat, cover with a lid and infuse for a further 5 minutes.

Pour through a fine-mesh sieve, pushing the juices through. Allow to cool down to room temperature, then add the lemon juice. Keep in the fridge until needed.

THE ELDERFLOWER SORBET

Combine the water and glucose syrup in a large pan over medium heat and bring to 45°C (110°F). Combine the sugar, dehydrated glucose and stabiliser in a bowl and add to the water, whisking as you do so.

Bring to a rolling boil, then remove from the heat, add the elderflower cordial and mix well. Chill for at least 4 hours or overnight.

Churn according to your ice-cream machine manufacturer's instructions and transfer to a plastic container. Freeze for a couple of hours before using.

THE BERRY COMPOTE

Bring all of the ingredients to the boil in a pan over low heat and simmer for 2–3 minutes.

Allow to cool to room temperature, then tip into a fine-mesh sieve (do not push through). Put the berries in a bowl and keep in the fridge until needed. Save the juices to add to the soaking syrup.

THE SOAKING SYRUP

Cook the strawberries and sugar in a large bowl set over a pan of simmering water on a low heat for 1 hour, stirring every now and then. Transfer to a sieve lined with muslin cloth and drain without pushing. Discard the strawberries and reserve the syrup.

Mix 150 g (5 oz) of the juices from the berry compote into the syrup and cool down.

THE BRIOCHE BASE

With a serrated knife, carefully slice away the crust from the brioche loaf and cut 6 x 2 cm (¾ in) slices. Cut the remaining brioche into 2 cm (¾ in) cubes – you'll need about 18 in total.

About 20 minutes before serving, add the slices of brioche to a dish of the soaking syrup, turning every few minutes to soak them evenly.

Meanwhile, heat a few tablespoons of sugar in a frying pan until it caramelises. Add a few brioche cubes to the pan and cook for a few minutes, turning to coat all sides in caramel. Transfer to a tray lined with baking paper and repeat with more sugar and more brioche cubes.

TO SERVE

Arrange a slice of brioche on each dessert plate. Carefully spoon on some berry compote and top with 3 cubes of caramelised brioche cubes. Finish with a quenelle of elderflower sorbet.

SALTED CARAMEL & MILK CHOCOLATE FLAN PÂTISSIER

Serves 10–12

300 g (10 oz) Puff Pastry (page 150)

FOR THE CHOCOLATE FILLING
200 g (7 oz) caster (superfine) sugar
850 g (1 lb 12 oz) whole milk
1 teaspoon sea salt
4 eggs
60 g (2 oz) cornflour (cornstarch)
150 g (5 oz) 70% dark chocolate
50 g (1¾ oz) 40% milk chocolate

Trips to the boulangerie would inevitably result in a slice of flan pâtissier. The kind with a golden – almost burnt – crust and soft – too yellow to be true – custard.

Here I've just infused my playground love with favourite flavours: salted caramel and milk chocolate.

If you already have puff pastry stashed away in your freezer, then it'll be super-easy to make. Essentially a simple crème pâtissière, where the sugar gets caramelised and then poured onto chocolate.

You could always use store-bought puff pastry, or even shortcrust pastry, as it's often seen at pretty much every street corner boulangerie.

The one thing you need to know, though, is that this crème pâtissière must be beaten for a good solid

Generously butter a 24-cm (9½-in) tart ring.

Roll the puff pastry on a well-floured work surface into a 28-cm (11-in) disk, approximately 5-mm (¼-in) thick. Gently lift the dough and line the prepared ring. Keep in the freezer for an hour or up to a month.

Preheat the oven to 180°C (350°F). Cut a large piece of baking paper and place on top of the puff pastry. Cover with rice or dried beans, packing with your hands, and bake for 20–30 minutes, or until golden brown around the edges.

In the meantime, make the crème pâtissière. Place the caster sugar in a large pan and cook over low heat until it turn a deep-brown caramel.

While the sugar is cooking, bring the milk and salt to the boil. Once the caramel is dark enough, take the pan off the heat and add with hot milk, a little at a time.

Return to medium heat and bring to the boil, stirring with a whisk to dissolve any bits of caramel that might have seized.

In a bowl, whisk the eggs and cornflour until combined. Pour the boiling caramel milk over the egg mixture and whisk well. Return to the pan and bring to the boil over medium heat, whisking constantly.

Pour over the chocolates and mix well, using either a stand-mixer fitted with the paddle attachment or hand-held electric beater, for around

10 minutes after it's been made. Both to cool it down and also to make it smoother and incorporate some air into it. I usually go the easy way and pump up my stand-mixer to full speed. However an electric hand-held beater works just fine too. Or if you're really desperate for the workout of your life, a wooden spoon. I've been there before!

10 minutes, or until almost cool to the touch.

Remove the paper and rice from the blind-baked pastry case. Scrape on the crème pâtissière and bake at 180°C (350°F) for 45 minutes, or until bubbling and dark patches have formed on the top.

Allow to cool down completely before unmoulding and slicing.

PUFF PASTRY

Makes around 1 kg (2 lb) of puff pastry

FOR THE DÉTREMPE
350 g (12 oz) plain (all-purpose) flour
150 g (5 oz) water
110 g (3½ oz) butter, melted
1 teaspoon sea salt

FOR THE BUERRE MANIÉ
310 g (11 oz) butter
150 g (5 oz) plain (all-purpose) flour

There is nothing quite as scary as making puff pastry for the very first time.

I've been there and really, after rolling and rolling some more, I thought it wasn't that hard ... if you're patient.

Puff pastry is the sort of thing that involves more resting time than effort. It's a labour of love and time, and a generous sprinkle of flour.

You start by making the détrempe, a simple dough made with flour, butter, and water, with the obvious pinch of salt, then leave it in the fridge to firm up for at least a couple of hours or a couple of days.

Then butter gets kneaded into flour, to make for an easier-to-work-with butter layer that won't set as hard.

And finally the magic happens, when you place the butter on top of your détrempe and start the very soothing rolling and folding. Trust me.

Start by making the détrempe. Place the flour in a large bowl. In a jug, combine the water, melted butter and salt. Using a wooden spoon, pour the water over the flour, mixing as you go until just combined. The dough should feel soft, but not sticky.

Place the dough onto clingfilm and, working quickly with the palm of your hands, form a rectangle approximately 30 x 20 cm (12 x 8 in) and 6 mm (⅓ in) thick. Wrap in clingfilm and refrigerate for at least 2 hours.

Once the détrempe is made, it's time to start making the beurre manié. Simply cream the butter for a couple of minutes. Then scrape the sides of the bowl, and tip in the flour and mix very briefly, until just combined. Transfer onto clingfilm and working very quickly – the last thing to want is the butter to melt – form a rectangle half the size of the one you just made with the détrempe. Wrap and chill for at least an hour.

After both doughs have rested enough, lightly flour your work surface. Place the rectangle of détrempe with its large end facing you and top the right side with the rectangle of butter. Fold the left panel of détrempe over the butter. You should now have something that sort of looks like a book.

Using a rolling pin, mark some indents into it. This will make the rolling easier and more even. Then starting from the centre-upwards and the centre-downwards, roll until the dough is less than 1 cm (½ in) thick. It should be a rectangle approximately 40 x 20 cm (15½ x 8 in).

The next step is called a tour double (literally, a double turn – read

151

fold). Brush the excess flour away and trim the ends so you have a neat rectangle.

Visualise the middle axis of the rectangle, grab the lower end of the dough and fold it over so it meets the middle axis. Do the same with the upper end. I'll call this an open book.

Finally, close the 'book' and wrap it in cling film. Chill for at least a couple of hours.

Now, you're going to make the second tour double.

Place the book look-alike dough in front of you, spine on the left and repeat the rolling and folding as above.

Once again, chill for a couple of hours.

To give the dough its final tour, place the 'book' in front of you, spine on the left and roll it into a rectangle slightly larger than a sheet of A4 paper. Brush the excess flour away and fold in three, just like you would do with a business letter.

Use a sharp knife to cut into 3 equal portions and wrap each well in clingfilm. You can either freeze for up to a month for later use, or keep refrigerated until needed for a couple of days.

MAKING A CARTOUCHE

A CARTOUCHE IS A ROUND PIECE OF
BAKING PAPER WITH A SMALL HOLE IN THE
CENTRE USED TO COVER FRUITS
DURING POACHING, MAKING SURE THEY
REMAIN SUBMERGED IN THE
POACHING SYRUP.
FOLD A SQUARE
OF BAKING PAPER IN HALF AGAIN AND AGAIN,
UNTIL YOU HAVE A TRIANGLE. TRIM THE
WIDER EDGE SO THAT THE TRIANGLE
HAS THE SAME LENGTH AS THE RADIUS
OF YOUR PAN, AND CUT A FEW MILLIMETRES
OFF THE POINT TO CREATE A HOLE.
UNFOLD THE PAPER AND YOU SHOULD
HAVE A CIRCLE THE DIAMETER OF YOUR
PAN WITH A HOLE IN THE MIDDLE.

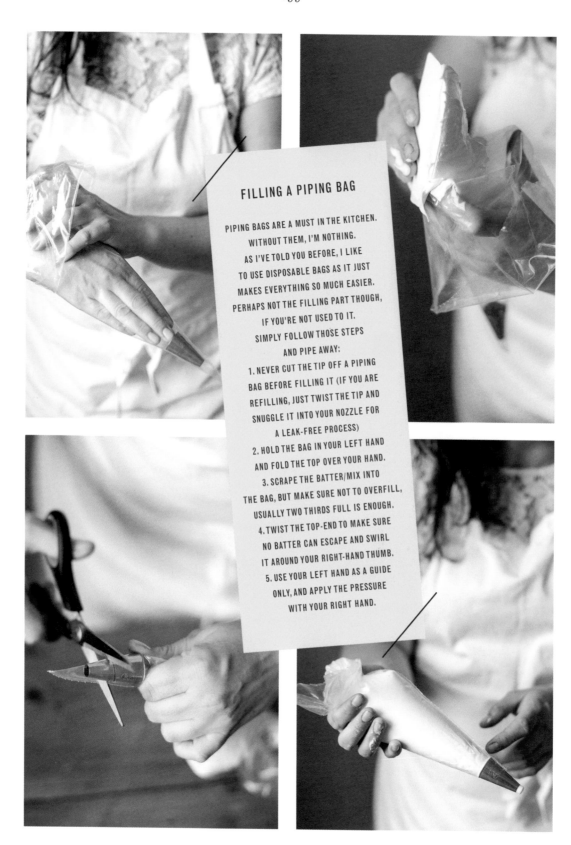

FILLING A PIPING BAG

PIPING BAGS ARE A MUST IN THE KITCHEN.
WITHOUT THEM, I'M NOTHING.
AS I'VE TOLD YOU BEFORE, I LIKE
TO USE DISPOSABLE BAGS AS IT JUST
MAKES EVERYTHING SO MUCH EASIER.
PERHAPS NOT THE FILLING PART THOUGH,
IF YOU'RE NOT USED TO IT.
SIMPLY FOLLOW THOSE STEPS
AND PIPE AWAY;
1. NEVER CUT THE TIP OFF A PIPING
BAG BEFORE FILLING IT (IF YOU ARE
REFILLING, JUST TWIST THE TIP AND
SNUGGLE IT INTO YOUR NOZZLE FOR
A LEAK-FREE PROCESS)
2. HOLD THE BAG IN YOUR LEFT HAND
AND FOLD THE TOP OVER YOUR HAND.
3. SCRAPE THE BATTER/MIX INTO
THE BAG, BUT MAKE SURE NOT TO OVERFILL,
USUALLY TWO THIRDS FULL IS ENOUGH,
4. TWIST THE TOP-END TO MAKE SURE
NO BATTER CAN ESCAPE AND SWIRL
IT AROUND YOUR RIGHT-HAND THUMB.
5. USE YOUR LEFT HAND AS A GUIDE
ONLY, AND APPLY THE PRESSURE
WITH YOUR RIGHT HAND.

HOW TO ...

ACKNOWLEDGMENTS

To my *grand-mère* Odette, my *grand-père* René, my great-grandmother *Mémé*
and my parents: with thanks for everything they've taught me, whether they know
it or not. *Je vous aime!* And to Aïda, my little sister, otherwise known
as the toughest food critic you'll ever meet.
Thank you Helen and April for turning the photoshoot into a dream. And to my
amazing colleagues and friends at Brasserie Chavot for supporting me. Through
days and nights, literally. And to Charlotte, for the stunning design.
And, perhaps most importantly, a never-ending *merci* to the fabulous team
at Hardie Grant, and especially to Kate.

ABOUT THE AUTHOR

Fanny Zanotti grew up in the south of France. She played with a kite on the beach;
she sat on the kitchen counter watching her *grand-mère* bake tarts; she rode her bike;
she fell in love. She milked goats and made cheese; she travelled the world;
she made cakes; she studied to become a product developer and then she studied again
to become a pastry chef. Since then, she's worked with the likes of Pierre Hermé,
Heston Blumenthal and Ben Spalding. She currently lives in London and works at Brasserie Chavot.
Fanny writes words in a black notebook and takes photos. She is a successful food blogger
at **likeastrawberrymilk.com**. She believes in magic, wishes and flour.

INDEX

Paris Pastry Club by Fanny Zanotti

First published in 2014 by Hardie Grant Books

Hardie Grant Books (UK)
Dudley House, North Suite
34–35 Southampton Street
London WC2E 7HF
www.hardiegrant.co.uk

Hardie Grant Books (Australia)
Ground Floor, Building 1
658 Church Street
Melbourne, VIC 3121
www.hardiegrant.com.au

British Library Cataloguing-in-Publication Data. A catalogue record
for this book is available from the British Library.

ISBN: 978-174270471-5

Publisher: Kate Pollard
Desk Editor: Kajal Mistry
Art Direction and design: Charlotte Heal Design
Design assistance: Kat Jenkins
Photography © Helen Cathcart
Prop styling: Helen Cathcart
Prop sourcing: Zoe Regoczy
Food Assistant: April Carter
Colour Reproduction by p2d

Printed and bound in China by 1010

10 9 8 7 6 5 4 3 2 1